CHARGED WITH TREASON

Jury Verdict: Not Guilty

John Carroll Elliott
and
Ellen Gale Hammett

mpc
McClain Printing Company
Parsons, West Virginia

1986

International Standard Book Number 0-9615630-0-1
Library of Congress Catalog Card Number 85-90938
Printed in the United States of America
Copyright © 1986 by John Carroll Elliott and Ellen Gale Hammett
St. Marys, West Virginia
All Rights Reserved

Foreword

Blennerhassett Island, located one mile south of the city of Parkersburg, West Virginia, is the setting for much of this story.

Schemes, designs, promotions, and conspiracy on the island culminated in a charge of treason brought against Colonel Aaron Burr, a former vice-president of the United States; and Harman Blennerhassett, owner of the island. Accumulating evidence of strange activities, both on the island and elsewhere, led directly to Colonel Burr's arrest. He was tried for treason in the Old Hall of the House of Delegates in Richmond, Virginia.

Never in history has such an array of eminent counsel appeared together in any one legal case as participated in the great trial which has been recounted in *Charged With Treason*. This book includes much of the proceedings of that trial—a dramatic application of the federal law of our land, as applied to an individual charged with the most heinous of crimes, treason.

From the month of March until September, the prosecution and the defense waged the most torrid legal debate ever staged in any courtroom. Historians have been amazed at the brilliance and learning of all counsel who appeared in that trial, both for the prosecution and for the defense.

The trial of Colonel Aaron Burr has, through the years, interested many people. Citizens of Richmond, today, speak of the trial as though it were a current event. This is understandable when one considers the fame of the man accused, the important people implicated with him, and the magnitude and daring of what they supposedly had proposed to do.

No trial for treason has taken place, in any country, in which more learning, ability, and eloquence have been displayed. All important decisions on treason, in America and England, were thoroughly examined and studied. Their application to the questions before the court was discussed with great talent and skill.

It is interesting to note the numerous ways in which England can prosecute for treason, as compared with the procedures that may be followed in America.

"Trial by jury," in America, is a bulwark of Justice—an example before the world that American principles are based upon the rights of men, regardless of their station in life. Great care was taken to make sure that the trial of Colonel Aaron Burr was a fair trial. He was both prosecuted and defended by the finest legal minds in the nation, all men of the highest ethical integrity.

When the debate was finished, when the evidence was in, the fate of Colonel Aaron Burr would be decided in only one way— by the verdict of the twelve jurors.

Introduction

In 1807, a Treason Trial was held in the Old Hall of the House of Delegates in Richmond, Virginia.

The person charged with treason was Colonel Aaron Burr, former Vice-President of the United States, former United States Senator from New York, and a decorated officer of the American Revolutionary War.

Presiding Judge at this trial was Chief Justice John Marshall of the United States Supreme Court.

A study review of Chief Justice John Marshall's life and of his application in judgments leads one to believe that John Marshall certainly was endowed with more than natural powers.

His learned opinions and decisions have influenced Judicial procedure in America to such an extent that historians have called him, "The Grandfather of the Courts."

With the exception of actual historical characters, the other persons named are entirely fictional and have no relation to any person in real life.

Charged With Treason

In part, this is the story of an island, the most sorrowful, the most romantic island in all the Ohio River. Neither time, nor tempest, nor mighty flood has been able to diminish the interest that our island holds for those who come this way. Many is the traveler, on his way along the Ohio today, who asks to have pointed out to him the island now known as Blennerhassett Island.

Melissa, the narrator of much of the story, may or may not have lived with the Blennerhassetts in their island home. Legendary or historical as the adopted daughter may have been, we have permitted her to relate much of the story as she could have personally experienced it. Melissa begins our narrative.

I must tell this story as it deserves to be told, for I, of all people living, know the story as it happened. I was there. I am Melissa.

Such a few years have passed since those frightening days, yet even this short time has been enough to cloud and distort the true happenings. One version that is already being accepted and even written as history, only touches the surface of the actual drama. That you may know what happened, and perhaps not as an onlooker but as one who lived in the midst of all its intimate details. In a peculiar way, I am qualified to do so, for I was of the household of Harman Blennerhassett. I was a member of his family.

It is my constant fear that this generation and the generations to come, having read what others have written, will believe that they are learning the whole of what happened. In my heart, I know that unless they read what I alone can write, unless they read for themselves my account of what really took place on our island during the weeks and months after Colonel Aaron Burr visited us, they cannot know our story.

Because I believe myself to be the only living person who experienced in its entirety, the hope and promise, the anguish and despair of those momentous days, I have undertaken this report. If at times it seems to become my own autobiography, it is not meant to be. As nearly as I can write it, my part is to be the story of Harman and Margaret Blennerhassett.

Growing out of our experiences on the island, and coming as a direct result of those same experiences and events, is a third story that I need not relate to you. I speak of the great treason trial of Colonel Aaron Burr. To the accurate account of what transpired in that courtroom, I can add little, nor shall I attempt to do so.

It was late in the eighteenth century that Harman Blennerhassett came, with his wife and children, to live on that island in the Ohio River, that has since borne his name. I came with them, as I had gone everywhere with them.

I remember the island as it was then, in all its beauty. The mansion, the wide lawn, the towering trees. I remember the culture and charm of the life that the Blennerhassetts lived there, for a few, short years. I remember, too, the turbulence and associations that later were to bring that life to an end.

I have known the joys and the sorrows of this unfortunate family, their hopes and their ambitions. I, who was one of them, have lived to see their story woven into the history and legend of the valley.

An island, a man, the man's wife, a mansion, harmony, culture, happiness. My story is about all of these—and more. Very much more! Ambition, scheming, distrust, conspiracy, loyalty, and—Colonel Aaron Burr.

It was a fateful morning in early June 1805 that a flatboat carrying two passengers slowly approached the tip of our island. Rain had fallen during the night, and drops still clinging to the trees glistened like jewels in the sunlight. The boat was almost to the landing when I discovered it from my window.

I saw, too, the well-dressed man and woman standing together on the bow. How could I have guessed the plans that were at that moment taking shape in the mind of the man? Much less could I have foreseen the part we were all to play in those plans, in the days to come. It was a strange discomfort, though, that I felt as I continued to watch from my window, and saw Colonel Burr come ashore. Could it have been premonition? That sensing, without reason, that something momentous, perhaps tragic, was about to happen?

I had no way of knowing who the visitors were, the brisk, neatly dressed, smiling man and the beautiful young lady, quite evidently his daughter. From the first, I felt a suspicion, a distrust that I was unable to understand. It was partly that he was too polite, too smiling. And always that restless eye that saw everything but revealed nothing. In the days that followed, he did nothing to cause me to revise my first impression.

The visitors could not have been more hospitably received if they had come to the island by special invitation. It was well known that we Blennerhassetts welcomed all visitors. Most certainly such a distinguished guest as Colonel Burr could have expected to be warmly received. Nor could anyone have found it possible to be anything but gracious to his lovely daughter.

Let me tell you first about our island as it was in the happy days before the stranger came. You would have liked it then as you would have liked the comforts and charm of any large estate. It was as though a bit from the East or South had been magically transported to this spot in the Ohio.

In those days the island was not overgrown with weeds and bushes as you see it today. The lawn looked as if it had been swept and brushed until each tiny blade of grass was a soft, living green. How can I best describe that lawn for you? It was shaped like a great fan that had been opened wide. With the mansion located at the handle of the fan, the fan itself spread out to embrace the entire northern end of the island—some one hundred acres in all.

The distance from the house to the river was one long, grassy slope, broken by a gravel walk that extended from the house to a wharf at the river's edge. Beds of bright-colored flowers, together with trees and shrubs, brightened the picture. I think I shall remember always the beauty of that view. I saw it so many times from a boat as we approached the wharf from the north. On this same view Colonel Burr must have gazed in wonder the first time he beheld it. Perhaps he might have passed us by had the island presented a less enchanting picture.

The mansion, semicircular in shape, stately, and gleaming white, was backed by a group of very tall trees. Extending both to the left and to the right from the house, these trees screened from view orchards, vegetable gardens, and stables at the back. It always came as a surprise to strangers who penetrated this background of virgin timber, to find how extensive was the cultivation beyond.

So much of our comfort and luxury we on the island obtained from that area that did not at first meet the eye. Fruit trees of every description produced quantities of the finest fruit, enough for the family table, for the servants, and to furnish gifts for our friends. In summer, vegetables fresh from the garden were never absent from our dinner table.

Beyond the gardens were stables and green meadows where the spirited riding horses were kept. Separate barns for cattle and sheep, and smaller houses for hogs furnished ample protection for all the animals. Acres and acres of meadow and pastureland, separated into fields by zigzagging rail fences, completed a pastoral scene that could have been equaled in but few places in the valley. In its way, the farm part of the island was just as beautiful as the more showy front lawn, and far more useful and conducive to our comfortable living.

Servants, mostly slaves, did the work that such an estate required. Their quarters, too, were in an area back of the mansion.

The year was 1805. The place was Blennerhassett Island. Harman Blennerhassett and his lady had been riding the length of their island estate on a routine tour of inspection. It was midafternoon of a sunny June day. As they sat on their horses in the shade of a great oak tree, each was busy with his own thoughts. It was their ability to draw closer to each other in a wordless harmony of spirit that had made them so companionable. Neither sought to intrude on the other's thoughts, yet frequently, as today, their minds were following in much the same channels.

Keen appreciation of beauty held them silent for the moment as their eyes circled the view before them. Harman was first to break the silence.

"Maggie, have you ever seen it look so beautiful?" He used a circular wave of his hand to include the farthest extent of the estate.

No one but her husband ever called Mrs. Blennerhassett Maggie. She was much too dignified, too beautiful, and withal too commanding of admiration and respect for any of her many friends to become quite so familiar. From the first, Harman had called her Maggie. Used by him, she loved the name; had anyone else used it, she would have hated it.

"So beautiful," she murmured, looking from the scene before them to her husband. From her tone of voice and the long moment that she looked at him, one could have imagined that she described some quality of the man, rather than the scenery.

"I wish you could have seen it this morning," she continued, returning to the view before them. "Sunlight came shimmering through the fog, giving everything a misty, golden look. I walked out here early just to enjoy the view.

"Everything was hidden by the fog, even the nearest trees, until the sunlight broke through; then it was like being suspended on a sunbeam."

"Could you paint it?" her husband asked.

"I don't think so, dear. It was too beautiful. There was an other-worldness about it impossible to capture."

Quickly her mood changed.

"Come, I'll race you to the house."

Harman Blennerhassett was always a little surprised by Margaret's quick change from gravity to playfulness, but he loved her the more for her very unpredictableness. He willingly joined in any diversions she suggested. It was Margaret who always won their little races since she was well on her way before Harman had recovered from his surprise. Today was no exception. She had dismounted and had tossed the reins to the groom when Harman pulled up beside her.

"Well, Maggie, you've beaten me again," Harman laughed. "But I like it. I couldn't lose to a more beautiful woman."

Arm in arm they went into the house, laughing together. Inside the door, Harman put his arms around her and held her close. It was a quick show of affection not usual to him.

"Maggie, Maggie, I wonder if you know how much I love you. I don't know what I would do if I were ever to lose you."

"Why, Harman," she cried, a little shaken by his tone of voice. "You are not going to lose me. I'm far too healthy for anything to happen to me."

"I know, I know," he quickly reassured her. "I just suddenly had such a funny feeling that you were going farther and farther away from me. I couldn't stand that."

They linked arms again and continued toward the stairway, but a slight chill remained with them, a dim sense of foreboding, of some strange, impending evil that neither was able to forget.

Only Melissa saw the flatboat as it approached the island early the next morning. From her window she watched it, strangely dreading its arrival yet not understanding why. Had the others seen it, could they have guessed that this was anything but an ordinary landing? Who could have recognized the drama already begun or suspected the parts they all would play?

Only the man on the boat could know the importance of his coming. He missed nothing of the scene before him, the well-kept lawn, the gravel walk, the trees, the flowers, the house. it was not the first time he had seen this same view, but he was still a little amazed at finding such a house here, west of the mountains. He knew what it must have cost to build such a mansion. The center part of the house was two stories tall. Extending from both sides to form a semicircle, were wings of one story. Fronting the whole of the house was a wide porch flanked by huge pillars. White and glistening in the early morning sunlight, the house was like a jewel set in the green of the lawn.

"This is the place I've been telling you about, Theodosia," Colonel Burr said as he turned to his daughter who stood beside him on the flatboat.

"It is beautiful!" she exclaimed. "But how did he ever build it here?"

"I asked him about that. Harman Blennerhassett told me that he brought most of the workmen from Philadelphia. It is truly a wonderful place."

Even as they talked, Colonel Burr's mind was busy with thoughts of a far different nature.

It is perfect, he thought. Among the trees in that little grove, we could store many provisions. All the supplies we would need for our expedition could be hidden there.

Now if I can just persuade the Blennerhassetts to join me. If I can convince Mrs. Blennerhassett that my enterprise is honorable and legal, there should be no trouble with him.

"We are going ashore there in a few minutes, Theodosia," her father told her. "You may as well know that I intend to talk with the Blennerhassetts about my colonizing expedition. Once I have told them about it, I think they will be ready to join with me."

"We have become pretty good friends, you know."

Theodosia's voice held a note of concern as she asked, "You are serious about those plans, Father? You are really going ahead with them?"

"Yes, I am, Theodosia. Ever since we left Pittsburgh, I have been planning the many details of my expedition."

"But the risk, Father! Something tells me that you are becoming involved in something that could be dangerous."

"Now what possible danger could there be? Even the Indians are pretty peaceable where we are going." Colonel Burr spoke lightly, choosing to ignore her real meaning.

"I wasn't referring to Indians, Father. Sometimes I wish you would be content with what we have and stop seeking for more."

"I'll do that someday," he promised her jokingly.

Colonel Burr's thoughts returned to the scene before him. It is just the setup I need, he mused. We will need troops and a place to train them. That little glade would be a perfect place to train the men. It is a large enough area, yet it is completely hidden from the river.

"I am so glad we are going ashore," Theodosia said cheerfully. "Tell me a little about the Blennerhassetts. Didn't we meet them in New York last winter? Is he that tall, stately Irish gentleman with the graceful wife so much younger than he?"

"Yes," Colonel Burr told her, "we met them at the Stanton's one afternoon. I hardly knew them then. He inherited an estate in Ireland, from an older brother, I believe, then sold it and came to this country."

"How much do you suppose it cost them to build that house?" Theodosia startled her father by asking.

"Hard to tell," he answered lightly.

Colonel Burr would have given a good deal to know, not so much what it had cost Harman Blennerhassett to build his island home, but the amount of money he had left. A friendly visit with the Blennerhassetts would be so much wasted time unless it produced financial aid for his expedition. But if most of the fortune had been spent, they could always borrow a substantial amount on that property.

"Are they expecting us, Father? Did you send them any word last night from Parkersburg?" Theodosia asked with some concern. Her father was a charming man to be around, but his daughter knew that he probably would not remember to inform his host and hostess that he intended visiting them.

"No. I did not think it necessary to send a messenger so late in the day. I am told that the Blennerhassetts are always ready to receive guests. Most people would be if they lived on an island," Colonel Burr said with a smile. It amused him to think for a moment of Theodosia on an island, away from the social life she loved.

Theodosia changed the subject.

"Harman Blennerhassett, if he planned all that, must be a man of refinement and good taste. That estate out here in the wilderness, is like a dream of fairyland."

"The island has possibilities," her father told her seriously. "Harman Blennerhassett recognized some of them. With his money he could make them a reality instead of a dream."

"I would guess, Father, that quite a lot of that vision was his wife's," Theodosia said. "I seem to detect the feminine touch here and there."

"That is exactly right," Colonel Burr agreed. "Her hand is there, all right. And a charming hand it is, my dear."

Theodosia cast a quick glance at her father, then decided to let the remark go unanswered. It probably had been but a teasing afterthought. Her father chose to be amused by her disapproval, often outspoken, of his liking for beautiful women.

I remember the peaceful harmony of our island that June morning in 1805. I can still hear the bobwhite calling from the edge of the lawn, a song sparrow trilling his small burst of music from a stump near the house. No single off-key note warned of approaching discord, so soon to shatter the tranquility of our island paradise.

Old Sam was first of the others to see the strange flatboat moving in toward our wharf. A quick look told him that the boat was a strange one. He was on his feet instantly, forgetting completely the rose bed he had been weeding. That his hands were grimy, made little difference to Sam. One or two quick brushes across his trouser legs, and he was off to help tie up the boat.

I have often wondered, did the strangers feel the coldness of Sam's voice in the short answers he gave to their questions? Did they recognize the distrust in his every glance? Probably not, for they had no way of knowing that Sam had seen one of his "omens" the night before. I wonder now, as I look back on all that has transpired, did Sam possess some strange understanding not granted to the rest of us?

"Yessuh, you is welcome to come ashore," Sam answered the stranger dutifully.

It took but a few minutes for the two boat hands and Sam to secure the flatboat to the small pier.

"You can come on up to the house," Sam said politely. "Mistah and Missus Blennerhassett is always happy to see people of quality. I'll tell the Missus you is here."

Sam motioned for them to precede him up the path to the house; he picked up the two bags and followed at a respectful distance. No one spoke. Each was busy with his own thoughts.

It is so beautiful, Theodosia was thinking, the island, the river, those hills beyond the river. But why is Father coming here? He could spoil everything with that plan of his. That big house is not reason enough for his friendliness.

Colonel Burr's piercing eyes looked only at the island. I begin to know this place pretty well, he was thinking. If we were to enclose that section over there on the far left, it would make a good place to store military equipment. Of course, there would have to be a large covered area, but that wouldn't be hard to build. We will need a drill ground—I know the very spot for that. Ah, Harman, little do you know that opportunity has come upon this fair isle today.

When they reached the veranda, Sam indicated some chairs and said, "Just you all set down there and I'll bring the Missus."

Neither Theodosia nor her father had any desire to relax in an easy chair. Instead, they moved about the veranda. Both went quickly toward the beautiful, stately Mrs. Blennerhassett as she came through the great center door.

"How nice to see you again, Colonel Burr," Margaret greeted her guest. He is as charming as ever, she thought as he bent to kiss her hand. I still wonder what is back of that wily, little smile of his. Does he think, perhaps, that he is about to make another conquest?

"I do hope, my dear madam, that you will forgive our coming so unexpectedly," the colonel apologized. "You see I have been telling everyone I meet about your island paradise. My daughter wished to come and see it for herself.

"Permit me to present my daughter, Theodosia, Mrs. Joseph Alston. Theodosia, this is Mrs. Blennerhassett."

"I am so happy to see you, my dear," Mrs. Blennerhassett said, extending her hand. "Welcome to our island home."

"Oh, I am glad that you said it just that way," exclaimed the impulsive Theodosia. "I have been worried about barging in on you in this way. Father has assured me that we should be welcome, but I feel much better having heard it from you."

"My dear, you are very welcome," Mrs. Blennerhassett smiled. With outspread hands she directed their eyes to the house and grounds. "It is yours to enjoy."

Even as she made her guests welcome, Margaret's mind continued to speculate. Why, really, have they come? The girl seems sincere enough, but I am not so sure of the colonel. I think I could like her very much. With all his charm, I doubt that I could ever bring myself to trust him completely. Ah, but here comes Harman.

"Harman, we have guests," she called to her husband as he came through the door. Mentally she could not resist comparing the two men, so opposite were they both in appearance and temperament. Colonel Burr, short, erect, quick of eye and movement, missed nothing that went on about him. Harman Blennerhassett, tall, a little stooped, given to thought and introspection, often seemed detached, remote to the people around him. However, today he was cordial in his greeting.

"Colonel Burr!" The warmth in Mr. Blennerhassett's voice was genuine. "This is a most pleasant surprise."

"My daughter and I have been presumptuous and have come to you without waiting for an invitation," Colonel Burr explained once more. Turning to Theodosia, he said, "Theodosia, this is Mr. Blennerhassett. Harman, my daughter, Mrs. Alston."

The silvery tones of a gong sounded from within the house.

"That is the signal for breakfast," Mrs. Blennerhassett said. "You must join us. I have told the servants to set places for you."

"How thoughtful you are," Theodosia exclaimed. "We shall be delighted to have breakfast with you. I hope you have not allowed our being here to disrupt your household."

Margaret Blennerhassett, for some reason that she did not quite understand, was pleased that Mrs. Alston appreciated that some slight adjusting had been necessary.

"Do not even mention such a thing," she said lightly. "We are always prepared for guests."

I saw the Burrs face to face for the first time as I came down the wide stairway, on that morning so long ago. I remember how beautiful Theodosia looked as she stood there beside my mother. I can hear, too, the love and pride in my mother's voice as she put her arm around my waist and said, "Permit me to present our daughter, Melissa Dale. Melissa has been one of our family since before we left Ireland."

It was the way my mother always introduced me. Thus did she tell them that I was their adopted daughter. Thus, too, did she spare me the embarrassment of having it put in plain words.

That first day of Colonel Burr's stay on the island gave no warning of events to come. Colonel Burr outdid himself in courtesy and charm of manner, while the warmth and friendliness of my father and mother put everyone at ease.

My father spent much of the morning in showing Colonel Burr about our island. Later the colonel continued his coverage of the island alone. Although none of us suspected it then, or could have given a reason for it, by nightfall there was little of the island that was not carefully catalogued in Colonel Burr's mind.

That evening we gathered in the living room of the great house. The day had been quite warm, but evening brought a chill that settled on us all. We were cold until Sam built a fire in the huge fireplace.

I think it was that evening that I first became aware that Colonel Burr never sat down. Sometimes he stood by the stone fireplace and joined in the conversation. But mostly he was by the window, peering into the darkness outside, as though there was still something he needed to learn about our island. The friendliness of the morning seemed to have been replaced for the moment with a sense of urgency far more grim. Something in Colonel Burr's manner as he stood there, made me cold with an icy foreboding that heat from the fire could not reach.

At the breakfast table the next morning, the tenseness of the evening before seemed to have disappeared. Colonel Burr was again smiling and courteous. As the women went through the hall after the meal, Mrs. Blennerhassett said, "Theodosia, it has become necessary for me to ride to Parkersburg this morning."

"Oh, do you ride there often?"

"Quite often. It is only about two miles from here, and the road is a good one. It would be a pleasure to have you go along, if you enjoy riding."

"Oh, I love it! I ride all the time when I am at home."

Theodosia's enthusiasm was almost childlike, then remembering she said, "But, Father! I had forgotten that he may want to leave today. I must ask him."

Her father, at the other end of the hall, had heard bits of the conversation and then Theodosia's cry of dismay. Now he called to her, "By all means, go, Theo. We shall not be leaving the island today. Mr. Blennerhassett and I have much we wish to discuss."

Colonel Burr could have added that their absence from the island would make it possible for him to talk privately with his host about a matter that he, Colonel Burr, was most anxious to discuss. Instead, he excused himself and retired to his room, using as an excuse some dispatches that he must prepare. No one thought that his use of the word dispatches was at all unusual or out of place. The Blennerhassetts, themselves, sometimes spoke of dispatching a letter by boat or the overland stage.

A short time later the two women, dressed in riding apparel, walked down to the wharf. Sam ferried them and the horses across to the Virginia shore. Once they were ashore, Mrs. Blennerhassett and Theodosia mounted and rode briskly along a road that paralleled the river.

The two women had not gone far when Theodosia reined in her horse, slowing it almost to a walk. She had reached a decision. Here was a woman with whom she could talk, and she did not intend to let the opportunity slip away. Perhaps her hostess was the one person who could advise her wisely.

"You have a beautiful estate, my dear," she began when Mrs. Blennerhassett, too, had slowed her horse's pace. "Is it true that you and your husband actually bought it in almost a wilderness state?"

"Yes, that is quite true. Of course, there had been a fort on the island. We lived in it while our own house was being built, but the whole island had gone back, almost to jungle." Margaret wondered why Theodosia had asked that particular question. Her next remark was clarifying.

"Father talks so much lately about a project he has been considering for some time. He talks of developing a large number of estates in some unsettled section of country much farther south and west. It all sounds so impractical to me. Has he mentioned it to you and Mr. Blennerhassett?"

"No," Mrs. Blennerhassett said, "he has not discussed his

project with us. Perhaps he means to do so later." It will be of little use for him to ask us for money, if that is what he wants, she thought to herself. If Colonel Burr wants financial assistance, he will need to convince Harman that his proposition is sound. That may not be an easy thing to do.

"Father has talked of nothing else for so long," Theodosia continued, "that I am incapable of deciding if his plans are practical or just visionary. Much as I love my father, I still am not too enthused over this dream of his."

I wonder who is wiser, the father or the daughter. Mrs. Blennerhassett studied the matter silently as they guided their horses over a rough spot in the road. It could be that she knows her father pretty well. We have always heard that the colonel is hotheaded and venturesome. And then there was that duel, but, on the other hand, we also know that he is an able man.

"Developing new territory is always interesting, Theodosia," she assured her companion. She thought it best not to discourage the girl unless there was some reason, and so far she could think of no very good one. "Our island was a wilderness when Harman and I first saw it. It took foresight and much work to make it what it is today.

"Do not be afraid to help your father if he undertakes something of the same nature. It is challenging to help in the expansion of civilization. That is really what we have done here in Wood County, you know—brought civilization a little farther into the West."

Theodosia sighed.

"You make it sound so right that I am almost convinced," she said, "but when I am alone, I begin thinking about everything. Then I am filled with misgivings. The whole undertaking seems strange and impractical."

The sudden sound of hoofbeats told them that they were not alone on the road. Theodosia was not prepared for the good-looking young man who rode rapidly toward them on a spirited bay.

"That is Neil Colton," Mrs. Blennerhassett explained. "His father was a judge or something in New York. When he was defeated for office, he came out here and buried himself in the wilds, hoping to forget. But Neil has refused to withdraw from life as his father has. He is living in Parkersburg and is reading law with Judge Wells. He apparently does not intend to let his father's political disappointment ruin him, too."

As the young man drew abreast of them, he bowed respectfully.

"Good morning, Neil," Mrs. Blennerhassett greeted him. "You are riding early today."

"Yes, madam, Judge Wells is gone for the day, and I am stealing a little time from my studies."

Turning to her companion, Mrs. Blennerhassett said, "Theodosia, may I present Mr. Colton? He is a neighbor of ours and often rides down to the island. Neil, this is Mrs. Alston. Mrs. Alston is visiting us along with her father, Colonel Burr."

Neil acknowledged the introduction with a slight bow and a friendly, "Good morning." Colonel Burr! The name echoed in his mind. Why was Colonel Burr visiting the Blennerhassetts?

"We are on our way to Parkersburg, Neil. Shall we see you at the island when we return?" Mrs. Blennerhassett's voice was warm, as though she meant to extend an invitation.

"With your permission, I should like to call on Melissa this morning," Neil answered respectfully.

"You have my permission," she said graciously, "and tell Melissa that I asked you to stay to dinner."

As the boat carrying my mother and Theodosia Alston pulled away from the shore that morning, Colonel Burr stood on the lawn watching them. I, in turn, was observing the colonel from my window. Even today, I am not sure what it was about the man that caused me to distrust him. It is enough to say that I did, almost from the first time I saw him. It was as though he had come upon our island to take something away with him, to rob us of some treasure. That he was seeking his own gain, I was certain; what he wanted from us, I knew not.

When the boat with its passengers had drawn well out from the island, Colonel Burr's whole manner suddenly changed. The suave gentleman disappeared, and in his stead I beheld a man, grim, determined, ruthless in his bearing. In one short moment he had become a determined leader, impatient of the slightest opposition, a man in great haste, with much he must accomplish.

Only for a moment did I see Colonel Burr stand there so revealed, then the smooth, polite, polished gentlemen returned. Moving quickly, as though he must hurry to grasp an unexpected opportunity, he went at once across the lawn and into the house. I heard his footsteps in the hall below. Without pausing to knock, he went at once into the library where my father was reading. I could not help reflecting that none of us ever entered that room without the formality of a light tap on the door.

Harman Blennerhassett was reading, which for him was much the same as being in another world. He had not heard Colonel Burr coming through the hall, nor did he realize that his guest was now standing but a few paces behind him. He was, however, not surprised, only startled, when the colonel spoke. He silently resolved that in the future, he would face the door when reading. For all his show of politeness, Colonel Burr did not choose to remember that among gentle people, an open door was not always an invitation to enter.

"Come in, Colonel," Harman said graciously, even though a little needlessly. "I hope you will excuse my neglect. I usually read during the morning, and I was inconsiderate enough to believe that you were perhaps occupying yourself in the same manner."

"I am an active man, Sir," Colonel Burr said. If he had any feeling of overstepping the privileges of a visitor, he in no way let it be known. "I have been out walking about the grounds."

"Are you interested in horticulture, Colonel?" Harman asked. "That interest and this book are responsible for my neglecting my duties as a host. The book, which came only yesterday, is filled with information that is quite valuable for anyone who tills the soil."

Just the opening I can use, thought Colonel Burr as he reached for the book. "Oh, yes, it is by Talman. I have found him to be one of the best authorities on the subject." He leafed rapidly through the small volume.

He closed the book and said more seriously, "I do not know if you realize it, Mr. Blennerhassett, but I am deeply interested in horticulture and all phases of developing the land."

Something in the colonel's manner seemed strange to Harman Blennerhassett, but he said with warmth, "I am glad to learn of your interest."

"Right now," Colonel Burr continued, "I am on my way south to begin the development of several huge estates. The territory I speak of can, I am sure, be developed into many estates, all of them as large or larger than the one you have here."

"This territory you speak of, Colonel, am I familiar with it? Is it in this area?" Blennerhassett was only politely interested in the colonel's conversation. He would much rather have continued with his reading.

Colonel Burr answered impatiently, speaking in a manner more familiar than he had used before. "Harman, for a time I have been deeply interested in a plan that I want to tell you about. This plan would operate to increase the wealth and the prestige of a choice few of our citizens. Not everyone who would desire to join with us will be asked to do so."

How much of what I say is the stupid fellow really getting? Colonel Burr's thoughts were angry, but his voice remained cool and persuasive, even as he spoke rapidly, "I want to extend to you and your wife an invitation to join my company."

Harman looked surprised, but the colonel gave him no time to interrupt as he continued, "I need not tell you that this would be a company, exclusive in its membership. Specifically, it would include you, your wife, my daughter, Theodosia, her husband, Governor Alston, my friend, Comfort Tyler, and myself."

Harman Blennerhassett was puzzled. What company was the man talking about? True, he had hinted at something big that first time he had spent a few hours on the island. Harman, however, had not given it a second thought.

In a puzzled voice, Harman asked, "You are inviting my wife and me to join you in promoting a colonizing expedition? I am not sure that I quite understand just what you are planning to do."

"I shall be glad to explain my proposal to you most carefully," Colonel Burr said agreeably. "This venture would, of course, be a financial investment for all of us. One which I am sure will pay off quite handsomely. That is why I am restricting it to a very few of my personal friends."

Harman Blennerhassett was not entirely satisfied with

Colonel Burr's explanation. The colonel doubtless had only his own interests at heart, but at that, it was worth inquiring further.

"In this company, Colonel Burr, is the division to be equal?" he asked shrewdly. "If I understand you correctly, my wife and I together would control one third of the company. Is that correct?"

"Yes, that is true," Colonel Burr answered. Better not count this fellow out on brains yet. He might prove to be shrewder than he looked.

In a more placating tone, the colonel explained, "There will be much landscaping of spacious grounds to be done on the estates, Harman. Someone who knows how it should be done will need to oversee the workmen. I can think of no one who could do it more efficiently, and artistically, than you.

"Your ability to landscape grounds has been most convincingly demonstrated here, in the planning of your own estate. With your experience, you could be of inestimable service in perfecting the contour and planting of the estates, thus making them more readily salable."

"I must confess an interest in what you are telling me," Harman said, relaxing a bit.

Colonel Burr was quick to catch the change in temper. Now, he thought, might be the best time to introduce the touchy part of his program. Blennerhassett was an idealist and a dreamer. Better approach him carefully.

"This next matter, Harman, I find myself a little reluctant to introduce lest you misunderstand me, but it is a necessary part of our little plan. You have ideal surroundings here on this island for training and equipping the five hundred volunteers necessary to control the territory. We will need half of this force of men to maintain control, once we are in possession."

Blennerhassett would have interrupted, but Colonel Burr did not pause. "I must continue hastily," he said. "In the Baron Bastrop Grant of land there are astounding possibilities for acquiring unlimited wealth. This area can be developed into at least one hundred huge estates, quite as large and just as beautiful as the one you have here.

"As you know, Harman, war between Spain and the United

States may be very near. That is something that we must not forget."

"War, Colonel Burr? Did you say war?"

"Now, Harman, that is nothing to become alarmed about. We would not start it; it is completely beyond our control." As he talked, Colonel Burr was appraising the strengths and weaknesses of the man before him. Quickly he came to the conclusion that here was one who would give and endure much for an ideal but very little for material gain. He would need someone to serve. How about the poor, down-trodden Mexicans?

"I only say, Harman," Colonel Burr continued, "if war should come, then we would be in a position to control the revolution that is sure to break out in Mexico. By so doing, we should be contributing a double service. Such a revolt would put heavy pressure on the small Spanish army now scattered over all of Mexico, thus eliminating them as a military threat to our United States forces. At the same time, we would be in a position to help free the poor, oppressed people of Mexico."

Harman Blennerhassett gave up trying to break into the colonel's lengthy discussion and contented himself with listening and watching. Colonel Burr had repeatedly paced the length of the library as he talked. Harman was beginning to feel a slight dislike for the colonel where previously he had felt only disinterest in him and in his venture.

The ambitious colonel was the sort of person who always succeeded in making Harman feel uncomfortable; it was his irrepressible energy that did it. Such a person was seldom content to be energetic alone. Just now, Harman could not quite understand why he had to be the victim. Does he want money? Is that it? Harman could think of no other reason why Colonel Burr had come to him.

Stopping now in front of his host, Colonel Burr said most earnestly, "Sir, I now seek your aid whole-heartedly. If you will come in with us, all is in readiness to proceed immediately. Through your influence, and with your financial aid, we will be able to secure the needed volunteers more quickly. Their training can begin at once."

"If you speak of soldiers, Colonel," Blennerhassett cried, jumping to his feet, "the idea is most abhorrent to me."

"Sir, I do not speak of soldiers. I am talking about men who will volunteer to occupy and colonize an area. Of course, they will need to be able to defend themselves, just as do any other pioneers."

Harman settled once more into his chair, at least partially convinced that there was nothing wrong with the plan. He was willing to listen a little longer. It might be worth money to them later.

Colonel Burr, finding his companion once more in a receptive attitude of mind, proceeded at once.

"We will ask first for two hundred volunteers. In the secluded groves here on your island, we can train these men in thirty days—not to be soldiers, but to take care of themselves in wild, undeveloped country.

"Do you realize what that means? It means that two weeks after they finish training, we can be on the banks of the Washita River."

Colonel Burr rushed on as though he feared his listener might again attempt to interrupt.

"There, in that region that is almost a wilderness, we will establish a permanent agricultural settlement which can serve as a base for our operations. It will be the beginning of a development such as this country has not seen.

"Having built our base, we shall then return to this island where we will equip and train three hundred more volunteers. Then, and not until then, we shall be ready to move to the Mexican border, there to await the possible outbreak of war between Spain and the United States. It is in this capacity of protector of our country that we can really be of service. If war comes, the people of Mexico will welcome our help."

Colonel Burr felt that he had presented a convincing story but he was not sure just how his companion had taken it. He paused and waited for comments.

"This is all very interesting, Colonel," Blennerhassett said noncommittally. "It could, I feel sure, prove profitable for my wife and me.

"However, you understand, I am sure, that I must have time to think the matter over carefully. Far too much is involved to warrant my making a hasty decision."

He stood up and then, almost as though it had been an afterthought, said, "Colonel Burr, I should like to ask you some questions."

"Go right ahead," Colonel Burr said amiably.

"You say, Colonel, that this undertaking will require several hundred volunteers. If it is as peaceful in purpose as you would have us believe, why is this so?"

"First, let me assure you that peaceful settlement of unoccupied land is our object in organizing this expedition. It is, however, going to be necessary for us to hold two places at the same time. For this, a fairly large group of men will be needed."

"Colonel, isn't the cost of this expedition going to be exorbitant, with such an extensive territory involved? My investment in this island and house alone, exceeds seventy thousand dollars.

"To build, as you plan, a group of one hundred such estates would require a great fortune. I just can't see where we can obtain all that money."

"I am glad you asked that," Colonel Burr told him. "We shall not attempt to develop a lot of these estates at one time, Harman. Instead, we will first build only two which we shall sell as soon as they are completed. Each estate, as we develop and sell it, will provide funds for the next step in the development."

"That sounds practical enough," Blennerhassett agreed, "but have you any real, substantial assurance that these estates can be sold?"

I made one small piece of wilderness into an estate, Harman was thinking. That was a big undertaking that required years of hard work. Yet this man proposes to develop hundreds of such properties. He has to have a market, and an exceptionally good one, or he is stopped before he starts. Either he is a genius or he is an impractical fool. I've got to know which.

"Certainly they can be sold," Colonel Burr replied sharply. Who did this book-reading, star-gazing dreamer think he was, asking all these questions? Better give him some convincing answers. He seems to have some sense of business, after all.

"First," the colonel explained in a quieter tone, "we will make the estates very exclusive, homes that only the rich can afford to buy. Then, Harman, we will advertise their very exclusiveness.

"Do you know, Harman, there is not a socially exclusive settlement east of the Alleghenies: you cannot help but know that you have, right here, the most beautiful home this side of the mountains. Yet who is there near you that is your equal socially or intellectually? Only in Marietta or Parkersburg can you find friends, and they live a different life, so different that you have little in common. Is it not so?"

Colonel Burr, expecting no reply, continued, "Harman, when you first came down the Ohio River from Pittsburgh, would you not have located in an exclusive settlement if there had been one in existence?

"Think how much easier it would have been for you and Mrs. Blennerhassett if you could have purchased a beautiful estate, all ready and waiting for you."

"True, I might have bought an estate already established," Harman mused. "Then again, I might not. We were looking for something special, and creating it ourselves has made it just that. There is a self-expression here, and a satisfaction, that we could never otherwise have achieved. As for the isolation, that, we like to believe, is part of the charm of this island."

Colonel Burr changed his approach.

"There is money to be made, you know." Maybe that would reach him! The Blennerhassett fortune must be pretty well spent—most of it right here on this island.

"Do you realize, Harman, that we have only to get two estates completed and sold?" Colonel Burr asked. "The rest will be easy. The publicity that our development will receive from those two sales will sell the other estates faster than we can get them into shape.

"Harman, believe me, our opportunities are vast and unlimited. We have only to grasp them. We must not, in a moment of indecision, allow them to escape us."

Blennerhassett, still showing little sign of having been convinced, questioned his companion further.

"Do you think that there are enough interested people in New York, Pennsylvania, and Virginia to buy all these estates?"

Colonel Burr was quick to reply. "It is true that we may not get enough buyers from those three states alone, but we should also be able to draw a limited number from the other states.

"However, there is another group not to be overlooked. We will advertise in Ireland, England, and Scotland. There are certain to be families of wealth in those countries who like yourself, would prefer to live in America if they could be sure that they would not need to sacrifice anything of their gracious way of life.

"You and I, Harman, have only to develop the estates. People will be waiting to buy them."

Colonel Burr strode the length of the room, then returned to stand directly in front of his host.

"This project requires great haste," he said sharply.

"I understand," Mr. Blennerhassett answered. "I shall not keep you waiting once I have reached a decision. However, I must have time to consider carefully before I can give you a definite reply."

Mrs. Blennerhassett and Theodosia, returning sooner than might have been expected, entered the hall in time to hear a little of the conversation between Colonel Burr and Mr. Blennerhassett. They were starting to withdraw when Colonel Burr noticed them. At once, he addressed himself to Mrs. Blennerhassett.

"Come in, Madam," he said.

When Colonel Burr came to the island, Neil Colton and I were engaged to be married. That the coming of this man could place an impassable barrier between us, would never have occurred to either of us. How little we knew! Had we suspected the power of this man, the very danger to all of us that his ambition was to become, would we have sat so unconcernedly on the veranda that morning?

Through the open window, there came suddenly to our ears the soft voice of my father, followed at once by the driving voice of Colonel Burr.

We did not listen voluntarily. The words thrust themselves upon our ears. Into my heart came a feeling of uneasiness that I was unable to put from me. It grew deeper with every word that came through the open window.

We might have gone in then, but Mother and Theodosia returned from their ride. We saw them enter the house by a side door. Colonel Burr must have seen them at once. I heard him speak to my mother.

"Come in, Madam. If you have time, I hope you will allow me to make you acquainted with my plans. I have just been explaining the details of them to your husband."

Mrs. Blennerhassett hesitated. Did she want to come face to face with this man with the enchanting smile, a smile that was so frequently replaced by a calculating glance? Was she ready to hear what he seemed to be so anxious to tell? No, not at this moment. Theodosia's conversation earlier in the morning had given her a hint of what he might want to discuss. She would exercise the privilege of a hostess and play for time.

"My dear Colonel, your daughter and I are much too hot and tired from our ride to listen with attention even to so good a conversationalist as you. I am sure you and Mr. Blennerhassett could also do with a rest until after lunch."

There was nothing for Colonel Burr to do except bow graciously and permit the ladies to withdraw.

"Someone to see Colonel Burr," Della, the maid interrupted the Blennerhassetts at lunch half an hour later.

"Show him into the reception room, Della," Mrs. Blennerhassett told her. "We have nearly finished."

"If I may be so rude, Madam, I'll ask you to excuse me," Colonel Burr interrupted, rising. "This may be important. Forgive me."

"Why, certainly," said his surprised hostess, not quite able to understand what matter could be that important.

The Blennerhassetts were not told who the man was or his reason for coming. They could, however, surmise that he was the bearer of some message, or messages, for Colonel Burr. What did not occur to them was that the messenger also bore away with him the letters that the colonel had written that morning. Ten minutes after his first words with the colonel, he was on his way back up the river toward Williamson, and the State Road that led directly to Winchester.

Neil and I were again on the veranda an hour later when Mother joined us. I was glad she had come just then—and alone.

I could not quite understand. Neil had been little or no help. All I could get from him was an expression of his strong dislike for and distrust of Colonel Burr.

"He puts on a good show," Neil had remarked, "but that is all it is, just show. The man himself is as treacherous as a snake."

"What do you suppose he wants here?" I had asked to keep him on the subject.

"I am not sure, but whatever it is, there is no good in it for the Blennerhassetts. Of that I am sure."

"Oh, there you are, Mother. Come over and sit down."

Mother was always beautiful. This afternoon she was like a princess, dainty and glowing.

"Mother," I said, trying to keep my voice natural, "can you tell us what all the discussion with Colonel Burr is about? I am so worried. We sat here on the veranda for about five minutes this morning. We heard some of the conversation between Father and Colonel Burr. The window was open, you see."

"Colonel Burr has been talking with your father about a colonizing expedition that he is organizing. He expects to develop a rich area in the Louisiana Territory."

Neil spoke up then.

"Mrs. Blennerhassett, can you and Mr. Blennerhassett trust the man? He has a reputation for taking care of himself at other people's expense, you know."

"We know about that, but people could be wrong. Mr. Blennerhassett likes him, and his proposal does sound good."

"But Mother, why is he in such a hurry? If there is nothing wrong with his plan, why can't he be a little more deliberate?"

"My dear, time can often be quite as valuable as money."

With that, Mother glided away, and we were alone. Without saying a word, we left the veranda and crossed the lawn to the arbor. Whom should we meet there but Colonel Burr himself!

"Well, my children," he said in a tone that neither of us liked, "have a seat. I find it very enlightening to talk with young people. Have you been told of my mission here?"

The thing that I most admired about Neil was his complete honesty and fearlessness. He never took the easy way out, just to avoid conflict. As a result, he was frequently getting himself involved in arguments and, sometimes, in more serious altercations. Colonel Burr had given him an opening; now the battle was on.

"We have been told a little, Colonel. I can't say that I like what we have heard. To be frank with you, there is a story going around to the effect that you are conspiring against the government. How do you answer that?"

Colonel Burr lost nothing of his calmness.

"Do you call settling new territory conspiracy against the government?" he questioned, smiling.

Neil came to the point.

"If you are just organizing a new colony of settlers, why are you in such a hurry? Why can't you give the Blennerhassetts more time to consider your proposition? Why all the urgency?"

Colonel Burr, showing the first signs of agitation, answered Neil's question sharply, "If you, Mr. Colton, were the owner of this island, I should gladly impart this information to you. Or if you should yourself consent to become a member of my company, the information would be made available."

He continued in a more pleasant tone, "I am happy to extend to you an invitation to come in with me. I like your clear thinking. I could use your straightforward honesty."

"I am not just being honest, Sir," Neil declared angrily, taking a step toward the colonel and clenching his hands into fists.

"I just plain do not trust you and your schemes. If I were to follow my desire, I would throw you bodily on that flatboat of yours and start you down the river."

"Young man," Colonel Burr said in a voice that had lost its friendliness, "I do not quite see just what business this is of yours."

"I intend to make it my business, Sir. I may not be able to make the Blennerhassetts see you for what I believe you to be, but I intend to do everything I can to prevent your schemes from wrecking their home on this island. Good day, Sir."

Two boatloads of young people from Belpre were tying up at the wharf when Melissa and Neil returned to the house. In the fun and laughter that followed, they were able to forget their earlier anxiety.

"We thought things needed livening up a bit of late here on

the island," one of the young men called to Neil. "I brought my fiddle along just so everyone can limber up a little."

"Jock, when you play that fiddle, no one can think of anything but dancing." Melissa called. "Come on up. We will dance on the veranda."

None of the young people could resist the magic of Jock's music, but after a time Jock tired of playing.

"That is all for now," he said as he put his violin back in its case. "You can amuse yourselves for a while."

Melissa and one of the other girls disappeared through the door. "Betty and I will get something cool to drink," Melissa said. "It is cool under the shade trees, if you would like to sit out on the lawn."

While the others strolled across the lawn, Neil and Jock sat on the porch and talked. After a few minutes, Neil asked the question that had begun going through his mind at the time Jock came ashore.

"What does your father think of Colonel Burr, Jock?"

"Colonel Aaron Burr?" Jock asked, a little puzzled.

"Yes," Neil answered. "Your father was a Revolutionary War officer. I'd just like to know his opinion of the colonel."

"Well, I don't think he cares much about him as a man," Jock said thoughtfully. "Father thought that the duel with Hamilton was uncalled for, a matter of vengeance.

"I have heard him say, though," Jock continued after a moment, "that he was a good officer."

"Did you know that Colonel Burr is here on this island now?" Neil asked.

"No, I didn't. What is he doing here?"

Neil hesitated, wondering how to tell Jock about Colonel Burr's project without also involving the Blennerhassetts.

"He asked me today to join him in a colonizing expedition that he is making into the Southwest. I don't like the looks of it.

"They are telling up in Parkersburg that he is conspiring with a certain army officer to set up a new empire. Do you suppose that there is any truth in it?"

"I don't know," Jock answered. "I do know that my father would never put any trust in what he says. Father does not believe him to be truthful except as it suits his own purpose.

"What did you tell him?"

"That I was not interested. I also told him of the rumors I had heard."

The young people had been gone for an hour when Colonel Burr joined the family on the veranda. Mrs. Blennerhassett was determined to learn all she could about Colonel Burr's plan. She also wanted to be certain that Melissa and Neil should hear the discussion. What she did not foresee was the active part Neil would take in the conversation.

"Colonel Burr," she said, coming directly to the point, "do you know how many boats and men your expedition will require?"

Completely surprised by her direct question, Colonel Burr quickly realized that now was the time to talk figures.

"Can you and your husband," he came back with another question, "raise one hundred thousand dollars? No, let me continue." He raised his hand as Mrs. Blennerhassett gasped.

"The money would reap you a rich return. Would you be willing to sell your estate here, including the island, for say sixty thousand dollars? If you can do so, we can afford a twenty-five percent greater moving force of both men and materials. Time can be shortened, too, if we can finance our move from here rather than from interests in the East."

Sell the island! She had not thought of that. Harman had said nothing about selling the island. The idea was something of a shock to her at first.

Sell the island? It is so beautiful here; but it does get lonely. So far to ride for suitable companionship. How nice it would be to be near people who had the same interests. No doubt there were many places that could be made just as beautiful as the island.

"Might we be exchanging this island for a home even more beautiful?" she asked.

"Indeed you would be, Madam. More than that, when war with Spain comes, and many think it is inevitable, we would be in a position to accomplish the liberation of the oppressed people of Mexico."

Neil interrupted.

"Why are you so sure that Spain and the United States are

going to war? Could you have, Colonel, information concerning this war that the people have not been given?"

Colonel Burr attempted to ignore the interruption, but Neil was insistent.

"This land you talk about. Do you propose to give it to the men who join with you?"

"I do. Five hundred acres to each volunteer."

"Do you have a clear title to that land, Colonel?" Neil was watching for the furtive look that crossed the colonel's face at that question.

"Do not try to answer, Colonel," he said raising his hand. "You have no title! Only the United States Government can give you a certified title. That you do not have?"

The colonel moved uncomfortably, and Neil was sure that he had guessed right. There was no title from the federal government consigning this territory to Colonel Burr. The whole venture was outside of the law.

"Colonel Burr," Neil was quick to continue, "I believe your plan to be contrary to the law of the land. Your scheme is costly; it is dangerous; it is unjust to those whom you hope to involve; and above all, it is seditious. Personally, I hope that someone will be able to stop you."

To say that Mrs. Blennerhassett was surprised at Neil's outburst, would be putting it mildly. She was also secretly pleased. She admired his spirit, even as she disagreed with what he was saying. The boy was evidently sincere enough but, of course, he had become alarmed over nothing.

"Neil," she said, "Colonel Burr is quite honorable. I feel sure that we have nothing to fear so far as the law is concerned. President Jefferson himself approves of your expedition, does he not, Colonel?"

"Most certainly he does, Madam. Why should he object to anything we might do to further the interests of our beloved country?"

"And I," Neil said quietly, "refuse to believe, without proof, that you have the approval of any government official. I do not believe that you have the slightest authority to go ahead with your plans."

Mrs. Blennerhassett spoke directly to the colonel, "I feel,

Colonel Burr," she said, "that your plans are reasonable and worthy of our consideration, but we would like a little more time to think about it before agreeing to join with you."

Colonel Burr impatiently struck one clenched fist into the palm of his other hand. "Permit me to excuse myself, my dear Madam, while you and your husband discuss the matter privately."

I, Melissa, shall remember forever the tenseness that settled over us that afternoon as Colonel Burr went down the veranda steps. We watched him in silence as he crossed the lawn and was lost from view among the shrubbery.

I think I knew then that, for good or evil, there went a man from whose influence my parents were powerless to escape. I do not think he had them charmed, nor did he coerce them. It was just that, when he talked, he painted such beautiful pictures that they had to go and see for themselves.

My mother, ever the perfect hostess, now took the best way she knew to relieve the strained, uncomfortable atmosphere that was threatening to engulf us. She invited our many friends to a dinner and ball. Governor Alston was to arrive that evening from Marietta to join his wife, Theodosia. What better way to show our guests a little extra attention than to entertain in their honor?

I can see it all now, as I watched it then. The servants dispatched to Parkersburg, Belpre, Marietta, with dozens of invitations; my mother and Cindy, the cook, planning the dinner; Jess and Liza clearing the dance floor, placing the chairs for Wilbur Macklefresh and his musicians.

I remember, too, watching Governor Alston as he stepped from the first boat that tied up at our wharf that afternoon. He came ahead of the other guests and was greeted by his wife and my mother. I thought that I had never seen so handsome a gentleman.

As though it were yesterday, I see once more the arrival of many boats that brought our friends—lovely ladies, gallant gentlemen, who landed at our wharf and strolled across the lawn to the house.

It was a happy group that sat at our table that evening. My mother, with charm and grace, kept the conversation lively and interesting. If anyone noticed an undercurrent of uneasiness, it was forgotten in the festivities of the evening.

Dinner was nearly finished when we heard soft strains of music coming from the drawing room. Half an hour later we were lining up for the grand march, with the governor and his beautiful lady leading. My mother, charming and stately, had chosen to dance first with Colonel Burr. I danced with my father and I saw Neil apparently quite happy with one of the other girls.

For a moment, I had forgotten the fear and anxiety in my heart. Sight of Neil brought it all to mind once more, with all the fear and dread. I had little heart left for dancing.

It was at the end of the second dance that Neil joined Melissa on the veranda. The music of the orchestra came through the open door, gay and happy, but neither Melissa nor Neil felt in tune with the music.

"Walk with me," Neil whispered, tucking Melissa's arm in his.

"Oh, Neil."

It was all she said, but the tremor in her voice spoke much more. Together, they went slowly down the steps, along the winding walk, toward the wharf. Behind them the music grew fainter. In the background, voices could be heard and, now and then, a burst of laughter. The voice of the river reached their ears in the soft lapping of the water against the island shore.

"The river, Neil, is like a friend tonight," Melissa said softly as they sat side by side on the edge of the wharf. "And yet, it has brought danger, perhaps unhappiness, into our midst."

"The river, Melissa, is first of all a thoroughfare and is concerned not at all with the danger or safety of those whom it serves. It is not the river that would betray your trust this night."

Melissa sighed.

"I know you are right, Neil. I am just feeling sad and a little silly. I don't know what is wrong with me."

"I can tell you what is wrong, Melissa," Neil said quickly. "You have the same letdown feeling that I have—only worse.

"Listen to all that music and the people laughing and talking.

Those people do not realize that this celebration tonight has a phony setting.

"Oh, Melissa, I wish you would let me take you out of all this."

Melissa's voice was gentle as she answered, "I know, Neil. Today, I almost would have gone. Now I know I cannot leave."

For the moment, they were quiet. It was Neil who broke the silence, his voice sounding strangely harsh.

"You know, Melissa, and I know that there are people up at the house tonight who should be dancing with heavy hearts. In my opinion, they are celebrating in their own sorrow."

Whether it was what he said or the tone of his voice, Melissa herself probably would not have known, but Neil's words aroused a sharp feeling of resentment in her. She knew that she was being unfair to Neil, that she was putting an interpretation into his words that he had not intended should be there.

She turned, her eyes flashing, and said almost in a whisper, "Neil, you can mean that for only one person—for my mother!"

Melissa ignored the look of surprise on Neil's face as she demanded, "Why do you dislike her, Neil? You know I am devoted to her. She has been a wonderful mother to me. The only real one I have ever known."

"Not so loud, Melissa," Neil cautioned her. He wanted no one to hear her making such wild accusations. Dislike Mrs. Blennerhassett? Neil reflected for a moment. He might not trust her judgment in all things, but he was really quite fond of her. He could not fail to recognize how kind she had been to Melissa.

"Melissa, please remember this one thing as I talk with you, I like and admire your mother very much. But please try to understand that you and I are engaged to be married. Our problem now is to plan for our own lives together. We cannot expect your mother to determine what is for our happiness. We have to decide that for ourselves. Melissa, knowing your mother as I do, I am afraid that she is going to make herself and those who love her most unhappy. Not purposely, but the result will be the same."

Melissa flushed angrily.

"Neil, you just do not like Mother. Everything you say is always against her."

Neil was becoming a little angry at Melissa's contrariness.

"I like your mother all right, Melissa," he said sharply. "I just do not like the mess she seems determined to get mixed up in. And I do not want her or anyone else involving you in any such dangerous scheme."

Neil arose and stood above her, erect and angry. I am glad that he gets so provoked with me, Melissa thought. His next question completely surprised her.

"Melissa, if I tell you that Mrs. Alston is completely opposed to her father's plans, will you believe me?"

"No," Melissa declared. "I do not believe you. That girl is too devoted to her father to oppose him. It would seem strange indeed for that to be true when she came here on the boat with him. She must be in agreement with what he is doing or she would not have come."

"It is true, Melissa. Theodosia is against this whole expedition. I have learned that she violently opposes all of her father's present plans. She believes the undertaking to be too dangerous.

"You and I, Melissa, have a decision to make, a direction to choose. We have need of making that decision very soon.

"I am convinced that this scheming, so-called Colonel Burr has only to get his way, and everything on this island will be sold, including the island itself."

Melissa was sad as she answered, "Oh, Neil, I am so worried! I don't know what to do."

There was no longer anger in Neil's voice, only earnestness as he said, "Melissa, dear, believe me. There is no future for you down the river. That can only end in unhappiness for everyone involved. Melissa, don't go.

"I do not want you to be unhappy. I want to marry you. Marry me, Melissa, and we will build our own happiness together."

Melissa slowly shook her head, too moved to speak. Hand in hand, they walked slowly back up the path toward the mansion. Half way to the house, they left the path and went to sit in chairs on the lawn.

Neil thought that Melissa had never looked more lovely, more beautiful than she did that night. He knew that she was accustomed to many luxuries that he could not give her, but he had dared to hope that she would be willing to share his life.

Neil had worked hard to provide for the future he had dreamed about. Tonight he was discouraged. It all seemed so hopeless. Sitting there on the moonlit lawn, Neil talked earnestly with Melissa. Gone was all the anger; only a deep seriousness remained.

"Melissa, I do not want to cause you any needless sorrow, but tonight I want you to give careful thought to our future.

"I must tell you once again that I am definitely opposed to the decision the Blennerhassetts seem to have made. I cannot, in any way, aid in their plans.

"I dislike and distrust Colonel Burr, probably because he has caused all this confusion. But I believe I am more angry with the Blennerhassetts for acting in such poor judgment that they have fallen in with all of his suggestions. No doubt there are those who will be in sympathy with them."

Melissa said nothing, although her thoughts were as deep as the river flowing near them.

Neil continued, "Melissa, I have bought that high knoll on the Ohio side, the one overlooking this island. You said once that it has the most beautiful view in the valley. I can begin our house tomorrow if you will just say the word.

"There, in the house I would build for you, we could make our home, just you and I, away from all the scheming, ambitious people. There we could raise our children, teaching them loyalty and service to the country we both love. You have only to say you will marry me, Melissa."

Neil moved over and sat on the lawn at Melissa's feet.

"I cannot go on until you give me an answer, Melissa."

Melissa stared out into the night, as if to read on the darkness the reply she must give. Presently she turned directly toward Neil, as though she had reached a decision.

"Neil," she said softly, "I do believe you and I do want to marry you, but that is impossible at the present time. That you may better understand, I shall try to tell you a little about myself. I think you will be able to see why my loyalties must always be with the Blennerhassetts.

"In your mind, come along with me to a little town in Ireland. I want you to see there, if you can, a ragged, dirty, neglected, little girl of twelve. She had a home, yes, but most of the time there was no one in it but her. Her father drank and her mother never stayed home. She had one older brother, but he was never around. He did write her one letter years later, after she had come to America.

"See, if you can, that little girl. On the street most of the day, wandering from place to place, always hungry, and often cold. Watch her at night slip into that dark, empty house, hoping but never expecting that her family would be there. Eat a bite or two of that cold, tasteless food or, better still, look into that cupboard when it holds no food at all.

"Walk up those dark stairs with her; feel the fear that stiffened her at the faintest sound. Know the hunger for affection that bored so deeply into her child's heart that it was many times more painful than her gnawing stomach.

"Go with her out into the street that morning when she had seen neither father or mother for five days. Go along with her to a place where some ladies of the church were feeding hungry people—the place she had walked past yesterday and could not go in. Follow her inside.

"Feel the embarrassment that she felt when the lady who knew her father and mother questioned her. Feel the humiliation of a child answering truthfully those terribly personal questions. Questions that no child should ever have the need to answer.

"Experience, if you will, that child's joy when, after she had eaten the warm, nourishing food, that same lady invited her to go home with her for the night. And then the warm bath, the clean clothes, the soft bed, the sound, untroubled sleep!

"It must have been an hour later that the child heard voices. Someone was talking with the kind lady and her husband. The new voice was so beautiful, so filled with kindness that it was sheer music to the ears of the child.

"That little girl fell in love with the voice even before she heard it say, 'Just as soon as we can sell out completely, we are going to America. My husband and I will do all within our legal power to take the little girl with us.'

"That voice, Neil, belonged to Mrs. Blennerhassett, and she was talking about me. Their voices drifted away, and I was soon asleep again, not to waken until noon the next day.

"Soon after I awoke, Mrs. Blennerhassett came in to see me. She told me the whole story of their selling their estate and going to America. They wanted me to go with them but they would first have to adopt me.

"Neil, I kept thinking, 'Can anyone leave their father and mother and go to a strange country to live, knowing that they are never to see them again?'

"Mrs. Blennerhassett arranged for me to stay with the same lady for a week. All the time I kept wondering where my parents could be. Mrs. Blennerhassett stopped in on the fifth day and told me that I would have to be declared a ward of the town. Then I would be put up for adoption. This could be arranged because a detective had stayed close to my home for five days and five nights. Neither of my parents came home during that time.

"Neil, I could offer no objection to all this planning because I had a warm bed and warm meals every day, and those people treated me just like they did their own children."

Neil interrupted.

"Did all those proceedings have the approval of Mr. Blennerhassett?" he asked.

"Yes, Mr. Blennerhassett was very much in favor of my adoption. In fact, he had the legal proceedings processed by one of Ireland's most noted attorneys.

"I was declared a ward of the town, eligible for adoption. I was permitted to continue living with the good people who were already taking care of me.

"If my father or mother read any of the legal proceedings concerning my adoption, they made no objection. Everything went through on schedule, and I became the adopted child of the Blennerhassetts. Two weeks later their sales were completed and we were on our way to America.

"On the day before we were to leave Ireland, I asked permission to visit a neighbor who lived close by my old home. I wanted to go back to see if Mother or Father was there. It was hard for me to believe that they were really guilty of the charge that the court had placed against them—deserting a minor.

"The neighbors told me that neither of my parents had been back. I went into the house where I had known so much loneliness and just rambled around for what seemed like hours. When I heard a knock on the front door, I was hoping to see my mother or father, but it was Mr. Blennerhassett.

"He sounded worried when he called my name. I wanted something from there to take with me so I hurried to the room that had been my own. When he called again, I answered and told him I would be out at once.

"I wanted so desperately to have some little keepsake to take with me from my old home. Looking around and trying to decide, I found a locket with my grandmother's picture in it. Grandmother had been gone for a long time, but I had always remembered how good she had been to me. I took the little locket. I thought if I wore the locket, I would not get so lonesome. I would always have with me something from home."

Both were silent for a few minutes after Melissa finished speaking. Neither was conscious of the sounds of music coming from the house, or of the night sounds around them. Each was too busy just thinking, Melissa of the past, Neil of all that she had told him, of what it must mean to their future. Neil was first to break the silence.

In a voice filled with tenderness, he said, "I am so glad you have told me all this, Melissa. It explains so many things. I think it has made me love you more than ever, but never again will I try to take you away from the Blennerhassetts."

Early in the morning, on the day Governor Alston and Theodosia were to depart for their home in South Carolina, Theodosia found her father alone on the lawn in front of the house. Colonel Burr greeted her warmly.

"You will be going soon, Theo, but it cannot be for long. When I get my plans into action, and it looks like that will be very soon, there will be an end to all this delay."

"Father," said Theodosia, "I cannot leave you without talking over some things that are worrying me. You have been wonderful about telling me all your plans, and everything seems good and proper, so far as I can tell. Because I trust you and believe in you, I have not hesitated to give my approval of your expedition."

Colonel Burr smiled. He who needed approval from no one, treasured that of his only daughter.

"Thank you, Theodosia," he said. "You know how much I appreciate your confidence in me."

"But, Father," Theodosia continued with a note of pleading in her voice. "I cannot say that I approve of your getting a loan from Mr. Blennerhassett. I keep thinking that it is wrong for you to ask him for so much money."

"Now, Theo," Colonel Burr answered her soothingly, "just you leave everything to me. The Blennerhassetts welcome the opportunity I offer them."

But Theodosia had not finished.

"Father," she continued, "I was so upset the other evening when I happened to see you looking at Mr. Blennerhassett with that calculating expression that you sometimes get. It was almost as if you were saying to yourself, 'How much is he worth to me?' "

"What are you talking about?" Colonel Burr's voice was impatient. Even Theodosia had no right to criticize.

Theodosia knew that she was pushing her father too far, but she had to say the things that had been bothering her ever since they had come to the island. She knew how relentless he could be where his ambitions were concerned.

"Father, I knew as I watched the expression on your face, that you regard Mr. Blennerhassett as a mere child instead of an equal partner. It is unfair for you to take advantage of this good man. Promise me, Father, that you will not do so."

Theodosia had tried. One look at her father's face was enough to convince her that she had failed in her attempt to protect the Blennerhassetts.

"Stop your sentimental dreaming," Colonel Burr told her angrily. "I have no designs on the Blennerhassetts. They are both adults, perfectly capable of making decisions, who stand to gain quite as much from this venture as any of us. Enough of your foolishness."

Theodosia persisted in spite of her father's anger.

"I know, Father, and you do, too, that Mrs. Blennerhassett

is an ambitious woman who listens earnestly to your plans. Then, just as earnestly, she discusses them with her husband, painting the picture even brighter than you have already presented it. We both know that he does as she says. He may be more mature, but she is the leader."

"You have really got this thing figured out, have you not, my dear?" Colonel Burr said scornfully.

Theodosia chose to ignore his sarcasm.

"It is true," she continued, "that you have not told me for sure that they are investing their money with you, but you do not need to tell me. The signs are too obvious. Father, do not take their money.

"I sometimes think that money means more to you than life itself."

"Why do you say that?" Colonel Burr demanded.

"I have been wondering, Father, much as I love you, if this very money that they are about to put into your hands may not be the ruin of all of us. Our two families are friends now, Father. Why can you not permit us to remain friends?"

"You are talking nonsense, Daughter, believe me," her father declared. He thought it best to reassure Theodosia. He knew her to be perfectly capable of going to the Blennerhassetts themselves if she were to become convinced that he was trying to trick them.

"Of course, we are friends, and there is every reason to believe that we shall be able to continue so. This project that we are all about to engage in will prove, I am sure, to be the means of strengthening our friendship with these fine people.

"Now, no more of this nonsense. How soon do you leave?"

Because she had thought about the situation so much and was still unconvinced, Theodosia did not answer her father's question. Instead, she argued further.

"Father, your plans are so uncertain. I have not said this before. In fact, I have hardly dared to think it, because of my loyalty to you, but to me these plans seem actually dangerous. If you have confided in me as completely as you say, I can see little in the proposed undertaking that is at all reassuring.

"You do not yourself have the necessary money to finance your venture. Instead, you are asking this man who has already established a permanent home for his family to dispose of it that he may share in this gamble with you.

"It is all very well for you to do something like this, Father, for you love the hazard of it, but leave the Blennerhassetts as they are."

"Young lady," Colonel Burr interrupted angrily, "you have said about enough."

Theodosia, determined to finish what she had to say, refused to be quieted.

"You say that the territory farther south has unlimited possibilities. I am sure that is true, but, Father, tell me what further opportunities do the people on this island need?

"You must agree that the paradise they already enjoy on this island would be hard to sacrifice. Why should they be persuaded to hazard this peace and comfort for the uncertainty you are prepared to offer them?"

"You seem to have all the answers," Colonel Burr said sharply.

Theodosia continued more calmly, "Father, I do not like to oppose you like this, but in the little time that we have been here, I have fallen in love with this island. Its beauty, its setting here in the middle of the river, the ideal life that this family live here fascinates me. I cannot bear to see it disturbed."

Colonel Burr seemed at a loss for words as he looked into the eyes of his daughter. Momentarily, it appeared that she might have persuaded him to change his mind. But not for long.

He slammed his fists together and said flatly, "Theodosia, go join your Governor. I shall not be longer detained."

In one final appeal, Theodosia pleaded, "Father, I beg you to go and see President Jefferson. If the president will approve your plans, I will join with you wholeheartedly."

Colonel Burr turned his back and did not answer.

"Good-bye, Father."

Theodosia's voice was scarcely audible as her father started slowly toward the house. She watched him for a moment then she went down the path toward the wharf where the governor and his party were waiting for her.

Late that same morning, Mrs. Blennerhassett was reading in the library when her husband joined her.

At once she asked, "Harman, how much thought have you given to Colonel Burr's wonderful idea—the expedition that he has invited us to join?"

"I have thought of little else, Margaret," her husband replied sharply. "Do you think we should give up this dream that has already come true for, let us say, a gamble of wishful thinking?

"We sold everything we owned in Ireland; we traveled thousands of miles to come here; we developed this beautiful island into the home of our dreams. It just does not seem sensible to sail away and leave all that we have built here.

"I will agree that Colonel Burr seems to be a sincere person, difficult to disagree with, but, Margaret, we have already realized our ambition. In this island Utopia, we now own the most beautiful home west of the Alleghenies.

"Colonel Burr's project will cost a lot of money. He has acknowledged that. Margaret, we cannot finance all of this by ourselves, and it would appear that that is just about what he would like us to do. If we go into this venture, it could turn out that we are trading riches and plenty for poverty and want. Let us not forget for one moment that that is the risk we would run."

Mrs. Blennerhassett was more determined than ever to influence her husband's thinking, so convinced was she that joining Colonel Burr's expedition was the proper course to follow.

"We have looked at the gloomy side now, Harman," she said lightly. "Let us take a look at the bright features that this plan appears to offer.

"You would no longer be buried here in the wilderness, miles from intellects that can interest you. Harman, you were educated in three universities. Your final degree made you a polished attorney. You are fitted for a cultured life, to be a leader among men.

"I know we are all happy here on this island, but it is so isolated. There is so little opportunity here for a man of your accomplishments."

"I have never been an ambitious man," Harman protested. "For myself, I am contented here with my books and my laboratory. It is for you and our children that I should be willing to make a change."

Margaret Blennerhassett understood perfectly her husband's willingness to remain on the island. She knew him to be a dreamer and a scholar rather than a man of action. She knew that it was up to her to furnish the drive, or their opportunity would be lost. Truly, she considered Colonel Burr's expedition a real opportunity. To gain her desire she resorted to a little flattery.

"Harman," she said, "you have such wonderful ideas. It is too bad there is here no way for you to put them into operation.

"In the Baron Bastrop territory that Colonel Burr has told us about, you can build many estates like this one. With your ability and this opportunity you will be able to develop a colony for our friends. The design of that community can take any form you desire."

Harman shook his head. "I am not so sure, Margaret. And," with an understanding smile, "do not try to flatter me."

Following another thought, the only one that had disturbed her, Margaret said, "Harman, you said yesterday that Colonel Burr's idea might be considered treasonable. You do not really believe that, do you? He is, as you know, a man who has held positions of high trust and I feel sure he is a man truly devoted to his country."

"Probably all you say is true," Harman agreed, "but Margaret, I sense something about him that I cannot completely trust. Maybe it is his ambition, but I am not sure that it is entirely ambition."

"Harman, you always distrust people until they have proved themselves," his wife complained, forgetting that she had asked her husband's opinion. "I am sure that Colonel Burr is deserving of our complete faith in him.

"Harman, do be reasonable. We have so much to gain if all that Colonel Burr has told us is true. Just think of all the land we would be helping to add to this great country. Let us take a chance, Harman, and join with him."

Harman had never been able to deny his wife anything she asked. Today was no exception.

"I shall not say yes, Margaret, just yet," he told her, "but you know that in the end, I always do what you say."

It was in the afternoon of the same day that Colonel Aaron

Burr impatiently waited in the library for the Blennerhassetts to appear. They had sent him word that they would meet him there. He was as usual, restlessly pacing the length of the room, but he stopped abruptly as Mrs. Blennerhassett entered, followed immediately by her husband. The colonel searched their faces intently for an instant, trying to read there something of what they were about to tell him.

Mrs. Blennerhassett spoke first.

"Colonel Burr, we will join you. My husband has consented to help."

"That is wonderful news, my dear lady," Colonel Burr said quietly, showing none of the elation he was feeling. Now he would be able to raise the money he needed. These people had saved his expedition.

It did not bother Colonel Burr that Harman Blennerhassett spoke somewhat less enthusiastically than his wife.

"I shall be able to assist you to the extent of eighty thousand dollars. That is all the cash that I can avail myself of at this time."

Colonel Burr was a little disappointed at the figure that Blennerhassett named; he had hoped for more. However, he did not allow his feelings to show. They must not know that he would need many times that amount before his project was to become a reality instead of a dream.

"Eighty thousand dollars will be a very considerable help to us," he said cheerfully. Then he added, "I shall go now to enlist the help of Governor Alston in our enterprise. I have every reason to believe that he wishes to be included in our venture."

As Colonel Burr shoved off from the island toward the small settlement of Parkersburg, he realized the necessity of overtaking Governor Alston and Theodosia. He urged his men to extreme effort, in his haste to overtake Governor Alston's party. Late in the afternoon they caught up with the governor's party at Neal's Crossing.

Theodosia was overjoyed when she saw her father coming toward them. She thought that he must have had a change of heart.

"Father, have you decided to abandon your plans and go to South Carolina with us?" she asked hopefully.

Colonel Burr replied firmly, almost impersonally, "No, Theodosia, I have come to talk directly with the governor. What I have to say, I will discuss with both of you.

"Let us withdraw from the party. We can talk over under that big shade tree."

When they were under the tree, Colonel Burr continued, "I hasten to inform you both that the Blennerhassetts have just agreed to invest eighty thousand dollars in my expedition."

At his statement, Theodosia cried, "Do you mean that those people have agreed to invest that much money with you?"

"They have," Colonel Burr replied.

Governor Alston said, "Colonel, I suppose you are wanting to secure the loan I promised you."

"Yes," Colonel Burr said brusquely, "I want the full amount, twenty thousand dollars."

"Father," Theodosia protested vigorously, "twenty thousand dollars is all the available money we have. You can not take all of it."

"I must have it all—and now," he said coldly.

"Why do you need an additional twenty thousand if the Blennerhassetts have already agreed to lend you eighty thousand dollars?"

Then, almost to herself, she added, "So they are going to let you have all that money. I think the Blennerhassetts are just plain stupid to sacrifice that island and all they have there. And for nothing but a wild adventure."

Colonel Burr ignored his daughter's remarks and turned to Governor Alston.

"Governor, I have all of the signed documents with me. Briefly, the original copy contains this: you and Theodosia, the Blennerhassetts, Comfort Tyler, and I, Aaron Burr, will share equally in this company. However, both of you must agree, as the others have already agreed, that I shall retain the presidency of the organization."

There was no hesitation in Governor Alston's answer.

"If the Blennerhassetts are willing to venture eighty thousand dollars on your project," he declared, "I am privileged to invest the twenty thousand you ask. I will also gladly sign the documents giving you the right to retain the presidency of the company.

"As you know, Colonel Burr, I have the duties of the governorship of my state to perform. I have little time for any other business."

"Governor," Colonel Burr hurriedly assured him, "no further aid will be asked of you, either physically or financially.

"However, we will contact you when we start construction on the first estate. Having invested so heavily, you will, of course, want to be kept informed of our progress."

Theodosia interrupted, speaking heatedly.

"Father, I insist, unless you go to see President Jefferson and get his approval, I will never agree to becoming a partner in your venture."

"I like your independence, Theo," Colonel Burr good-humoredly answered his daughter. "You are right to oppose me in this, feeling the way you do. However, time will reveal who is right and who is wrong. With or without your agreeing, we are now ready to proceed with our plans.

"I now bid you both a fond adieu. You must be on your way for your journey will be long. I shall return at once to the island."

Colonel Burr's boat left Neal's Crossing in the dim light of early evening. Several hours later, the colonel once more landed on the wharf in front of the Blennerhassett home. The family was at supper when Colonel Burr returned. No one knew that he was near until he walked into the dining room.

Harman rose to his feet to greet him.

"Good evening, Colonel. How are you? You are just in time for supper."

Colonel Burr seemed more stern than they had previously seen him as he replied, "Fine, Sir. I have already eaten, thank you. Just as soon as you have finished, Harman, I should like to talk with you."

Colonel Burr appeared to be more uneasy than at any time since he had first arrived on the island. The Blennerhassetts exchanged sharp glances as they noticed how restless he had become. As usual, he refused their invitation to sit down. However, Colonel Burr's ever-persistent walking was no indication that he was even slightly agitated. By this time the Blennerhassetts had become accustomed to the fact that Colonel Burr never did sit down when he was talking with them.

Harman Blennerhassett finished his meal hurriedly then followed Colonel Burr into the library. Colonel Burr did most of the talking.

"Harman," he said, beginning at once to give orders, "I want you and your wife to decide on one of your personal friends who is best qualified to be our captain. We want a man who can, and will, go out and recruit two hundred volunteers in the next thirty days.

"These volunteers must be of good character and also men who want to advance themselves. They will have special assignments because they will be the nucleus of our agricultural settlement on the banks of the Washita.

"They will also have key positions, for many of them will be offered the opportunity to homestead land as compensation for their efforts in our enterprise."

When Colonel Burr finished talking, Harman turned to his wife and asked, "Margaret, do you not think that Ned Fox would be our best choice? I feel sure he will agree to our plans. More than that, he is a man whom we can trust."

"Yes," Mrs. Blennerhassett agreed. "I think Ned is just the man we need. From now on, he should be referred to as Captain Fox."

Mr. Blennerhassett called Sam and handed him a letter that he had hurriedly written.

"Sam, I want you to take this letter to Mr. Ned Fox. If he is not at home, find him. Give him the letter, then bring him back with you to this island."

"Yessuh, Mistah Harman, I'll do that," Sam said as he left the room.

Next evening Ned Fox arrived to confer with the Blennerhassetts. The purpose of the expedition was explained to him, also his own duties as leader of the volunteers. Because he both trusted and respected the Blennerhassetts, Ned Fox readily agreed to do what they asked of him.

Mrs. Blennerhassett then said, "You are now to be known as Captain Fox. You will be so addressed by all of us."

"It will be your responsibility to recruit the volunteers," Harman explained further. "Since you know everyone in the locality and have the confidence of all, that will best be accomplished by your seeing each one of the men personally."

Captain Fox asked, "Shall I inform the volunteers that they will be quartered on the island, or will they be permitted to return to their homes each evening?"

Blennerhassett thought for a moment before replying.

"The answer is both yes and no. We will have quarters available for them if they wish to remain on the island at night. However, any who wish to return to their homes each evening will be permitted to do so.

"Of course, Captain Fox, we will entrust to your judgment the advisability of your requiring an oath of allegiance from each volunteer to you."

Captain Fox, completely convinced of the opportunity the volunteers would have, found it an easy task when he went from home to home detailing plans for the expedition. By the end of the week, one hundred thirty-two volunteers had enlisted for aid to the Blennerhassetts.

If Ned Fox had thought that he was to do all of the recruiting, he was wrong. Harman Blennerhassett, too, worked quietly among his friends, influencing a number of them to join. Colonel Burr, on a number of occasions, actively sought volunteers. He was a most persuasive talker.

There was the day in Marietta when the local militia had assembled for their annual training. Colonel Burr addressed the gathering of militia and local citizens.

"My good friends," he said in part. "It is a pleasure for me to be allowed the privilege of telling you of a great opportunity that has come your way. The opportunity to join in an undertaking like none you have ever known before.

". . . and need I tell you of the beauties of that wonderful country of Mexico? Perfect climate, rich soil, gorgeous flowers, wealth beyond description—all waiting to be liberated from the Spaniard's yoke. The time is at hand. . . .

"And then there is the land that we will settle. Five hundred acres to every man of you who comes with me to that untrodden paradise. A paradise bequeathed to the white man by Indians who have moved on farther into the West.

"But I shall talk no more for the present of my expedition. Proceed with your drill. Let me see what you young men have learned in your training."

With that, Colonel Aaron Burr took command of the raw troops and drilled them in a way that left no doubt in the mind of any observer that he was a competent and skilled officer.

With the coming of the volunteers, life on our island changed. Entertainment and social gatherings at the mansion were no more. Gaiety was a thing of the past. The very air grew somber and foreboding. Cindy had stopped singing at her work in the kitchen, and laughter was no longer heard in the servants' quarters.

In one of the shops guns were being repaired and stored. Day after day, the sound of hammering and sawing told us that the building of boats was continuing. Boats were being fitted with storage compartments for food, supplies, and—guns. Drilling and conditioning exercises for the volunteers were now a daily routine.

How I hated seeing them involved, those men who were our neighbors. Their good humor was evidence enough that they were acting in the best of faith. They could know nothing of the dread that lay so heavily on my heart.

I grieved for my father who had forsaken his books and his letters. I wept for all that was gone, and feared for what was yet to come.

Neil Colton had ridden out to Coalton's Range to visit his father. It was a ride of some twenty-five miles from Parkersburg, over the lately completed State Road, to the spot where his father lived. Neil had never talked with his father about his reasons for buying himself in such a secluded location. Today he meant to ask him a few questions.

As he rode up to the house, large as a mansion but built entirely of hewn logs, Neil could not escape the beauty of its setting at the very edge of a tract of virgin timber. The house looked to be almost a part of the dark forest rising behind it.

Within the house, Neil was fondly greeted by his mother and sister, but today his mission was not with them. He tarried but a few minutes before he crossed the room to knock on the door of his father's study.

"Come in," he heard his father's voice solemn and sonorous, as coming from a great distance or from the depths of some serious book he might have been reading.

"Neil, it is good to see you, my boy." His father rose to greet him. "To what do we owe this unexpected visit? Does your mother know that you are here?"

Neil answered the last question first. "I talked with Mother and Jane for a few minutes in the living room just now. They are at the moment bustling around getting something for me to eat."

"That is what makes your mother happiest now, Neil, cooking and working for her family. It is her only regret that you cannot be with us more. But why are you here today? I thought you were studying all the time."

"There are some things I want to talk over with you, Father, important things, I believe. That is why I have taken the time this morning to ride out here to see you."

Believing that his first question might surprise his father, Neil watched his father's face as he asked, "Father, did you ever know Aaron Burr?"

"Yes, I knew Colonel Burr," the older man answered guardedly after a slight pause. "Why do you ask?"

"Because," Neil said, "I must know what kind of man he really is. I must know just how far he can be trusted. For some reason, I had the feeling that maybe you could tell me."

"Why is it so important that you know about him?" Neil's father asked a little anxiously. "Have you seen him, or have you been hearing something about him?"

Neil leaned forward as he answered, "Colonel Burr is in the valley, Father. He is staying on the island with the Blennerhassetts. From there he goes to Belpre, Marietta, Parkersburg, and all the surrounding areas recruiting men for some kind of expedition. More than that, he is drilling a number of these same recruits on the island, volunteers he calls them.

"Not everyone believes the story he tells, that he is organizing a peaceful, colonizing expedition. Enough have believed, however, that he has been able to persuade several hundred men to join with him, including Harman Blennerhassett."

"And you, my son, do you believe that he speaks the truth?" the father asked.

"No, Sir. I have distrusted him from the first, but it is only a feeling. I have no knowledge that anything is wrong. Rumors are being circulated in both Marietta and Parkersburg that Colonel Burr is heading a conspiracy against the government, but they are only rumors. I need proof."

"I met Colonel Burr only once," the father said quietly. "He probably does not remember that I even exist, but I should not be living here in this secluded place today except for him.

"I have never talked about it. For a long time it was much too painful, but that is over now. It was the Colonel's man who defeated me in the ambition of a lifetime. He kept me from the office that should rightfully have been mine. I have been able to forgive and partially to forget, but my confidence in either of them can never be restored.

"You know, of course, the life we have made for ourselves here in this new country. Through my editors and through personal correspondence I have kept in touch with that other world of politics and, at times, intrigue."

He drew a letter from his pocket and handed it to Neil.

"This letter came by the morning post. It is from Sylvester Connor, a news reporter in Richmond. I know him well and feel that he can be trusted to tell the truth."

Neil unfolded the letter and read it quickly.

"This is the proof, Father," he said a little sadly. "Now I need delay no longer. Maybe what I say will be listened to without so much skepticism. Thus far my words have had very little influence."

Neil's heart was heavy the next morning as he left the Ohio shore and headed his canoe toward the island. He had hoped to find Ned Fox at his home in Belpre and talk with him there. Instead he had been told that Ned was on the island and was not expected home for several days. Neil found several canoes tied at the water's edge and immediately borrowed one for quick crossing to Blennerhassett Island.

As Neil paddled, his mind was busy with everything but the river; his paddling was automatic and required no thought. Where, he wondered, would he find Ned Fox? How should he approach him? Ned had never been at all interested in any of Neil's objections. In fact, he had been quite scornful of the attitude Neil had persisted in taking toward the expedition.

A quiet approach, Neil was convinced, would gain him nothing. Ned would not even listen. What Neil had to say would have to be sharp, brusque, even rude. He must be prepared to startle or scare the other man into attention.

The wharf where Neil landed could not be seen from the house because of a grove of trees that grew between. He pulled the canoe from the water and went directly to the camp of the volunteers.

Might as well let the camp know he had arrived, Neil reasoned as he called loudly at the edge of the camp. "Captain Fox, are you here? I have a message for you."

It was no surprise to Neil that Ned Fox did not appear in answer to his call. He had thought it hardly likely that he would find the captain of the volunteers so near the outskirts of the camp. As he walked along through the camp, he saw here and there a man emerging from one of the cabins where some of the volunteers had elected to stay, but he did not see Ned Fox. Few of the men astir paid any attention to Neil, and none of them was concerned enough to help in locating the man he was seeking. He had walked the length of the camp before he saw Captain Fox talking to some of the volunteers.

At the last moment, Neil decided to try a courteous approach. He waited a moment until Fox had finished speaking then said calmly, "Captain Fox, I should like to talk with you."

The two men had never been friends. Of late, there had been a feeling almost of enmity between them. This morning Ned chose to ignore Neil. With but a glance in Neil's direction, he turned again to the group of ten volunteers and continued his instructions to them.

Neil interrupted him angrily.

"Ned Fox!" he purposedly omitted the title of captain, "I have news for you, Ned, and for your army."

"Just a minute, Colton," Ned was angry, "can't you see that I'm busy?" He turned again to the volunteers.

More of the volunteers began to gather about them, curious to know what was happening. Neil, angered by being brushed off so lightly, called again, "Captain Fox! You are called Captain Fox, I am told."

As Ned Fox continued to ignore him, Neil could feel the curiosity of the men changing to amusement. They were pleased that the smart young lawyer was proving to be no match for their leader.

"Captain Fox!" Neil said again derisively. "Did Colonel Burr give you that title? He could, you know! But he is the only one around here who could confer such a rank. It is doubtful if even he could do it legally and make it stick."

"Captain Fox!" There was a sneer in Neil's voice this time. "Captain," he mused. "That is quite a promotion—an elevation no doubt, *Sir*."

Captain Fox's face reddened. With a word or two of command, he sent the men away. Then he turned to answer Neil.

"Why are you here, Colton? Don't you know that I can have you thrown off the island if I choose? I happen to know that you were told to stay away."

The man's arrogance angered Neil.

"I'll come on this island whenever I choose. You are not the one to stop me."

"Didn't Melissa tell you that she is not interested in you any more?"

"You keep her name out of this, Fox," Neil said in a low voice. The lout! What right had he to include Melissa in their argument?

"Sure, sure," Fox agreed. "I'll keep her name out of it, but if you think you can come here with some wild story to impress her and scare us, it won't work. She won't be impressed, and we don't scare. She is going down the river with the rest of us one of these days."

With an effort, Neil controlled his anger. "Listen, Fox," he said impatiently. "What I have come to tell you this morning is too big for you and me to stand here fighting over."

"Nothing's that big, Colton. You and I are on opposite sides of a mighty worthwhile question—this expedition that has been planned and is supported by Colonel Burr and the Blennerhassetts. When they believe in it, it is good enough for me. You're wasting your time, Neil."

"Listen to me, Ned," Neil said earnestly. "I have big news this morning. It can be good news if, because of it, you decide to stop drilling these men like soldiers."

They were by this time almost surrounded by a group of men who had gathered a few at a time. At Neil's words, they murmured angrily. Neil gave no indication of having heard them.

"What I have to tell you, Ned, is so serious," he said gravely, "that I want Colonel Burr and Jay Mahoney present when I tell you. I want to see Mahoney, too, because he is in charge of your supplies. It is up to you to arrange a meeting between us. I'll wait for you over there by the hedge fence."

As Fox hesitated, Neil said sternly, "Consider this a command, a command that Colonel Burr would insist you obey, once he understands the important news I bring. Go, Fox. Make my mission known to them at once!"

Captain Fox did not argue further. Realizing Neil's deadly seriousness and impressed by the gravity of his tone, Ned went himself to inform the colonel. A few minutes later Fox returned followed by Colonel Burr and Jay Mahoney. Neil did not wait for them to reach him but walked to meet them.

"What is this about your wanting to see me, Colton?" Colonel Burr asked brusquely.

"I have come to warn you, Colonel Burr, not to go ahead with your expedition." Neil knew that he sounded ridiculous, but his intention was to startle them.

"In all my acquaintances," Colonel Burr sneered, "I have never seen a man so dense as you, Colton. You tell me to stop my expedition! Ha! You tell me! Hear this, young man. I stop for no one. Furthermore, I shall ask Harman Blennerhassett this morning to order your permanent banishment from this island."

"When you have heard what I have to say," Neil warned, "you may not want to order my removal."

Jay Mahoney spoke up sneeringly, "Neil, if you've got somethin' to say, why don't you say it? Why all this beatin' about the bush?

"A jilted lover does always seem to be in a mess, don't he?" Mahoney laughed at his own joke. "Or are you maybe sufferin' from indigestion, Neil?"

"Forget any mess I may be in," Neil warned. "The mess you three men have got yourselves into is a lot worse. Colonel Burr, Captain Fox, if you should like to know the truth, here it is, just as plain as I can give it to you.

"Your whole plan, Colonel Burr, the preparations you are making here, the expedition down the river, the settlements you propose to make, the whole enterprise has now been branded as *TREASON!*"

"Preposterous," shouted the colonel. "Who says so? You, Neil Colton? You cannot come here making statements like this. I demand that you produce your evidence."

It was the moment that Neil had been anticipating. With a flourish, he drew from an inner pocket the letter his father had given him.

"Here, Sir," he said quietly, "is your evidence."

Colonel Burr took the letter, then turning it over and over, he examined the address on the front, the postmark, and lastly the sealing wax on the back. It was apparent that he was trying to determine if he held in his hand a genuine letter that had passed through regular mail channels, or a fake.

Neil was quick to see that Colonel Burr would question everything about the letter. Better give it to him straight.

"That letter," he explained, "was sent to my father by Sylvester Connor who is a news reporter for a Richmond paper. The information in it is reliable, it is in detail, and it says that a treason charge will be placed against you, Colonel Burr, and the Blennerhassetts if you attempt to go ahead with your expedition."

Without replying to Neil, Colonel Burr read and then reread the letter. Then, without saying a word to anyone, he turned and walked toward the mansion. His head was slightly bowed in thought but he, nevertheless, walked briskly. Neil realized that the letter, however it might have disturbed him, had in no sense diminished the man's resolute purpose and determination. With the others, Neil watched in silence as Colonel Burr entered the house through a side door.

Ned Fox was plainly disturbed as he turned to Neil.

"What does that mean?" he said more to himself than to Neil. "What was in that letter?"

Neil saw no reason for softening the blow. Perhaps a blunt statement of the dangers involved would bring Ned Fox to his senses.

"I'll tell you what it means," he said sharply. "It means just one thing, Ned. You and your men may all be arrested for treason. The man who just went through that door will be the ruin of all of you unless you break away soon. Tomorrow could be too late."

"I don't believe you," Ned said shortly.

"Maybe you will believe me when someone comes on this island with a warrant for the arrest of you and all your men.

"Ned, now is your chance to square things for yourself and for these men who have followed you. There is still time to get out before things begin to happen."

Neil thought that he could detect a wavering in Fox's attitude. "Call your men together and let me talk to them. Then if they decide to stay, it will be their own responsibility."

"Maybe I'm crazy," Fox said angrily. "If I'm not, then you are. If you want to talk to the men, get them together yourself. I'll not stop you, but I'll not assemble them for you."

Neil waited to hear no more but walked rapidly down to where a group of the volunteers had stood watching. Jumping lightly up on a long, outdoor, dining table not yet cleared of its dishes, he started pacing back and forth the length of it. Dishes flew to right and left.

Neil was being purposely dramatic as he cried, "Men, you have all been duped. Colonel Aaron Burr has involved you in an undertaking that is not the innocent expedition you have believed it to be. It is a conspiracy against the government of the United States. If you men continue to support and engage in this expedition, it will surely bring ruin to you and to your families."

Neil watched their faces closely as he spoke. He could see that they were not convinced. They probably thought him disgruntled because he was not one of them.

"Did you see the letter I gave to Colonel Burr?" he snapped the question.

"Did you see your colonel when he read that letter?" This time his voice was quiet. He fairly shouted the next question. "Do you want to know what is in the letter? Would you like to know what sent him to the Blennerhassetts in such a hurry?

"Well, I'll tell you! That letter says that you, every man of you, are going to be arrested and tried for treason against the United States of America.

"Do you believe yourselves to be what that letter says you are, treasonable cowards? Why then do you continue to listen to fabled promises made by an unscrupulous man who cares nothing about you or the country he once served? If you persist in following Aaron Burr, I tell you in truth that you follow him to your ruin."

At this point, Neil was angrily interrupted by one of the men who crowded to the front of the group. Neil recognized him as Acker Knoost, a hunter and trapper from the Virginia shore. He wondered how old Acker could have been persuaded to join the volunteers.

"Neil Colton," Acker called out, "who are you to come here tellin' us that we're traitors? We all know what we're doin'. Since when is it treason for a man to homestead land?"

"Yeah, what business is it of yours?" another sneered.

There was muttering from the crowd as Knoost went on, "Neil, we got a chance to homestead five hundred acres of land apiece and we ain't lettin' you or no one else talk us out of it. We're goin' to git rich."

"Acker, you and all these men are headed for the penitentiary if you stick with Colonel Burr. That is where he is headed for," Neil warned, "and he is perfectly willing to let you follow him right on in behind the bars."

"Don't you tell me I'm a goin' to jail," one of the younger

men in the crowd yelled. In an instant, he was on the table confronting Neil. "Take that back before I knock you off of here." "I take back nothing," Neil answered him. "You'll go to jail if you stay with Colonel Burr. Go ahead and knock me off if you think you can, but I still say this is treason."

The fight did not last long since there were older and more sensible men there to stop it. When they had subdued the volunteer, and Neil was once more on the table, they stood quietly, waiting for him to continue. Neil observed what he thought was a change in the temper of the crowd. Even Acker Knoost appeared ready to listen.

What he did not notice was that Sam and Zeke, two of the Blennerhassett servants, stood at the edge of the wood anxiously observing him and the volunteers. They had listened to Neil as he talked to the men and, during the fight, they had stood as if glued to the ground. A kind of terror seemed to hold them almost spellbound as Neil now continued his talk to the men.

"You have one chance," he told them quietly, "to save yourselves. If you don't care what happens to you, think of your families. Are you willing to disgrace them by getting yourselves arrested for treason?"

There was no answer from the men. They glanced anxiously at each other but no one moved.

"Don't stand there a minute longer," Neil shouted. "Go! Get in those boats and leave these shores before someone arrives to serve a warrant on you. I have brought you the only warning you are likely to receive. Now get out while there is still time."

With angry mutterings and some arguing, the men broke up into small groups. Some of them soon started for the boats. Others began packing and getting ready to leave.

A few minutes later, a very worried-looking Harman Blennerhassett walked down the path with Colonel Burr. The unusual activity among the volunteers, which they noticed immediately, added to the concern of the two leaders.

"This letter, Neil," Mr. Blennerhassett said anxiously when they had reached the table where Neil was still standing. "How long has it been in your possession?"

"The letter came by post to my father only yesterday, Sir,"

Neil said respectfully. "It came into my possession when I had occasion to visit him later in the day."

"And Sylvester Connor?" Mr. Blennerhassett continued, "is he a man who can be trusted? I have never heard of him."

"My father believes that he can be trusted. More than that, Connor is in a position to get the inside story of what is happening. When he says that the orders have gone out to arrest you and Colonel Burr, you may be sure that someone will arrive on this island shortly for just that purpose."

As they were talking, a continuous stream of men had begun filing by on their way to the boats.

"Men! Men!" Colonel Burr attempted to stop them. "You lose all if you leave now! Consider the future that you are throwing away!"

"We ain't hankerin' fer a future in any jail," one of the older men called without pausing.

"We are sorry, Sir," another man said, stopping briefly in front of Harman Blennerhassett, "but we can't afford to take the risk. Most of us have families, and we have to think of them first."

In all, eighty-two men deserted the camp in an interval of less than thirty minutes. The others appeared restless and undecided as they watched their friends load into boats and row toward either the Virginia or the Ohio shore.

As darkness settled over Blennerhassett Island that night, it was a solemn group that sat at the supper table in the big mansion. Margaret Blennerhassett, for almost the first time in her life, found herself unable to cheer those around her. They are all so frightened, she thought. Why can I not think of something to say that will reassure them? Can it be that I, too, am frightened? I who have never been afraid in all of my life? Poor Harman! How desolate he looks.

"Harman," she broke abruptly into his thoughts, "come, eat your supper. We are all here; no one has bothered us. I for one am convinced that no one is going to bother us. We are honorable and respected people whom everyone knows to be just that.

"Colonel Burr," Margaret Blennerhassett turned to their distinguished guest and confederate, "isn't it ridiculous even to suggest the word treason in connection with your name? Do they forget that you were once vice-president of the United States?"

"Madam," the colonel answered her gravely, "the memories of one's friends can be very short. By the same measure, the memories of one's enemies can be quite long. I have not been without my share of both. However, it would seem that some of my enemies are now vocal. I do not fear them but I do sadly regret any unhappiness or worry that they may cause you."

Colonel Burr knew the unspoken question in the minds of all who sat at the table with him that evening. Plainer than words, the food they left untouched told him what they were thinking. He knew that he must answer their question. He knew, too, that he must make that answer sound plausible. If he should fail to speak convincingly, the Blennerhassetts, too, might be lost to his cause.

"I am sorry to cause you this uneasiness," he said, speaking directly to Mrs. Blennerhassett. "It makes me very sad because it is so uncalled for; we have done nothing treasonable."

Colonel Burr addressed his host. "They can charge us with these things, Harman, but you are a lawyer. As such, you know that they cannot make the charges hold in any court.

"Our men are not soldiers; they are volunteers who are aiding us for one purpose only, the right to homestead land in the territory we shall develop. They want but one thing—an opportunity to go south and stake claims to new, rich territory."

Harman Blennerhassett spoke musingly, "I am glad that all the men who are doubtful about the legality of our project have felt free to leave us."

"More of them went just at dusk," his wife said. She wondered if Harman realized just how many had actually deserted them. "Their desertion shows how much we can depend on our friends," she added bitterly.

"I would not have it different," Mr. Blennerhassett said, sensing her mood. "I am opposed to encouraging anyone to participate with us except freely, on his own initiative, and strictly as a volunteer. We may end up without anyone, but if any do stay, we shall know that they are really one of us."

Even as they were speaking, the last of the local volunteers had gone from the island. Only Captain Fox remained of the local men. He had watched regretfully as he saw his friends and neighbors one by one leave the island. He watched but he made no attempt to stop them or to try to persuade them to remain.

There were on the island thirty-nine other men who had traveled a great distance from their homes in the East to take part in Colonel Burr's journey south. For them it was too late to withdraw. They were far from home; they had staked everything; they did not intend to quit now.

If Harman Blennerhassett had not decided to go for a walk that night after supper, he would not have been present when Sam and Zeke beheld their omen. The night was clear and bright with almost a full moon, one of those nights when just the bright stars can be seen. Standing at the edge of the lawn, in the shadow of the shrubbery, Mr. Blennerhassett heard the voices of Sam and Zeke as they passed along the path a little to his right.

Almost at the same time that he saw Sam and Zeke, Mr. Blennerhassett's attention was attracted by a large shooting star streaking across the sky. It was one of the slowest moving stars he had ever watched and one of the most brilliant. The trail of light it left seemed almost like the tail of a comet.

As the star vanished into nothingness, Harman heard Sam's voice, low and quavery. At first he was unable to distinguish words. He was a little amused when he understood what was being said.

"Zeke, what is it? Is it an omen?"

"It's a omen, all right," Zeke groaned. "We better git out of here. Looked like it was about to hit Mistah Harman's house."

"Mistah Harman's house?" Sam cried in alarm. "All them sparks a flyin'. They won't be nothin' left of the big house if one of them sparks hit it."

"Oh, Lord," it was Zeke's voice, "save the big house; don' let none of them sparks hit it."

"Oh, Lord," he moaned, "git us out of here. I can't run; my feet won' go. Lord, Lord!"

Zeke's eyes were shut and he swayed back and forth to the rhythm of his words. Sam became suddenly brave now that he was sure the star had disappeared.

"Zeke, git up from there," he said in a voice that he tried to make sound brave. "What you scared of? That was just a shootin' star."

It was then that they heard the owl. Sam froze in his tracks. "You hear that, Zeke?" he whispered. "What you think it is?"

"I hears it. It sound like a lost soul."

"Oh-o-o-o," Zeke moaned as Cindy, without a sound, suddenly moved in beside them from the shadows. "Don' you ever do that to me again, Cindy. You tell me you is here before I sees you."

"Who-o-o-o, Who-o-o-o," the call of the owl came loud and much nearer. Shaking with fear, the three huddled together.

Cindy whispered, "Zeke, who is that? What you spose they wants?"

"I don't know, Cindy. You jus' pray."

All Cindy could say was "Lord, I's afraid. I's jus' plain scared to death."

"Shut up, Cindy," Sam said disgustedly. "That ain't prayin'; that is jus' moanin'. I's scared mos' to death, too."

"Who-o-o-o! Who-o-o-o!"

This time the call was almost overhead, loud and tremulous. "Cindy, is that a hoot owl?" Sam asked, rolling his eyes.

"That ain't no hoot owl," Cindy said, her teeth chattering. "I ain't never heard no hoot owl that sounded like that. That's a hant; that's what it is. Somethin' bad is sure a goin' to happen. Oh, Lawdy, Lawdy!"

"Whoo-oo," this time the call was far in the distance.

"It is goin' away," Zeke said hopefully.

"It is goin' away. I does believe," Cindy agreed. "Le's us all go back to the cabin before it changes its mind. I don' want to meet up with no more hants."

"We better go right away," Sam said solemnly. "It's a bad omen. Somethin' terrible is a goin' to happen. I don' want to be here if it comes back."

"Maybe it's mad about all those soldier men on the island," Cindy ventured. "I never did like to see them here."

"I know trouble was a comin' when that Colonel Burr first come on this island. Things ain't never been right since." Sam spoke sadly. "I saw a omen that night, too, but it wasn't near as bad as this one. I don' want to see no more omens."

From where he was standing, Harman Blennerhassett had been unable to hear all of what the three servants were saying, but he had heard enough to tell him that they were badly frightened. I had better talk with them, he thought. That owl did sound pretty scary. They probably think it was a ghost.

He had not foreseen the added fright that his sudden appearance would cause the three.

"Oh-o-o," Cindy screamed, throwing her arms over her head and all but swooning.

"Go 'way from here," Zeke cried, "we didn't do nothin'."

Only Sam recognized Mr. Blennerhassett.

"Mistah Blennahassett," he said when he could speak, "you sure does walk mighty quiet."

"Mistah Blennahassett," Cindy said excitedly, regaining her voice, "did you hear that hant? It is a bad omen. Somethin' bad is about to happen to—."

"Cindy," Mr. Blennerhassett interrupted her, "that was no hant. I heard it. It was only an owl, a big hoot owl. It is not an omen. It does not indicate that anything bad is about to happen. Now go back inside and forget it."

"But, Mistah Blennerhassett," Sam, emboldened by the darkness, objected, "we don' like all those soldier men. We is afraid of them."

"They shoot, Mistah Harman," Zeke added. "When you leave in the daytime, they shoot much—at jus' everything. We stays inside then; we is afraid to come out."

"They will not hurt you, Zeke. They are just practicing."

Sam said, "We hear those men talkin' today, Mistah Harman, an' what they say we don' like. They say you and Missus Blennahassett is a goin' away, down the river with that Colonel Burr. Goin' to Mississippi, they say. Cindy knows about Mississippi. She say that a long way off."

Cindy interrupted, "Mistah Blennahassett, we don' want you and Missus Blennahassett to go away. Don' go away an' leave us. If you does go, take us with you. Don' leave us here. This place gettin' too scary."

The fright of the servants, Harman Blennerhassett realized,

was genuine. They needed reassurance, probably more than he was at the moment prepared to give them. How could he tell them everything was all right when the morrow might bring the end of all their hopes?

"No harm will befall you," he told the servants who were beginning to wonder at his hesitation. "You will be protected as long as you are on this island. If it becomes necessary for us to leave the island, you will all be quartered on the boat that I shall use."

"This may be our last morning on the island for many days to come," Harman Blennerhassett told Melissa. She had come up beside him as he stood on the veranda in the early morning light.

"Hear the island awakening," he said. "The birds sing just as beautifully this morning as they did the first time I heard them from this veranda.

"But why are you down so early, Melissa?"

"I heard you come down, Father."

More words were not necessary. He sensed her understanding and her concern as they stood there looking at the scene before them. He was first to break the silence, speaking more to himself than to Melissa.

"I wonder what will become of all this when we are gone."

Melissa knew he did not expect her to answer.

"All the trees and flowers—the house! I wonder if I shall ever build another house that we shall like so well.

"It is a beautiful place. If it were possible, by some magic, to pick it up and place it on one of those estates down the river, I could go with a lighter heart."

"It has been such a happy place," Melissa said, "until recently."

"If we could go back," her father mused, "I wonder, would I make the same decision? I was doubtful of its wisdom then. Could I be more certain now?"

"You must not blame yourself, Father." It hurt her to see him so despondent.

"There is no one else to blame, Melissa. I have made the decisions. It has been my responsibility to make them prudently.

The happiness and prosperity of my family have depended on my judgment, and mine alone.

"I have known that. If I have listened to others; if I have allowed myself to be over-persuaded; if by so doing, I have brought my loved ones to the brink of disaster; no one but me shall assume the blame. I alone am responsible."

It was at that moment that they noticed the small boat that had tied up at the wharf. Even as they talked, a strange man had approached the house.

"Go in, Melissa, I'll talk with him," her father said.

"My name is Barker," the stranger introduced himself when he had reached the house.

"Come in. I am Harman Blennerhassett. Did you wish to see me?" He was sure he had heard Colonel Burr mention a recruit named Barker. This must be the man.

"My business is with both you and Colonel Burr," the newcomer stated. "They told me in Parkersburg that I should find him here."

"Colonel Burr left early this morning but he should be back here by early evening. I'll be glad to help you in any way I can," Mr. Blennerhassett offered.

If Barker was surprised at Blennerhassett's willing cooperation, he in no way let it be known. Instead he took advantage of the opportunity by asking a few questions.

"You are Colonel Burr's partner in this venture, are you not, Mr. Blennerhassett?" he inquired respectfully.

"I am. He has, of course, told you much about what we plan to do." Harman did not quite understand what the visitor said since his words were somewhat mumbled.

"You do know, no doubt, that we are going to colonize new territory in the Louisiana country—thousands of acres of it. Everyone stands to make a great deal of money," Harman spoke enthusiastically, having for the moment forgotten the desertion of the men the evening before.

"There is, too, an association of men in New Orleans waiting for us to join them. Should war with Spain come, this force will be ready to liberate the unfortunate people of Mexico from their Spanish oppressors."

Government Agent Barker had heard enough to establish to his own satisfaction, his government's suspicion that this was no innocent colonizing expedition. It had been so described to him by some of the men involved, but many others with whom he had talked believed it to be a traitorous scheme.

"Mr. Blennerhassett," he hastened to explain, "you apparently believe me to be one of the men associated with Colonel Burr. I must be honest with you and tell you that I am not. I am an agent of the United States Government. I have been sent here to investigate what goes on on this island. It is my duty to determine if you and Colonel Burr are, as you have been reported to be, conspiring against the government that I represent."

For the moment Harman Blennerhassett was speechless, aghast at the confidence he had mistakenly placed in this man. How much had he told him? Why had he believed the man to be one of Colonel Burr's recruits? Harman felt bewildered by what had happened. Such a foolish thing to do—to take the man into his confidence without finding out anything about him. Just because he was friendly and made a good appearance. Who was the man he had mistaken him for? What would be his next move?

Harman was totally unprepared for what Barker said next.

"Mr. Blennerhassett, it is my opinion, after talking with you, that you have been deceived by Colonel Burr, that you have not been fully informed of the gravity of what he proposes to do. There is yet time for you to withdraw from the partnership, thus avoiding being criminally involved. I respectfully urge you to do so immediately."

Harman Blennerhassett shook his head.

"Even if all you say is true, it is too late now for me to withdraw. One does not go back on an agreement just because a few difficulties arise."

"Difficulties, Sir! You put it mildly. The word is treason. Colonel Aaron Burr is accused of conspiring against the United States Government."

Harman Blennerhassett thought he had misunderstood. True, Neil Colton's letter had said the same thing, but he had refused to believe that. Now here was this man, Barker, using almost the same words.

"Treason!" Harman exclaimed. "It cannot be that! No sane man would call what we propose to do treason. It was not treason when I settled on this island. Why should it be called treason to settle in the Bastrop Grant?"

Barker shook his head. "There is more to this plot than just settling land," he said. "You appear to be innocent of any treasonable intent. If that is so, my friend, you are being grossly deceived. Colonel Burr does not appear to be so innocent.

"I am going next to Marietta where I intend to conduct further investigation. Should I find things there as they have been reported to be, my report to Washington cannot be in favor of Colonel Burr. I hope you will follow my advice and reconsider. Good day to you, Sir."

Harman watched Government Agent Barker return to the wharf and untie his boat. It did not occur to him to think it queer that Barker should visit him before he went to Marietta. Nor did he foresee that the man would soon be on his way to Chillicothe, where he would make a full report to the governor of Ohio. He could hardly have guessed that the governor would soon ask the legislature to empower him to prevent certain acts of a treasonable nature within the state of Ohio.

Withdraw! Harman Blennerhassett would have liked to withdraw but he felt it was too late. It had been too late ever since he had handed his money over to Colonel Burr. Or had it? He had thought so before, but now things were beginning to look different. He was not so sure as he had been even so short a time ago as last night.

"Who was that man, Harman?"

Margaret Blennerhassett had come out on the veranda without her husband's having heard her. One glance at him was enough to tell her that he was in a depressed mood. Probably because of something the strange man had said.

It was becoming more and more difficult for her to reassure Harman that they were doing the right thing by going with Colonel Burr. Margaret was finding it a little exhausting, this constant bolstering of her husband's confidence. She was inclined to believe that her husband might be lacking in courage.

"Why was that man here just now?" Margaret asked as she slipped her arm through her companion's.

Glad of the interruption in his thoughts, Harman placed his own hand over hers and said lightly, "Oh, just someone to see Colonel Burr. The Colonel left for Marietta at daybreak this morning, so he has gone there to find him."

"Will the boats be ready for Colonel Burr today, Harman?" Margaret asked. If only they could get the boats and get started down the river before something happened to keep them from going. Everything moved so slowly. If they could get under way, there would be an end to this uncertainty.

"Colonel Burr expects to have the boats moved down to the island at dusk," her husband told her. Secretly he was wondering if even Colonel Aaron Burr would be able to exert enough influence to move the boats out of the Marietta docks.

Margaret, sensing her husband's uncertainty, said with more confidence than she felt, "We must be prepared to load the boats as soon as they arrive. If we do that, we can get under way by midnight."

"Can you be ready, Maggie, on such short notice?" Harman asked quickly. "It is what Colonel Burr wishes us to do."

"I will be ready," Margaret Blennerhassett's voice was determined. In her mind, she was already planning the packing of the most essential of their belongings. It would be no fault of hers if the expedition failed to get away tonight. Nothing must be allowed to hinder their departure.

Late in the evening of the same day, Harman Blennerhassett went to the stables to instruct Jess, his horseman, about the selection and loading of the saddles and other equipment that they would take with them. Horses they could obtain downriver, but saddles and bridles might not be too easily available.

Mr. Blennerhassett had completed his directions to Jess and was leaving the stable when he met Colonel Burr. This was the opportunity he had been wanting. Since early morning, his mind had been filled with questions that the colonel might be able to answer. He wasted no time in greetings but spoke directly about the misgivings uppermost in his mind.

"I have some questions I should like to ask you, Colonel,

about the letter that Neil Colton brought here yesterday. You are a lawyer, Colonel, in some ways more experienced than I. I should appreciate your giving me your analysis of that letter as you would give it legally, if you had no personal interest in it."

"I told you last night, Harman, what I think about that letter," Colonel Burr said impatiently. What a nuisance this man, Blennerhassett, could be! Was he, too, getting ready to back out?

"Just what does the letter mean?" Harman insisted. "Is it probable that the government will be able to establish proof of the charges that, according to the letter, are to be made?"

"There is no proof. Any evidence they might produce will be of their own making." Colonel Burr spoke brusquely, not bothering to hide his impatience.

"I have given you my opinion," he continued. "It is still the same. We have in no way done anything treasonable. Nor will we be committing any treasonable act in the promotion and carrying out of our already formulated plan."

In an attempt to dispel his partner's apprehension, Colonel Burr continued in a more pleasant tone of voice, "Harman, not one of us has been charged with being a traitor. True, we have seen a letter filled with rumors, a letter written by some reporter who thinks the state will so charge us. That is all. I suggest that we stop thinking about rumors and get ready to move. The boats will be here within the hour."

"Did a man named Barker reach you in Marietta today?" Harman asked, noting the quick change of expression on Colonel Burr's face.

"Barker?" The colonel's voice rose on a note of concern.

"Yes, Barker," Harman replied. "He came early this morning, a little more than an hour after your own departure. He, too, talked of treason.

"He said that he is a government agent and that he had been sent here to investigate our actions here on this island." It was not in Harman Blennerhassett's nature to deceive, but he saw no reason to disclose his own misplaced confidence in Barker.

"Barker is here for no good to us," Colonel Burr said grimly. "I know the man. His presence means that steps are being taken to stop our enterprise. We have no time to lose."

Colonel Burr was thoughtful for a moment before he said, "We are to be charged with having committed an act of resistance against the Union of States, according to that Richmond reporter. Why? Because we have an assemblage of volunteers here on this island."

"Yes," Harman agreed, "and Barker said the same thing."

"You and I know how absurd that charge would be," the colonel declared. "We both know that not one shot has been fired in defiance of, or in attack upon, our government. Nor has any such resistance been planned."

Colonel Burr could have been trying to convince himself as well as Harman Blennerhassett that they had done nothing wrong. But he knew that their only hope, now that an investigation had begun, was to get on their way down the river without any more delay. They must go tonight. Tomorrow could bring interference, even arrest.

What we ourselves know to be true of our expedition will not help us if they come after us," he said with conviction. "We will load at once the boat that is already at the wharf. We will prepare to load the others just as soon as they arrive."

They had by now walked out to where the few volunteers yet remaining on the island were awaiting orders. For the first time, Colonel Burr waited for Harman Blennerhassett to direct them.

Harman thought he knew why Colonel Burr did not himself tell the men to begin loading the boats. It could be that he wanted another on whom he could place a share of the blame. Or was it, perhaps, that he was putting his partner to some sort of test. Whatever the reason, the next move was up to Harman Blennerhassett, and he knew it. Harman had not been entirely convinced by Colonel Burr's reasoning, but he saw nothing to do but give the orders. Reluctantly, he turned to the waiting volunteers.

"Men," he said, "begin at once to load the boat that is tied up at the wharf. Further orders will be given when you have finished."

Almost at once, everyone on the island became engaged in some activity connected with preparations for a hasty departure. A feeling of urgency had communicated itself to men and women alike. Work must be done; they would do it.

Mrs. Blennerhassett was glad that the time had come for action. She had grown impatient of all the talk about things they were going to do. Always in the future. At last there was something that she could do now.

With her usual energy and enthusiasm, Margaret went from room to room, from house to wharf, from wharf to house, helping, encouraging, organizing, giving orders, and seeing that directions were carried out with speed and efficiency. In her heart she rejoiced that the day had at last arrived.

On one of her errands down to the wharf, Margaret suddenly realized that her husband was no longer there. She remembered having seen him last more than an hour earlier. No one could tell her where he was. She had to find him. More than once in the past weeks he had wavered in his resolve, had spoken of his desire to free himself from all entanglements. Only her own firm determination had encouraged him to continue.

"Harman, you are not upset again, are you?" Margaret asked when she had found him resting on a bench in the garden. "You just can not get discouraged now. We must go on, you know."

"No, Margaret, I do not know. I see no good reason why we cannot stop now."

Harman knew all the arguments; he had heard them so many times. Just now he had been repeating them to himself, trying in vain to make some sense out of them. But what was the use of repeating them? Reasoning that had once sounded logical, was no longer convincing.

Margaret was quick to sense the change in her husband's thinking. She realized that idealism could no longer be the appeal by which she could influence him. She would resort to stark reality.

"Every penny we own is invested in this undertaking, Harman," she told him. "You know that. And you know, too, that the only way we shall ever get the money back is to continue with the expedition. Harman, we cannot afford to be afraid.

"We cannot stay here now, Harman. I could never be content again on this island. I could not bear to face these people, knowing that their desertion had been our defeat. I should always be sure that they were secretly laughing at me. Truly, my happiness lies down the river. Harman, your does, too."

She knew that he was truly unhappy and skeptical about the whole thing, but he must not be allowed to withdraw now. Margaret knew her husband to be perfectly capable of doing just that if he should become convinced that it was the honorable thing to do.

"Harman," she said determinedly, "if I am to keep my self-respect, we must go through with this. We must not stop because the going has become a little rough. Think what triumph awaits us at the completion of this undertaking. Our cry must ever be, Onward, onward to happiness and fortune."

She knew the instant that Harman's mood changed; knew that she had won this hardest battle. Her own reaction was reflected in the note of triumph in her voice as she said, "Come, my love, no more of this pining for the past. It is behind us. Let us set our house down the Ohio, into the future."

Harman had never been able to resist her pleading. Today was no different. Hiding his reluctance, he returned to the wharf and the loading.

Melissa hated leaving the island, but she had found much more distasteful the idea of deserting the Blennerhassetts. In her loyalty to them, she had not once considered remaining behind. Tonight she was just as busy as the others, doing all that she could to help prepare for their journey.

On her way down to the wharf, Melissa was startled to hear her name called in a low voice, by someone in the shadows. She realized almost at once that it must be Neil. No other person ever said her name quite like that. She had not seen him for days and was surprised to know that he was again on the island. She was pretty sure that he had been told to stay away. If he had only stayed away, how much easier he would have made everything for her. She did not want to see him, but she knew she could not avoid it now.

"Melissa, I must talk with you," his voice came again. "Walk with me over to the big maple. The others are busy and will not miss you. There is so much that we must talk about."

After first making sure that none of the others was observing her, Melissa left the path and joined Neil. Together they walked toward the big tree. Neither spoke until they had reached a rustic bench. There they could not be seen from either house or wharf, nor were they likely to be noticed by anyone walking along the gravel path.

"Why did you come, Neil?" Melissa asked, anxiety making her voice sharp. She knew that she could not be away from the others very long without her absence being discovered. She must some way persuade Neil to leave the island at once.

"I came, Melissa, because I had to see you and talk with you." Neil carefully kept all emotion out of his voice, for one look had been enough to tell him that Melissa was very tired and a little afraid.

"It does so little good for us to talk," Melissa said with a sigh. "We always end up quarreling and hating each other."

Neil let that pass. "If what I have heard is true," he said, "you and just about everyone on this island will be gone from this island before morning. The boats are leaving at ten, are they not?"

Melissa did not answer.

"Oh, I don't expect you to say so," Neil said impatiently. He rose and stood looking down at her. Almost at once, he sat down again and took her hands in his own.

"All I want, Melissa, is for you to tell me that you will stay here and marry me."

"You know I cannot do that, Neil. When the others go, and they are going, I shall be with them. My place is with them at this time, not with you." Melissa knew that she had said too much but she did not care. She was sure that Neil loved her, and because he loved her, she wanted him to know what she had determined to do.

"You can't go," he declared. "I will not let you."

"I must go," she said earnestly. "You promised, Neil. Do you not remember? You promised not to try to stop me."

"I promised, yes," Neil said, "but do not forget what that promise was—only that I would not take you away from the Blennerhassetts. I am not taking you away from them, Melissa. They are taking you away from me.

"Things have changed, Melissa. You cannot go down that

river into danger and uncertainty. If the others want to go, it is their own business. You must not be allowed to go." He made his voice sound more determined than he felt. In his heart, Neil knew that Melissa would make her own decision. Nothing he could say would stop her if she was sure her duty lay with the Blennerhassetts.

"Neil, for me nothing has changed," she told him sadly. "My obligation is the same as it was on that other night when we talked about it. Do not try to persuade me that it is otherwise."

"Persuade!" Neil jumped to his feet. He was angry at his own helplessness. "Persuade you! I'll stop you! I'll take you with me!"

"If you try that, Neil, I'll never forgive you." Melissa was angry, too. She watched him warily, knowing that he was capable of doing just what he had threatened. She knew, too, that no outcry she might make could be heard by the men at the wharf.

"Get your things, Melissa," he ordered brusquely. "I saw you put that box on the porch an hour ago. It is all you are taking with you on the boat, is it not?"

"Oh, don't bother to answer unless you want to, but get something, anything you need, and let's get out of here."

Melissa flushed angrily.

"How dare you spy on me that way, Neil Colton?" she cried. "I told you that I intend to stay with the Blennerhassetts and I mean to do just that. If my mother goes, I go, and don't you try to stop me."

Neil seemed to spin in his tracks, so quickly did he grab Melissa. With his arms firmly about her, he said, "Melissa, I am taking you to the other side of the island where I left my boat. From there, I am going to take you to my father's home where you will be safe. I shall come back for your clothes some time later. Or you can wear some of my sister's things until you get new ones."

Melissa knew that she had to stop him. Once more in command of her own emotions, she undertook to calm the angry Neil.

"Neil, let me down," she said. "I will not try to run away from you. You and I have to look at this calmly."

"Calmly!" he barked, releasing her.

"Yes, Neil, calmly. Not in a fit of temper. You do not want it said that you had to kidnap me, do you? What else would it be if you carry me off by force? Oh, Neil, I know you too well to believe that you would take me away with you against my will."

"You just think I will not, Melissa," Neil answered angrily. But in his heart, he knew that she had won, that he would never force her to go with him.

"Do not stop me, Neil." Melissa put her hand on his arm. "Let me go for now, but not—forever. I promise to write."

This time Neil was gentle as he took her in his arms and held her close, but his heart was heavy. He felt the damp of the evening breeze as it brushed Melissa's hair against his cheek. The sound of the river chilled him as it had never done before. So soon it would take all happiness from him, and he was powerless to stop it. For the moment, he had a strange feeling that the river was his enemy, an enemy that was trying to destroy him and all happiness, an enemy against whom he was powerless to strike back.

"I'll write to you, Neil," Melissa was saying softly, "every time I get an opportunity. I'll let you know where we are. Maybe, when we are settled, and no one is in trouble, you can come down. That is if you want to come—," her voice lost its assurance.

"I do not know, Melissa," Neil said thoughtfully. "I have so little hope for the future that lies ahead of you down the river. Listen to it, Melissa. It sounds cold, and dark, and dangerous, almost as if it were warning you of evil."

"Oh, Neil, how silly!" Melissa scoffed. "You will be coming down this same river to see me some day. Then, if you still want to marry me, I will leave the Blennerhassetts and come back with you. They would want me to do that."

"What would they say if you were to tell them that you are staying tonight?" Neil asked.

"Even tonight, they might tell me to marry you," Melissa said. "But I shall not ask them. They have troubles enough. Tonight my place is with them."

A little of the anger that Neil had felt a few minutes before, returned. Pacing back and forth in front of Melissa, he questioned the motives back of the decision she had made.

"Melissa, could it be that you are actually in sympathy with this expedition? You must be in it whole-heartedly or you would not be so determined to join it." He knew that he was hurting her, that he was being unreasonable. It was what he wanted most to do—for the hurt that she had caused him.

Stopping abruptly in front of her, he continued, "Melissa, are you going down that river just because Mrs. Blennerhassett wants you to go?"

Tears were near as Melissa tried to explain, "Can you not understand, Neil, or is it that you will not believe me? I do not want to stay here and let these people, my family, leave me. Maybe there is danger. If they are in danger, I have no desire to be safe."

Melissa turned away from him, sadly shaking her head.

"I know you do not agree with me," she said, "but I thought I could at least make you understand."

"But treason!" Neil exclaimed. "I can understand everything but that. It is treason, you know. And yet, you go along with it."

"Do not say that word!" Melissa cried. "Do not say it."

"I will say it," Neil declared. "Treason! Not a pretty word, is it? I cannot understand you, Melissa. There can be no honor in your going along with these traitors. Can you not see that? They betray your trust in them, even as they betray their country."

Melissa was weeping softly. Neither saw the six husky volunteers until they had closed in on Neil.

Colonel Burr, in walking back to the mansion, unobserved by either Neil or Melissa, had heard voices. He had listened just long enough to recognize Neil. Backtracking quickly, he had dispatched six of the volunteers, enough to overpower Neil without hurting him. Neil did not submit without a struggle, but he was no match for the six strong men.

Colonel Burr met his men and their prisoner just beyond the stables where there was none to observe them. He was curious about Neil, even to the point of admiring his stubbornness and determination. Neil's eyes blazed with anger. So furious was he at his rough handling that he missed the unspoken admiration that shone for an instant in the Colonel's eyes.

"Colton," Colonel Burr said, not unkindly, "we are leaving here, all of us, in just one hour. Your interference can in no way prevent that departure. I have given orders that you are to be taken to the Virginia side of the river where, one hour from now, you will be released unharmed.

"The time will come, young man, when you will realize that your judgment has been wrong. We intend no harm to our country. We seek instead her growth and honor."

Neil shook off the hand of the volunteer, and faced Burr squarely.

"I think you are a traitor and a hypocrite, Colonel Burr," he said angrily. "You, who have caused so much sorrow to so many people, talk of honor. I only hope that the day is near when I can see you brought into the court and tried for treason."

Colonel Burr shrugged but did not bother to reply. Instead, he turned and disappeared into the night.

Of all things that happened on our island, saddest by far, was our leave-taking. It came so suddenly! There was indecision, questioning, wondering what to do—to go or to stay? And then, almost before we realized what was happening, we were going. We were running away! The strange sense of foreboding danger had changed into an awareness of calamity about to overtake us.

It was the arrival of the drums that forced our decision. From somewhere up the river they came—from Marietta or Parkersburg, probably. Huge they looked and many of them, bobbing along in the water and most of them headed straight for our shore. They might have appeared smaller if we could have been sure that they contained no explosives. Had they been released by pranksters, or were they a crude weapon being directed against us? They proved to be harmless, and we relaxed a bit, only to grow tense at each new sound from the river. No one felt safe as the dusk of evening thickened into darkness.

The chill I felt that night came not from the mist rising over the water. It came from the depths of my own heart. Sad was the tragedy that had befallen us!

How forlorn my father looked as he directed the loading of the boats. He had dreamed of honor and fortune; he was facing disgrace and failure.

For the first time, I saw my mother for the tragic figure she had become. I noticed in her face that night, lines that I was to watch deepen into furrows, in the days ahead. Seeing her so, I knew that I could never leave her, regardless of what the future might hold.

There was one note of cheer in our departure, there in the darkness. We were almost ready to go when they came, all of our neighbors that we thought had deserted us. It was not us, the Blennerhassetts, whom they had deserted; it was the cause we had embraced.

As they pulled in to our shore, boatload after boatload of them, I thought of the night not so long ago when these same friends had come to the ball. Only there were more of them tonight, and they were not dressed in their best clothes. They wore the plainest of garb as they came, bearing baskets and baskets of food for our journey. We felt their good will and knew that they regretted our going.

Few words were spoken there in the moonlight; hearts were too heavy. My mother tried to tell them how much we appreciated what they had done, but her voice quavered and broke. A swift embrace here, a clasp of the hand there, such was our farewell to those good people. No one told us how they had known that we were leaving, but it did not matter. It mattered only that we knew them again for our friends—friends who were truly concerned about our welfare.

It was one of the volunteers so recently withdrawn from our cause who conveyed the word of warning to my father.

"It is best that you do not tarry, Sir," he said. "There are forces gathering tonight in a town south of here who mean to intercept you before morning." He was one whose word my father could not doubt.

"They seek both you and Colonel Burr," he warned. "Go quickly if you would go at all."

At once, we were being hurried on to the larger of the two boats—the one where Colonel Burr had been standing, impatiently waiting for us to come on board. But for once, our friends had meant more to us than his displeasure. As our boats pulled out from the shore, we looked back to see them waving to us. A few of the women were weeping, as were some of us on the boats. As we watched, they turned and began loading into their own boats.

Thus we left the island; thus we left forever the great house. It broke my heart to see it standing there in the moonlight, deserted, reproachful, abandoned. I thought once that I heard it calling to us to come back, but it was only a night bird in one of the trees on the lawn, voicing its usual mournful cry. A dismal farewell, in keeping with the sorrow in our hearts!

It was cold on the river that night. Our hastily constructed quarters offered very little of protection and nothing of comfort. We could only shiver in the darkness and pray that the morning would bring nothing worse.

All was quiet as our boats moved along swiftly and almost silently with the current. Luckily, our course lay downstream. I noted the skill with which certain of the volunteers handled the heavily loaded craft. At least, it appeared that we had nothing to fear from incompetent boatmen.

Realization that we had become fugitives and were being sought by federal authorities weighed heavily on my father. For most of the night, he stood by himself at one side of the flatboat staring out into the darkness. From time to time, he glanced quickly back upriver, as though he had heard somthing or he was expecting someone to appear from behind us. If there had been any doubt in his mind that an order for our arrest had been issued, that doubt was dispelled as we approached the river town of Point Pleasant.

From far up the river, we were able to see the glow of campfires built by the soldiers waiting for us there. Why they had been so careless as to blaze such a warning, we could not imagine. Could it be that they had not really wanted to capture us? They could not have warned us better, had they chosen to do so.

Hugging the Ohio shore line, we allowed ourselves to drift silently toward the lighted section of the river. When Colonel Burr felt that we could not safely go any farther, he gave the order to stop.

"Pull into that clump of willows," he directed. "We will wait until they have quieted down for what is left of the night. It should then be easy to steal by their sleeping sentinels."

"Get some rest," my father told us, looking anxiously at my mother.

"Our danger lies in front of us. Now that we have located our hazard, we should have but little difficulty in avoiding it. It is the unseen trap that catches even the most wary."

I was sure that I could not sleep, but I must have closed my eyes almost at once. It was nearly dawn when the motion of the moving boat wakened me. We were on our way once more. The men allowed the boats to drift slowly, soundlessly, close in against the tree-lined Ohio shore.

A quick look toward the little town told me that all was quiet in the camp. Fires had burned down until only a faint glow shone here and there. No sound of voices reached our ears.

If there were sentinels on duty, they did not see or hear us as we passed slowly and stealthily along the opposite shore. Once we were beyond the town, we made good time. Confident that we had left all danger behind us for the present, we continued our journey for an hour beyond the dawn. Then we got another scare. Two men on horseback watched us from a bank high above the river. We had no way of knowing if they were seeking us, or just idly looking at our boats. It must have been the latter for we did not see them again. Half an hour later Colonel Burr gave the order to tie up the boats.

"We will keep out of sight through the day," he said, "and travel at night."

Such was the pattern of our journey for the next three days. But then, as danger seemed far away, we grew bolder. It was much more pleasant traveling by day and sleeping at night. Had it not been for the insects that plagued us, I believe I could have enjoyed the days we spent on the river.

Then came the morning when we awoke to find that Colonel Burr was gone. At first, we told ourselves that he and his two aides had gone ashore on some errand. They would soon return. In our hearts, we knew that this was not so. We knew that we had been deserted, left to get out of our desperate plight as best we could.

Our start was late that morning, and we made only a few

miles. The boats seemed almost without direction, so uncertain were all on board. No one knew where we were going, or if we were going anywhere. Without Colonel Burr to direct our course, our trip down the Ohio had lost all purpose.

That evening, when we tied up for the night, we did not speak of the morrow. It was just as well. Could we have known what the day would bring, I doubt that any of us would have slept.

We woke to find two strangers on board, and Father standing, pale and drawn, beside them. In a tired voice, Father explained what everyone had guessed—that all plans were now canceled, abandoned. He told us, too, that Colonel Burr had been apprehended by the federal authorities; that he would be taken directly to Richmond, Virginia, there to be tried for treason. Treason! The very word made me shudder.

Father's voice did not falter as he continued, "I, too, am now being taken into custody by these two gentlemen. Again, the charge is treason."

The hardships we endured on that journey across the mountains will remain in my memory forever. There were no comforts; we just plodded on, on toward a distant courtroom, the very thought of which filled us with dread. Added to the physical hardships of the journey was the realization that Father had mortgaged all of his property to finance Colonel Burr's ill-fated adventure. At last, I realized that for my father, failure of the enterprise had meant complete financial ruin.

More than once, on that long trip, did the words my father had spoken to my mother back on the island return to haunt me. How almost prophetic he had been when he warned her that to join in Colonel Burr's expedition could result in their exchanging riches and plenty for poverty and want.

We arrived in Richmond tired, bedraggled, and friendless, on the night before the trial of Colonel Aaron Burr began. I think none of us slept much that night, and it was all but impossible to remove from our persons the ravages of the long, hard journey. What few clothes we still possessed had lost all of their former richness and style. Even the quality of fine cloth disappears when the garment becomes dusty and torn.

But people are not like cloth. The inborn quality of the person can shine from beneath frayed and tattered garments. So it was with my mother and father that morning as they entered the courtroom. My mother held her head high, even proudly, as she walked down the aisle in front of all those people. She might have been entering her own ballroom to greet her guests, so completely natural were her grace and self-possession.

My father, ever the quiet one, seemed to have borrowed, for the moment, a larger amount than usual of Mother's stamina and spirit. His head, too, was up, and he looked once more to be what he had ever been—the perfect gentleman, the proud, studious, somewhat impractical man of letters. I think that everyone in that room felt, as I did, that the clothes mattered not, that they were viewing the proud entry of true aristocrats.

But the trial itself! The endless days of it! The helpless feeling of being on exhibition and, worse than that, on trial ourselves. For we were, in a sense, everyone of us on trial from the time that Colonel Burr, to save himself, named Harman Blennerhassett as the instigator of his undertaking, the planner of his expedition. It was then that the droop in my father's shoulders became more pronounced, and the lines in my mother's face grew deeper. Our hearts were cold in the knowledge that we had been betrayed.

On that first morning, we little guessed the many weeks that we were to spend inside that courtroom. It was better that we did not know; our courage might have failed us. Scarcely had we reached our places when everyone stood, and the judge entered the courtroom.

How strange it all seemed to me—the rising group, the rustle of movement as they seated themselves once more, the somber atmosphere, the deep silence, broken a moment later by the sharp sound of the judge's gavel. I was glad that Mother and I were allowed to sit by Father. We needed each other.

The courtroom in Richmond was packed on that morning when the sound of the gavel warned that the trial of Colonel Aaron Burr was about to begin. Instantly, the room was quiet.

The Trial of Colonel Aaron Burr

CITY OF RICHMOND, Monday, March 30, 1807.
Court of the United States for the fifth circuit and district of Virginia.
PRESIDING JUDGE—JOHN MARSHALL who was chief justice of the United States; and Cyrus Griffin, judge of the district of Virginia.

The court was opened at half past twelve o'clock; when Colonel Aaron Burr appeared, with his counsel, Messrs. Edmund Randolph, John Wickham, Benjamin Botts, and Luther Martin.

Counsel for the prosecution; Messrs. Caesar A. Rodney, George Hay, district attorney, William Wirt, and Alexander Mac Rae.

Because of limited seating capacity in the Federal Court House, the final decision was made to hold the trial in the Old Hall of the House of Delegates which is located in the Virginia State Capitol.

Attorneys for the Prosecution

CAESAR A. RODNEY

Caesar A. Rodney was a lawyer of such distinguished ability that few attorneys have attained his stature. He is described as a most impressive man, handsome in appearance and an agile actor before a jury. Rodney blended together his wit, his knowledge of law, and a dynamic mannerism in a skillful presentation of facts. It was said that upon his entrance, the atmosphere of the courtroom appeared to reflect some of Rodney's charm.

Rodney gave such a polished performance that opposing counsel complimented him at the conclusion of the trial.

Mr. Rodney, the Attorney General of the United States, then addressed the judge. He observed, that when he considerd the numerous and attentive audience, the public anxiety so strongly excited, the character charged, and the crime of which he was accused, he was more than usually embarrassed; that he had never felt more for any person than for the prisoner, who was no less than the late vice-president of the United States, esteemed for his transcendent talents, and whom he once considered as his friend, and treated as such in his own house.

That he now stood charged with the most heinous crime; that it was incumbent on those who prosecuted, to prove probable cause to believe his guilt, and that the chain of circumstances showed, without doubt, that he was guilty; that, however, he would endeavor to convince him, by his manner of conducting the prosecution, that the government was not influenced by malicious or vindictive passions, to persecute him.

That the gentlemen on the other side had argued as if they

were then before a jury upon the principal trial, and demanded such legal evidence as would be sufficient to convict him on such trial; that the law, however, required no such plenary testimony in this incipient stage of the proceedings; that to show probable cause to authorise a commitment, exparte testimony was admissible; and unless it manifestly appeared that he was innocent, he ought to be committed; whereas before a jury, such testimony would be excluded, and his innocence would be presumed till his guilt appeared.

That on the trial the law required two witnesses to an overt act of treason; and that his confession would be unavailing unless made in open court; that on the present inquiry, two witnesses were not requisite to prove an overt act, and that exparte evidence of his confession must be admitted.

That it was true, that the constitution required two witnesses of an overt act to convict the prisoner; but that the sixth article of the amendments to the constitution rendered probable cause only necessary to justify the issuing a warrant to take a man into custody, and of course to commit him for trial.

That there were two charges against him; one for a crime against the constitution; the other for a violation of the Act of Congress passed in 1794, to prevent the safety and peace of the United States from being put in jeopardy, by the daring enterprises of unauthorized individuals; on both of which he would make a few remarks.

In the first place he contended, that the mystery in which this business was enveloped, afforded just grounds of suspicion. If the settlement of lands merely was intended, why were dark and corruptive messages sent to military commanders? Why was a letter in cypher sent to the Commander in Chief, when he was supposed to be at St. Louis? Why, when it was found he was not there, was another sent to Natchitoches, and from thence to New Orleans?

That it was an important fact, that Colonel Burr in the preceding year had been throughout that whole country; that it was the practice every day to take the confession of accomplices as evidence against their principals, though made to escape punishment themselves.

That here the case was much stronger, for the confessions of

Bollman and Swartwout to General Wilkinson were perfectly voluntary—with the design of engaging him in the criminal projects of Colonel Burr.

Their disclosure ought to have the more weight, because they knew the contents of the letters which they delivered, which stated them to be in his confidence; and they declared themselves his partizans; that the affidavit of General Wilkinson, by which these facts are proved, was certainly good as a piece of exparte testimony in this stage of the business, though inadmissible on the trial.

That the declaration of Swartwout, as stated in that affidavit, proves the intention of the prisoner to have been to seize on New Orleans, and plunder it, as preparatory to his expedition against Mexico. That the Supreme Court, in the case of Bollman and Swartwout, had adjudged, that if an end cannot be accomplished without treasonable means, the end itself was treasonable; and of course the project of the prisoner must have been to perpetrate treason.

Mr. Rodney further contended, that the treasonable intention thus proved by Wilkinson was strongly fortified by the deposition of General Eaton. . . .

WILLIAM WIRT

William Wirt assisted in the trial of Colonel Burr at the request of President Jefferson. Wirt at that time was thirty-five years old and was fast rising in eminence. No other lawyer, on either side, so commanded the attention and won the admiration of the spectators who daily attended the trial, as did Wirt. He was handsome with graceful manners, a pleasing wit, and his brilliant declamations invariably captivated the bystanders. Never retreating in argument, he made his points relentlessly. William Wirt's presentation of the evidence in this trial has long been regarded as a legal "classic."

". . . if any man commit high treason and thereby becometh a traitor, if any other man knowing him to be a traitor, doth receive comfort and aid him, he is guilty of treason, for that there be no accessory in high treason."

". . . The gentlemen appear to me to feel a very extraordinary and unreasonable degree of sensibility on this occasion. They seem to forget the nature of the charge, and that we are the prosecutors. . . . Treason is the charge; when we speak of treason, we must call it treason; when we speak of a traitor, we must call him a traitor; when we speak of a plot to dismember the Union, to undermine the liberties of a great portion of the people of this country, and subject them to an usurper and a despot, we are obliged to use the terms which convey these ideas. . . .

"It is my duty to proceed on the part of the United States. . . .

"Who is Blennerhassett? A native of Ireland, a man of letters, who fled from the storms of his own country to find quiet in ours. His history shows that war is not the natural element of his mind. . . .

"Possessing himself of the beautiful island in the Ohio, he rears upon it a palace and decorates it with every romantic embellishment of fancy. An extensive library . . . a philosophical apparatus . . . peace, tranquility . . . a wife . . . graced with every accomplishment. . . .

"In the midst of all this peace, this innocence, and this tranquility, this feast of the mind, this pure banquet of the heart—the destroyer comes—he comes to turn this paradise into a hell—yet the flowers do not wither at his approach and no monitory shuddering through the bosom of their unfortunate possessor, warns him of the ruin that is coming upon him. A stranger presents himself. Introduced to their civilities by the high rank which he had lately held in his country, he soon finds his way to their hearts by the dignity and elegance of his demeanor, the light and beauty of his conversation, and the seductive and fascinating power of his address. The conquest was not a difficult one. Innocence is ever simple and credulous; conscious of no designs itself, it suspects none in others. . . .

"There is no man who knows anything of this affair, who does not know that to everybody concerned in it, Aaron Burr was as the sun to the planets which surround him. He bound them in their respective orbits, and gave them their light, their heat and their motion. Let him not then shrink from the high destination which he has courted; and having already ruined Blennerhassett in fortune, character and happiness forever, attempt to finish the tragedy by thrusting that ill-fated man between himself and punishment.

"I will make this remark upon the act of Congress; [mentioned in Mr. Wickham's argument for the defense] whenever it mentions accessories to any crime it is for the purpose of distinguishing between the guilt and consequently the punishment of accessories before and after the fact. I mentioned before, the line which reason had drawn between them. Congress has observed this line. Accessories before the fact in piracy, are punished with death: those after it by fine and imprisonment. The XXIII Section of that act is confined merely to the case of rescues after acquital, and its object is simply to keep the course of justice clear. *Congress* knew that in *treason,* all were *principals* from the nature of the crime, and that it was therefore unnecessary to implicate them in detail by a special act."

GEORGE HAY

The leader of the prosecution was George Hay, Attorney of the United States for the District of Virginia. A man of sound ability, Hay was a profound and dedicated public official. He was the son-in-law of James Monroe, and a "zealous" Democrat of the Jefferson school.

He prosecuted this trial with a driving determination. In the charge that he delivered to the court was perhaps an "intemperate zeal"; at least it was so intimated by the counsel for the defense. Hay presented the evidence with a "zest" seldom equaled in legal annals.

Hay's charge to the court was that the prisoner should be committed in order to take his trial upon two charges, exhibited against him on the part of the United States:

First, For a high misdemeanor, in setting on foot, within the United States, a military expedition against the dominions of the King of Spain, a foreign prince, with whom the United States, at the time of the offense, were and still are, at peace.

Second, For treason in assembling an armed force, with a design to seize the city of New Orleans, to revolutionize the territory attached to it, and to separate the western from the Atlantic states.

He stated the first offense to be a violation of the Fifth Section of an Act of Congress, passed on the 5th of June, 1794, entitled, "an Act in addition to the Act for the punishment of certain crimes against the United States," continued for limited periods by several laws, and continued without limitation by an act passed in 1799.

The said section provided, "that if any person shall, within the territory or jurisdiction of the United States, begin or set on foot, or provide or prepare the means for any military expedition or enterprize, to be carried on from thence against the territories or dominions of any foreign prince or state, with whom the United States are at peace, every person so offending shall, upon conviction, be adjudged guilty of a high misdemeanor, and shall suffer fine and imprisonment, at the discretion of the court in which the conviction shall be had, so as that such fine shall not exceed three thousand dollars, nor the term of imprisonment be more than three years."

He supported this charge by the letter of the prisoner addressed to General Wilkinson, and insisted that it showed probable cause to suspect him of having committed this offense; nay, that he had actually committed it, and that this construction of the letter was deliberately adopted by the Supreme Court of the United States; that the intention of the prisoner to commit these offenses was perfectly clear from the evidence.

But secondly, Hay insisted, that there was probable cause to suspect, that the prisoner had committed an act of treason; that he intended to take possession of New Orleans, make it the seat of his dominion, and the capital of his empire; and that this charge was proved by the affidavits exhibited in the cases of Bollman and Swartwout, and he referred to the opinion of the Supreme Court in those cases, as supporting the doctrine for which he contended, that there was just ground of suspicion against him. He went minutely into an examination of the evidence, to show that he was correct, and among other circumstances mentioned his flight from justice.

"Sir, a great deal has been said in the newspapers upon this transaction; and a great deal will yet be said. But are the presses shut against Colonel Burr, when even in this very city certain presses have been found to vindicate his motive and designs?

"But what of all this? The public mind is hostile to any encroachment upon the liberty of the press; and it ought to be so. Where a crime of such gigantic enormity, as that attributed to Aaron Burr, arises in this country, the printers will speak. If there have been publications against Colonel Burr, innumerable communications have also appeared in his favour; and if the publications against him have contained the severest strictures, they have resulted from his own character and conduct; and he has no right to complain.

"He stands on the fairest ground which his conduct and character can reach. But if in truth prejudices have been improperly excited against him, why does he wish to close the only door to his own vindication, by excluding the evidence?

"His counsel exclaim, 'Send the evidence to the Grand Jury.'

"Surely if Colonel Burr wishes to have the evidence before the jury, he should be much more anxious to have it before the court. The jury will have one side of the evidence only before them; and that will be completely against himself. Both, however, will go before the court. Why, then, does he shrink from the evidence? If an unjust prejudice assails him, the light of truth and evidence will dissipate it. Why does he shrink?

"The gentlemen on the other side," continued Mr. Hay, "do not do us justice. They charge us with persecution and oppression. I hold it my duty to proceed—for the sake of the court, for the sake of vindicating the trial by jury, now sought to be violated, for the sake of full and ample justice in this particular case, for the sake of the future peace, union and independence of these states, I hold it my bounden duty to proceed. . . .

"Having ascertained that the prisoner can in no view of *the law* be considered as an accessory in this case, let us enquire whether he can be so considered *in reason.*

"A plain man who knew nothing of the curious transmutations which the wit of man can work, would be very apt to wonder by what kind of legerdemain Aaron Burr had contrived to shuffle himself down to the bottom of the pack as an accessory, and turn up poor Blennerhassett as principal in this treason. It is an honor, I dare say, for which Mr. Blennerhassett is by no means anxious; one which he has never disputed with Colonel Burr, and which I am persuaded, he would be as little inclined to dispute on this occasion, as on any other. Since, however, the modesty of Colonel Burr declines the first rank, and seems disposed to force Mr. Blennerhassett into it in spite of his blushes, let us compare the cases of the two men and settle this question of precedence between them. . . .

"Who then is Aaron Burr, and what the part which he has borne in this transaction, He is its author; its projector; its active executor. Bold, ardent, restless and aspiring, his brain conceived it; his hand brought it into action. Beginning his operations in New York, he associates with him, men whose wealth is to supply the necessary funds. Possessed of the main spring, his personal labour contrives all the machinery . . . and in the autumn of 1806, . . . he meets with Blennerhassett. Sir, I never contemplated or wished to hurt Aaron Burr. I scorn it. I look not to him. I look only to the duties which I am solemnly bound to perform.

"One remark more, Sir, and I have done: Gentlemen on the other side, insist upon the insufficiency of our evidence; because we have withheld our indictments from the grand jury, they have hastily inferred, that we feel our evidence to be too feeble to satisfy the jury. They are mistaken, Sir. I assure them that they are mistaken. I conscientiously believe, that we have evidence enough, even throwing out the depositions themselves, to satisfy the grand jury of the guilt of Aaron Burr."

ALEXANDER MAC RAE

Alexander Mac Rae, "the son of a Scotch parson, was distinguished in the Revolutionary War, first, for being himself a hot Tory, and secondly, for being the father of seven sons, all of whom are ardent Whigs." He was described as "a lawyer of respectable ability and a sharp tongue—sharp from ill-nature more than wit." He was neither pleasing nor powerful in argument. At the time of the trial he was Lieutenant Governor of Virginia.

Mac Rae had a good mind, keen and direct in its grasp of legal matters. His participation in a trial was often marked by heated exchanges with opposing counsel. However, in the Burr trial he served in an advisory capacity, taking very little active part in the argument. Instead he served as consultant to the other lawyers for the prosecution. Throughout the trial, they were frequently guided by Mac Rae's interpretations and advice.

"The gentlemen seem to consider the recognisance already taken as sufficient for all circumstances, and that Colonel Burr will comply with it at any rate; but we have not the same expectation that he will appear, in case he discovers that sufficient evidence for his conviction has been obtained.

"When they speak of the sum in which he was bound on a former occasion, they do not recollect the circumstances which induced the judge to take bail in so small a sum. It was expressly mentioned by Your Honor, that his having been brought to a place at a distance from the circle of his friends, and the nature of the offense, [a misdemeanor only] induced you to hold him to bail in that sum; and the charge of treason was altogether excluded from view in taking the recognisance."

Attorneys for Defense

EDMUND RANDOLPH

Edmund Randolph, in point of age, experience, and position, deserves to be mentioned first, of the counsel who assisted in the defense. He was a dignified Virginia gentleman of the old school. He had been a member of the Continental Congress during the Revolution, Attorney General and Secretary of State under Washington, and Governor and Attorney General of his own state. He was a man of much learning and fair ability; but his powers were then rather on the wane.

Politically, he had been popular among the voters of his state for years. As a lawyer he was considered one of the best of his profession. Randolph's appearance for Colonel Burr in the trial was a morale booster for the defense.

"Mr. Hays says, our tone is changed. And how, Sir? We demand a trial now. We demand a fair trial. But must we not, therefore protest against a measure, which is calculated to defeat this object? Certainly, Sir. You are called upon to prejudice the minds of the grand jury. But, Sir, in this interesting case, where libery and life themselves are endangered, I trust that some hard-mouthed precedents, from old black letter books, will be found in opposition to this procedure. We have come here to answer to every charge, which may be urged against us; we come here to answer in a precedented and constitutional manner.

"Little did we expect that the court would decide in the first instance, instead of the grand jury; that the sentiments of the grand jury were to be prejudicated by an unconstitutional decision; and that the court itself was to commit its opinion on certain points, which would be regularly brought before them for argument and for decision at some of the ulterior stages of the prosecution.

" 'Why,' said Mr. Wirt, 'do you shrink?' Sir, trace the course of the prosecution, and see who it is that retires from the contest. On Friday the United States' attorney was not ready; on Saturday he was not ready; and now indeed he will not probably be ready before Monday next. Sir, who is it that shrinks? And yet does the attorney positively aver that he has evidence enough!

"We are charged, Sir, with addressing the multitude. Mr. Wirt says that he could, but would not imitate the example; but neither he nor Mr. Hay hath spared the theme. Sir, I will not deny the justness of his eulogiums upon the administration; but permit me only to remark, that there has been a certain conduct observed towards Colonel Burr which excites my deepest astonishment.

"When I look at the first man in the government, I behold an individual whom I have long known, and whose public services have commanded my admiration. When I look at the second, Sir, he has my whole heart. But, Sir, the inquiry which is now before us relates not so much to the intention as to the effect. An order has been given to treat Colonel Burr as an outlaw, and to burn and destroy him and his property.

"And Sir, again; when the House of Representatives demanded certain information, as it was their right and their duty to do, the President granted it; and would to God, Sir! that he had stopped here, as an executive officer ought to have done. He proceeded, however, to say that Colonel Burr was guilty of a crime; and consequently to express an opinion, which was calculated to operate judicially upon the judges and the juries. Such was the substratum of all the censures which have been heaped upon Colonel Burr.

"Colonel Burr was arrested in the Mississippi Territory. Was there no court there? Was there no judge of integrity to try him? [He was] arrested, too, after he had been acquitted by a grand jury! Well! He was transported thence [with humanity it has been said], dragged on by eight musqueteers, who were ready to shoot him at a moment's warning. [He was] refused any appeal to the judicial authority; denied even the melancholy satisfaction of writing to his only child. Was all this humanity?

"Dragged before this court, which derives its only jurisdiction from a little speck of land on the Ohio. Yes! Sir, but for that little spot of an island, Virginia never would have enjoyed this honour! What is all this, Sir, but oppressive and bitter inhumanity?

"I trust, Sir, from what I have said, that no one will think with Mr. Wirt, that I am shifting the question from Colonel Burr to Mr. Jefferson. I should not have made the observations which have escaped me, [except] to show that my client is justified by his situation in stating every objection that he can to the present measure.

"At least one disadvantage will result from this inquiry. It is not clear, as Mr. Hay asserted, that the affidavits will be laid before the court only, and not before the grand and petit juries, for the grand jury will soon be possessed of the substance of them. It will be next to impossible for them to separate the impressions thus illegally to be produced on their minds, from the weight of the legal viva voce testimony."

JONATHAN WICKHAM

Second among Burr's counsel should be ranked Jonathan Wickham, of Richmond, in whom was combined, more than in any one else engaged in this trial, on either side, all the elements which constitute the able and accomplished barrister. He was an Englishman by birth, and "had learning, logic, wit, sarcasm, eloquence, a fine presence, and persuasive manner."

Although Wickham was not of the barrel-chested type, he was a fencer for points and his arguments were exceedingly well pinpointed to fit the occasion.

"The common law is part of the law of Virginia and the Act of Congress has adopted the laws of Virginia as the rule of decision in cases where they apply.

1. "... under the Constitution of the United States no person

can be guilty of treason, by levying war, unless he was personally present when and where an overt act of war was committed, and participated therein.

2. "Even admitting this construction of the Constitution to be wrong, and that a person who was not present at the committing of the overt act may be guilty of the crime of treason by relation, still the facts must be specially charged in the indictment, and proved as laid. And inasmuch as the indictment charges Mr. Burr with personally levying war with others on Blennerhassett's island, no evidence to charge him with the act by relation, he being absent at the time it was committed, is relevant to the indictment. He should not only be charged specially with the accessorial acts imputed to him, but charged and tried in the district where said acts were committed.

3. "If aiders, abettors, and procurers in treason be considered as principals, yet their guilt is derivative, and can only be established by legal proof that the persons whose acts they are answerable for have committed treason; which legal proof can consist of nothing less than a record of their conviction.

4. "The evidence has wholly failed to prove that an overt act of levying war has been committed on Blennerhassett's island; hence no evidence can be received to charge Colonel Burr, by relation, with an act which has not been proved to have been committed.

"The clauses of the Constitution which declare that 'treason against the United States shall consist only in levying war against them, or in adhering to their enemies, giving them aid and comfort,' and that, 'no person shall be convicted, unless on the testimony of two witnesses to the same overt act,' must be construed according to the plain, natural import of the words.

"The Constitution is a new and original compact between the people of the United States, and is to be construed, not by the rules of the art belonging to a particular science or profession, but like a treaty or national compact, in which words are to be taken according to their natural import, unless such a construction would lead to a plain absurdity. In being new and original, and having no reference to any former act or instrument, [the Constitution] forbids a resort to any other rules of construction than such as are furnished by the Constitution itself, or the nature of the subject. Hence, artificial rules of construction statutes, cannot be resorted to, to prove that these words of the Constitution are to be construed, not according to their natural import but that an artificial meaning, drawn from the statute and common law of England, is to be affixed to them, entirely different.

"But even if these words of the Constitution are to have an artificial meaning, such as it is contended has been given them in the courts of England, in that country the rule has not practically obtained that all persons aiding and abetting others in the act of levying war against the government are guilty of treason, though not personally present, notwithstanding some dicta of the law writers to that effect.

"Lord Coke, and after him some other writers who are deservedly revered, have laid down the general proposition that there are no accessories in treason, either before or after the fact, but that all are principals. No adjudications in the case of an accomplice in the nature of an accessory before the fact bear them out in it, except that of Sir Nicholas Throgmorton, reported in Vol. I State Trials, pp. 63 to 76.

"The conduct of the court on that occasion was so obviously contrary, not only to the rules of law and justice, but even to those of decency, that I am persuaded counsel for the prosecution will not rely on it as an authority.

"In Tremaine's Pleas of the Crown, p. 3, is found an indictment against Mary Speke for treason, in aiding the Duke of Monmouth and others in levying war, with provisions; neither before nor after, but at the time when the treason was committed by the principals. She was not an accessory in fact, but an 'aider' in the commission of the treason. The case comes within the definition of 'an aider or procurer,' and belongs to the class of accessories before the fact. But neither history nor any report of the decision of the court, as far as I have been able to discover, informs us how the case was decided.

"It was in the fourth year of the reign of James II, when the spirit of prosecution was very high, and was probably one of the cases decided by the execrable Jeffries, on the occasion of Monmouth's rebellion. Whether he carried this doctrine to the utmost length or not, I cannot say, but I presume the counsel for the United States would not rely on it as a precedent, even if it applied.

"I have been unable to find any other decisions that go to this point with respect to accomplices, in the nature of accessories before the fact, to treason in 'levying war.' As to the other great class of treasons in England, that of compassing the death of the king, the crime does not admit of an accessory before the fact, as distinguished from a principal. The crime consists in the intention, and every person concerned is a party to the agreement, and therefore, from the nature of things, a principal...."

COLONEL AARON BURR

On the part of the defense, the real leader and principal tactician was Burr himself. "No step was taken, not a point conceded, without his express permission. He appeared in court attired with scrupulous neatness, in black.... His manner was dignity itself—composed, polite, confident, impressive. He had the air of a man at perfect peace with himself, and simply intent on the business of the scene. It was observed that he never laughed at the jokes of counsel, which at some stages of the trial, were numerous and good."

He never lost his temper, and never, under any provocation, was betrayed into an offensive personal retort. He brought forward nearly every motion made on his side, and stated the grounds of it with remarkable brevity and clearness. He was equally happy in briefly summing up, at the close of a debate, and presenting in order the strong points brought forward in the more elaborate arguments of his counsel. He never, in the whole course of the trial, indulged in an argument of any considerable length. Deep, abstruse, metaphysical reasoning was not his forte. He left all that to more competent hands.

The following plea was made by Colonel Burr in his own behalf:

"I am not, I hope, Sir, wasting the time of the court upon the present occasion. The motion proposed, is admitted on all hands, to be important; and it is certainly a new one. Perhaps it was to have been expected, that on a point so novel, some precedents would have been produced; but, in this expectation we have been disappointed. Its novelty will, however, be productive of another effect. It will still better qualify it for making another small feature in a picture of oppressions and grievances, which have never been paralleled in the records of criminal law.

"The case is this; no man denies the authority of the court, to commit for a crime; but no commitment ought to be made, except on probable cause. . . . The question in the present case, is, whether there is probable cause of guilt; and, whether time ought to be allowed to collect testimony against me. This time ought generally to be limited; but there is no precise standard on the subject; and much is, of course, left to the sound discretion of the court.

"Two months ago, however, you declared, that there had been time enough to collect the evidence necessary to commit on probable cause; and surely, if this argument was good then, it is better now.

"As soon as a prosecutor has notice of a crime, he generally looks out for witnesses. It is his object to obtain probable cause for committing the accused. Five months ago, a high authority declared, that there was a crime; that I was at the head of it; and it mentioned the very place, [on Blennerhassett Island] where the crime was supposed to be in a state of preparation. The principal witness against me, is said to be General Wilkinson. . . ."

"There are other serious objections to my situation. Must I be ready to proceed to trial? True, Sir, but then it must be in their own way. Are we then on equal terms here? Certainly not.

"And again, as to affidavits. The United States can have compulsory process to obtain them; but I have no such advantage. An ex parte evidence, then, is brought before this court, on a motion for commitment. The evidence on one side only is exhibited; but if I had mine also to adduce, it would probably contradict and counteract the evidence of the United States.

"Well, Sir, and these affidavits are put into the newspapers, and they fall into the hands of the grand jury. I have no such means as these, Sir. Where then is the equality between the government and myself?"

". . . A sufficient answer, Sir, has been given to the argument about my delay; and its disadvantages to myself have been ably developed. But my counsel have been charged with declamation against the government of the United States. I certainly, Sir, shall not be charged with declamation; but surely it is an established principle, Sir, that no government is so high as to be beyond the reach of criticism. It is more particularly laid down, that this vigilance is more peculiarly necessary, when any government institutes a prosecution; and one reason is, on account of the vast disproportion of means which exists between it and the accused.

". . . if ever there was a case which justified this vigilance, it is certainly the present one, when the government has displayed such uncommon activity. If, then, this government has been so peculiarly active against me, it is not improper to make the assertion here, for the purpose of increasing the circumspection of the court."

BENJAMIN BOTTS

Benjamin Botts was another distinguished lawyer who took a prominent part in conducting the defense. He was the youngest of Burr's counsel; a ready, bold, dashing man, who always charged his adversary on the "double quick," and generally dealt effective blows. He had great power of caricaturing the arguments of his opponent, and exposing them in a ludicrous light. At a very early age, he had displayed legal maturity. Able to express himself better than most, his verbal exchanges with opposing counsel held the interest of all who heard him.

". . . Although we sustain considerable inconvenience by being thus suddenly and unexpectedly called upon without reflection, or authorities, yet we should experience greater by a day's delay. I shall, therefore, beg leave to make a few remarks on this extraordinary application, and the pernicious effects such an extraordinary measure, if generally practiced, would inevitably produce.

"The organ particularly appropriated for the consideration of the evidence which this motion calls for, is the grand jury; and the motion is to divest the grand jury of the office, which the constitution and laws have appropriated to them, and to devolve it upon the court.

"The grand juror's oath is to inquire into all crimes and misdemeanors committed within the district of the state of which they are freeholders. Their office is to perform that which the court is now called upon to perform. To them belongs the exclusive duty of inquiring and examining into all species of evidence, which may lead to a conviction of the crime of which Colonel Burr is now charged; but there is a great objection to the exercise of this examining and committing power by a high law officer, who is to preside upon the trial, when the grand jury, the appropriate tribunal, is in session. He is obliged, previously, without a full hearing of both sides of the case, to commit himself upon the case of the accused. Every one will agree, that a judge should, if possible, come to the office of trial as free from prepossession, as if he had never heard of the case before.

"It is true, that when a grand jury is not embodied, in order to avoid a failure of justice, and to prevent the guilty from escaping, the measure which the gentleman now proposes, would not only be proper but necessary. The examining and committing office of the judge is, in such cases, justified by the necessity of the case; but then it is because the appropriate body of inquest is not impaneled to perform the office.

"The necessity does not exist here. This novel mode of proceeding would give the attorney for the United States the chance of procuring an opinion from the court, unfavorable to the accused. Failing in that chance, he would then resort to his only legal one—before the grand jury.

"Why should this court step out of its ordinary course to forestall or influence the deliberations of the grand jury and the public? The motion is without precedent, or reason to warrant such a precedent; it is oppressive and against all principle; it is unreasonable and oppressive that the functions of the grand jury should be suspended, in order that the court should assume them.

"Although in the absence of the grand jury, it would be

proper in the court to determine a question of commitment, yet the history of our criminal jurisprudence yields no instance of such a motion during the session of the grand jury. I did expect, that some solitary reason would have been given, by the gentleman for the prosecution, in support of his motion; I did expect, Sir, that all the books of England would have been ransacked; I did suppose, Sir, that the musty pages of folios and quartos would have been opened to support his argument; I did expect, at least, Sir, that one case of state justice would have been produced. In this expectation I am disappointed.

"I say then, Sir, that the motion before the court is without precedent, unreasonable in its nature, inconvenient in its effects, and oppressive in its end. [It is] of a piece with the long course of oppression which has been practiced against Colonel Burr, but has been hitherto unknown in this country; unheard of in any country which enjoys the blessings of freedom, and which, I trust, will never again be repeated in these states.

"Colonel Burr appears in this court ready to go on with his trial; he wishes no delay; he is opposed to every measure which may occasion delay, or procrastinate the business. His great object is to satisfy his country, the minds of his fellow citizens, and even his prosecutors, that he is innocent. We have suffered already two or three days to pass away in idle discussion, or without doing anything. Yet we are told, at last, after the lapse of several months; after a grand jury have been convened and gone into their room; after attending with great inconvenience to themselves and expense to the state; after *all this*, we are told, that the business of commitment is again to be gone over; that the evidence which ought to be given to the grand jury, the only proper tribunal at this time for its consideration, is to be submitted to the court.

"We have, Sir, made enough of sacrifices; we have been deprived of our legal rights; our person and papers have been seized; we have been subjected to a military persecution unparalleled in this country; given into the custody of the satellites of military despotism, and guarded by the rigid forms of military law. Surely our wrongs ought now to end. It was rumored that he would not appear; but he has appeared. We come to ask a legal trial: an examination into the charges which have been preferred against us.

"The government has had the time and necessary means of preparation, and they ought to be prepared. Our pleasure was, to await the pleasure of the prosecution, unless that pleasure should be found to be oppressive. But we are told now, that the indictment cannot go up; but in the mean time an inquisition must be held.

"Permit me to advert, for a solitary moment, to one circumstance: If we had sought every legal advantage, our motion would have been preceded theirs; our motion would have been, that, if they were not ready to present their evidence before the grand jury, Colonel Burr should be discharged from the recognisance already given."

LUTHER MARTIN

Luther Martin of Maryland, ". . . in the single particular of legal learning, was the first lawyer of his day. His memory was as wonderful as his reading, so that his acquirements were at instantaneous command. Burr had become acquainted with him at Washington three years before, during the trial of Judge Chase, in whose defense he greatly distinguished himself."

He was coarse in his manners, ungrammatical in his language, verbose and addicted to repetitions in his style, and utterly regardless of order in the arrangement of his arguments. These defects were aggravated by an unfortunate impediment in his speech, arising from an excessive flow of saliva. Withal, he was "a mighty drinker," and though able to carry an incredible cargo of brandy, often exhibited unmistakable signs of being overladen.

One record says, "Fancy has been as much denied to his mind as grace to his person or habits. These are gross and incapable of restraint, even on the most solemn public occasions. Hence his invectives are rather coarse than pointed, his eulogiums more fulsome are pathetic."

Nevertheless, he was a great and powerful man, possessing many excellent qualities of the heart as well as of the head. He entered upon the defense of Colonel Burr with all the zeal that the warmest personal friendship for his client, and intense political enmity to Jefferson and his administration, could inspire in his ardent and passionate nature.

"The gentleman may now think himself perfectly safe, by the prevalence of his party and principles; but the day very possibly may come, when he may find himself as obnoxious as the gentleman whom I defend. He may possibly, by the same means, the malice, injustice, and violence of party spirit, like my client, not only find himself reviled and calumniated, but his dearest friends abused and persecuted. I should be sorry that such prediction should be realized with respect to any gentleman; but such are the natural consequences of his own pernicious doctrines; and these we oppose.

"It is for the security of innocence that we contend. If innocence had never been persecuted, if innocence were never in danger, why were so many checks provided in the Constitution for its security? We know the summary and sanguinary proceedings of former times, as recorded in faithful history. In those times of oppression and cruelty, they never troubled courts or juries with their accusations, proofs and legal forms, but declared the intended victim guilty of treason, and proceeded to execution at once. We wish to prevent a repetition of those scenes of injustice and horror.

". . . it has been my intention to argue the cause correctly, without hurting the feelings of any person in the world. We are unfortunately situated. We labor against great prejudices against my client, which tend to prevent him from having a fair trial. I have with pain heard it said that such are the public prejudices against Colonel Burr, that a jury, even should they be satisfied of his innocence, must have considerable firmness of mind to pronounce him not guilty. I have heard it not without horror.

"God of heaven! Have we already under our form of government [which we have so often been told is best calculated of all governments to secure all our rights] arrived at a period when a trial in court of justice, where life is at stake, shall be but a solemn mockery, a mere idle form and ceremony to transfer innocence from the gaol to the gibbet, to gratify popular indignation, excited by bloodthirsty enemies!

"But if it require in such a situation firmness in a jury, so does it equally require fortitude in judges to perform their duty. And here permit me again, most solemnly, and at the same time most respectfully, to observe that, in the case of life and death, where there remains one single doubt in the minds of the jury as to facts, or of the court as to law, it is their duty to decide in favor of life. If they do not, and the prisoner fall a victim, they are guilty of murder *in foro coeli* whatever their guilt may be *in foro legis*.

"When the sun mildly shines upon us, when the gentle zephyrs play around us, we can easily proceed forward in the straight path of our duty; but when bleak clouds enshroud the sky with darkness, when the tempest rages, the winds howl, and the waves break over us—when the thunders roar over our heads and the lightnings of heaven blaze around us—it is then that all the energies of the human soul are called into action. It is then that the truly brave man stands firm at his post. It is then that, by an unshaken performance of his duty, man approaches the nearest possible to the Divinity.

"Nor is there any object in the creation on which the Supreme Being can look down with more delight and approbation than on a human being in such a situation and thus acting. May the God who now looks upon us, who has in his infinite wisdom called you into existence and placed you in the seat to dispense justice to your fellow citizens, to preserve and protect innocence against persecution—may that God so illuminate your understandings that you may know what is right; and may He serve your soul with firmness and fortitude to act according to that knowledge."

The Examination of Colonel Aaron Burr

RICHMOND, Monday, March 30th, 1807

COLONEL AARON BURR, who had been arrested on the Tombigbee river, in the Mississippi Territory, on the 19th day of February last, and brought to this city under a military escort on Thursday evening the 26th instant, remained under guard until this day, when he was delivered over to the civil authority, by virtue of a warrant issued by the chief justice of the United States, grounded on the charges of a high misdemeanor, in setting on foot and preparing, within the territories of the United States, a military expedition, to be carried on from thence against the dominions of the king of Spain, with whom the United States then were and still are at peace; and also of treason against the United States.

Between the hours of twelve and one o'clock, major Scott, the marshal of the district of Virginia, attended by two of his deputies, waited on colonel Burr, at his lodgings at the Eagle Tavern, and, after informing him in the most respectful manner, of the nature and object of his visit, conducted him through an awfully silent and attentive assemblage of citizens to a retired room in the house, where he was brought before chief justice Marshall for examination. The counsel and a witness for the United States, the counsel for the prisoner, the marshal and his deputies, and a few friends invited by the counsel of colonel Burr, were alone admitted.

This mode of proceeding occasioned some degree of dissatisfaction among the citizens; but the following statement of facts, which we are authorised to say is correct, will readily account for it. When the attorney for the district applied to the chief justice for a warrant, some conversation ensued on the manner of examination. Mr. Marshall observed that it was indifferent to him whether it was held at the capitol or at the Eagle Tavern. Mr. Hay objected to the latter, that no room was sufficiently large to receive the crowd that would attend, which would be a source of considerable inconvenience. Mr. Marshall observed, that if there were a discussion by counsel, they should adjourn to the capitol.

The evidence introduced on this occasion consisted of a copy of the record in the case of Bollman and Swartwout in the supreme court of the United States, (containing the affidavits of general Eaton, general Wilkinson, and others); and also of the verbal testimony of major Perkins, the gentleman by whom colonel Burr was apprehended, the substance of which we are authorised to assert, is correctly as follows: On the night of the 18th or 19th of February last, he was at Washington courthouse. At about 11 o'clock, as he was standing at the door of the house occupied by the sheriff, he observed two men coming down the road. The moon afforded him light enough to see objects at some distance. The foremost man, who was thirty or forty yards before his companion, and who turned out to be colonel Burr, passed near the door without stopping or speaking. Burr's companion stopped and inquired the way to major Hinson's: the way was pointed out, but Perkins informed him that the major was from home, and that, in consequence of a late rise in the waters, he would experience some difficulty in getting there that night; the stranger, however, went on. Perkins, struck with this midnight journey, the silence of the person who had first passed, the unwillingness of the travellers to stop at a public place, where they and their horses might have been accommodated, and their determination to continue their route to Hinson's after information was given that he was from home, communicated to the sheriff his suspicion, that these men must be under the influence of some extraordinary motive. Possibly they might be robbers, or perhaps one of them was Burr endeavoring to effect his escape. He had been informed that Burr had left Natchez. Impressed by these suspicions, he urged the sheriff, who had gone to bed, to rise and go with him to Hinson's. After some time the sheriff agreed to accompany him, and they went to Hinson's, where they found both the travellers. Burr, who had been in the kitchen to warm himself, soon came into the room where his companion and Perkins were. He spoke very little, and did not seem willing to be observed. Perkins eyed him attentively, but neve got a full view of his face. He discerned that Burr once glanced his eye at him, apparently with a view to ascertain whether Perkins was observing him; but withdrew it immediately. The latter had heard Mr. Burr's eyes mentioned as being remarkably keen, and this glance from him strengthened his suspicions. He determined immediately to take measures for apprehending him. He accordingly left the place, after mentioning in a careless manner the way he meant to take. The way he indicated was opposite to the course he thought Burr would pursue. After getting beyond the reach of observation, he took the road to Fort Stoddart, and obtained the aid of the commandant and four soldiers. The circumstances of the arrest have been already stated to the public.

Perkins further said, that, while they were on their way to Washington, at Chester Town or courthouse, in the back part of South-Carolina, Mr. Burr, observing a small collection of people, got off his horse, went into the company, asked for a magistrate, and complained of being under an illegal arrest and military guard. Perkins, however, soon reinstated him on his horse, and directed the guard to proceed. The people manifested no disposition to interfere.

After the evidence was gone through, Mr. Hay submitted to the chief justice a motion in writing for the commitment of the prisoner on the two charges above mentioned. A discussion was then agreed, on both sides, to be necessary; and, in pursuance of the arrangement previously made, Mr. Hay moved for an adjournment to the capitol, to which the counsel of colonel Burr readily assented. Colonel Burr was then admitted to bail in the sum of five thousand dollars for his appearance on the following day at ten o'clock.

TUESDAY, 31st March, 1807.—Present, John Marshall, chief justice of the United States. Counsel for the prosecution, Caesar A. Rodney, attorney general for the United States; George Hay, attorney of the United States for the district of Virginia. Counsel for colonel Burr, Edmund Randolph, esquire, John Wickham, esquire.

At ten o'clock, the chief justice was seated on the bench, and the court room crowded with citizens. Colonel Burr arrived at half past ten o'clock, and apologized for the delay, declaring that he had misapprehended the hour at which he was bound to appear.

On the suggestion of the counsel, that it would be impossible to accommodate the spectators in the court room, the chief justice adjourned to the hall of the house of delegates.

Mr. Hay, the attorney for the United States, for the district of Virginia, moved, that the prisoner should be committed in order to take his trial upon two charges, exhibited against him on the part of the United States: 1st, For a misdemeanor, in setting on foot, within the United States, a military expedition against the dominions of the king of Spain, a foreign prince, with whom the United States, at the time of the offence, were, and still are, at peace. 2d, For treason in assembling an armed force, with a design to seize the city of New Orleans, to revolutionize the territory attached to it, and to separate the western from the Atlantic states.

He stated the first offense to be a violation of the fifth section of an act of congress, passed on the 5th of June, 1794, intitled, "an act in addition to the act for the punishment of certain crimes against the United States," continued for limited periods by several succeeding laws, and continued without limitation by an act passed in 1799. The said section provides, "that if any person shall, within the territory or jurisdiction of the United States, begin or set on foot or provide or prepare the means for any military expedition or enterprize, to be carried on from thence against the territories or dominions of any foreign prince or state, with whom the United States are at peace, every person so offending shall, upon conviction, be adjudged guilty of a high misdemeanor, and shall suffer fine and imprisonment, at the discretion of the court in which the conviction shall be had, so as that such fine shall not exceed three thousand dollars, nor the term of imprisonment be more than three years." He supported this charge by the letter of the prisoner addressed to general Wilkinson, and insisted that it showed probable cause to suspect him of having committed this offense; nay, that he had actually committed it, and that this construction of the letter was deliberately adopted by the supreme court of the United States; that the intention of the prisoner to commit these offences was perfectly clear from the evidence.

But, secondly, he insisted, that there was probable cause to suspect, that the prisoner had committed an act of treason; that he intended to take possession of New-Orleans, make it the seat of his dominion, and the capital of his empire; and that this charge was proved by the affidavits exhibited in the cases of Bollman and Swartwout, and he referred to the opinion of the supreme court in those cases, as supporting the doctrine for which he contended, that there was just ground of suspicion against him. He went minutely into an examination of the evidence, to show that he was correct, and among other circumstances mentioned his flight from justice.

Mr. WICKHAM, in behalf of the prisoner, contended, that there was no evidence of treason committed by colonel Burr; that there was nothing like an overt act, or probable ground to believe him guilty of such an offense; that the letter in cypher to general Wilkinson was not delivered by Mr. Burr, nor proved to be written by him; that a comparison of the handwriting was inadmissible evidence; that if it were written by him, the contents of it might be mistaken, and general Wilkinson acknowledged that it could not be fully interpreted; that the definition of treason was clearly marked out by the constitution itself, and could not be mistaken. He contested the propriety and effect of the evidence relied on by the attorney for the United States, and insisted, that if any thing could be inferred from it, an invasion of the territories of the king of Spain, a power with which we were in an intermediate state between war and peace, was by far the most probable; that if his intention were to attack the Spanish settlements, it was not only innocent, but meritorious; that there were strong circumstances at that time to justify the expectation of a war with Spain; and he appealed to the message of the president of the United States, at the opening of the session of congress, to prove the provocations on the part of Spain, and the probability of such an event; that if we remained at peace with that power, still colonel Burr might very innocently contemplate some individual enterprize, and the president recommended strong settlements beyond the Mississippi; that as to what was deemed a flight, he only exercised a right in endeavoring to escape from military despotism. He concluded, that there was not a shadow of evidence to support the charge of treason; and as to the other, the evidence was trivial; but if deemed sufficient to put him on his trial, it was a bailable offence; and as, unfortunately for colonel Burr, he was brought to the place where he had fewer friends or acquaintances, than in almost any other part of the United States, it would be cruelty in counsel to insist on his giving bail in a considerable sum.

Mr. RANDOLPH enforced the same principles in behalf of the accused. He denied that there was any evidence to support either of the charges; that, though long conversant with criminal jurisprudence, he never before heard of a conjecture of an overt act of treason attempted to be proved from a supposed intention! which was an inconsistent with law and justice as with charity. But whatever the intention might have been, the law required, that a criminal act must be proved to support a prosecution; that the government, who had caused him to be brought such a great distance from his friends and the scene of intelligence, ought not to avail itself thereof to oppress him; that as treason was of all crimes the most heinous, it required the strongest evidence to support it; whereas here there was no proof except what was vague, weak, and unsatisfactory; that he had not fled from justice, but from military oppression, (which he had a right to resist) after he had been acquitted in Kentucky, and a grand jury in the Mississippi Territory had found him not guilty. Notwithstanding the alarm excited, nothing like an overt act of treason in levying war was proved. No military preparations existed, not a single soldier was enlisted; nay, not even a servant extraordinary has been shown to have attended him; that there was no evidence that Swartwout's communication with Wilkinson was authorised by Burr, or that he faithfully delivered the message, if entrusted with one; that therefore the affidavit of Wilkinson proved nothing; that his being in the western country, and engaged in collecting persons to settle some valuable lands, were the only circumstances which remained to subject him to the slightest shade of suspicion; and these were strangely converted into act of "levying war"; that the terrible alarm at New-Orleans was imputable to the conduct of general Wilkinson, whose arbitrary and violent proceedings, and magnifying accounts of danger, were calculated to make the people tremble for their personal safety. As to his attempt to escape in South Carolina, Mr. Randolph concluded that any other man would in the same circumstances have endeavoured to escape from military persecution and tyranny; and that the manner in which he was treated was barbarous, inhuman and oppressive, to the last degree. That, according to the doctrine contended for by the counsel for the United States, a man might be apprehended in the district of Maine, and carried as far as the Tombigbee, illegally, without redress any where between those places, for want of evidence; and when brought to the place appointed for his trial, the court would not try him, but wait for further evidence, if the commitment appeared to be right on the face of it, which would annihilate, altogether, the benefit of the writ of habeas corpus. He concluded, that there was no evidence of an overt act to support the charge of treason, and that it ought to be renounced. As to the other point, the fitting out an expedition against the dominions of the king of Spain, he asked, where it was prepared? in what state? Virginia, Ohio, Kentucky, or the Mississippi Territory? That they had no arms, no ammunition; that they had some boats calculated only to accommodate families removing to form new settlements. He hoped, that if the judge should think that a recognisance ought to be required, it should be in as small a sum as possible.

Colonel BURR rose, he said, not to remedy any omission of his counsel, who had done great justice to the subject. He wished only to state a few facts, and to repel some observations of a personal nature. The present inquiry involved a simple question of treason or misdemeanor. According to the constitution, treason consisted in acts; that an arrest could only be justified by the suspicions of acts, whereas, in this case, his honour was invited to issue a warrant upon mere conjecture; that alarms existed without cause; that Mr. Wilkinson alarmed the president, and the president alarmed the people of Ohio. He appealed to historical facts. No sooner did he understand that suspicions were entertained in Kentucky of the nature and design of his movements, than he hastened to meet an investigation. The prosecution not being prepared, he was discharged. That he then went to Tennessee. While there he heard that the attorney for the district of Kentucky was preparing another prosecution against him; that he immediately returned to Frankfort, presented himself before the court, and again was honourably discharged; that what happened in the Mississippi Territory was equally well known; that there he was not only acquitted by the grand jury, but they went farther, and censured the conduct of that government; and if there had been really any cause of alarm, it must have been felt by the people of that part of the country; that the manner of his descent down the river, was a fact which put at defiance all rumours about treason or misdemeanor; that the nature of his equipments clearly evinced that his object was purely peaceable and agricultural; that this fact alone ought to overthrow the testimony against him; that his designs were honourable, and would have been useful to the United States. His flight, as it was termed, had been mentioned as evidence of guilt. He asked, at what time did he fly? In Kentucky he invited inquiry, and that inquiry terminated in a firm conviction of his innocence; that the alarms were at first great in the Mississippi Territory, and orders had been issued to seize and destroy the persons and property of himself and party; that he endeavoured to undeceive the people, and convince them that he had no designs hostile to the United States, but that twelve hundred men were in arms for a purpose not yet developed; the people could not be deceived; and he was acquitted, and promised the protection of the government; but the promise could not be performed; the arm of military power could not be resisted; that he knew there were military orders to seize his person and property, and transport him to a distance from that place; that he was assured by the officer of an armed boat, that it was lying in the river ready to receive him on board. Was it his duty to remain there thus situated? That he took the advice of his best friends, pursued the dictates of his own judgment, and abandoned a country where the laws ceased to be the sovereign power; that the charge stated in a hand-bill, that he had forfeited his recognisance, was false; that he had forfeited no recognisance; if he had forfeited any recognisance, he asked, why no proceedings had taken place for the breach of it? If he was to be prosecuted for such breach, he wished to know why he was brought to this place? Why not carry him to the place where the breach happened? That more than three months had elapsed since the order of government had issued to seize and bring him to that place; yet it was pretended, that sufficient time had not been allowed to adduce testimony in support of the prosecution. He asked, why the guard who conducted him to that place, avoided every magistrate on the way, unless from a conviction that they were acting without lawful authority? Why had he been debarred the use of pen, ink, and paper, and not even permitted to write to his daughter? That in the state of South Carolina, where he happened to see three men together, he demanded the interposition of the civil authority; that it was from military despotism, from the tyranny of a military escort, that he wished to be delivered, not from an investigation into his conduct, or from the operation of the laws of his country. He concluded, that there were three courses that might be pursued,—an acquittal, or a commitment for treason, or for a misdemeanor; that no proof existed in support of either, but what was contained in the affidavits of Eaton and Wilkinson, abounding in crudities and absurdities.

Mr. RODNEY, the attorney general of the United States, then addressed the judge. He observed, that when he considered the numerous and attentive audience, the public anxiety so strongly excited, the character charged, and the crime of which he was accused, he was more than usually embarrassed; that he had never felt more for any person than for the prisoner, who was no less than the late vice president of the United States, esteemed for his transcendent talents, and whom he once considered as his friend, and treated as such in his own house; that he now stood charged with the most heinous crime; that it was incumbent on those who prosecuted, to prove probable cause to believe his guilt, and that the chain of circumstances showed without doubt, that he was guilty; that, however, he would endeavour to convince him, by his manner of conducting the prosecution, that the government was not influenced by malicious or vindictive passions, to persecute him.

That the gentlemen on the other side had argued as if they were then before a jury upon the principal trial, and demanded such legal evidence as would be sufficient to convict him on such trial: that the law however, required no such plenary testimony in this incipient stage of the proceedings; that to show probable cause to authorise a commitment, ex parte testimony was admissible; and unless it manifestly appeared that he was innocent, he ought to be committed; whereas before a jury, such testimony would be excluded, and his innocence would be presumed till his guilt appeared; that on the trial the law required two witnesses to an overt act of treason; and that his confession would be unavailing unless made in open court; that on the present inquiry, two witnesses were not requisite to prove an overt act, and that ex parte evidence of his confession must be admitted; that it was true, that the constitution required two witnesses of an overt act to convict the prisoner; but that the sixth article of the amendments to the constitution, rendered probable cause only necessary to justify the issuing a warrant to take a man into custody, and of course to commit him for trial. That there were two charges against him: one for a crime against the constitution; the other for a violation of the act of congress passed in 1794, to prevent the safety and peace of the United States from being put in jeopardy, by the daring enterprises of unauthorised individuals; on both of which he would make a few remarks. In the first place he contended, that the mystery in which this business was enveloped, afforded just grounds of suspicion. If the settlement of lands merely was intended, why were dark and corruptive messages sent to military commanders? why was a letter in cypher sent to the commander in chief, when he was supposed to be at St. Louis? why, when it was found he was not there, was another sent to Natchitoches, and from thence to New-Orleans? That it was an important fact, that colonel Burr in the preceding year had been throughout that whole country; that it was the practice every day to take the confession of accomplices as evidence against their principals, though made to escape punishment themselves; that here the case was much stronger, for the confessions of Bollman and Swartwout to general Wilkinson were perfectly voluntary—with the design of engaging him in the criminal projects of colonel Burr: Their disclosure ought to have the more weight, because they knew the contents of the letters which they delivered, which stated them to be in his confidence; and they declared themselves his partizans; that the affidavit of general Wilkinson, by which these facts are proved, was certainly good as a piece of ex parte testimony in this stage of the business, though inadmissible on the trial; that the declaration of Swartwout, as stated in that affidavit, proves the intention of the prisoner to have been to seize on New-Orleans, and plunder it, as preparatory to his expedition against Mexico; that the supreme court, in the case of Bollman and Swartwout, had adjudged, that if an end cannot be accomplished without treasonable means, the end itself was treasonable; and of course the project of the prisoner must have been to perpetrate treason. Mr. Rodney further contended, that the treasonable intention thus proved by Wilkinson was strongly fortified by the deposition of general Eaton, which was unquestionable evidence in this stage of the prosecution; that there could be no doubt of the truth of the statements of this gallant soldier; this man of true honour and most respectable character, who had rendered such memorable services to his country by traversing the deserts of Lybia, and by the conquest of Derne; that his communications to him were begun in the same cautious manner with those to general Wilkinson; that in both instances, he pretended at first to be in the confidence of the government, but afterwards proceeded by degrees to develop his treasonable plans; that the territory of Orleans, or some other territory belonging to the United States, was to be revolutionized; that there was to be some seizure at New-Orleans; that no doubt remained of the treasonable intention; that the only doubt was, whether there was sufficient proof of force having been actually embodied, and that all the circumstances rendered that fact very probable. Mr. Rodney here expatiated on the evidence; the letter of colonel Burr written in July; his intention to wait till he heard from the military commander at New-Orleans; Swartwout's statement; Eaton's deposition; the activity of colonel Burr in Ohio, Kentucky, Tennessee, and the Mississippi Territory, and his cautious mysterious conduct; and that in this incipient stage of the proceedings, stronger testimony could not be reasonably expected; that the government, however vigilant it had been, had not had sufficient time to obtain it; and that he ought to be put on his trial; that if he should be acquitted by a jury of his country, it would give no man more heartfelt pleasure than himself.

When Mr. Rodney concluded, Mr. Hay observed, that if the judge should be of opinion, that the prisoner ought to be put on his trial, and that he might be admitted to bail, he wished to make some observations on the amount of the sum in which the recognisance should be taken. He cited the 1st vol. of the laws of the United States, p. 144, and 2d vol. p. 275, to show, that it was discretionary with the judge to admit to bail, whether he should be of opinion that he ought to be tried for treason or misdemeanor. The chief justice answered, that he would certainly give him an opportunity to make the observations he desired; and that he intended himself, to deliver his opinion in writing, to prevent any misrepresentations of expressions which might fall from him. As it could not be prepared till the next day, colonel Burr's recognisance was renewed for his appearance at the capitol on the following day at ten o'clock.

WEDNESDAY, 1st April, 1807.—The chief justice delivered the following opinion in the presence of a numerous audience:

I am required on the part of the attorney for the United States to commit the accused on two charges:

1st. For setting on foot and providing the means for an expedition against the territories of a nation at peace with the United States.

2d. For committing high treason against the United States.

On an application of this kind I certainly should not require that proof which would be necessary to convict the person to be committed, on a trial in chief; nor should I even require that which should absolutely convince my own mind of the guilt of the accused: but I ought to require, and I should require, that probable cause be shown; and I understand probable cause to be a case made out by proof furnishing good reason to believe that the crime alleged has been committed by the person charged with having committed it.

I think this opinion entirely reconcileable with that quoted from judge Blackstone. When that learned and accurate commentator says, that "if upon an inquiry it manifestly appears that no such crime has been committed, or that the suspicion entertained of the prisoner was wholly groundless, in such cases only it is lawful totally to discharge him, otherwise he must be committed to prison or give bail," I do not understand him as meaning to say that the hand of malignity may grasp any individual against whom its hate may be directed, or whom it may capriciously seize, charged him with some secret crime, and put him on the proof of his innocence. But I understand that the foundation of the proceeding must be a probable cause to believe there is guilt; which probable cause is only to be done away in the manner stated by Blackstone. The total failure of proof on the part of the accuser would be considered by that writer as being in itself a legal manifestation of the innocence of the accused.

In inquiring therefore into the charges exhibited against Aaron Burr, I hold myself bound to consider how far those charges are supported by probable cause.

The first charge stands upon the testimony of general Eaton and general Wilkinson.

The witness first named proves that among other projects which were more criminal, colonel Burr meditated an expedition against the Mexican dominions of Spain. This deposition may be considered as introductory to the affidavit of general Wilkinson, and as explanatory of the objects of any military preparations which may have been made.

I proceed then to that affidavit.

To make the testimony of general Wilkinson bear on colonel Burr, it is necessary to consider as genuine the letter stated by the former to be, as nearly as he can make it, an interpretation of one received in cypher from the latter. Exclude this letter, and nothing remains in the testimony, which can in the most remote degree affect colonel Burr. That there are to the admissibility of this part of the affidavit great and obvious objections, need not be stated to those who know with how much caution proceedings in criminal cases ought to be instituted, and who know that the highest tribunal of the United States has been divided on them. When this question came before the supreme court, I felt the full force of these objections, although I did not yield to them. On weighing in my own mind the reason for and against acting, in this stage of the business, on that part of the affidavit, those in favour of doing so appeared to me to preponderate, and, as this opinion was not overruled, I hold myself still at liberty to conform to it.

That the original letter, or a true copy of it accompanied by the cypher, would have been much more satisfactory, is not to be denied: but I thought, and I still think, that, upon a mere question whether the accused shall be brought to trial or not, upon an inquiry not into guilt but into the probable cause, the omission of a circumstance which is indeed important, but which does not disprove the positive allegations of an affidavit, ought not to induce its rejection or its absolute disbelief, when the maker of the affidavit is at too great a distance to repair the fault. I could not in this stage of the prosecution absolutely discredit the affidavit, because the material facts alleged may very well be within the knowledge of the witness, although he has failed to state ixplicitly all the means by which this knowledge is obtained.

Thus, general Wilkinson states that this letter was received from colonel Burr, but does not say that it was in his hand writing, nor does he state the evidence which supports this affirmation. But, in addition to the circumstance that the positive assertion of the fact ought not perhaps, in this stage of the inquiry, to be disregarded, the nature of the case furnishes that evidence.

The letter was in cypher. General Wilkinson it is true, does not say that a cypher had been previously settled between colonel Burr and himself, in which they might correspond on subjects which, though innocent, neither of them might wish to subject to the casualties of a transportation from the Atlantic to the Mississippi; but when we perceive that colonel Burr has written in cypher, and that general Wilkinson is able to decypher the letter, we must either presume, that the bearer of the letter was also the bearer of its key, or that the key was previously in possession of the person to whom the letter was addressed. In stating particularly the circumstances attending the delivery of this letter, general Wilkinson does not say that it was accompanied by the key, or that he felt any surprise at its being in cypher. For this reason, as well as because there is not much more security in sending a letter in cypher accompanied by its key, than there is in sending a letter not in cypher; I think it more reasonable to suppose that the key was previously in possession of Wilkinson. If this was the fact, the letter being written in a cypher previously settled between himself and colonel Burr, is, in this stage of the inquiry at least, a circumstance which sufficiently supports the assertion, that the letter was written by colonel Burr.

The enterprize described in this letter is obviously a military enterprize, and must have been intended either against the United States, or against the territories of some other power on the continent, with all of whom the United States were at peace.

The expressions of this letter must be admitted to furnish at least probable cause for believing, that the means for the expedition were provided. In every part of it, we find declarations indicating that he was providing the means for the expedition; and as these means might be provided in secret, I do not think that further testimony ought to be required to satisfy me, that there is probable cause for committing the prisoner on this charge.

Since it will be entirely in the power of the attorney general to prefer an indictment against the prisoner, for any other offence which he shall think himself possessed of testimony to support, it is in fact, immaterial whether the second charge be expressed in the warrant of commitment or not; but as I hold it to be my duty to insert every charge alleged on the part of the United States, in support of which probable cause is shown, and to insert none in support of which probable cause is not shown, I am bound to proceed in the inquiry.

The second charge exhibited against the prisoner, is high treason against the United States in levying war against them.

As this is the most atrocious offence which can be committed against the political body, so is it the charge which is most capable of being employed as the instrument of those malignant and vindictive passions which may rage in the bosoms of contending parties struggling for power. It is that, of which the people of America have been most jealous, and therefore, while other crimes are unnoticed, they have refused to trust the national legislature with the definition of this, but have themselves declared in their constitution that "it shall consist only in levying war against the United States, or in adhering to their enemies giving them aid and comfort." This high crime consists of overt acts which must be proved by two witnesses or by the confession of the party in open court.

Under the control of this constitutional regulation, I am to inquire whether the testimony laid before me furnishes probable cause in support of this charge. The charge is, that the fact itself has been committed, and the testimony to support it must furnish probable cause for believing that it has been actually committed, or it is insufficient for the purpose for which it is adduced.

Upon this point too, the testimony of general Eaton is first to be considered. That part of his deposition which bears upon this charge is the plan disclosed by the prisoner for seizing upon New-Orleans, and revolutionizing the western states.

That this plan, if consummated by overt acts, would amount to treason, no man will controvert. But it is equally clear, that an intention to commit treason is an offence entirely distinct from the actual commission of that crime. War can only be levied by the employment of actual force. Troops must be embodied, men must be assembled in order to levy war. If colonel Burr had been apprehended on making these communications to general Eaton, could it have been alleged that he had gone further than to meditate the crime? Could it have been said that he had actually collected forces and had actually levied war? Most certainly it could not. The crime really completed was a conspiracy to commit treason, not an actual commission of treason.

If these communications were not treason at the instant they were made, no lapse of time can make them so. They are not in themselves acts. They may serve to explain the intention with which acts were committed, but they cannot supply those acts if they be not proved.

The next testimony is the deposition of general Wilkinson, which consists of the letter already noticed, and of the communications made by the bearer of that letter.

This letter has already been considered by the supreme court of the United States, and has been declared to import, taken by itself or in connexion with Eaton's deposition, rather an expedition against the territories of the United States. By that decision I am bound, whether I concurred in it or not. But I did concur in it. On this point the court was unanimous.

It is, however, urged that the declarations of Swartwout may be connected with the letter and used against colonel Burr. Although the confession of one man cannot criminate another, yet I am inclined to think that, on a mere inquiry into probable cause, the declaration of Swartwout made on this particular occasion, may be used against colonel Burr. My reason for thinking so is, that colonel Burr's letter authorizes Mr. Swartwout to speak in his name. He empowers Mr. Swartwout to make to general Wilkinson verbal communications explanatory of the plans and designs of Burr, which Burr adopts as his own explanations. However inadmissible therefore, this testimony may be on a trial in chief, I am inclined to admit it on this inquiry.

If it be admitted, what is its amount? Upon this point too, it appears that the supreme court was divided. I therefore hold myself at liberty to pursue my own opinion, which was, that the words "this territory must be revolutionized," did not so clearly apply to a foreign territory as to reject that sense which would make them applicable to a territory of the United States, at least so far as to admit of further inquiry into their meaning. And if a territory of the United States was to be revolutionized, though only as a mean for an expedition against a foreign power, the act would be treason.

This reasoning leads to the conclusion that there is probable cause for the allegation that treasonable designs were entertained by the prisoner so late as July last, when this letter was written.

It remains to inquire whether there is also probable cause to believe, that these designs have been ripened into the crime itself by actually levying war against the United States.

It has been already observed, that to constitute this crime, troops must be embodied, men must be actually assembled; and these are facts which cannot remain invisible. Treason may be machinated in secret, but it can be perpetrated only in open day and in the eye of the world. Testimony of a fact which in its own nature is so notorious ought to be unequivocal. The testimony now offered has been laid before the supreme court of the United States, and has been determined in the cases of Bollman and Swartwout, not to furnish probable cause for the opinion that war had been actually levied. Whatever might have been the inclination of my own mind in that case, I should feel much difficulty in departing from the decision then made, unless this case could be clearly distinguished from it. I will, however, briefly review the arguments which have been urged, and the facts now before me, in order to show more clearly the particular operation they have on my own judgment.

The fact to be established is, that in pursuance of these designs previously entertained, men have been actually assembled for the purpose of making war against the United States; and on the showing of probable cause that this fact has been committed, depends the issue of the present inquiry.

The first piece of testimony relied on to render this fact probable, is the declaration of Mr. Swartwout, that "colonel Burr was *levying* an armed body of 7,000 men from the state of New-York and the western states and territories, with a view to carry an expedition against the Mexican provinces." The term *"levying"* has been said, according to the explanation of the lexicons, to mean the embodying of troops, and therefore to prove what is required. Although I do not suppose that Mr. Swartwout had consulted a dictionary, I have looked into Johnson for the term, and find its first signification to be "to raise," its second "to bring together." In common parlance, it may signify the one or the other. But its sense is certainly decided by the fact. If when Mr. Swartwout left colonel Burr, which must be supposed to have been in July, he was actually embodying men from New-York to the western states, what could veil his troops from human sight? An invisible army is not the instrument of war, and had these troops been visible, some testimony relative to them could have been adduced. I take the real sense then in which this term was used to be, that colonel Burr was raising, or in other words engaging or enlisting men through the country described, for the enterprize he meditated. The utmost point to which this testimony can be extended is, that it denotes a future embodying of men, which is more particularly mentioned in the letter itself, and that it affords probable cause to believe that the troops did actually embody at the period designated for their assembling, which is sufficient to induce the justice to whom the application is made to commit for trial. I shall readily avow my opinion, that the strength of the presumption arising from this testimony ought to depend greatly on the time at which the application is made. If soon after the period at which the troops were to assemble, when full time had not elapsed to ascertain the fact, these circumstances had been urged as the ground for a commitment on the charge of treason, I should have thought them intitled to great consideration. I will not deny, that in the cases of Bollman and Swartwout, I was not perfectly satisfied that they did not warrant an inquiry into the fact. But I think every person must admit that the weight of these circumstances daily diminishes. Suspicion may deserve great attention, when the means of ascertaining its real grounds are not yet possessed; but when those means are or may have been acquired, if facts to support suspicion be not shown, every person, I think, must admit, that the ministers of justice at least ought not officially to entertain it. This, I think, must be conceded by all; but whether it be conceded by others or not, it is the dictate of my own judgment, and in the performance of my duty I can know no other guide.

The fact to be proved in this case is an act of public notoriety. It must exist in the view of the world, or it cannot exist at all. The assembling of forces to levy war is a visible transaction, and numbers must witness it. It is therefore capable of proof; and when time to collect this proof has been given, it ought to be adduced, or suspicion becomes ground too weak to stand upon.

Several months have elapsed, since this fact did occur, if it ever occurred. More than five weeks have elapsed, since the opinion of the supreme court has declared the necessity of proving the fact, if it exists. Why is it not proved?

To the executive government is intrusted the important power of prosecuting those, whose crimes may disturb the public repose, or endanger its safety. It would be easy, in much less time than has intervened since colonel Burr has been alleged to have assembled his troops, to procure affidavits establishing the fact. If, in November or December last, a body of troops had been assembled on the Ohio, it is impossible to suppose that affidavits establishing the fact could not have been obtained by the last of March. I ought not to believe that there has been any remissness on the part of those who prosecute, on this important and interesting subject; and consequently, when at this late period no evidence, that troops have been actually embodied, is given I must say, that the suspicion, which in the first instance might have been created, ought not to be continued, unless this want of proof can be in some manner accounted for.

It is stated by the attorney for the United States, that, as affidavits can only be voluntary, the difficulty of obtaining them accounts for the absence of proof.

I cannot admit this position. On the evidence furnished by this very transaction of the attachment felt by our western for their eastern brethren, we justly felicitate ourselves. How inconsistent with this fact is the idea, that no man could be found who would voluntarily depose, that a body of troops had actually assembled, whose object must be understood to be hostile to the union, and whose object was detested and defeated by the very people who could give the requisite information!

I cannot doubt that means to obtain information have been taken on the part of the prosecution; if it existed, I cannot doubt the practicability of obtaining it; and its nonproduction, at this late hour, does not, in my opinion, leave me at liberty to give to those suspicions which grow out of other circumstances, that weight to which at an earlier day they might have been entitled.

I shall not therefore insert in the commitment the charge of high treason. I repeat, that this is the less important, because it detracts nothing from the right of the attorney to prefer an indictment for high treason, should he be furnished with the necessary testimony.

The chief justice having delivered his opinion, observed, that, as colonel Burr would be put on his trial for carrying on a military expedition against a nation with whom the United States were at peace, his case was of course bailable.

Mr. Wickham wished to say something to the sum in which colonel Burr should be recognised to appear.

CHIEF JUSTICE.—I have thought a good deal on the subject, but have formed no very deliberate opinion. Bail ought certainly to be required in a sum sufficiently serious to insure the appearance of the party, but not so large as to amount to oppression. It has occurred to me, that, under all the circumstances of the case, ten thousand dollars would be about right, and would avoid the two extremes.

Mr. HAY.—I have no doubt of Mr. Burr's ability to procure bail for any sum which might be exacted, even without asking for it: I do not think ten thousand dollars adequate; nor would I ask a larger sum if I did not think it could be obtained without subjecting colonel Burr to any kind of inconvenience. From the facility with which bail was offered a few days ago, I have discovered a disposition in certain gentlemen of this place to relieve colonel Burr from the humiliation of an imprisonment.

Mr. WICKHAM.—I should suppose, sir, that five or six thousand dollars would be sufficient. It should be recollected, that colonel Burr is to give bail to answer the charge of a misdemeanor only. He is here among strangers. Perhaps, in no part of the United States, has colonel Burr fewer acquaintances than in Richmond. And however easy it might be for him to procure bail among his friends or connexions, I am very apprehensive he will not be able to obtain it here for so large a sum as ten thousand dollars. With respect to his ability to procure bail for any amount, as stated by Mr. Hay, I do expect that that observation, like some others of that gentleman, is not well warranted. Upon this point I am unable to express any decided opinion, as it is a subject with which I am personally unacquainted. But as to the *spirit*, which, it is insinuated by Mr. Hay has been shown by certain gentlemen to relieve colonel Burr, I am enabled explicitly to state the opinions of others, of a very different nature. It is true that two gentlemen stepped forward a few days ago, and relieved colonel Burr from the horrors of a dungeon. Their sole object was to assist a gentleman in distress, who had been dragged here by a military force more than a thousand miles. Gentlemen might be willing to be bound for two days, who would reluctantly engage for a longer time. Besides, I have heard several gentlemen of great respectability, who did not doubt but colonel Burr would keep his recognisance, express an unwillingness to appear as bail for him, lest it might be supposed they were enemies to their country. I hope this sentiment is incorrect; but it certainly will have its influence. I doubt very much whether he can procure bail, considering his remote situation from his friends, and the apprehensions just mentioned.

Mr. HAY.—I did state, sir, my belief to be, that colonel Burr could find bail for any sum which might be demanded. Mr. Wickham has been pleased to say, that this observation, like some others of mine, is not well warranted. I therefore consider it my duty to state candidly and correctly the reasons which have induced me to form that opinion. In the first place; two gentlemen, having no acquaintance with colonel Burr, on the first day of the examination voluntarily stepped forward, and offered themselves as his bail. This proves the prevailing sentiment among certain gentlemen. This sentiment, we may fairly presume, is not confined to those two gentlemen alone. Secondly; I have been well informed, that colonel Burr could give bail in one hundred thousand dollars. Mr. Wickham has not mentioned names, nor shall I state the source of my information. I do not pretend to say, that this large sum should be required. But when it is considerd, that, at the next court, evidence of assembling troops may be adduced, which will constitute the crime of treason, and prevent the appearance of colonel Burr, I do think that a sum sufficiently large should be fixed on to insure that object.

Colonel BURR.—I had no expectation, sir, that any thing would be taken into consideration but the subject immediately.

CHIEF JUSTICE.—If colonel Burr had been in the circle of

his friends, it might have made a difference as to the sum in which bail would be required. It is supposed that, under his present circumstances, bail to the amount of ten thousand dollars may be given. On a mere question as to bail, in this stage of the business, and from the proofs already adduced, the charge of treason ought not to be considered.

If bail for ten thousand dollars cannot be had, I will hear an application to reduce the sum.

Mr. HAY.—As long as that impression remains, no person will offer till the sum shall be reduced to its *minimum*.

CHIEF JUSTICE.—I shall certainly not very readily yield to an application to reduce the sum. And should it be made, you shall have notice of it.

The judge adjourned till three o'clock, in order to give the prisoner an opportunity to procure bail. At the hour appointed, he again attended at the capitol, when colonel Burr, with five securities, entered into a recognisance in the sum of ten thousand dollars for his appearance at the next circuit court of the United States for the Virginia district, which will commence on the 22d day of May next.

OPINION
OF SUPREME COURT OF THE UNITED STATES

Delivered by Chief Justice Marshall, on the 21st of February, 1807, referred to in the trials of colonel Burr.

The United States
vs.
Bollman and Swartwout.

Habeas corpus, on a commitment for treason.

THE prisoners having been brought before this court on a writ of *habeas corpus,* and the testimony on which they were committed having been fully examined and attentively considered, the court is now to declare the law upon their case.

This being a mere inquiry, which, without deciding upon guilt, precedes the institution of a prosecution, the question to be determined is, whether the accused shall be discharged or held to trial; and if the latter, in what place they are to be tried, and whether they shall be confined, or admitted to bail. "If," says a very learned and accurate commentator, "upon this inquiry it manifestly appears that no such crime has been committed, or that the suspicion entertained of the prisoner was wholly groundless, in such cases only it is lawful totally to discharge him; otherwise he must either be committed to prison or give bail."

The specific charge brought against the prisoners is treason in levying war against the United States.

As there is no crime which can more excite and agitate the passions of men than treason, no charge demands more from the tribunal before which it is made a deliberate and temperate inquiry. Whether this inquiry be directed to the fact or the law, none can be more solemn; none more important to the citizen or to the government; none can more affect the safety of both.

To prevent the possibility of those calamities which result from the extension of treason to offences of minor importance, that great fundamental law which defines and limits the various departments of our government, has given a rule on the subject, both to the legislature and the courts of America, which neither can be permitted to transcend.

"Treason against the United States shall consist only in levying war against them, or in adhering to their enemies, giving them aid and comfort."

To constitute that specific crime for which the prisoners now before the court have been committed, war must be actually levied against the United States. However flagitious may be the crime of conspiring to subvert by force the government of our country, such conspiracy is not treason. To conspire to levy war, and actually to levy war, are distinct offences. The first must be brought into operation by the assemblage of men for a purpose treasonable in itself, or the fact of levying war cannot have been committed. So far has this principle been carried, that in a case reported by Ventris, and that mentioned in some modern treatise on criminal law, it has been determined, that the actual enlistment of men to serve against the government does not amount to levying war. It is true, that in that case the soldiers enlisted were to serve without the realm, but they were enlisted within it, and if the enlistment for a treasonable purpose could amount to levying war, then war had been actually levied.

It is not the intention of the court to say, that no individual can be guilty of this crime who has not appeared in arms against his country. On the contrary, if war be actually levied, that is, if a body of men be actually assembled for the purpose of effecting by force, a treasonable purpose, all those who perform any part, however minute or however remote from the scene of action, and who are actually leagued in the general conspiracy, are to be considered as traitors. But there must be an actual assembling of men for the treasonable purpose, to constitute a levying of war.

Crimes so atrocious as those which have for their object the subversion, by violence, of those laws and those institutions which have been ordained, in order to secure the peace and happiness of society, are not to escape punishment because they are not ripened into treason. The wisdom of the legislature is competent to provide for the case; and the framers of our constitution, who not only defined and limited the crime, but with jealous circumspection attempted to protect their limitations, by providing, that no person should be convicted of it, unless on the testimony of two witnesses to the same overt act, or on confession in open court, must have conceived it more safe that punishment in such cases should be ordained by general laws, formed upon deliberation, under the influence of no resentments, and without knowing on whom they were to operate, than that it should be inflicted under the influence of those passions which the occasion seldom fails to excite, and which a flexible defintion of the crime, or a construction which would render it flexible, might bring into operation. It is therefore more safe as well as more consonant to the principles of our constitution, that the crime of treason should not be extended by construction to doubtful cases; and that crimes not clearly within the constitutional definition should receive such punishment as the legislature in its wisdom may provide.

To complete the crime of levying war against the United States, there must be an actual assemblage of men for the purpose of executing a treasonable design. In the case now before the court, a design to overturn the government of the United

States in New-Orleans by force, would have been unquestionably a design which, if carried into execution, would have been treason; and the assemblage of a body of men for the purpose of carrying it into execution, would amount to levying of war against the United States; but no conspiracy for this object, no enlisting of men to effect it, would be an actual levying of war.

In conformity with the principles now laid down have been the decisions heretofore made by the judges of the United States.

The opinions given by judge Patterson and judge Iredell, in cases before them, imply an actual assembling of men, though they rather designed to remark on the purpose to which the force was to be applied, than on the nature of the force itself. Their opinions, however, contemplate the actual employment of force.

Judge Chase, in the trial of Fries, was more explicit.

He stated the opinion of the court to be, "that if a body of people conspire and meditate an insurrection to resist or oppose the execution of any statute of the United States by force, they are only guilty of a high misdemeanor; but if they proceed to carry such intention into execution by force, that they are guilty of the treason of levying war; and the *quantum* of the force employed, neither lessens nor increases the crime; whether by one hundred, or one thousand persons, is wholly immaterial. "The court are of opinion," continued judge Chase, on that occasion, "that a combination or conspiracy to levy war against the United States is not treason, unless combined with an attempt to carry such combination or conspiracy into execution; some actual force or violence must be used in pursuance of such design to levy war, but it is altogether immaterial whether the force used is sufficient to effectuate the object; any force connected with the intention, will constitute the crime of levying war."

The application of these general principles to the particular case before the court will depend on the testimony which has been exhibited against the accused.

The first deposition to be considered is that of general Eaton. This gentleman connects in one statement the purport of numerous conversations held with colonel Burr throughout the last winter. In the course of these conversations were communicated various criminal projects which seem to have been revolving in the mind of the projector. An expedition against Mexico seems to have been the first and most matured part of his plan, if indeed it did not constitute a distinct and separate plan, upon the success of which other schemes still more culpable, but not yet well digested, might depend. Maps and other information preparatory to its execution, and which would rather indicate that it was the immediate object, had been procured; and for a considerable time, in repeated conversations, the whole efforts of colonel Burr were directed to prove to the witness, who was to have held a high command under him, the practicability of the enterprize, and in explaining to him the means by which it was to be effected.

This deposition exhibits the various schemes of colonel Burr, and its materiality depends on connecting the prisoners at the bar in such of those schemes as were treasonable. For this purpose the affidavit of general Wilkinson, comprehending in its body the substance of a letter from colonel Burr, has been offered and was received by the circuit court. To the admission of this testimony great and serious objections have been made. It has been urged, that it is a voluntary, or rather an extrajudicial affidavit made before a person not appearing to be a magistrate, and contains the substance only of a letter, of which the original is retained by the person who made the affidavit.

The objection that the affidavit is extrajudicial, resolves itself into the question, whether one magistrate may commit on an affidavit taken before another magistrate: For if he may, an affidavit made as the foundation of a commitment, ceases to be extrajudidicial, and the person who makes it would be as liable to a prosecution for perjury as if the warrant of commitment had been issued by the magistrate before whom the affidavit was made.

To decide that an affidavit made before one magistrate would not justify a commitment by another, might in many cases be productive of great inconvenience, and does not appear susceptible of abuse if the verity of the certificate be established. Such an affidavit seems admissible on the principle that before the accused is put upon his trial, all the proceedings are ex parte. The court therefore overrule this objection.

That which questions the character of the person who has on this occasion administered the oath is next to be considered.

The certificate from the office of the department of state has been deemed insufficient by the counsel for the prisoners; because the law does not require the appointment of magistrates for the territory of New-Orleans to be certified to that office; because the certificate is in itself informal, and because it does not appear that the magistrate had taken the oath required by the act of congress.

The first of these objections is not supported by the law of the case, and the second may be so easily corrected, retaining however any final decision, if against the prisoners, until the correction shall be made. With regard to the third, the magistrate must be presumed to have taken the requisite oaths, since he is found acting as a magistrate.

On the admissibility of that part of the affidavit which purports to be as near the substance of the letter from colonel Burr to general Wilkinson as the latter could interpret it, a division of opinion has taken place, in the court. Two judges are of opinion that as such testimony delivered in the presence of the prisoner on his trial would be totally inadmissible, neither can it be considered as a foundation for a commitment. Although in making a commitment the magistrate does not decide on the guilt of the prisoner, yet he does decide on the probable cause, and a long and painful imprisonment may be the consequence of his decision. This probable cause therefore ought to be moved by testimony in itself legal, and which, though from the nature of the case it must be ex parte, ought, in most other respects to be such as a court and jury might hear.

Two judges are of opinion that in this incipient stage of the prosecution an affidavit stating the general purport of a letter may be read, particularly where the person in possession of it is at too great a distance to admit of his being obtained, and that a commitment may be founded on it.

Under this embarrassment it was deemed necessary to look into the affidavit for the purpose of discovering whether if admitted, it contains matter which would justify the commitment of the prisoners at the bar on the charge of treason.

That the letter from colonel Burr to general Wilkinson relates to a military enterprize mediated by the former has not been questioned. If this enterprize was against Mexico, it would amount to a high misdemeanor; if against any of the territories of the United States, or if in its progress the subversion of the government of the United States, in any of their territories was a mean clearly and necessarily to be employed, if such mean formed a substantive part of the plan, the assemblage of a body of men to effect it would be levying war against the United States.

The letter is in language which furnishes no distinct view of the design of the writer. The cooperation, however, which is stated to have been secured, points strongly to some expedition against the territories of Spain. After making these general statements the writer becomes rather more explicit and says, "Burr's plan of operations is to move down rapidly from the falls on the 15th of November with the first 500 or 1000 men in light boats now constructing for that purpose, to be at Natchez between the 5th and 15th of December, there to meet Wilkinson: then to determine whether it will be expedient in the first instance to seize on or to pass by Baton Rouge. The people of the country to which we are going are prepared to receive us. Their agents now with Burr say that if we will protect their religion and will not subject them to a foreign power, in three weeks all will be settled."

There is no expression in these sentences which would justify a suspicion that any territory of the United States was the object of the expedition.

For what purpose seize on Baton Rouge? why engage Spain against this enterprize, if it was designed against the United States?

"The people of the country to which we are going are prepared to receive us." This language is peculiarly appropriate to a foreign country. It will not be contended that the terms would be inapplicable to a territory of the United States, but other terms would more aptly convey the idea, and Burr seems to consider himself as giving information of which Wilkinson was not possessed. When it is recollected that he was the governor of a territory adjoining that which must have been threatened, if a territory of the United States was threatened, and that he commanded the army, a part of which was stationed in that territory, the probability that the information communicated related to a foreign country, it must be admitted, gains strength.

"Their agents now with Burr say that if we will protect their religion and will not subject them to a foreign power, in three weeks all will be settled."

This is apparently the language of a people who, from the contemplated change of their political situation, feared for their religion, and feared that they would be made the subjects of a foreign power. That the Mexicans should entertain these apprehensions was natural, and would readily be believed. They were, if the representation made of their dispositions be correct, about to place themselves much in the power of men who professed a faith different from theirs, and who by making them dependent on England, or the United States, would subject them to a foreign power. That the people of New-Orleans, as a people, if really engaged in the conspiracy, should feel the same apprehensions, and required assurances on the same points, is by no means so obvious.

There certainly is not in the letter delivered to general Wilkinson, so far as that letter is laid before the court, one syllable which has a necessary or a natural reference to an enterprize against any territory of the United States.

That the bearer of this letter must be considered as acquainted with its contents, is not to be controverted. The letter and his own declarations evince the fact.

After stating himself to have passed through New-York and the western states and territories, without insinuating that he had performed on his route any act whatever, which was connected with the enterprize, he states their object to be "to carry an expedition to the Mexican provinces."

This statement may be considered as explanatory of the letter of colonel Burr, if the expressions of that letter could be thought ambiguous.

But there are two other declarations made by Mr. Swartwout, which constitute the difficulty of this case. On an inquiry from general Wilkinson, he said, "this territory would be revolutionized, where the people were ready to join, and that there would be some seizing, he supposed, at New-Orleans."

If these words import that the government, established by the United States in any of its territories, was to be revolutionized by force, although merely as a step to, or a means of executing some great projects, the design was unquestionably treasonable, and any assemblage of men for that purpose would amount to a levying of war. But on the import of the words a difference of opinion exists.

Some of the judges suppose they refer to the territory against which the expedition was intended, others to that in which the conversation was held. Some consider the words, if even applicable to the territory of the United States, as alluding to a revolution to be effected by the people, rather than by the party conducted by colonel Burr.

But whether this treasonable intention be really imputable to the plan or not, it is admitted that it must have been carried into execution by an open assemblage of men for that purpose, previous to the arrest if the prisoner, in order to consummate the crime as to him; and a majority of the court is of opinion, that the conversation of Mr. Swartwout affords no sufficient proof of such assembling.

The prisoner stated, that "colonel Burr, with the support of a powerful association, extending from New-York to New-Orleans, was levying an armed body of 7,000 men, from the state of New-York and the western states and territories, with a view to carry an expedition to the Mexican territories."

That the association, whatever may be its purpose, is not treason, has been already stated. That levying an army may or may not be treason, and that this depends on the intention with which it is levied, and on the point to which the parties have advanced, has been also stated. The mere enlisting of men without assembling them, is not levying war. The question then is, whether this evidence proves colonel Burr to have advanced so far in levying an army, as actually to have assembled them.

It is argued, that since it cannot be necessary that the whole 7,000 men should have assembled, their commencing their march by detachments to the place of rendezvous, must be sufficient to constitute the crime.

This position is correct, with some qualification. It cannot be necessary that the whole army should assemble, and that the various parts which are to compose it should have combined. But it is necessary there should be an actual assemblage, and therefore this evidence should make the fact unequivocal.

The travelling of individuals to the place of rendezvous would perhaps not be sufficient. This would be an equivocal act, and has no warlike appearance. The meeting of particular bodies of men, and their marching from places of partial to a place of general rendezvous, would be such as assemblage.

The particular words used by Mr. Swartwout are, that colonel Burr was levying an armed body of 7,000 men. If the term levying, in this place, imports that they were assembled, then such fact would amount, if the intention be against the United States, to levying war. If it barely imports that he was enlisting or engaging them in his service, the fact would not amount to levying war.

It is thought sufficiently apparent, that the letter is the sense in which the term was used. The fact alluded to, if taken in the former sense, is of a nature to force itself upon the public view, that, if the army had been actually assembled, either together, or in detachments, some evidence of such assembling would have been laid before the court.

The words used by the prisoner in reference to seizing at New-Orleans, and borrowing perhaps by force from the bank, though indicating a design to rob, and consequently importing a high offence, do not designate the specific crime of levying war against the United States.

It is, therefore, the opinion of a majority of the court, that, in the case of Samuel Swartwout, there is not sufficient evidence of his levying war against the United States to justify his commitment on the charge of treason.

That both the prisoners were engaged in a most culpable enterprize against the dominions of a power at peace with the United States, those who admit the affidavit of general Wilkinson cannot doubt. But that no part of this crime was committed in the district of Columbia, is apparent. It is therefore the unanimous opinion of the court, that they cannot be tried in this district.

The law read on the part of the prosecution is understood to apply only to offences committed on the high seas, or in any river, haven, bason, or bay, not within the jurisdiction of any particular state. In these cases there is no court which has particular cognizance of the crime, and therefore the place in which the criminal shall be apprehended, or, if he be apprehended where no court has exclusive jurisdiction, that to which he shall be first brought, is substituted for the place in which the offence was committed.

But in this case, a tribunal for the trial of the offence, wherever it may have been committed, had been provided by congress; and at the place where the prisoners were seized by the authority of the commander in chief, there existed such a tribunal. It would too be extremely dangerous to say, that because the prisoners were apprehended, not by a civil magistrate, but by the military power, there could be given by law a right to try the persons so seized in any place which the general might select, and to which he might direct them to be carried.

The acts of congress, which the prisoners are supposed to have violated, describe as offenders those who begin or set on foot, or provide or prepare the means for any military expedition or enterprize to be carried on from thence against the dominions of a foreign prince or state, with whom the United States are at peace.

There is a want of precision in the description of the offence, which might produce some difficulty in deciding what cases would come within it. But several other questions arise, which a court, consisting of four judges, finds itself unable to decide; and therefore, as the crime with which the prisoners stand charged has not been committed, the court can only direct them to be discharged. This is done with the less reluctance, because the discharge does not acquit them from the offence, which there is probable cause for supposing they have committed; and if those whose duty it is to protect the nation by prosecuting offenders against the laws shall suppose those who have been charged with treason to be proper objects for punishment, they will, when possessed of less exceptionable testimony, and when able to say at what place the offence has been committed, institute fresh proceedings against them.

The order of the court was as follows:

The United States
   vs.   On a writ of *habeas corpus.*
Swartwout.

The arguments of the attorney general, and of the attorney of the United States for the district of Columbia, and the arguments of the counsel for the prisoner having been heard; and the record of the circuit court for the county of Washington, containing the order by which the said Samuel Swartwout was committed on the charge of treason in levying war against the United States, and the testimony on which the said commitment was made, having been inspected and attentively considered, the court is of opinion that the said Samuel Swartwout levied war against the United States, and doth therefore direct, that he be forthwith discharged from the custody of the marshal.

The same order with regard to Bollman.

The Trial of Colonel Aaron Burr

CITY OF RICHMOND, FRIDAY, 22d MAY, 1807

Court of the United States for the fifth circuit and district of Virginia

PRESENT—JOHN MARSHALL, chief justice of the United States; and Cyrus Griffin, judge of the district of Virginia.

The court was opened at half past twelve o'clock; when colonel Aaron Burr appeared, with his counsel, Messrs. Edmund Randolph, John Wickham, Benjamin Botts, and John Baker.

Counsel for the prosecution; Messrs. George Hay, district attorney, William Wirt, and Alexander Mac Rae.

The clerk having called the names of the gentlemen who had been summoned on the grand jury, Mr. Burr's counsel demanded a sight of the panel; which was shown to them: when Mr. Burr addressed the court to the following effect:

May it please the court,

BEFORE any further proceeding with regard to swearing the jury, I beg leave to remark some irregularity that has taken place in summoning part of the panel. This is the proper time to make the exception. I understand that the marshal acts not under an act of congress, but a law of the state of Virginia, by which he is required to summon twenty-four freeholders of the state to compose the grand jury. When he has summoned that number, his function is completed. He cannot on any account summon a twenty-fifth. If, therefore, it can be made to appear, that the marshal has struck off any part of the original panel, and substituted other persons in their stead, the summons is illegal. Such is the law and the dictate of true policy; for in important cases, like the present, a different course would produce the most injurious consequences. I consider it proper to ask the marshal and his deputies, what persons they have summoned, and at what periods: whence it may be known, whether some have not been substituted in place of others struck off the panel. When we have settled this objection, I shall proceed to exceptions of a different nature.

Mr. BOTTS observed, that it was the 29th section of the judicial act, which refers to the state law, besides a distinct act which enumerates other duties; that neither of these laws specified any particular mode by which marshals were to summon juries in different districts. By the first section of the Virginia act, the sheriff is to summon twenty-four freeholders, any sixteen of whom appearing are to constitute a grand jury. The first section does not state that he is to make a return, but a distinct section inflicts a penalty, if he violate the duties prescribed by the first section; that is, if he fail "to summon a grand jury, and return panel of their names." Colonel Burr is anxious to have nothing more than a fair trial. The reports circulated, and prejudices excited against him, justify a strict attention to his rights. He therefore asks the strictest scrutiny into past and subsequent measures. An important interest is involved in the authority of the grand jury. And if there be any irregularity in the marshal's summons, it ought now to be rectified. By the act of Virginia, a sheriff, and by the act of congress a marshal, are mere ministerial officers bound to discharge certain duties. He is to summon twenty-four jurors. When that act is done, it is irrevocable, and his duty at an end. This court only possesses the authority to excuse any of those who have been summoned, and to direct the marshal to substitute others, till the necessary quorum be completed.

Mr. Botts further observed, that he had no intention of casting the slightest imputation on the marshal for his conduct in this transaction; that his honourable character placed him above suspicion, and the fault, if any, must have arisen from official misconceptions; that he did not propose to interrogate Major Scott in any manner that might possibly criminate him; but that the court had a right to inquire, and, if any error was committed, to correct it. That if he was overruled in this motion, he would then crave leave of the court to produce testimony as to the facts: that he took it for granted, that if a single moment intervened between the summoning of a juror and the meeting of a court, the court alone had the power to discharge him; that with regard to the present panel it would appear, that the marshal after summoning one individual, had notified another to attend; in other words, he had summoned him according to the legal definition of the term "summons." That this was not the duty of the marshal; that when the original panel was complete, his duty was at an end, and he must return that very panel precisely, without any addition. What mischiefs might not result from a different practice, particularly in cases of extreme importance, where the government was concerned, since the marshal himself depended on the government for the duration of his commission?

Mr. Botts therefore contended, that the ministerial duties of a marshal ceased with the summons which he gave; and that, if the jurors did not appear, it was the privilege of the court to supply any deficiency. He cited the decision of the supreme court of the United States in the case of Marbury v. Madison, to show, that when the ministerial duties of an officer were discharged, his power necessarily ceased, and his act was irrevocable. This doctrine was of universal application in law, both in America and England. It was applicable to a sheriff, after he had served a common writ of *fieri facias.* If he summon a petit juryman, who fails to appear before the court, it is the right of the court alone to fine or to excuse him. Mr. Botts then concluded, that he would ask the marshal, who were the twenty-four whom he had first summoned; for that may constitute the grand jury. Every one beyond that number was illegally summoned. It was the right of colonel Burr to demand such a purgation of the panel.

Mr. Hay, the district attorney, observed, that he was not prepared to make any observations upon this question, as it was a point which he had never before had any occasion to consider; that the proposition was, however, of no great importance, since, if any of them were set aside, there would still be a sufficient number to constitute a grand jury; or the deficiency might be supplied by a new summons among the bystanders. If there were, in reality, any objection to the regularity of the summons, he was willing to accommodate the opposite counsel; that he was not certain how far it was strictly proper to interrogate, or examine into the time of summoning the different members of the panel, as he had not been very conversant with business of this kind. He was, however, content that the court should decide; and if it should be their opinion that the marshal should be interrogated, how many jurymen he had summoned, and when he had discharged them, he should feel perfectly satisfied.

Mr. Wickham.—Before we go into this inquiry, we declare, that we mean no personal imputation upon the respectable gentleman who is the marshal. His intentions were certainly pure. It is an error of judgment alone to which we object. But in the present case, where such important interests are at stake, and where such unjustifiable means have been used to prejudice the public mind against Colonel Burr, it is his right to take every advantage which the law gives him. We are prepared to show, that when a person is bound in a recognisance, he has a right, at this period of the business, to come before the court with his exceptions to the grand jury; and if in any other case, why not in one of such deep importance as the present: In support of this position, Mr. Wickham cited 2 Hawkin's Pleas of the Crown, page 307, sect. 16, and 3 Bacon's Abridgment, page 725. Whether we might afterwards file a plea in abatement for the error admitted, is not now to be discussed. It is Colonel Burr's anxious desire, that this whole affair should terminate here, and that this grand jury may determine his case.

The chief justice called for the law of Virginia.

MR. HAY read it.—Revised Code, page 100, sect. 2.—The construction put upon this part of the law seems to me far more rigid than sound sense warrants. By this law, the marshal is empowered to select twenty-four freeholders, legally qualified to serve on the grand jury. The officer, in many cases necesarily ignorant of the situation of an individual, summons him to attend. The person informs him, that, from some personal misfortune, some domestic calamity, or some indispensable business, it is impossible for him to attend. We ask, whether the accurate construction of this law forbids him to summon another in his place? Where is the legal authority to prove, that when he has once summoned twenty-four jurymen, his ministerial function is at an end? The moment it appears in court, that the legal number of jurors is not present, he is to fill up his panel from the bystanders. We appeal to the candour of the opposite counsel, to point out the real distinction between the two cases. Why should the marshal have the right to fill up his panel, when it is once ascertained before the court, that some of the jurymen have not actually attended, and yet deny him the right of substituting others in the place of those he has summoned, but who, he is satisfied, before the meeting of the court, cannot attend? Instead of a difference, the two cases are strikingly parallel. What the fact was, Mr. Hay said he knew not, but he believed that some of those who were said to be substituted had not been positively summoned by the marshal, but had been merely applied to, to know whether they could attend.

Mr. Wickham contended, that the counsel for the United States had not fairly met the question. There is a doubt whether Colonel Burr has not a right to come forward with his exceptions *now* to the grand jury. As the authorities on this subject are short, he would take the liberty of reading them to the court. (He read those he before cited.) From these authorities it manifestly appears, that a person bound in a recognisance, had a right, before the grand jury were sworn, to state his exceptions to the mode of impaneling them. It is for this reason that Colonel Burr has, in this stage of the business, come forward with his objections.

Mr. Hay contends, that our construction of the law is more rigid than sound policy demands. But when the words of the law are obvious, why should we resort to a dubious construction? *"Ita lex scripta est."* But if we are to wander into the wide field of policy, how completely would it bear against the gentleman's cause! God forbid, sir, that I should utter the slightest imputation upon the character and official conduct of Major Scott; they soar above suspicion. But if once the marshal, who holds his commission at the will of the government, were permitted to alter the panel as he pleased, the life of every citizen in this state would be held at his pleasure. It is therefore essentially important, that the ministerial officer should rigidly pursue the statute from which he derives his authority. And what is his duty in the present instance? He is to summon twenty-four freeholders to serve on the grand jury, any sixteen of whom may constitute a quorum. Mr. Hay had declared, that this provision was mere matter of forum; for if there be not a sufficient number present to constitute a quorum, the marshal may make up to the full number twenty-four. But that is not the fact. If sixteen jurymen attend, the marshal cannot add one more. Let us then apply a suppositious case.

The marshal, if notified that one of the jury whom he has summoned cannot attend, is authorised, according to Mr. Hay's doctrine, to summon a substitute. It is no impediment to the exercise of this authority, that there be the legal quorum of sixteen remaining upon the panel; he may proceed to summon substitutes till he completes the whole number twenty-four. And yet, if the case were to happen in court, the marshal would certainly have no authority, to complete the whole number. Why then suppose such a difference of authority in and out of court? Why not rather suppose, that the marshal has no authority to do *that* out of court, which he cannot do before the court.

Let us suppose another case. A grand juror has been summoned for several weeks before the meeting of the court. The bare authority of the marshal is sufficient, according to this doctrine, to excuse him from serving, and to substitute another in his place, only one hour before the meeting of the court. Mr. Wickham declared he could mention the case of a man who had been excused from this very panel.

Major Scott (the marshal.)—Name him, sir: I demand his name.

Mr. Wickham declared, that he meant no imputation upon Major Scott, but he would not submit to such interruptions. If no sufficient excuse is given by the absent juror, he is subject to a fine. Is it then contended, that the marshal is to judge in the place of the court? not only to relieve the person of the juror, but his property also from the fine? The words of this law are too plain to be mistaken. It admits of no latitude of construction. But if the marshal has really transcended his authority, yet I do not hesitate to declare my opinion, that he intended to discharge his duty with fidelity. It was only an error in judgment, to which all men, however well versed in the law, are liable.

MR. HAY.— Will the court indulge me with a single additional remark? I stated before, that when the marshal found, that one of the jury whom he had before summoned could not attend, he was authorised to summon a substitute. Mr. Wickham, however, contends, that the marshal cannot summon others, after sixteen have appeared. But for what reason? Because there is, in reality, no occasion for it. The object of the law is already attained. The grand jury is complete, and it is unnecessary to take up further time, when the grand jury is legally full. But before the court convenes, how is it possible for the marshal to know how many of those summoned will attend? According to the doctrine of the opposite counsel, there may be no grand jury.

The chief justice inquired, whether the question had ever come before the state courts?

MR. RANDOLPH.—Not, sir, to my knowledge. In nearly thirty years practice, (and a considerable part of that time I was attorney general for the commonwealth) no occasion has occurred for an objection. I have never seen a case where it was so absolutely necessary to assert every privilege belonging to the accused, as in this. But as to the *right* itself, abstractedly considered, I have never hesitated a moment about its existence. It is written in broad intelligible characters. Sir, if we ever submit to these relaxations of the rights of the accused, a time may possibly come, when we may lament the precedent we have established; when men less virtuous than the present respectable marshal, shall succeed to his functions. But the question in the present case, is not what has been the practice in the state courts, but what is the right? If this right has never been before asserted, it is because there never was an occasion which so imperiously demanded it as the present; because there never was such a torrent of prejudice excited against any man, before a court of justice, as against Colonel Burr, and by means which we shall presently unfold.

CHIEF JUSTICE.—As this question has never been decided before the state courts, we must refer to the words of the act of assembly. There can be no doubt that this is the time when the accused has a right to take exceptions to the jury; and the only doubt can be, is this a proper exception? The marshal is authorised by law to summon twenty-four jurymen; but he is not to summon a twenty-fifth. Of course, the twenty-fifth is not legally summoned, unless he has the power to discharge a person already summoned. He has no such power, unless the jury be composed of bystanders. The twenty-four first summoned must compose the jury, sixteen of whom constitute a quorum. It follows, therefore, that no one can be on the grand jury, unless he be one of the twenty-four first summoned, or one who has been selected from the bystanders by the direction of the court. When the panel has been once completed by the marshal, its deficiencies can be supplied only from the bystanders.

The chief justice further observed, that he was not well acquainted with the practice in the state courts; but he believed the practice of sheriffs to be, to excuse a man summoned on the jury, if they are satisfied that his excuse is reasonable. So it may have been with the officer of this court, who acted, he had no doubt, with the most scrupulous regard to what he believed to be the law. That the court, however, thought the marshal had no such dispensing power. One very obvious reason against the marshal's possessing this power of substitution, is, that if a person summoned should come into court, and prove that he had been actually summoned, he certainly would be on the grand jury, if one of the twenty-four first summoned. The general principle is, that when a person is put in the panel he stands upon it, and cannot be displaced by the marshal. There is an evident distinction between actually summoning a grand juryman, and merely talking to a person about summoning him. The court is therefore of opinion, that a person substituted in the place of one actually summoned, cannot be considered as being on the panel.

MR. BURR.—The court having established the principle, we must ask their aid to come at the facts. We wish to know, when certain persons were summoned, when discharged, and whether other persons' were substituted in their stead.

The marshal said, that he had not the least objection to state all the facts necessary to be known on this occasion. A few days ago he had received a letter from Colonel John Taylor, of Caroline, one of those whom he had summoned on the jury, in which he states, that a hurricane of wind had destroyed his carriagehouse, and with it his carriages, so that he could not use them; and that his indisposition prevented his riding to Richmond on horseback. This letter he had laid before both their honours, and the chief justice had deemed his excuse reasonable. He had then summoned Mr. Barbour to serve in Colonel Taylor's place. He had also received a letter from Mr. John Macrae, informing that he was going to leave the state for his health. He had in consequence summoned Doctor Foushee in his place. The marshal added, that he felt it to be his duty to bring twenty-four jurymen into court, and acted upon this principle.

The court decided, that Mr. Barbour and Dr. Foushee, the substituted persons, were not on the grand jury.

MR. BURR.—I understand that the panel is now reduced to sixteen, and that this is the proper time to make any other exceptions to the panel. It is with regret, that I shall now proceed to exercise the privilege of challenging for favour. In exercising this right, I shall perhaps appeal to the authority of the court to try these jurors. Lest it may be contested, it is better to settle the principle first.

Mr. Hay, without directly contesting, called for the law to justify the application.

MR. BURR.—Let it be distinctly understood, that I claim the same right of challenging "for *favour*" the grand jury, that I have of challenging the petit jury. I admit, that it is not a peremptory challenge, but that I must show good cause to support the challenge. It will be of course necessary to appoint triers to decide, and before whom the party and the witnesses to prove or disprove the favour, must appear.

MR. BOTTS.—There can be no question, that a person standing in the situation of Colonel Burr, may challenge the jury for favour. In civil cases, any individual may challenge a jury for favour or partiality to his antagonist; a *fortiori*, it must exist in criminal cases. Mr. Botts here cited authority in support of his principle, and admitted, that the cause of challenge must be proved by testimony; that it was necessary to prevent such impurity from creeping into the commencement of this trial, as must contaminate all its subsequent stages; that no reflection against the integrity of the present jurors was intended; but in principles of plain common sense it was proper to remove every cause that might defeat the purposes of justice.

Mr. Hay disavowed the intention of opposing substantial exceptions, and admitted the law to be as stated by the opposite counsel.

MR. BURR.—I shall, then, proceed to name the persons and causes of challenge. The first I shall mention is William B. Giles, against whom there are two causes of challenge. The first is a matter of some notoriety, because dependent on certain documents or records: the second is a matter of fact, which must be substantiated by witnesses. As to the first, Mr. Giles, when in the senate of the United States, had occasion to pronounce his opinion on certain documents by which I was considered to be particularly implicated. Upon those documents he advocated the propriety of suspending the writ of habeas corpus. The constitution however forbids such suspension, except in cases of invasion or insurrection, when the public safety requires it. It was therefore to be inferred, that Mr. Giles did suppose, that there was a rebellion or insurrection, and a public danger, of no common kind. It is hardly necessary to observe, that with this rebellion, and this supposed danger, I myself had been supposed to be connected. Perhaps this may be a sufficient reason to set aside Mr. Giles. But if not, I shall endeavor to establish by evidence, that he has confirmed these opinions by public declarations; that he has declared that these documents, involving me, contained guilt of the highest grade.

MR. BOTTS.—There is no necessity of adding any thing to the observations of Colonel Burr. If the right of challenge exists, the right to try the challenge exists also. But while I am up, I will declare, that no reflection is intended to be made on the character or conduct of Mr. Giles. That gentleman will be candid enough to admit, that there is not the least design to wound his feelings. It is with the utmost reluctance that Colonel Burr has prevailed upon himself to advance this exception. I have authorities, however, to prove, that these two causes are sufficient to disqualify Mr. Giles. The first relates to his public, the second to his individual conduct.

MR. HAY.—How many of the panel does the counsel mean to object to?

MR. BOTTS.—Only two.

MR. GILES.—As to exceptions to myself personally, I can have no objection to have them tried. The court will, however, perceive the delicate situation in which I shall be placed. The triers will have to interrogate witnesses, and the result either way is ineligible. I have no objection to state to the court every impression I have ever had upon this subject. But to culling witnesses to detail loose conversations, so liable to be misunderstood, forgotten, or misrepresented, I am certainly opposed.

MR. HAY.—I was about to make a proposition which might relieve us from all this useless embarrassment, and which might gratify the views of the accused. If the gentlemen who are challenged on the jury will consent to withdraw themselves, I can have no objection. I am content that every one who had made declarations expressive of decisive opinion, should be withdrawn from the jury. I am not disposed to spend time on such points as these.

MR. BURR.—It will certainly save time, and I assent to the proposition.

MR. GILES.—The circumstances which have just occurred place me in an unpleasant situation. I have no objection to disclose, in the usual way, with candour, the real state of my mind in relation to the accused. But I have an objection to the introduction of witnesses to prove casual expressions, which are so liable to be misconceived. In the *present* state of things, expressions might be imputed to me which I never used, or expressions which I really used might be mistaken or misrepresented by the witness; or the witness might deduce inferences from my expressions which they did not justify. It was by no means agreeable to me to have been summoned on this grand jury. But for some time past I have invariably pursued this maxim: *"neither to avoid nor to solicit any public appointment; but when called to the discharge of any public duty by the proper authority, conscientiously to attempt its execution.*" In undertaking to serve on the present grand jury, I was influenced by the same consideration.

With respect to my public conduct, I presume it is of public notoriety, and will speak for itself. I not only voted for the suspension of the privilege of the writ of *habeas corpus,* in certain cases, but *I* proposed that measure. I then thought, and I still think, that the emergency demanded it; that it was fully justified by the evidence before the senate; and I now regret that the nation had not energy enough to support the senate in that measure. This opinion was formed upon the state of the evidence before the senate, which, in all questions of a general nature, is of a very different character from the legal evidence necessary in a judicial investigation. My mind is, however, free to receive impressions from judicial evidence.

In relation to the accused, I feel very desirous, and have often so expressed myself, that the various transactions imputed to him should undergo a full and fair judicial investigation; and that, through that *medium,* they should receive their just and true *character,* whatever in point of fact it might be, and that he should be presented in that character to the world. I have no personal resentments against the accused; and if he has received any information inconsistent with this statement, it is not true. However, as it is left to me to elect, whether to serve on the grand jury or not, I will certainly withdraw.

CHIEF-JUSTICE.—The court thinks, that if any gentleman has made up and declared his mind, it would be best for him to withdraw.

MR. BURR.—A gentleman who has prejudged this cause, is certainly unfit to be a juryman. It would be an effort above human nature for this gentleman to divest himself of all prepossessions. I believe his mind to be as pure and unbiased as that of any gentleman under such circumstances. But the decisive opinion he has formed upon this subject, though in his public character, disqualifies him for a juryman. But he is one of the last men on whom I would wish to cast any reflections. So far from having any animosity against him, he would have been one of those whom I should have ranked among my personal friends.

The other gentleman whom I shall challenge is Wilson Cary Nicholas.

Mr. Nicholas desired that the objections against him should be stated.

MR. BURR.—The objection is, that he has entertained a bitter personal animosity against me; and therefore I cannot expect from him that pure impartiality of mind which is necessary to a correct decision. I feel the delicacy of my situation; but if the gentleman will consent to withdraw, I will waive any further inquiry.

COLONEL WILSON C. NICHOLAS rose, and addressed the court as follows:

My being in this situation certainly was not a thing of choice. When I was summoned by the marshal, I urged him in the strongest manner to excuse me. I mentioned to him, that it would be extremely inconvenient to me to attend the court, and that it would be very unpleasant to serve on the jury, on account of the various relations in which I had stood to Colonel Burr. I had been in congress at the time when the attempt was made to elect Colonel Burr president of the United States. My feelings and opinions on that occasion are well known. I had served three years in the senate while Colonel Burr was president of that body, and was one of those who, previous to the last election, had taken a very decided part in favour of the nomination of the present vice president, for the office at that time filled by Colonel Burr. Moreover, from the time that Colonel Burr first went to the western country, my suspicions were very much excited as to his probable objects, in that part of the United States; in consequence of which I gave early and perhaps too great credit to the charges which were brought against him. Such was my opinion of the importance of New-Orleans, not only to the prosperity, but to the union of the states, that I felt uncommon anxiety at what I believed to be the state of our affairs in the west, and had expressed my impressions very freely in conversation, and in letters to my friends during the last winter.

Under these circumstances, I doubted the propriety of my being put on the jury; *but I felt no distrust of myself,* as I was confident that I could discharge the duty under a just impression of what I owe to my country, to the accused, and to my own character.

The marshal assured me, that he felt the strongest disposition to oblige me, but that he thought he could not do it, consistently with his duty. He supposed there was scarcely a man to be found, who had not formed and expressed opinions about Colonel Burr. That he, too, was in a situation of great delicacy and responsibility, and that, without the utmost circumspection on his part, he would be exposed to censure. I renewed my application to the marshal several times, and always conceived the same answer. Thus situated, I determined to attend the court, both from a sense of duty, and because I would not put it in the power of the malicious, and those disposed to slander me, to assign motives for absenting myself, which had no kind of influence on me.

Another reason for pursuing this course presented itself some time after I had formed this determination. I conceived that an attempt had been made to deter me from attending this court. I was informed by a friend in the city, that he had heard, that one of the most severe pieces which had ever been seen, was preparing for publication, if I did attend, and serve on the grand jury. From what quarter this attack was to come, I do not know. The only influence which that circumstance had, was to confirm me in the determination I had made; as I was much more inclined to defy my enemies, than to ask their mercy or forbearance. From the first I hesitated, whether I ought not to make the same representation to the court, that I had made to the marshal. As I was in doubt on the subject before I came from home, I committed to paper the substance of what I have now said, and consulted three gentlemen who were lawyers, men of honour, and my personal friends. Their advice to me was not to mention it, for they did not believe that the court would or ought to discharge me for the reasons I had mentioned.

As I was in doubt myself, I determined to follow their advice, and the more readily as they seemed confident that I would not be discharged, and I was not scrupulous of acquiring, in this way, a reputation for scrupulous delicacy. I was perfectly willing, that my reputation should rest on the general tenor of my life, and did not believe that my character required such a prop.

At present I feel myself embarrassed how to act. I certainly was, and am, anxious not to serve on the jury, but am unwilling to withdraw, lest it should be thought that I shrink from the discharge of public duty of great responsibility, and I am not willing to be driven from the discharge of that duty in a way which should lead to a belief, that the objection to me is either acknowledged to be well founded, or has been sustained by the court. Upon this subject, the example of Mr. Giles has great weight with me. That consideration, and a hope that my motives cannot now be misunderstood or misrepresented, will induce me to do as he has done.

COLONEL BURR.—The circumstances mentioned by the gentleman, that an attempt has been made to intimidate him, must have been a contrivance of some of my enemies, for the purpose of irritating him, and increasing the public prejudice against me; since it was calculated to throw a suspicion on my cause. Such an act was never sanctioned by me, nor by any of my friends. I view it with indignation, and disclaim any knowledge of the fact in question.

The court established the following, as being the proper questions to be put to the jurors: First, Have you made up your mind on the case, or on the guilt or innocence of Colonel Burr, from the statements you have seen in the papers or otherwise? and finally, Have you formed and expressed (or delivered) an opinion on the guilt or innocence of Colonel Burr (or the accused)?

MAJOR JOSEPH EGGLESTON now addressed the court to this effect:

I understood the court to say, that this was the proper time to apply to be excused from serving on the grand jury. Having been summoned by the marshal to serve as a grand juror, I wrote a letter to that officer, desiring him to excuse me; but he refused. In addition to some private reasons, there is one of a public nature, which I hope will exempt me from being retained on the jury. As soon as I read the deposition of General Eaton in the newspapers, I felt and expressed considerable warmth and indignation on the subject likely to come before the grand jury; and on that account it might be both delicate and improper in me to serve on the grand jury, however correct the decision of that body might be.

The chief justice having asked whether he had formed and expressed an opinion on this subject, Major Eggleston repeated what he had said as to his warmth after reading General Eaton's deposition, and said, that he had expressed his opinion in public company; yet he declared his belief, that he could so far divest himself of his previous opinions and feelings, as to be able to decide according to the testimony and the law. It had been said, that a bias might imperceptibly remain upon the minds of men of the purest intentions, and as it might possibly be the case with him, he again desired to be excused.

MR. BURR.—Under different circumstances, I might think and act differently; but the industry which has been used through this country to prejudice my cause, leaves me very little chance, indeed, of an impartial jury. There is very little chance that I can expect a better man to try my cause. His desire to be excused, and his opinion that his mind is not entirely free upon the case, are good reasons why he should be excused; but the candour of the gentleman, in excepting to himself, leaves me ground to hope, that he will endeavour to be impartial. I pray the court to notice, from the scene before us, how many attempts have been made to prejudge my cause. On this occasion I am perfectly passive.

CHIEF-JUSTICE.—What are your impressions now? Have you formed a decisive opinion on this case?

MR. EGGLESTON.—I have formed some opinion on the statement and evidence I have seen; and if no other evidence were to be produced, I should probably retain it. I am willing to hear other testimony, but I wish to be excused.

The court did not excuse him.

The panel was here called over, and fourteen only appeared: upon which the marshal requested the clerk to add thereto the names of John Randolph and William Foushee. The court then instructed the clerk to place Mr. Randolph as foreman, who being called on to take the foreman's oath, addressed the court thus:

May it please the court,

I wish to be excused from serving. I will state the reasons of that wish. I have formed an opinion, not on the case now before the court, because I know not what that case is; but concerning the nature and tendency of certain transactions imputed to the gentleman now before you. I do trust, that without arrogating to myself any thing more than becomes a man, I would divest myself of this prepossession upon evidence. But I should be wanting in candour to the court and the party accused, if I did not say, that I had a strong prepossession.

MR. BURR.—Really I am afraid, that we shall not be able to find any man without this prepossession.

CHIEF-JUSTICE.—The rule is, that a man must not only have formed, but declared an opinion, in order to exclude him from serving on the jury.

MR. RANDOLPH.—I do not recollect to have declared one.

Upon which Mr. Randolph was sworn as foreman, and the rest of the panel called to the book, until it was Dr. Foushee's turn. He stated to the court, that he felt some difficulty about the propriety of serving on the jury; that, after hearing the number of excuses which were made and overruled by the court, he was unwilling to bring himself before the court, to claim an exemption from serving. But having the same feelings with other gentlemen, he must move the court to excuse him.

After a few desultory remarks by Mr. Burr and Mr. Wickham, Doctor Foushee stated, that after having read the presidents' message, General Eaton's deposition, and the publications in the newspapers respecting Colonel Burr, and having heard little but from those publications, he had formed an opinion of Colonel Burr's guilt; and unless other testimony were adduced, his impression would probably be retained. That his present opinion might, however, be said to be merely hypothetical, and predicated on the supposition of the truth of General Eaton's testimony, and those other publications: but that he would as easily divest his mind of prejudice as any other man; and that, on the exhibition of other testimony, he might change his opinion.

Mr. Wickham and Mr. Randolph delivered their opinions as to the impropriety of the doctor serving as a grand juror. And

Mr. Hay insisted, that he was a proper juror; that there was not a man in the United States, who probably had not formed an opinion on the subject: and if such objections as these were to prevail, Mr. Burr might as well be acquitted at once.

MR. BURR.—This gentleman has said, that from the evidence he has already seen, he has made up his mind; but that, on hearing other testimony, he may change it. But as a grand juror, he will only hear testimony on one side. The evidence which will be laid before the grand jury, will be altogether on the part of the United States, and ex parte; and no testimony to remove the impressions, which he has already imbibed, will be offered. There will be an accumulation of evidence on the same side to increase the bias already on his mind, and nothing on the other to counteract it. I hope therefore the court will suffer him to withdraw.

DR. FOUSHEE.—I have stated what other gentlemen have done: that if the testimony I have seen be true, and nothing brought to counteract it, my impression will of course remain unchanged. I ask, if others are not excused, why this discrimination against me? However indisposed I may be to serve, I shall not withdraw but by the direction of the court.

After some observations by Messrs. Wickham, Randolph and Hay, the chief justice observed, that the difference seemed to be, that Dr. Foushee had made up an opinion both as to law and fact; whereas other gentlemen had formed an opinion only as to certain facts. Consequently Dr. Foushee was permitted to withdraw.

Colonel James Barbour being next called, excepted to himself on a principle in some degree similar to that on which Dr. Foushee claimed to be excused: that of being impressed with sentiments unfavourable to Colonel Burr. But his excuse was deemed insufficient by the court.

The grand jury were then sworn, and were as follows:

John Randolph, Junior, foreman.
Joseph Eggleston,
Joseph C. Cabell,
Littleton W. Tazewell,
Robert Taylor,
James Pleasants,
John Brockenbrough,
William Daniel,
James M. Garnett,
John Mercer,
Edward Pegram,
Munford Beverly,
John Ambler,
Thomas Harrison
Alexander Shephard,
and
James Barbour.

The Chief Justice then delivered an appropriate charge to the grand jury, in which he particularly dwelt upon the definition and nature of treason, and the testimony requisite to prove it. After which they retired.

Colonel Burr then addressed the court, and stated his wish, that the court should instruct the grand jury on certain leading points, as to the admissibility of certain evidence which he supposed would be laid before the grand jury by the attorney for the United States.

Mr. Hay hoped, that the court would proceed as they had always done before, and that they would not grant particular indulgences to Colonel Burr, who stood on the same footing with every other man charged with a crime. That they had already charged the jury on certain material principles, and he trusted that the court would not depart from established rules, or adopt a new precedent, to oblige the accused.

MR. BURR.—Would to God that I did stand on the same ground with every other man. This is the first time I have ever been permitted to enjoy the rights of a citizen. How have I been brought hither?

The Chief Justice said it was improper to go into these digressions.

Mr. Burr said, that the attorney for the United States had mistaken his meaning, if he supposed that he wished to be considered as standing there on a different footing from other citizens; that he viewed himself as only entitled to the same privileges and rights which belonged to every other citizen; that how much soever he may have disapproved of certain principles laid down by the supreme court in their late decisions, he should not at present insist on his objections to them; that there were many points on which the best informed jurymen might be ignorant, or entertain doubts. All he wished the court to do now was, to instruct the jury on certain points relating to the testimony; for instance, as to the article of papers.

Mr. Hay pledged himself that no attempt should be made to send up any testimony to the jury without the knowledge of the court.

Mr. Randolph observed, that it was not on particular parts, but on certain principles of testimony, that he wished instructions from the court to the jury: for instance, to instruct them how many witnesses were necessary to satisfy them that an overt act was committed; how far facts committed in different districts, should be suffered to bear upon a single act committed in one district; how far facts done in one district, ought to be admitted as evidence to confirm the commission of other facts in another district; and what in short was proper evidence to be laid before them.

Mr. Hay objected to this proceeding as extraordinary; that the opposite counsel would require from the court a dissertation on the whole criminal law, upon every point which might possibly occur; that the jury were the proper judges, and if they had doubts let them apply to the court for instructions.

Mr. Wickham observed, that this was not an ordinary case as had been said; that the man who thought so must have shut his eyes against the host of prejudices raised against his client; that the attorney for the United States had said, that there was no man who had not formed an opinion on it; that he did not require a dissertation on criminal law in general, but merely that the court would instruct the jury on certain points of law and evidence; that the necessity of instructing arose from the peculiarity of this case; that there might be witnesses from different parts of the United States, who would state facts not connected with Colonel Burr; that there were witnesses to show what was done in the western country when he was hundreds of miles distant; that the jury ought to know from the court how much of this vast mass of testimony ought to have a legal application.

Mr. Hay inforced his former objection, that if the law was to be laid down by the court, they would certainly wish to have it explained by both sides; that the gentlemen on the other side wished the court to decide without argument, on matters the most important; that as the jury were very intelligent, and the court had already given a general definition of principles, the correct course was to proceed in the usual way, without wasting time in unnecessary argument.

Mr. Botts said, that in a case of such unexampled importance, which was sufficiently attested by the busy crowd around them, the noise in the country, the curiosity of the people, and the activity of the government, no reasonable objection could be made to even wasting a few minutes; that it was a case where the prisoner required, and ought to receive, the benefit of every legal right which the court could furnish.

Chief Justice observed, that there would certainly be a difficulty in the court's giving dissertations on criminal or penal laws; that he was not prepared at present to say, whether the same evidence was necessary before the grand jury as before the petit jury; whether two witnesses to an overt act were required to satisfy a grand jury: this was a point which he would have to consider. That he had not made up his mind on the evidence of facts said to be done in different districts, how far the one could be adduced as evidence in proof or confirmation of the others; but his present impression was, that facts done *without* the district, may be brought in to prove the material fact said to be done *within* the district, when that fact was charged.

The question was postponed for further discussion, on Mr. Hay pledging himself, that no evidence should be laid before the grand jury, without notice being first given to Colonel Burr and his counsel.

Several witnesses on behalf of the United States were called and recognised to appear to-morrow, at eleven o'clock A.M.

The court adjourned till then.

SATURDAY, 23D MAY, 1807

Present the same Judges as on yesterday.

The proceedings of yesterday being read, and the names of the jury called over, several witnesses on the part of the United States appeared and were recognised to attend on the court.

The counsel for Colonel Burr observed, that if it met the approbation of the court, the discussion on the propriety of giving special instructions to the grand jury would take place on Monday next.

This proposition was assented to, and it was understood that Mr. Burr's counsel were to give due notice of the propositions they intended to submit.

The grand jury appearing pursuant to adjournment, the chief justice informed them, that the absence of General Wilkinson, a witness deemed important by the counsel for the United States, and the uncertainty of his arrival at any particular period, made it necessary that they should be adjourned.

Some conversation ensued between the court and bar, with respect to the propriety of adjourning the grand jury to some future day in the term.

The Chief Justice stated it as his opinion, that as there was no necessity for calling over the names of the grand jury every day, they might be considered in contemplation of law, still in their chambers till they were called into court, and it might be understood that they would not be called till some particular day. This he said was the practice in some of the states, nor did he know any sound objection to it: but unless it was considered by counsel on both sides, that this course was free from *all exception*, he should be unwilling on any account to adopt it.

The counsel for Colonel Burr stated that they knew no objection to the measure, but were unwilling to express any decided opinion, especially as Colonel Burr was not then in court.

The chief justice said, that he felt much inclined to accommodate the grand jury; but until further consideration of the subject, they would stand adjourned till Monday following.

The court adjourned till then accordingly.

MONDAY, 25TH MAY, 1807

The court met according to adjournment: present the same judges as on Saturday.

The grand jury appeared in court, and on its being stated by their foreman, that they had been two days confined to their chambers, and had no presentment to make or bill before them, Mr. Hay observed, that he had two bills prepared, but wished to postpone the delivery of them till the witnesses were present, and it was ascertained that all the evidence relied on by the counsel for the prosecution could be had. He thought it probable, that in the course of a week, he should hear of General

Wilkinson, who was still absent, and whose testimony was deemed very important.

A further conversation took place, as to the propriety of adjourning the grand jury to a distant day of the term, and Monday next was mentioned, as the time when they would probably be required to attend.

The Chief Justice observed, that from the researches which he had been able to make, he was still inclined to favour the opinion which he had expressed on Saturday, that there was no necessity for *calling* the grand jury *every day*. This opinion was the result of his reflection upon principle, not formed from any positive authority on the subject.

Mr. Wickham having stated, that as a number of witnesses were attending at a considerable distance, on the part of Colonel Burr, it might be important to know when the grand jury would be again called.

Mr. Hay observed, that a motion might be made, which would render their presence necessary, even on that day.

Mr. Wickham then requested, that before any order should be taken in relation to the adjournment of the grand jury, the counsel for the United States might state the nature and object of his motion.

MR. HAY.—The object of my motion is to commit Mr. Burr on a charge of high treason against the United States. On his examination there was no evidence of an overt act, and he was committed for a misdemeanor only. The evidence is different now.

Mr. Wickham hoped, that the application might be made and counsel heard.

MR. HAY.—Gentlemen may be assured that they will be apprised of the application; but is it their wish that it should be made, and the subject discussed in presence of the grand jury?

COLONEL BURR.—The gentleman has mistaken the object of my counsel as far as it is comprehended in my motion. The design was not that the grand jury might hear, but that the impropriety of mentioning the subject in the presence of the grand jury, might be made more manifest. I think it may be demonstrated, that while there is a grand jury attending, before whom a question may be determined, there is an obvious impropriety in submitting it to any other tribunal for any other purpose.

The grand jury were requested to withdraw.

Mr. Hay renewed his application, stating more at large the grounds on which it was made; and moved the court to commit Mr. Burr on a charge of high treason against the United States, on the evidence formerly introduced, and on additional testimony to be now brought forward.

Mr. Wickham inquired what sort of evidence was intended to be introduced: whether that of witnesses to be examined *viva voce,* or affidavits in writing? Mr. Hay answered, that where the witnesses were present he intended to examine them *viva voce;* but where they were absent to make use of their affidavits regularly taken and certified.

MR. BOTTS.—We may have cause of much regret, that the attorney of the United States, has not given us some previous notice of this application. From the engagements between the prosecuting and defending counsel, to interchange information of the points intended to be discussed, we had a right to expect, that upon a subject like this, involving questions new and important, we should not have been taken by surprize. Indeed, from the common courtesy and candour of the attorney of the United States, we might have reasonably calculated on a previous communication. This interchange of civility and information, usual even in cases of inferior importance, was more necessary in this case, because the application is as unfortified by precedent as it is unexpected; and because it involves questions of deep consideration and weighty importance.

MR. HAY interrupted Mr. Botts.—Since the gentleman complains of being taken by surprize, I am willing to postpone the motion till to-morrow.

MR. BOTTS.—Not a moment's postponement. Although we sustain considerable inconvenience by being thus suddenly and unexpectedly called upon without reflection, or authorities, yet we should experience greater by a day's delay. I shall therefore beg leave to make a few remarks on this extraordinary application, and the pernicious effects such an extraordinary measure, if generally practised, would inevitably produce. The organ particularly appropriated for the consideration of the evidence which this motion calls for, is the grand jury; and the motion is to divest the grand jury of the office, which the constitution and laws have appropriated to them, and to devolve it upon the court. The grand juror's oath is to inquire into all crimes and misdemeanors committed within the district of the state of which they are freeholders. Their office is to perform that which the court is now called upon to perform. To them belongs the exclusive duty of inquiring and examining into all species of evidence, which may lead to a conviction of the crime of which Colonel Burr is now charged; but there is a great objection to the exercise of this examining and committing power by a high law officer, who is to preside upon the trial, when the grand jury, the appropriate tribunal, is in session. He is obliged, previously, without a full hearing of both sides of the case, to commit himself, upon the case of the accused. Every one will agree, that a judge, should, if possible, come to the office of trial as free from prepossession, as if he never heard of the case before.

It is true, that when a grand jury is not embodied, in order to avoid a failure of justice, and to prevent the guilty from escaping, the measure which the gentleman now proposes, would not only be proper but necessary. The examining and committing office of the judge is, in such cases, justified by the necessity of the case; but then it is because the appropriate body of inquest is not impaneled to perform the office.

The necessity does not exist here. This novel mode of proceeding would give the attorney for the United States the chance of procuring an opinion from the court, unfavourable to the accused. Failing in that chance, he would then resort to his only legal one—before the grand jury. Why should this court step out of its ordinary course to forestall or influence the deliberations of the grand jury and the public? The motion is without precedent, or reason to warrant such a precedent; it is oppressive and against all principle; it is unreasonable and oppressive that the functions of the grand jury should be suspended, in order that the court should assume them.

Although in the absence of the grand jury, it would be proper in the court to determine a question of commitment, yet the history of our criminal jurisprudence yields no instance of such a motion during the session of the grand jury. I did expect, that some solitary reason would have been given, by the gentleman for the prosecution, in support of his motion; I did expect, sir, that all the books of England would have been ransacked; I did suppose, sir, that the musty pages of folios and quartos would have been opened to support his argument; I did expect, at least, sir, that one case of state practice would have been produced. In this expectation I am disappointed. I say then, sir, that the motion before the court is without precedent, unreasonable in its nature, inconvenient in its effects, and oppressive in its end; of a piece with the long course of oppression which has been practised against Colonel Burr, but has been hitherto unknown in this country; unheard of in any country which enjoys the blessings of freedom, and which, I trust, will never again be repeated in these states.

Colonel Burr appears in this court ready to go on with his trial; he wishes no delay; he is opposed to every measure which may occasion delay, or procrastinate the business. His great object is to satisfy his country, the minds of his fellow citizens, and even his prosecutors, that he is innocent. We have suffered already two or three days to pass away in idle discussion, or without doing any thing: and yet we are told, at last, after the lapse of several months; after a grand jury have been convened and gone into their room; after attending with great inconvenience to themselves and expense to the state; after *all this,* we are told, that the business of commitment is again to be gone over; that the evidence which ought to be given to the grand jury, the only proper tribunal at this time for its consideration, is to be submitted to the court.

We have, sir, made enough of sacrifices; we have been deprived of our legal rights; our person and papers have been seized; we have been subjected to a military persecution unparalleled in this country; given into the custody of the satellites of military despotism, and guarded by the rigid forms of military law: surely our wrongs ought now to end. It was rumored that he would not appear; but he has appeared. We come to ask a legal trial: an examination into the charges which have been preferred against us.

The government has had the time and necessary means of

preparation, and they ought to be prepared. Our pleasure was, to await the pleasure of the prosecution, unless that pleasure should be found to be oppressive. But we are told now, that the indictment cannot go up; but in the mean time an inquisition must be held. Permit me to advert, for a solitary moment, to one circumstance: If we had sought every legal advantage, our motion would have preceded theirs; our motion would have been, that, if they were not ready to present their evidence before the grand jury, Colonel Burr should be discharged from the recognisance already given.

The laws of congress have adopted our rules and practice in the states, in proceedings upon indictments for misdemeanors. You were of opinion, you well remember, sir, that nothing more than probable cause of suspecting a misdemeanor appeared against Colonel Burr. Even after an indictment in Virginia for a misdemeanor, nothing more than a summons can go against the person indicted. No court, in the commonwealth, ever permitted a capias to go in the first instance, unless the case passed *sub silentio*. Now arrest and bail are utterly incompatible with a summons; and surely, if an *indictee* cannot be arrested, one merely suspected, cannot be held to bail. The conduct of Judge Chase, in awarding a *capias* against Callender, was the subject of one of the charges in his impeachment. Mr. Hay, vehemently and ably contended, that a summons only ought to have been issued against him.

I know that the court may have an impression that I am wandering from the subject. I will soon show what application the recognisance already taken has to the motion to examine witnesses, in order to commit for treason.

Notwithstanding Colonel Burr was committed upon a charge of misdemeanor, when according to the state laws he would not have been committed, a public prejudice has been excited against the lenity of the measure; and attempts have been made, through newspapers and a popular clamour, to intimidate every officer who might have any concern in the trial. This public prejudice would be increased by the present motion rather than allayed, if the necessary explanation should not be made. The multitude around us must hear what is passing, and we cannot submit to a course which would further invest the public mind with the poison already too plentifully infused. I do not charge the attorney of the United States with a design to excite or increase this public prejudice; but I know it will be increased, unless care be taken to show, that the public clamour has been groundless. I take it for granted, that after this view of the subject, whatever motive dictated the application, it will now be abandoned, and that the gentleman will withdraw his motion. I will not weary out the patience of the court, but conclude by saying, that I sit down in anxious hope, that the success of this motion may not add to the catalogue of Colonel Burr's grievances.

The chief justice inquired whether the counsel for the prosecution intended to open the case more fully?

Mr. Hay had not intended to open it more fully; he did not himself entertain the least doubt, that if there was sufficient proof produced to justify the commitment of Colonel Burr, the court had completely the right to commit him. That the general power of the court to commit, could not be questioned; and if gentlemen contended, that it ought not to be exercised in the present case, it was incumbent on them to show it. That Mr. Botts himself had not denied it. That his whole argument turned on the question, not whether the court had the right, but whether it was expedient now to exercise it. Its expediency depended on the evidence; if that was sufficient, there could be no doubt of the power. That if the court once admitted, as an exception to this principle, that the grand jury was in session, they would establish a precedent fraught with the most injurious consequences.

MR. WICKHAM.—It certainly would have been an accommodation to us, if the gentlemen had given us notice of their intended motion. We come into this discussion completely off our guard, completely unprepared; and it may be presumed, that it was merely an omission in the opposite counsel, not to have given us notice of the motion which they intended to bring forward. Because it was distinctly understood between us, (by an argument made, I believe, in the hearing of the court), that if any specific motion was to be made on either side, timely notice of its nature and object was to be given. I am sorry that they have departed from their agreement in the present instance; but if I have not forgotten every principle of law which I ever learnt, of every principle of common justice, this motion cannot be supported.

MR. HAY.—The gentleman will permit me to set him right. He might have relied on my candour, that when I was about to lay my indictments before the grand jury, I would have given him timely notice of my intention. They might then have moved for the instruction to the jury, which they are so anxious to obtain. This was the only understanding between us on the subject; our agreement extended no further; much less to the particular case before the court. On the other hand, there was a very strong reason against our making this communication. I feel no hesitation, sir, in assigning this reason: and I hope that it will wound neither the feelings of the prisoner, nor of his counsel. I did not intend to have laid it before the court, but I now conceive myself called upon to be thus explicit.

The fact is this. Mr. Wilkinson is known to be a material witness in this prosecution; his arrival in Virginia, might be announced in this city, before he himself reached it. I do not pretend to say what effect it might produce upon Colonel Burr's mind; but certainly Colonel Burr would be able to effect his escape, merely upon paying the recognisance of his present bail. My only object then was to keep his person safe, until we could have investigated the charge of treason; and I really did not know, but that if Colonel Burr had been previously apprised of my motion, he might have attempted to avoid it. But I did not promise to make this communication to the opposite counsel, because it might have defeated the very end for which it was intended. I have said, that the only pledge I gave, merely related to the indictments to be sent up to the grand jury.

Mr. Wickham observed, that after this explanation, he must suppose, that he had misapprehended the extent of their agreement. He knew the gentleman too well to think that he had intentionally misled him; but what could he think of the motion he had made? It was a strange episode which he weaved into his tale; it may be a good poetry indeed, but it was not certainly proper matter of argument. Every man who hears me, every man who has ever read on the subject, must know, what are the feelings which dictate these suspicions of Colonel Burr.

Some mortification was felt by his enemies, (not that the attorney for the United States himself ever felt it), that he returned here for trial. But here Colonel Burr *is,* and always will be ready to meet every charge they may think proper to bring against him; and to face every man who dares to say any thing against him. The gentleman will not open his case, and why? Because when he has heard our arguments against his motion, he may come out with the adverse arguments against us. If they do not choose to open their case, we hope the court will grant us the right of concluding the argument.

Here a desultory conversation ensued upon the order of proceeding.

Mr. Edmund Randolph observed, that the power of the court to commit, was not denied; but that the expediency of committing, while a grand jury was in session, was denied; that it was improper that an inquiry which belonged exclusively to that body, should be transferred to the court.

Mr. Hay said, that it made no difference in law, whether the grand jury were in session or not; that the grand jury being in session could not deprive the court of the power with which they were vested. Let me state a case, said Mr. Hay. Suppose Colonel Burr had only arrived at Richmond this morning, instead of having been brought at the period of his first examination, would his consel contend, that the court would not think it proper to commit him, instead of bringing the question immediately before the grand jury, when the prosecutor was not furnished with the necessary evidence? This is precisely the case at present. From additional evidence, which has come into my possession since his examination, it appears to me, that upon a disclosure of it to the court, they will see proper that he should be committed on the charge of treason; but to complete this evidence still more, the testimony of General Wilkinson is essential; and until his arrival, it would be improper to submit it to the grand jury; although it is necessary, for the reasons I have stated, that it should be submitted at present to the court.

Mr. Wickham meant to support his arguments on the grounds of law and precedent: he read the revised code of Virginia, page 103, sect. 10, which he contended were plainly in his favour. He observed, that the present motion was unprecedented in a system of criminal jurisprudence, which was upwards of one hundred years old. If this motion be a proper one, there must be some precedents in this country or in England. If there be none such their motion cannot be supported; and as the gentlemen have not produced them, it is fair to infer, that there are none such. It is therefore obvious that the present motion is contrary to the acts of Virginia, as well as to the common law. The attorney for the United States says, that he can take no final measures, till General Wilkinson is present. His deposition is greatly relied upon. Now, sir, I refer to you as well as to the supreme court of the United States, where you presided, that the facts contained in that deposition did not amount to treason, but to a probable proof of a misdemeanor only. As to General Eaton's it is not relied on; the sole reliance of the prosecution is on Wilkinson's: of course, if Wilkinson himself were present, he would prove nothing new. But if General Wilkinson be so material a witness, why are they not prepared to go with him before the grand jury? Why is he not here? He is a military officer, bound implicitly to obey the head of the government. In the war of Europe, a general has been known to march the same distance at the head of his army, in a shorter time than General Wilkinson has had to pass from New-Orleans to this place. He is bound to go wherever the government directs him: to march to Mexico; to invade the Floridas; or to come to this city. Perhaps there are other reasons for his not coming; but let us not press this subject.

What, sir, is the tendency of this application? What is the motive? I have no doubt, the gentlemen mean to act correctly. I wish to cast no imputation; but the counsel and the court well know, that there are a set of busy people, (not I hope employed by the government) who, thinking to do right, are labouring to ruin the reputation of my client. I do not charge the government with this attempt; but the thing is actually done. Attempts have been made. The press, from one end of the continent to the other, has been enlisted on their side to excite prejudices against Colonel Burr. Prejudices? Yes, they have influenced the public opinion by such representations, and by persons not passing between the prisoner and his country, but by *ex parte* evidence and mutilated statements. Ought not this court to bar the door, as much as possible, against such misrepresentations? to shut out every effort to excite further prejudices, until the case is decided by a sworn jury? not by the floating rumours of the day, but by the evidence of sworn witnesses? The attorney for the United States offers to produce his testimony: no doubt, the most violent; no doubt, the least impartial which he can select: testimony, which is, perhaps, to be met and overthrown by superior evidence. Do they, besides, wish that the multitude around us should be prejudiced by garbled evidences? Do precedents justify such a course as this? Produce your witnesses, they may say. No, sir, Colonel Burr is ready for a trial; but he wishes that trial to come before a jury. I do not pretend to understand the motives which led to those things: it is enough, that they produce these mischievous effects upon ourselves. Should government, hereafter, wish to oppress any individual; to drag him from one end of the country to the other by a military force; to enlist the prejudices of the country against him; (interrupted by William Wirt, attorney for the prosecution)

MR. WIRT.—May it please your honours,

The attorney for the United States, believing himself possessed of sufficient testimony to justify the commitment of Aaron Burr for high treason, has moved the court to that effect. In making this motion, he has merely done his duty. It would have been unpardonable in him to omit it; yet the counsel for the defense complain of the motion and the want of notice. As to the latter objection, it must be palpable, that the nature and object of the motion rendered notice improper. The gentlemen would have the attorney to announce to the party accused, that he was, at length, in possession of sufficient evidence to justify his commitment for high treason; and, that being apprehensive he might not be disposed to stand this charge, he intended, as soon as the accused came into court next morning, to move his commitment! This would really be carrying politeness beyond its ordinary pitch. It would not have deserved the name of candour, sir; it would, in fact, have been an invitation to the accused to make his escape. But, as gentlemen seem to doubt, at least with an air of some earnestness, the propriety of this motion at this time, and express their regret that they have not had time to examine its legality, the attorney has offered to waive the motion until tomorrow, to give gentlemen the opportunity which they profess to desire; but no, sir, they will not even have what they say they want, when offered by the attorney. Another gentleman, after having demanded why this motion was made, and by that demand drawn from the attorney an explanation of his motives, has been pleased to speak of the attorney's statement, of his apprehensions, as an episode, which "though good poetry," he says, "had better have been let alone, when such serious matters of fact were in discussion." It may be an episode, sir; if the gentleman pleases, he is at liberty to consider the whole trial as a piece of epic action, and to look forward to the appropriate catastrophe. But it does not appear to me to be very fair, sir, after having drawn from the attorney an explanation of his motives, to complain of that explanation; if a wound has been inflicted by the explanation, the gentlemen who produced it, should blame only themselves. But, sir, where is the crime of considering Aaron Burr as subject to the ordinary operation of the human passions? Towards any other man, it seems, the attorney would have been justifi(ed) in using precautions against alarms and escapes; it is only improper when applied to this man. Really, sir, I recollect nothing in the history of his deportment, which renders it so very incredible, that Aaron Burr would fly from a prosecution. But at all events, the attorney is bound to act on general principles, and to take care that justice be had against every person accused, by whatever name he may be called, or by whatever previous reputation he may be distinguished. This motion, however, it seems, is not legal, at this time, because there is a grand jury in session. The amount of the position is, that though it may be generally true, that the court possesses the power to hear and commit, yet, if there be a grand jury, this power of the court is suspended; and the commitment cannot be had unless in consequence of a presentment or bill of indictment found by that body. The general power of the court being admitted, those who rely on this exception, should support it by authority; and therefore, the loud call for precedents, which we have heard from the other side, comes improperly from that quarter. We ground this motion in the general power of the court to commit; let those who say that this general power is destroyed by the presence of a grand jury, show one precedent to countenance this original and extraordinary motion. I believe, sir, I may safely affirm, that not a single reported case or dictum can be found, which has the most distant bearing towards such an idea. Sir, no such dictum or case ought to exist. It would be unreasonable and destructive of the principles of justice; for if the doctrine be true at all, that the presence of a grand jury suspends the power to hear and commit by any other authority, it must be uniformly and universally true in every other case as well as this, and in every case which can be proposed while a grand jury is sitting. Now, sir, let us suppose, that immediately on the swearing of this grand jury, and their retiring to their chamber, Aaron Burr had for the first time been brought to this town; the members of the evidence scattered over the continent; the attorney, however, in possession of enough to justify the arrest and commitment of the accused for high treason, but not enough to authorise a grand jury to find a true bill. What is to be done? The court disclaims any power to hear and commit, because there is a grand jury; the grand jury cannot find a true bill, because the evidence is not sufficient to warrant such a finding; the natural and unavoidable consequence would be, that the man must be discharged; and then, according to Mr. Wickham's principles of ethics, that every man must be supposed to intend the natural consequences of his own acts, the gentlemen who advocate this doctrine intend, that Aaron Burr shall be discharged without a trial.

I beg you, sir, to recollect what was said by gentlemen the other day, when you were called upon to give an additional charge to the grand jury. You were told that a grand jury should require the same evidence to find a true bill, which a petty jury would require to convict the prisoner. Connect this principle with the doctrine in question; the sitting of the grand jury suspends all power to commit by any other body, and the grand jury cannot find a true bill, unless on evidence on which they would convict as a petit jury; connect these two principles, and consider the immaturity of evidence, which always exists at the period of arrest and commitment; and the sitting of the grand jury, instead of being a season of admonition and alarm, becomes a perfect jubilee to the guilty. But it is said, that this is "an attempt to divest the constitutional organ of its just and proper power." I believe, sir, it was never before heard, that an application to commit for safe keeping, was an encroachment on the power of the grand jury. Would the gentlemen have us to address this motion to the grand jury? They might as well propose, that we should submit the bill of indictment to the court, and desire them to say, whether it is a true bill or not? This would be indeed, the "shifting of powers," of which the gentleman complains. As it is, sir, there is no manner of collision between the power, which we call upon the court to exercise, and the proper power of the grand jury. The justices arrest and commit, for safe keeping; then comes the function of the grand jury, to decide on the truth of the indictment exhibited against the prisoner. The two offices are distinct in point of time, and totally different in their naure and objects. But it is said, that "there is a great inconvenience in submitting a great law officer to the necessity of expressing an opinion on the crime, on a motion like this—that the judge like the juror, should come to the trial with his mind pure and unbiased." This argument does not apply to the legality of the power, which we call upon the court to exercise; it goes merely to the expediency of exercising it; and if the argument be true, the court ought never to commit, whether the grand jury be sitting or not. This, however, sir, is a matter for legislative, not for judicial consideration. Whenever the legislature shall decide, by the force of this argument, that the court which commits shall not sit on the trial in chief, a motion like this will become improper. At present, however, the legislature has left this power with the court, and we claim its exercise for considerations of the most serious importance to truth and justice.

But, sir, we are told, that this investigation is calculated to keep alive the public prejudices; and we hear great complaints about these public prejudices. The country is represented as being filled with misrepresentations and calumnies against Aaron Burr; the public indignation it is said, is already sufficiently excited. This argument is also inapplicable to our right to make this motion; it does not affect the legality of our procedure. But if the motion is likely to have this effect, we cannot help it. No human institution is free from inconveniences; the course we hold is a legal one, a necessary one; we think it a duty. It is no answer to us to say, that it may produce inconveniences to the prisoner. But let us consider this mournful tale of prejudices, and the likelihood of their being excited by this motion. Sir, if Aaron Burr be innocent, instead of resisting this motion, he ought to hail it with triumph and exultation. What is it that we propose to introduce? not the rumours that are floating through the world, nor the bulk of the multitude, nor the speculations of newspapers; but the evidence of facts. We propose, that the whole evidence exculpatory as well as accusative, shall come before you; instead of exciting, this is the true mode of correcting prejudices. The world, which it is said has been misled and influenced by falsehood, will now hear the truth. Let the truth come out, let us know how much of what we have heard is false, how much of it is true; how much of what we feel is prejudice, how much of it is justified by fact. Whoever before heard of such an apprehension as that which is professed on the other side? prejudice excited by evidence! Evidence, sir, is the great corrector of prejudice. Why then does Aaron Burr shrink from it? It is strange to me that a man, who complains so much of being, without cause, illegally seized and transported by a military officer, should be afraid to confront this evidence; evidence can be promotive only of truth. I repeat it then, sir, why does he shrink from the evidence? The gentlemen on the other side can give the answer. On our part, we are ready to produce that evidence. Permit me now, sir, to turn to the act of assembly which has been read by Mr. Wickham. Into what embarrassment must the ingenious and vigorous mind of that gentleman have been driven, before he would have taken refuge under this act of assembly? It is but to read it to see that it has no manner of application whatever to this motion; that it applies to the case of a person already committed; declaring that such person shall be bailed, if not indicted at the first term after his commitment, and discharged if not indicted at the second term. Revised code, page 103, sec. 10. It begins thus, "When any person committed for treason."—Now, sir, is Aaron Burr committed for treason? If not, it is obvious that the clause has no manner of application to him. Why, sir, the object of this motion is to commit him; gentlemen must have been in strange confusion when they resorted to this law. Mr. Wickham asks, if General Wilkinson be a material witness, why he is not here? Who is General Wilkinson? says that gentleman. Is he not the instrument of the government, bound to a blind obedience? I am sorry for this and many other declamatory remarks which have been unnecessarily and improperly introduced; but the gentleman assures us, that no imputation is meant against the government. Oh no, sir; Colonel Burr indeed has been oppressed, has been persecuted; but far be it from the gentleman to charge the government with it. Colonel Burr indeed has been harassed by a military tyrant, who is "the instrument of the government bound to a blind obedience"; but the gentleman could not by any means be understood as intending to insinuate aught to the prejudice of the government. The gentleman is understood, sir; his object is correctly understood. He would divert the public attention from Aaron Burr, and point it to another quarter. He would, too, if he could, shift the popular displeasure which he has spoken of, from Aaron Burr to another quarter. These remarks were not intended for your ear, sir; they were intended for the people who surround us; they can have no effect upon the mind of the court. I am too well acquainted with the dignity, the firmness, the illumination of this bench, to apprehend any such consequence. But the gentlemen would balance the account of popular prejudices; they would convert this judicial inquiry into a political question; they would make it a question between Thomas Jefferson and Aaron Burr. The purpose is well understood, sir; but it shall not be served. I will not degrade the administration of this country by entering on their defence. Besides, sir, this is not our business; at present we have an account to settle, not between Aaron Burr and Thomas Jefferson, but between Aaron Burr and the laws of his country. Let us finish his trial first. The administration too will be tried before their country; before the world. They, sir, I believe, will never shrink, either from the evidence or the verdict. Let us return to Aaron Burr. "Why is not General Wilkinson here?" Because it was impossible in the nature of things for him to be here by this time. It was on the first of April that you decided on the commitment of Aaron

Burr for the misdemeanor; until that decision was known, the necessity of summoning witnesses could not be ascertained. General Wilkinson is the commander in chief of the American troops, in a quarter where his presence is rendered important by the temper of the neighborhood; to summon him on the mere possibility of commitment would have afforded a ground of clamour, perhaps a just one, against the administration. The certainty that Aaron Burr would be put upon his trial, could not have been known at Washington till the 5th or 6th of April. Now, sir, let the gentlemen on the other side make a slight calculation. Orleans is said to be 1500 or 1600 miles from this place. Suppose the United States mail travelling by a frequent change of horses and riders, a hundred miles per day, should reach Orleans in 17 days from the federal city, it would be the 24th or 25th of April (putting all accidents out of the question,) before General Wilkinson could have received his orders to come on. Since that time until this, he has had thirty days to reach Richmond. Could a journey of 1500 or 1600 miles be reasonably performed in thirty days? Who can bear a journey of 50 miles per day for thirty days together? But sir, General Wilkinson is not here; due means have been used to bring him hither; his materiality is ascertained by his affidavit, and the attorney does not choose to send up the indictment in his absence. But we admit, it seems, that we are not ready to make good our charge. In my opinion there is evidence enough to prove the treason independently of General Wilkinson. But it is important in every point of view, that that gentleman should be here. It is important to his own reputation; it is important to the people of the United States that he should be here; and on the part of the grand jury, sir, there is no calculating what inferences unfavourable to the prosecution might be drawn from the mere circumstance of his absence. The attorney is therefore, in my opinion, very right not to hazard the justice and the fair trial of this case, by sending up the indictment in General Wilkinson's absence.

But it seems that Wilkinson's affidavit has been already decided to have no relation to the charge of treason. To what General Wilkinson's affidavit tended while it was inomalated [*sic*], insulated, or connected only with that of General Eaton, is no proof of what its tendency may be now, in connection with the great mass of additional testimony which we have collected. Sir, we say that it is the key-stone which binds the great arch of evidence now in our possession. As to sending up the indictment, it is out of the question; truth and justice require that it should not now be sent up. But we hope, sir, that the motion to commit Aaron Burr will be received, because we think it not only a legal, but also a just and necessary measure of precaution.

MR. HAY.—On this occasion, I beg leave to make one or two preliminary remarks. I stand here engaged in the performance of a very serious duty. The duty I have to perform is, indeed, most serious and important. The subject now before us is one which deeply affects the character of the government; and the charge is the most solemn and interesting that can be exhibited against any individual. The motion I have to make is, that Aaron Burr may be committed on a charge of treason against the United States!

Sir, it was natural to suppose, that such a serious charge would have a most serious impression upon Aaron Burr's mind; that he would have roused all the energies of his understanding in his service, in vindicating himself, and not in casting imputations upon the government. Why then does he turn from defending himself to attack the administration? Why these complaints of persecution which have fatigued our ears? I most solemnly deny the charge. I most confidently avow, that there is not a tittle of evidence to support it. None can be produced, unless it be a persecution, that the government brings him before a legal tribunal, where his guilt or innocence will be impartially established. Aaron Burr stands accused of the highest crimes and misdemeanors; he stands charged with a deliberate design of involving his country in all the horrors of a civil insurrection, or of entangling her in a war with a foreign nation. This is the true question before the court; and instead of meeting this charge with the energy and firmness which became him; instead of confronting it with his evidence, he complains forsooth of persecution! And where, sir, is this tremendous persecution? "Because he was sent here by a military authority?" But Aaron Burr has been tried in the country where he was arrested? Was Blennerhasset's island in the Mississippi territory? Or ought he not to have been conveyed to that judicial district, which possessed a competent jurisdiction? But if Aaron Burr ought to have been sent hither, by what number of men should he have been escorted? Was it by one man only; from whom he could have been so easily rescued, and whose vigilance he could most probably have eluded? Or ought he to have been conveyed, as he really was, by the energy of men, like Perkins, whose unshrinking firmness, and whose humanity (in the presence of Aaron Burr himself I avow it, let him deny it if he can) had completely qualified him for the safe transportation of his prisoner? But, sir, when this cry and yell of persecution is once excited, it is not easy to set bounds to its fury. Not contented with inveighing against the pretended persecution of the government; a government which never did persecute; a government which cannot persecute, and which will forever stand firm in the affections of the people, from the integrity and intelligence which mark its measures. Not contended with lavishing their complaints against that government, the counsel for the prisoner have even turned against the humble instruments, who conduct the prosecution. They seriously complain, that we have given them no previous notice of this motion; and these are the very men, who have so often offered motions to this court, without the slightest intimation to ourselves. Sir, I most positively assert, that no notice in the present case ought to have been given. I shall not pretend to assert, that Aaron Burr was disposed, under the present state of things, to effect his escape. But, I say, that supposing such to have been the fact, and supposing that, availing himself of the information which we had imparted, he should have taken to flight; I appeal to the candour of every impartial man; I appeal to the candour of the opposite counsel themselves, whether I should not have been guilty of a most gross violation of my duties?

But they say, he ought not to be committed, because the presence of the grand jury suspends the authority of this court. But where are the precedents which justify this position? I have not made many researches into this case; because I did not suppose that there was a single sceptic at this bar who would deny the universality of the proposition that we have laid down; that it was the right of the court to commit in every case where they deemed it proper. They say, that in this case, the power of the grand jury and the court are concurrent. Strange that they should forget the immense difference between their powers! the evidence which is sufficient before the latter, is widely different from that which is necessary to be produced to the former. The testimony requisite to induce the court to commit the person accused is less than we are bound to submit to the grand jury, and much less than that which alone is admissible before the petit jury. I will quote the authority of the gentlemen against themselves. They say, that stronger evidence is necessary before the grand jury than before a court for the examination of a prisoner. I think differently myself; but certain it is, that affidavits are not admissible to be sent to the grand jury; although they may be used to convince the court that it is proper to commit. For my part, I think we are already in possession of *viva voce* evidence not only sufficient to commit Colonel Burr, but to induce the grand jury to find in favour of both the indictments; but I will boldly inquire, whether I should discharge my honest duty, were I to submit my indictments before the grand jury at this moment, when I have not all the material evidence which we may possess? Sir, these gentlemen may cast their groundless censures upon me; but in vain; all their clamours will never move me from my purpose. The course which I am pursuing is sufficient to satsify my own conscience; and it is indifferent to me whether ten or ten thousand men should join in my condemnation.

Mr. Botts asserts, that we have produced no authorities to prove our position; and that we have none to produce. But is it right to be continually recurring to precedents? Is there no allowance to be made for the operations of common sense, in any case? Where cases of doubt and difficulty occur, a reference of this kind is certainly proper to enlighten and fortify our own judgments. But even admitting the propriety of introducing precedents in the whole extent for which gentlemen contend, it is their business and not ours to comply with the requisition for precedents. We stand upon the broad, general principle, that courts have the power to commit. If gentlemen contest this principle in the present case, why do they not introduce their countervailing authorities?

I regret that my duty did not permit me to give my friend

Mr. Wickham notice of this motion, that he might have more seriously meditated upon the subject before he urged his objections. If he had understood it with his usual correctness, he never would have troubled the court with the law of Virginia; for this law has not the slightest bearing upon the specific proposition before you.

Mr. Wickham inquires why we do not at once send up our indictments before the grand jury? Suppose, sir, we should pursue the course which he recommends; suppose we should send up our indictments on the evidence which is now in our possession; several days might elapse before they would be able to investigate this body of evidence. In the mean time, some of those numerous persons, who are prying into every hole and corner of this city, might probably catch some distant hint of the probable decision of the jury. They have certainly too much discretion not to keep their own counsel; but it is absolutely impossible to exclude completely the busy eye of curiosity. Some vague insinuations may probably escape; something which might justify a suspicion of their determination. Suppose, then, that Aaron Burr was to be actuated by these considerations; suppose that his fears (if fears he can feel) should prompt him to escape; what, sir, would become of our indictment? Mr. Burr may quit the United States; he may flee for ever beyond the jurisdiction of this country; and in that case, the whole world would ridicule us for the course we had pursued. Or let us even suppose that we were to withdraw this motion, where would be our sincerity? Must we trust to the indulgence of Mr. Burr himself for remaining in this city and standing his trials?

We expect General Wilkinson here in a few days. We have an affidavit which positively states, that an express to New-Orleans, to command his presence on this trial, was met on the frontiers of the Mississippi Territory; we have also letters from the attorney general of the United States, explicitly stating, that General Wilkinson has been officially authorised to leave the army of the United States, and select whatever mode of transportation he might think proper. (Here Mr. Hay read the affidavit, showing that the express to General Wilkinson, had been seen in Athens, in the state of Georgia.) In the mean time, what is Colonel Burr's situation? It is completely optional with him, whether to stay here and face his accusers, or to avail himself of his liberty and leave the United States. We call upon this court to exercise the authority with which they are invested; and by binding over Colonel Burr, as well on the charge of high treason, as of a misdemeanor, to detain him here for a satisfactory trial.

We scarcely expected to have been asked, why General Wilkinson was not here? The gentleman himself has said, that he is a general. Can he then leave his army at any time, and without the permission of the government? Make, however, a computation of time. The attorney general left this city on the 4th or 5th of April. He reached Washington on the 7th or 8th. Allow then a reasonable time for an express from Washington to New-Orleans; and for a man of General Wilkinson's age and bulk to travel to this city; and is it probable that he could have arrived here before this period? If he availed himself of the liberty and means to come by water; the gales have been lately very severe. And even two of the grand jury have assured me, that if General Wilkinson was exposed to the late tempestuous weather, he will probably never see the United States. Mr. Wickham has expatiated upon the attempts made to prejudice the public opinion through the medim of the press. Sir, a great deal has been said in the newspapers upon this transaction; and a great deal will yet be said. But are the presses shut against Colonel Burr, when even in this very city certain presses have been found to vindicate his motive and designs? But what of all this? The public mind is hostile to any encroachment upon the liberty of the press; and it ought to be so. Where a crime of such gigantic enormity, as that attributed to Aaron Burr, arises in this country, the printers will speak, and they ought to speak; the purest motives will command them to speak. If there have been publications against Colonel Burr, innumerable communications have also appeared in his favour; and if the publications against him have contained the severest strictures, they have resulted from his own character and conduct; and he has no right to complain.

He stands on the fairest ground which his conduct and character can reach. But if in truth prejudices have been improperly excited against him, why does he wish to close the only door to his own vindication, by excluding the evidence. His counsel exclaim, "Send the evidence to the grand jury." Surely if Colonel Burr wishes to have the evidence before the jury, he should be much more anxious to have it before the court. The jury will have one side of the evidence only before them; and that will be completely against himself. Both, however, will go before the court. Why, then, does he shrink from the evidence? If an unjust prejudice assails him, the light of truth and evidence will dissipate it. Why does he shrink?

The gentlemen on the other side, continued Mr. Hay, do not do us justice. They charge us with persecution and oppression. Sir, I never contemplated or wished to hurt Aaron Burr. I scorn it. I look not to him. I look only to the duties which I am solemnly bound to perform. One remark more, sir, and I have done: Gentlemen on the other side, insist upon the insufficiency of our evidence; because we have withheld our indictments from the grand jury, they have hastily inferred, that we feel our evidence to be too feeble to satisfy the jury. They are mistaken, sir. I assure them that they are mistaken. I conscientiously believe, that we have evidence enough, even throwing out the depositions themselves, to satisfy the grand jury of the guilt of Aaron Burr. But, sir, puerile indeed would it be for us, under the present state of things, to submit our case before the grnd jury, on the evidence before us, when we are every moment expecting better.

Mr. Edmund Randolph addressed the court to the following effect:

Sir, it would have been impossible for us, even had we received due notice of this motion, to have availed ourselves of the time that was allowed to us. That would have been impossible, because the enormity of the proposition itself, would have baffled all our consideration, and all our researches. Mark the course, sir, which has been pursued towards my unfortunate client. First he was brought here under a military escort. Then that little folio of depositions and affidavits, was laid before your honour; then the charge of treason; and then that little cock-boat which was destined to attend this great ship, on a foreign expedition. You heard it all, sir, and what did you say? You bound Colonel Burr to bail, simply on the charge of a misdemeanor, to appear here at the opening of court; but not contented with this security, you superadded, that he was not to leave the court until it had discharged him. You opened the door, too, for an ulterior prosecution; you declared, that if the attorney for the United States should obtain any additional evidence, the judgment which you then rendered, would not prevent his indicting Colonel Burr on the charge of treason.

Sir, thus stands the case, as it was understood by the whole universe. On Friday, we came here to meet the whole world; Friday, however, passes away, and nothing is done. On Saturday, we came here again; Saturday, also, passes away, and nothing is done. But on Sunday, sir, (for it seems that day, which, to the generality of mankind, is a day of rest, is a day of activity to some,) is broached this new fangled doctrine, which now excites our astonishment. They demand precedents, sir, for our conduct; and who are they that require it? Why, sir, they that take things out of the ordinary course of the law. For thirty years, I never saw such a proceeding; I have never read of such a one in the English books; and yet, these gentlemen call upon us for precedents. If we were asked for our reasons sir, we should have enough to offer; and first, a judge in the federal court, sitting in the capacity which your honour now fulfills, in the same relation to the accused, as an examining judge is in the state courts. But, sir, who ever invited a single magistrate, or a state court to augment the bail of any individual in the situation of Colonel Burr? If a man was bound, in a distant county, to answer to a misdemeanor, and another crime was to be brought against him, to be predicated on the very same evidence, have you, sir, ever known the trying court to increase his bail? There never was such an example, sir.

Mr. Botts' remark, sir, is not to be answered. You are changing the constitutional organ of justice. You are completely blotting out the functions of a grand jury. The witnesses will be all produced before you; but no, improper as this proceeding will be, it is still less so, than that which they will actually pursue. None of the United States' witnesses will be brought before you, but those whom they may think it politic to introduce; and depend upon it, that such testimony will be garbled for the ears of this court, as may be expected to bias their judgment. Well, sir, and what will be the consequence? When the grand jury are about to retire to their own chamber, they will be told that you have demanded additional bail. Are you then, sir, to be a pioneer of blood for the grand jury? Is not this precedent outrageous, sir? The boasted principle, that no man is to be condemned but upon the verdict of twenty-four of his peers, is gone. Throughout this town, it will be universally reported, that you have solemnly declared Aaron Burr to be guilty of high treason against the United States; and some of those, to whom the rumour may extend, may hereafter be impaneled on the petit jury. And will they feel themselves altogether unbiased by your judgment? Why, sir, let it be declared at once, that the grand jury is to be struck out as an intermediate organ of justice.

Do not, I pray you, sir, let us suffer for the delays and negligence of other people. I cannot blame the United States' attorney. It is his business to obey the instructions of the government; and if the witnesses are not here, it is certainly no fault of his; but surely there is time enough to travel from New-Orleans to this city in seventeen days; even with the gigantic "bulk" of General Wilkinson himself.

Mr. Hays says, our tone is changed. And how, sir? We demand a trial now. We demand a fair trial. But must we not, therefore protest against a measure, which is calculated to defeat this object. Certainly, sir. You are called upon to prejudice the minds of the grand jury. But, sir, in this interesting case, where liberty and life themselves are endangered, I trust that some hard-mouthed precedents; from old black letter books, will be found in opposition to this procedure. We have come here to answer to every charge, which may be urged against us; we come here to answer in a precedented and constitutional manner; but little did we expect that the court would decide in the first instance, instead of the grand jury; that the sentiments of the grand jury were to be prejudicated by an unconstitutional decision; and that the court itself was to commit its opinion on certain points, which would be regularly brought before them for argument and for decision at some of the ulterior stages of the prosecution. "Why," said Mr. Wirt, "do you shrink?" Sir, trace the course of the prosecution, and see who it is that retires from the contest. On Friday the United States' attorney was not ready; on Saturday he was not ready; and now indeed he will not probably be ready before Monday next. Sir, who is it that shrinks? and yet does the attorney positively aver, that he has evidence enough! We are charged, sir, with addressing the multitude. Mr. Wirt says that he could, but would not imitate the example; but neither he nor Mr. Hay hath spared the theme. Sir, I will not deny the justness of his eulogiums upon the administration; but permit me only to remark, that there has been a certain conduct observed towards Colonel Burr which excites my deepest astonishment. When I look at the first man in the government, I behold an individual whom I have long known, and whose public services have commanded my admiration. When I look at the second, sir, he has my whole heart. But, sir, the inquiry which is now before us relates not so much to the intention as to the effect. An order has been given to treat Colonel Burr as an outlaw, and to burn and destroy him and his property. And sir, again; when the house of representatives demanded certain information, as it was their right and their duty to do, the president granted it; and would to God, sir! that he had stopped here, as an executive officer ought to have done. He proceeded, however, to say that Colonel Burr was guilty of a crime; and consequently to express an opinion, which was calculated to operate judicially upon the judges and the juries. Such was the substratum of all the censures, which have been heaped upon Colonel Burr.

Mr. Randolph proceeded to touch upon a subject to which Mr. Hay had referred. Colonel Burr was arrested in the Mississippi Territory. Was there no court there? was there no judge of integrity to try him? arrested too after he had been acquitted by a grand jury! Well! he was transported thence (with humanity it has been said), dragged on by eight musqueteers, who were ready to shoot him at a moment's warning; refused any appeal to the judicial authority; denied even the melancholy satisfaction of writing to his only child. Was all this humanity? Dragged before this court, which derives its only jurisdiction from a little speck of land on the Ohio. Yes! sir; but for that little spot of an island, Virginia never would have enjoyed this honour! What is all this, sir, but oppressive and bitter inhumanity?

I trust, sir, from what I have said, that no one will think with Mr. Wirt, that I am shifting the question from Colonel Burr to Mr. Jefferson. I should not have made the observations which have escaped me, but to show that my client is justified by his situation in stating every objection that he can to the present measure.

Mr. Randolph observed, that at least one disadvantage would result from this inquiry; that it was not clear, as Mr. Hay had asserted, that the affidavits would be laid before the court only, and not before the grand and petit juries, for the grand jury would soon be possessed of the substance of them; and that it was next to impossible for them to separate the impressions thus illegally to be produced on their minds, from the weight of the legal viva voce testimony.

Mr. Randolph said, that he did not understand Mr. Hay's expressions about certain persons in holes and corners; that if however he meant spies, there were none such employed by Colonel Burr; but, although the government certainly had employed no spies, yet it has excited so much prejudice against Colonel Burr, that it was sufficient to make every man in the country desirous of contributing his full quota of information against him. Mr. Randolph concluded with remarking, that the present argument had perhaps been permitted to embrace too wide a field of discussion; and that there were two great questions which he should submit to the consideration of the court: 1st, Whether there were any precedents in favour of the present motion? and 2d, If a proposition like this, and of such great importance, was adopted without any precedent to support it, whether it would not expose every man in the country to the danger of oppression?

Mr. Randolph contended, that this was a charge which the judge had already decided, on a former examination; that it was not a supplemental crime, but the old one; that perhaps there might be some little affidavit to splice out some defect in the former evidence; but what would be the consequence of this proceeding? Day after day, another and another affidavit would be brought forth. Facts like polypi, are easily cut into two or three pieces; each of which may be made to form a new and entire body; and each of those atoms is to require a new recognisance.

For one affidavit there must be a bail of 1000 dollars: another affidavit, another 1000 dollars; until the burden of bail is so oppressive as to leave no other resource, but in the four walls of a prison.

Mr. Hay observed, that he should simply notice one remark of Mr. Randolph's. That gentleman had used the expression of "pioneer of blood"; but surely it would not have escaped him, had he but for one moment seriously reflected upon the court whom he addressed, upon the counsel he opposed, or the government. Satisfied of this, Mr. Hay said he should pass the observation by, without further notice.

Mr. Randolph had stated, that no similar case had occurred in his thirty years practice. It was not wonderful that such a case had not occurred in the time when that gentleman was attorney for the commonwealth. A great change has taken place in the system of our government. At that time no federal court existed. The mode of proceeding in the state courts is different from that here. In the system of penal law established in the commonwealth of Virginia, there is an examining court intervening between the arrest and commitment of a prisoner, and his being charged before the grand jury; but this court has the power to examine as well as to commit. Moreover, the United States are a most extensive country, compared to that of Virginia; a most material witness may now be 1500 miles from the court, before which he is to appear; and may be at the same time at the head of an army; in all which circumstances, the federal and the state sovereignties are different. So that this difference altogether defeats the application of Mr. Randolph's experience to this subject, even if that experience had been admitted as a good authority in the state courts. But even that gentleman would admit, that had a similar case occurred before the state courts, the accused would have been committed. Mr. Randolph asserts, that this motion is made to draw forth the opinion of the court, and thus to prejudicate the minds of the grand jury. But Mr. Randolph has certainly forgotten, that this intelligent and impartial jury are on their oaths and their consciences; and surely this court will not pay so little compliment to their independence, as to admit, that its own opinion will be sufficient to bias their judgment; more particularly too, when the point before the court is so different from that before the jury. It is the business of the court to commit; and of the jury to indict: and it is certainly the privilege of the court to decide upon written testimony, although that point may not be perfectly established and settled as it relates to the grand jury. How the court would decide upon this point, Mr. Hay said, he could not pretend to know. There is another consideration, which should be weighed by the opposite counsel. The grand jury is now already embodied. They are ready to proceed with any business which may be brought before them; but my great object, said Mr. Hay, is to prosecute Colonel Burr on the charge of treason. I make this declaration, because I believe him to have been guilty of it. Let us suppose, however, that the grand jury was to discharge Colonel Burr, from the misdemeanor; and then that I was to bring the present motion before the court; what resource then would Mr. Randolph have? From the present proceeding, however, Mr. Burr would derive the advantage of an immediate trial; whereas, according to the other mode of proceeding, weeks and months might escape, before he would be brought to trial; and certainly it is, in every point of view, more desirable, both for the government and himself, to terminate this business at once, than to impose upon us the necessity of moving for an adjourned trial.

Mr. Randolph says, "We are ready; we were ready on Friday; we were ready on Saturday, &c." Sir, there are two sorts of readiness: one in point of fact, and one under certain circumstances. Now these gentlemen will scarcely persuade me, that they could be ready to resist the weight of evidence, if it were ready to be laid before them; but there is certainly no difficulty in believing, that they are now ready to proceed to trial, when the whole evidence, and particularly General Wilkinson's, is not present. One more remark: Mr. Randolph has expressed a reverence for Mr. Jefferson, which is not certainly derived from trifling considerations. I will make but one remark, and that gentleman will agree with me in the opinion: Survey the many peopled globe, through all the ages and nations, and you will not find a man more anxiously bent upon promoting the liberty of the people. This was certainly the idea which Mr. Randolph intended to convey. Mr. Randolph next proceeded to Mr. Madison, upon whom he has not hesitated to lavish the most unreserved encomiums. Surely then, after this solemn declaration of the oldest counsel for the prisoner, we shall hear no more about persecution. Sir, it is a state of things, which it is impossible to reconcile with the amiable character ascribed to the two first officers in the government.

Mr. Wickham observed, that he should offer a few remarks on the supplementary arguments of Mr. Hay. That in this case Colonel Burr's counsel had called, they had a right to call, for precedents; that Mr. Randolph, who had so ably represented this commonwealth, as a criminal prosecutor for many years, had never known a single one to justify this motion; that however true it might be, that the state of Virginia was now of smaller extent than the whole of the United States, yet it was then cut up into as small judicial districts, as the United States at present are, and that the witnesses in a criminal prosecution might have been scattered over those districts, as they are said to be in the present circumstances; that Mr. Randolph had represented not one of those districts, but the whole; not only on this side of the mountains, but beyond them; and even the uncultivated region of Kentucky, where travelling was at that time liable to so many difficulties, and from which it was so extremely laborious to transport the witnesses to this side of the mountains; that it was not until Kentucky had been more thickly populated, that a particular court had been established there. And what is the case in England and her dependencies? Certainly that island is not equally extensive with the United States; but her subjects may, at all events, be scattered over the world. Why then, is there no precedent in that country? Is it not probable, that a man might happen to be as far from the court of king's bench, as General Wilkinson is from this court? and yet there is no precedent to justify this motion. What is the crime? Is it of so little importance that this court, upon the production of every little affidavit, should consent to hear new motions for a commitment? This crime is treason! it is "a levying of war" against the United States! and where is the proof of it? where were Colonel Burr's forces? was his army like that of Bayes, kept in disguise? Wilkinson's testimony cannot establish this fact; for it is the opinion of the chief justice, that his affidavit does not at all bear upon this subject; and yet two months have since elapsed, and no testimony has been collected. Wilkinson's deposition contains an improbable, mysterious tale, about a key and cypher. Mr. Wickham said, that he would not, at present, expose this transaction; but does this mysterious tale constitute treason? "You, sir, have already decided, that there is no treason in Wilkinson's deposition; but were the man himself in court, what could he establish further, than his deposition can do?" Mr. Hay is satisfied, that he has sufficient evidence to convict Colonel Burr. No man doubts his ability, or his inclination to discharge his duty. Why, then, does he not lay his indictments before the jury? Because, there happens to be a man in New Orleans, and one, perhaps, in the East Indies; and, therefore, "to make assurance doubly sure," he must wait for their appearance; and all this too, whilst the gentleman most seriously protests against oppression and delay. Though the gentleman may not be conscious of such a sentiment, as that of wishing to oppress Colonel Burr, there must still be something like it in his heart; but whatever the motive may be, the result to ourselves is the same. It produces delay, and all its consequent oppressions. No court should sanction this proceeding. This case is like that of a man, whose cause stands for trial. When subpoenas after subpoenas have been issued; when sums after sums have been expended; he moves for a continuance of his suit, and at the very same time, he insists upon the sufficiency of his evidence. Surely the court would rule him to trial. Why is not the attorney for the United States ready for trial? He has, indeed, made a computation of time, to show, that Wilkinson could not have been here before this period; and he has besides, introduced an affidavit to show, that an express was on his way to Orleans, to give him an early summons. There is however, nothing in proof, that the drawer of this affidavit was not imposed on, by this express; or that the express himself was not mistaken, as to the contents of his dispatches. And how stands the computation as to time? The post goes from Washington to New Orleans, in seventeen days. Mr. Rodney left this city, in the last of March. The express must, therefore, have reached New Orleans, about the 20th of April; and yet, where is Wilkinson? Though the Mississippi runs down to New-Orleans and opposes a strong current to those who ascend it, yet it is surely a reasonable proposition, that on land it requires no longer time to come than to go, and yet General Wilkinson is not here!

Mr. Hays says, it is of no consequence, whether the grand jury is present or not. But is this consonant with the sound principles of law? Is it constitutional, sir, where there is a particular body, set apart for the investigation of facts, for the court to step in, and rudely take this power from them? He says, that, perhaps, he shall not send up his bills before the present grand jury. But I trust in God, sir, that this determination will be overruled by the court; and that if this prosecution is ever to be closed, we may see the curtain dropt upon it now and for ever! If, sir, the counsel for the prosecution obtain a postponement of this trial, and for want of evidence on their part, we might probably contend, that Colonel Burr, if bound to bail at all, should be held in a smaller recognisance than at present. But we shall waive this right. It is not our wish to discharge the grand jury, but to set this question at rest forever.

We have said, that we were ready for trial. We are so, sir, in fact, as well as in the abstract. The prosecutors say, that we do not believe them to be ready; but how can the gentleman suppose, that we mean to pay so poor a compliment to his veracity, as to believe, that he acts upon his own facts, as if he, himself, did not believe them to be true?

The gentleman, sir, has warmly eulogized the present administration. As a private citizen, sir, no man has less to say with the politics of this country than myself. That gentleman has drawn a picture of our national prosperity; and I am happy to hope, that it is true to the life, in every thing, one feature only excepted. What, however, will be say of the persecution of my client? Sir, let that gentleman draw the most animated picture of our happiness, which his imagination can supply; let it be howsoever cheering, or howsoever just, it will be but little alleviation to the wounds of my persecuted client, that he is the only man in the nation whose rights are not secure from violation.

Mr. Burr then rose and addressed the court to the following effect:

I am not, I hope, sir, wasting the time of the court upon the present occasion. The motion proposed, is admitted on all hands, to be important; and it is certainly a new one. Perhaps it was to have been expected, that on a point so novel, some precedents would have been produced; but, in this expectation we have been disappointed. Its novelty will, however, be productive of another effect. It will still better qualify it for making another small feature in a picture of oppressions and grievances, which have never been paralleled in the records of criminal law.

The case is this; no man denies the authority of the court, to commit for a crime; but no commitment ought to be made, except on probable cause. This authority is necessary; because policy requires, that there should be some power to bind an accused individual for his personal appearance, until there shall have been sufficient time to obtain witnesses, for his trial; but this power ought to be controlled as much as possible.

The question in the present case, is, whether there is probable cause of guilt; and, whether time ought to be allowed to collect testimony against me? This time ought generally to be limited; but there is no precise standard on the subject; and much is of course left to the sound discretion of the court. Two months ago, however, you declared, that there had been time enough to collect the evidence, necessary to commit, on probable cause; and surely, if this argument was good then, it is still better now.

As soon as a prosecutor has notice of a crime, he generally looks out for witnesses. It is his object to obtain probable cause for committing the accused. Five months ago, a high authority declared, that there was a crime; that I was at the head of it; and it mentioned the very place, too, where the crime was in a state of preparation. The principal witness against me, is said to be Mr. Wilkinson. Now, from what period is the time to be computed? If, from the time I was suspected, five months; if, from the time when I was seized, three months; or is it to be only computed from the time when I was committed? So that it is near forty days since the notice must have arrived at New Orleans. But a vessel navigates the coast, from New Orleans to Norfolk, in three weeks. I contend, however, that witnesses ought to be procured, from the very time when the crimes are said to be committed. There is, then, no apology for the delay of the prosecution, as far as it respects the only person for whom an apology is attempted to be made.

There are other serious objections to my situation. Must I be ready to proceed to trial? True, sir, but then it must be in their own way. Are we then on equal terms here? Certainly not. And again, as to affidavits. The United States can have compulsory process to obtain them; but I have no such advantage. An *ex parte* evidence, then, is brought before this court, on a motion for commitment. The evidence on one side only is exhibited; but if I had mine also to adduce, it would probably contradict and counteract the evidence of the United States. Well, sir, and these affidavits are put into the newspapers, and they fall into the hands of the grand jury. I have no such means as these, sir; and where then is the equality between the government and myself.

The opinion of the court, too, is to be committed against me. Is this no evil?

A sufficient answer, sir, has been given to the argument about my delay; and its disadvantages to myself have been ably developed. But my counsel have been charged with declamation against the government of the United States. I certainly, sir, shall not be charged with declamation; but surely it is an established principle, sir, that no government is so high as to be beyond the reach of criticism; and it is more particularly laid down, that this vigilance is more peculiarly necessary, when any government institutes a prosecution; and one reason is, on account of the vast disproportion of means which exists between it and the accused. But, if ever there was a case which justified this vigilance, it is certainly the present one, when the government has displayed such uncommon activity. If, then, this government has been so peculiarly active against me, it is not improper to make the assertion here, for the purpose of increasing the circumspection of the court.

Mr. Burr observed, that he meant by persecution, the harassing of any individual, contrary to the forms of law; and that his case, unfortunately, presented too many instances of this description. He would merely state a few of them. He said, that his friends had been every where seized by the military authority; a practice truly consonant with European despotisms. He said, that persons had been dragged by compulsory process before particular tribunals, and compelled to give testimony against him. His papers, too, had been seized. And yet, in England, where we say they know nothing of liberty, a gentleman, who had been seized and detained two hours, in a back parlour, had obtained damages to the amount of one thousand guineas. He said, that an order had been issued to kill him, as he was descending the Mississippi, and seize his property. And yet, they could only have killed his person, if he had been formally condemned for treason. He said, that even post-offices had been broken open, and robbed of his papers; that, in the Mississippi Territory, even an indictment was about to be laid against the postmaster; that he had always taken this for a felony; but that nothing seemed too extravagant to be forgiven by the amiable morality of this government. All this, said Mr. Burr, may only prove that my case is a solitary exception from the general rule. The government may be tender, mild and humane to every one but me. If so, to be sure it is of little consequence to any body but myself. But surely I may be excused if I complain a little of such proceedings. Mr. Burr said, there seemed to be something mingled in those proceedings, which manifested a more than usual inclination to attain the ends of justice: as far as it related to himself, perhaps, these things were of no account; but what was then to be said of those and other measures, such as the suspension of the habeas corpus act, which concerned the whole nation? If in the island of Great Britain such a measure was calculated to produce so much disturbance, what kind of sensation ought it to produce in this country.

Our president, said Mr. Burr, is a lawyer, and a great one too. He certainly ought to know what it is, that constitutes a war. Six months ago, he proclaimed that there was a civil war. And yet, for six months have they been hunting for it, and still cannot find one spot where it existed. There was, to be sure, a most terrible war in the newspapers; but no where else. When I appeared before the grand jury, in Kentucky, they had no charge to bring against me, and I was consequently dismissed. When I appeared for a second time, before a grand jury, in the Mississippi Territory, there was nothing to appear against me; and the judge even told the United States attorney, that if he did not send up his bill before the grand jury, he himself would proceed to name as many of the witnesses as he could, and bring it before the court. Still there was no proof of war. At length, however, the Spaniards invaded our territory, and yet, there was no war. But, sir, if there was a war, certainly no man can pretend to say, that the government is able to find it out. The scene to which they have now hunted it, is only 300 miles distant, and still there is no evidence to prove this war.

Mr. Burr requested the court to consider the consequence which would now result from a commitment for treason; that if he were bound now, the law of Virginia declared, that he should so remain until the next term; that this delay was the very inconvenience he would wish to avoid; and that he presumed he was to remain in prison six months, until they could find out this war.

Here the arguments closed, and the court then adjourned till to-morrow morning at ten o'clock.

TUESDAY, MAY 26TH, 1807

The following Opinion was delivered by the Chief Justice of the United States, on Mr. Hay's motion to commit Colonel Burr.

In considering the question which was argued yesterday, it appears to be necessary to decide:

1st, Whether the court, sitting as a court, possesses the power to commit any person charged with an offence against the United States.

2dly, If this power be possessed, whether circumstances exist in this case which ought to restrain its exercise.

The first point was not made in the argument, and would, if decided against the attorney for the United States, only change the mode of proceeding. If a doubt can exist respecting it, that doubt arises from the omission in the laws of the United States to invest their courts, sitting as courts, with the power in question. It is expressly given to every justice and judge, but not to a court.

This objection was not made on the part of Colonel Burr, and is now mentioned, not because it is believed to present any intrinsic difficulty, but to show that it has been considered.

This power is necessarily exercised by courts in discharge of their functions, and seems not to have been expressly given; because it is implied in the duties which a court must perform, and the judicial act contemplates it in this light. They have cognisance of all crimes against the United States; they are composed of the persons who can commit for those crimes; and it is obviously understood, by the legislature, that the judges may exercise collectively the power which they possess individually, so far as is necessary to enable them to retain a person charged with an offence in order to receive the judgment which may finally be rendered in his case. The court say, this is obviously understood by the legislature; because there is no clause expressly giving to the court the power to bail or to commit a person, who appears in discharge of his recognisance, and against whom the attorney for the United States does not choose to proceed; and yet the thirty-third section of the judicial act evinces a clear understanding in the legislature, that the power to take bail is in possession of the court.

If a person shall appear in conformity with his recognisance, and the court passes away without taking any order respecting him, he is discharged. A new recognisance, therefore, or a commitment on the failure to enter into one, is in the nature of an original commitment, and this power has been uniformly exercised.

It is believed to be a correct position, that the power to commit for offences of which it has cognisance, is exercised by every court of criminal jurisdiction, and that courts as well as individual magistrates are conservators of the peace.

Were it otherwise, the consequence would only be, that it would become the duty of the judge to descend from the bench, and, in his character as an individual magistrate, to do that which the court is asked to do.

If the court possesses the power, it is certainly its duty to hear the motion which has been made on the part of the United States; for, in cases of the character of that under consideration, its duty and its power are coextensive with each other. It was observed when the motion was made, and the observation may now be repeated, that the arguments urged on the part of the accused rather prove the motion on the part of the United States unnecessary, or that inconvenience may result from it, than the want of a legal right to make it.

The third is, that the grand jury being now in session ready to receive an indictment, the attorney for the United States ought to proceed by bill instead of applying to the court, since the only purpose of a commitment is to bring the accused before a grand jury. This statement contains an intrinsic error which destroys its operation. The commitment is not made for the sole purpose of bringing the accused before a grand jury; it is made for the purpose of subjecting him personally to the judgment of the law, and the grand jury is only the first step towards that judgment. If, as has been argued, the commitment was simply to detain the person until a grand jury could be obtained; then its operation would cease on the assembling of a grand jury; but such is not the fact. The order of commitment retains its force while the jury is in session, and if the prosecutor does not proceed, the court is accustomed to retain a prisoner in confinement, or to renew his recognisance to a subsequent term.

The arguments drawn from the general policy of our laws; from the attention which should be bestowed on prosecutions, instituted by special order of the executive; from the peculiar inconveniences and hardships of this particular case; from the improper effects which inevitably result from this examination, are some of them subjects for the consideration of those who make the motion, rather than of the court; and others go to the circumspection with which the testimony in support of the motion ought to be weighed, rather than to the duty of hearing it.

It has been said that Colonel Burr already stands charged with treason, and that, therefore, a motion to commit him for the same offence is improper. But the fact is not so understood by the court. The application to charge him with treason was rejected by the judge to whom it was made, because the testimony offered in support of the charge did not furnish probable cause for the opinion, that the crime had been committed. After this rejection, Colonel Burr stood, so far as respected his legal liability to have the charge repeated, in precisely the same situation as if it had never been made. He appears in court now as if the crime of treason has never before been alleged against him. That it has been alleged, that the government had had time to collect testimony for the establishment of the fact, that an immense crowd of witnesses are attending for the purpose, that the prosecutor in his own judgment has testimony to support the indictment, are circumstances which may have their influence on the motion for a commitment, or on a continuance, but which cannot deprive the attorney for the United States of the right to make his motion. If he was about to send up a bill to the grand jury, he might move that the person he designed to accuse, should be ordered into custody, and it would be in the discretion of the court to grant or to reject the motion.

The court perceives and regrets that the result of this motion may be publications unfavourable to the justice, and to the right decision of the case; but if this consequence is to be prevented, it must be by other means than by refusing to hear the motion. No man, feeling a correct sense of the importance which ought to be attached by all to a fair and impartial administration of justice, especially in criminal prosecutions, can view, without extreme solicitude, any attempt which may be made to prejudice the public judgment, and to try any person, not by the laws of his country and the testimony exhibited against him, but by public feelings, which may be and often are artificially excited against the innocent, as well as the guilty. But the remedy, for a practice not less dangerous than it is criminal, is not to be obtained by suppressing motions, which either party may have a legal right to make.

If it is the choice of the prosecutor on the part of the United States to proceed with this motion, it is the opinion of the court that he may open his testimony.

Mr. Hay then rose, and observed, that he was struck with the observations of the court relative to "publications," and he would attempt if possible to make some arrangement with the counsel on the other side to obviate that inconvenience; and he understood they were disposed to do the same.

The counsel on both sides then retired by permission of the court for this purpose. They returned in a short time; and Mr. Hay informed the court that the counsel for the United States, and for Colonel Burr, not having yet been able to agree upon any arrangement which would attain his object, namely, that of having Colonel Burr recognised in a sum sufficiently large to insure his appearance to answer the charge of high treason against the United States, without incurring the inconvenience resulting from a public disclosure of the evidence at this early stage of the proceeding, wished to have further time for that desirable purpose. This was granted by the court, and it then adjourned till next day.

Upon proof against Colonel Burr touching a crime, part of which was committed in this district, he may be tried and acquitted. In Ohio he may be indicted, and evidence may be prepared touching the same crime. Can he plead *autrefois acquit* in bar, by averring, that the crimes charged in the two states was one and the same? His averment would be against the record of the indictment charging a complete separate crime in each district. Will you, sir, put upon the constitution such a construction as will subject a citizen to be hunted down, by trial after trial, in state after state, as long as the persecuting spirit of a wicked executive may last? Do not understand me to allude, in this, to the present administration, the characters of which I have been in the habit of admiring; but the construction now to be fixed must go down to posterity, and may be made instrumental in effecting the worst of state oppressions.

Remember that Colonel Burr has forborn to avail himself of this legal principle in Kentucky and in the Mississippi Territory, in order that the merits of his case might come before the inquests; but it ought now to be agreed that he should protect himself from being harassed further, by calling into exercise the great principles of the constitution, declaring that no man shall be twice put in jeopardy of his life for the same offence. See amendments to constitution. Now, what part of the affidavit speaks of a fact within the district?

Fourthly, The overt act of treason by Colonel Burr within the district must be proved by two witnesses. The constitution and act of congress require two witnesses, not only to the act, but to the treasonable quality of the act. After full time has been afforded to collect all the witnesses in the power of the government, the accused ought not to be deprived of his liberty, unless it was believed that the evidence collected would convict him: imprisonment is only intended for trial and not for punishment.

By what does General Wilkinson's affidavit make out intentions? The answer is, by the confessions of the accused or of his supposed associates. The confessions of the accused, by the express words of the constitution, are not evidence, unless made in open court. Confessions are often admitted, from necessity, to get at crimes that deal in secrecy; as larceny, forgery and robbery: but the safety of the people requires that crimes, which deal in publicity, as does the crime of a treasonable war, should not be proved by evidence so incapable of exculpatory proof. When an honourable gentleman (Mr. Giles) was challenged the other day upon a suggestion of his having expressed himself upon the case of the accused, he said he was indisposed to hear evidence of unguarded expressions, in which the witness might have mistaken his meaning; have misunderstood what he said, or not have heard all that he said; or have substituted his own inferences for the words of the speaker.

Blackstone and Foster have characterised it to be the most dangerous species of evidence, ever liable to misconstruction and abuse. But if the constitution has proscribed it, why now question its exclusion? If the confessions of the accused, out of court, could not be evidence, against him, could the confessions of real accomplices be evidences against him? Yet the evidence of Wilkinson relates, in part, to the confession of pretended accomplices, no way proved to have been authorised by Colonel Burr to say or to do any thing.

But why, it may be asked, is Colonel Burr afraid to hear illegal evidence, if he is consciously innocent?

We see witnesses from different and distant parts of the United States, whose names, faces and characters, are alike unknown to Colonel Burr. He cannot ascertain upon what parts of his life or conduct they are expected to speak, or upon what information their evidence may rest. His character has long been on public torture; and wherever that happens, with either a good or a bad man, the impulses to false testimony are numerous. Sometimes men emerge from the sinks of vice and obscurity into patronage and distinction by circulating interesting tales, as all those of the marvelous kind are. Others, from expectations of office and reward, volunteer; while timidity, in a third class, seeks to guard against the apprehended danger, by magnifying trifling stories of alarm. These works of exaggeration and propagation are frequently the subjects of idle amusement. The authors, until they commit themselves, have no just conception of the mischiefs they are hatching; but when they are afterwards called to give testimony, perjury will not appal them, if it be necessary to save their reputations for consistency or veracity. If the evidence be restricted within the legal limits, the purest of characters, under accusation of treason, will have hazard enough to run.

A judge, whose experience of these dangers was great, thus speaks on the subject: "The rule of rejecting all manner of evidence in criminal prosecutions, that is foreign to the point in issue, is founded on sound sense and common justice. For no man is bound, at the peril of life or liberty, fortune or reputation, to answer, at once, and unprepared, for every action of his life." Few, even of the best of men, would choose to be put to it. And had not those concerned in the state prosecutions, out of their zeal for the public service, sometimes stepped over this rule in the case of treason, it would, perhaps, have been needless to have made an express provision against it in that case. Foster's C. L. 246.

Mr. Wickham regretted that so much time had been consumed; but hoped the court would acquit them of any intention to waste it. When any illegal motion was introduced by the opposite counsel, he felt it as a serious duty due to his client to resist it with firmness. That for his own part he should not forget that he was before the circuit court of the United States, nor should he so far lose his respect for their discernment as to bring forward motions, which he believed to be illegal, only to waste the time of the court; that he hoped none but legal evidence would be suffered to be introduced; none but competent witnesses to be heard; and if this rule was not rigidly adhered to, what was to prevent the counsel on the other side from producing any and every kind of evidence that they pleased?

It cannot be supposed, said Mr. Wickham, that we are afraid of this affidavit. What is in it, which has not been already known and scattered in every loose sheet of a newspaper throughout the United States? It is not that we resist it in point of fact; but on the ground of principle. We wish two points to be settled: are affidavits to be read at all on such a motion, and at such a crisis of the prosecution as this? and if so, ought they to be read if the witnesses themselves were present? Would it be right, if they were in the next street or the next county? Would it in fact be right if there was time enough to produce the '*viva voce*' testimony itself? Mr. Burr had a right to be confronted with General Wilkinson. He had a right to crossquestion and examine him on all the statements which he has made. The government had power to bring him here. Why is he not here? Ought not some satisfactory excuse to be made for him? He is an officer of this government; and the government might have procured his attendance, as well by a special order as by a civil process. Has any subpoena been taken out, inquired Mr. Wickham, addressing himself to the clerk?

The clerk replied, that no subpoena filled up with General Wilkinson's name had been issued from his office; but that blank subpoenas had been taken out.

MR. WICKHAM.—No one knows, sir. There was time enough to have him here. The mail travels from Washington to New-Orleans in seventeen days. He might have come; but if he has not, why is not some satisfactory excuse brought forward? We want, sir, to see this gentleman crossexamined. We want to see him confronted with other witnesses. This is one ground on which we object to the production of this affidavit.

Another ground is, that according to the decision of the supreme court of the United States, this affidavit does not bear upon the present motion. Mr. Swartwout, who was said to be connected with Colonel Burr, was discharged by them, because this affidavit did not apply to the charge of treason. Are counsel then to be suffered to produce testimony on any subject that they please? A third objection is, that General Wilkinson does not relate a single act, committed in the district of Virginia. In Virginia? No, nor any where else. The attorney for the United States says, that he will prove the overt act hereafter. But, sir, I repeat it, that the rules of evidence apply not only to the admissibility of evidence, but to the order in which it is to be produced. Let them first prove an overt act, if they can; and then they are at full liberty to prove the colour of it.

Again, sir, this deposition is not the best evidence which could be produced, and which the laws require. General Wilkinson speaks of a cyphered letter, and of its contents, as well as he can make them out. Now, sir, where is this letter; and where is the key to it? Why are they not here? Why are they not produced before you? For these reasons, Mr. Wickham hoped, that the court would not suffer the affidavit to be read in evidence.

MR. HAY.—We shall not, sir, be carried from our course by speeches, however long or animated they may be. But, sir, permit me to give those gentlemen a little information. Why talk of the affidavit before you? Do these gentlemen know, that we can positively prove the astonishment, the regret, and the denunciation which escaped from Mr. Burr, when he first heard of the publication of his cyphered letter! Let them first know what we can prove, before they abandon themselves to their triumph. General Wilkinson's affidavit is the first in the series of our proofs, and it is for this reason that we wish to commence with it.

MR. EDMUND RANDOLPH.—Sir, we do not know what those gentlemen expect to prove; but we do object to the production of General Wilkinson's affidavit from what is already known: we know it to be perfectly inapplicable to the present question. Sir, this species of evidence is directly in the face of our bill of rights, and of the constitution of the United States. "In all criminal prosecutions, the accused shall enjoy the right to a speedy and public trial, by an impartial jury of the state and district wherein the crime shall have been committed; which district shall have been previously ascertained by law; and to be informed of the nature and cause of the accusation; to be confronted with the witnesses against him, &c." Colonel Burr, then, sir, has a general constitutional right to be confronted with the witnesses against him. Let gentlemen show any exception to it, if they can. And what have they done? Why, they have shown here an obsolete, an evaporated affidavit, for which there is no necessity and no law. The law positively declares, that the best evidence is always to be had; that when a witness is attainable, his affidavit is not to be admitted as testimony. We stand, therefore, sir, upon the bill of rights. Gentlemen may, indeed, attempt to evade its provisions by saying, that they can hereafter prove the material act; but I hope that this court will never countenance such illegal proceedings.

The Chief Justice stated, that the supreme court of the

United States had already decided, that an affidavit might be admitted under certain circumstances; but they had also determined, that General Wilkinson's affidavit did not contain any proof of an overt act; that he was certainly extremely willing to permit the attorney for the United States to pursue his own course in the order of drawing out his evidence, under a full confidence that he would not waste the time of the court by producing any extraneous matter; but where was the necessity of producing General Wilkinson's affidavit first? If there was no other evidence to prove the overt act, Wilkinson's affidavit goes for nothing; for so the supreme court of the United States have already decided; and by that decision he should have conceived himself bound, even if he had dissented from it. Why then produce this affidavit?

Mr. Hay observed, that there was a great difference between the course prescribed by the court, and the one which he would himself have pursued; and that he seriously believed, if he had been left to himself, he would at least have satisfied the court itself that his own course was the best. That as to General Wilkinson's affidavit, it might even now be confronted with witnesses; as Messrs. Bollman and Swartwout were present, and would say whether such and such conversations were ever held, as are detailed in this affidavit. That he was now before an examining court, and not before the petit jury: why then the same strictness of evidence now as would be required on the trial in chief? That he really believed it was the intention of the opposite counsel, by dint of long speeches, to attempt to drive him into their course: but that they ought to know he never consulted the counsel opposed to him; and that they would be the last persons in the world, whose opinions he would consult on the present occasion. That he seriously believed, that the evidence which he possessed, would, beyond the possibility of a doubt, convince the mind of the court, not only of the existence of a traitorous design, but of an overt act; and that all that he asked, was the liberty of producing this evidence in the order which he thought best. Is no part of this deposition, then, admissible? Not a word?

The Chief Justice observed, that he thought no part of it admissible at this time; that General Wilkinson's affidavit either contained proof of the treasonable design, which was no proof of the overt act, or it related to conversations, which, however strongly they might bear upon those who held them, did not bear upon Colonel Burr.*

Mr. Hay asked, how the court was to be satisfied of the contents of any paper, before it was read to them. An affidavit might contain both the proof of the overt act, and a traitorous design. Was such a paper as this to be read under the decision of the court? or how was the court to know, whether a paper might not contain some proof of the overt act satisfactory to them, unless they had an opportunity of inspecting that paper?

MR. WICKHAM.—These gentlemen talk of delay; and yet they would produce to this court whole masses of evidence that are perfectly irrelevant to the present question. They declare that they will not pursue our advice; and that we are the last persons whom they would take for counsellors. Sir, we do not ask them; all that we want is, that they would pursue the strict principles of law and legal evidence. One of the best rules of evidence is the order of evidence. If a man is charged with a crime, must not the deed itself exist before any testimony is produced as to the intention with which it is done? I hope that no testimony will be suffered to be introduced before the act itself shall be produced; and I call upon this court to inforce the strict order of evidence.

Mr. Burr observed, that in point of fact, it was very immaterial to him, whether this affidavit was read or not; that what he particularly wanted, was, that the great principles of evidence should be laid down, which would be equally applicable to this, and to all other affidavits. He consented that the court might have this deposition read, if they thought proper.

MR. HAY.—This deposition will prove that it was one of Aaron Burr's objects to seize upon Mexico. Then, if we can prove by some other evidence, that this object was connected with an attack upon the United States, is not this deposition of

---

*The chief justice observed, in a subsequent stage of this business, that an idea had since struck his mind, which he thought it material to state; that he had not recollected that these conversations were said to be held by persons who were said to be authorised by Colonel Burr, and of course that their conversations would bear upon him.

material importance in that point of view? If both must be proved, does it make any difference which we begin with? If a conspiracy has been planned of a misdemeanor and of treason so strongly combined that they are made to go on together, and the accomplishment of the one facilitates the accomplishment of the other, is it not of material consequence to prove the misdemeanor? I have not myself seen Mr. Taylor, or Mr. Allbright; but I am credibly informed, that they will prove an armed assemblage of men on Blennerhassett's island.

The Chief Justice observed, that if there was no fact, or no overt act of treason before the court, the court could have nothing to say to the present motion; that if therefore, no fact, was proved, the court could not grant the motion for the prosecution; that he should be extremely sorry to waste the time of the court, and to launch into a variety of irrelevant subjects, when there was actually no testimony to prove the overt act itself, and thus to give the court a competent jurisdiction over the case.

MR. HAY.—I am bound, sir, to obey the decision of the court. However much I may lament that decision, I shall certainly acquiesce in their order. If I understand the court—

The Chief Justice said, that he was of opinion, that unless there be a fact to be proved, no testimony ought to be produced. The question before the court was not whether there had been a treasonable intent, but an overt act. That fact itself must be proved, before there can be any treason, or any commitment for treason. General Wilkinson's affidavit was, accordingly, put aside.

Mr. Hay then called Peter Taylor, who was Mr. Blennerhassett's gardener, and Jacob Allbright, a labourer, who had worked on his island, who gave their testimony. (It is omitted here, because it will be fully detailed in a subsequent and more important part of the report.) After these witnesses had been examined, the affidavit of Jacob Dunbaugh was offered, which was "taken on the fifteenth of April, 1807, before B. Cenas, a justice of the peace," to which was subjoined a certificate of Governor William C. C. Claiborne, dated "at New-Orleans, the sixteenth of April, 1807," stating "that B. Cenas was a justice of the peace for the county of New-Orleans."

To the reading of this affidavit several objections were taken by the counsel for Colonel Burr, but those most relied on were the following: 1st, That an affidavit could, under no circumstances, be read, unless it were shown, that the witness could not be produced, and that the government had not had sufficient time to produce the attendance of Jacob Dunbaugh. 2dly, That though the governor of New-Orleans had certified that B. Cenas was a justice of the peace, yet he had not said, that it was the same B. Cenas before whom that affidavit was taken. 3dly, That B. Cenas had not stated in the caption of his certificate, or elsewhere, that the affidavit was taken "at New-Orleans," so as to show, that he was acting within his jurisdiction.

The argument on these points was continued to the adjournment of the court, who took time to consider the subject till the next day.

THURSDAY, MAY 28TH, 1807

The court met according to adjournment.

Luther Martin, Esq. appeared as the counsel of Colonel Burr.

On the motion made yesterday, to exclude the evidence of Jacob Dunbaugh, the Chief Justice delivered the opinion of the court as follows;

On the part of the United States, a paper, purporting to be an affidavit, has been offered in evidence, to the reading of which two exceptions are taken:

1st, That an affidavit ought not to be admitted, where the personal attendance of the witness could have been obtained.

2dly, That this paper is not so authenticated as to entitle itself to be considered as an affidavit.

That a magistrate may commit upon affidavits has been decided in the supreme court of the United States, though not without hesitation. The presence of the witness, to be examined by the committing justice, confronted with the accused, is certainly to be desired; and ought to be obtained, unless considerable inconvenience and difficulty exist in procuring his attendance. An *ex parte* affidavit, shaped, perhaps, by the person pressing the prosecution, will always be viewed with some suspicion, and acted upon with some caution; but the court thought, it would be going too far to reject it altogether. If it was obvious, that the attendance of the witness was easily attainable, but, that he was intentionally kept out of the way, the question might be otherwise decided.

But the particular case before the court does not appear to be of this description. The witness resides at a great distance; and there is no evidence, that the materiality of his testimony was known to the prosecutors or to the executive in time to have directed his attendance. It is true, that general instructions, which would apply to any individual, might have been sent, and the attendance of this, or any other material witness, obtained under those instructions; but it would be requiring too much, to say, that the omission to do this ought to exclude an affidavit. This exception, therefore, will not prevail.

The second is, that the paper is not so authenticated as to be introduced as testimony on a question, which concerns the liberty of a citizen. This objection is founded on two omissions in the certificate.

The first is, that the place at which the affidavit was taken does not appear.

The second, that the certificate of the governor does not state the person who administered the oath to be a magistrate; but goes no farther than to say, that a person of that name was a magistrate.

That, for aught appearing to the court, this oath may, or may not, in point of fact, have been legally administered must be conceded. The place, where the oath was administered, not having been stated, it may have been administered where the magistrate had no jurisdiction, and yet the certificate be perfectly true. Of consequence, there is no evidence before the court, that the magistrate had power to administer the oath, and was acting in his judicial capacity.

The effect of testimony may often be doubtful, and courts must exercise their best judgment in the case; but of the verity of the paper there ought never to be a doubt. No paper writing ought to gain admittance into a court of justice as testimony, unless it possesses those solemnities which the law requires. Its authentication must not rest upon probability, but must be as complete as the nature of the case admits of: this is believed to be a clear legal principle. In conformity with it is, as the court conceives, the practice of England and of this country, as is attested by the books of forms; and no case is recollected, in which a contrary principle has been recognised. This principle is, in some degree, illustrated by the doctrine with respect to all courts of limited jurisdiction. Their proceedings are erroneous, if their jurisdiction be not conclusively shown. They derive no validity from the strongest probability that they had jurisdiction in the case: none, certainly, from the presumption, that being a court, an usurpation of jurisdiction will not be presumed. The reasoning applies in full force, to the actings of a magistrate, whose jurisdiction is local. Thus, in the case of a warrant, it is expressly declared, that the place where it was made ought to appear.

The attempt to remedy this defect, by comparing the date of the certificate given by the magistrate with that given by the governor cannot succeed. The answer given at bar to this argument, is conclusive: the certificate wants those circumstances, which would make it testimony; and without them no part of it can be regarded.

The second objection is equally fatal. The governor has certified, that a man of the same name with the person who has administered the oath is a magistrate; but not, that the person, who has administered it, is a magistrate.

It is too obvious to be controverted that there may be two, or more persons of the same name, and, consequently, to produce that certainty, which the case readily admits of, the certificate of the governor ought to have applied to the individual, who administered the oath. The propriety of this certainty and precision in a certificate, which is to authenticate any affidavit to be introduced into a court of justice, is so generally admitted, that I do not recollect a single instance in which the principle has been departed from. It has been said, that it ought to appear that there are two persons of the same name, or the court will not presume such to be the fact. The court presumes nothing. It may or may not be the fact, and the court cannot presume that it is not. The argument proceeds upon the idea, that an instrument is to be disproved by him who objects to it, and not that it is to be proved by him who offers it. Nothing can be more repugnant to the established usage of courts. How is it to be proved, that there are two persons of the name of Cenas in the territory of Orleans? If, with a knowledge of several weeks, perhaps months, that this prosecution was to be carried on, the executive ought not to be required to produce this witness, ought the prisoner to be required, with the notice of a few hours, to prove that two persons of the same name reside in New-Orleans?

It has been repeatedly urged, that a difference exists between the strictness of law, which would be applicable to a trial in chief, and that which is applicable to a motion to commit for trial. Of the reality of this distinction, the present controversy affords conclusive proof. At a trial in chief, the accused possesses the valuable privilege of being confronted with his accuser. But there must be some limit to this relaxation, and it appears not to have extended so far as to the admission of a paper not purporting to be an affidavit, and not shown to be one.

When it is asked, whether every man does not believe that this affidavit was really taken before a magistrate? it is at once answered, that this cannot affect the case. Should a man of probity declare a certain fact within his own knowledge, he would be credited by all who knew him; but his declaration could not be received as testimony by the judge who firmly believed him. So a man might be believed to be guilty of a crime, but a jury could not convict him, unless the testimony proved him to be guilty of it. This judicial disbelief of a probable circumstance does not establish a wide interval between common law and common sense. It is believed in this respect to show their intimate union.

The argument goes to this, that the paper shall be received and acted upon as an affidavit, not because the oath appears to have been administered according to law, but because it is probable that it was so administered.

This point seems to have been decided by the constitution: "The right of the people" says that instrument, "to be secure in their persons, houses, papers, and effects, against unreasonable searches and seizures, shall not be violated; and no warrants shall issue but upon probable cause, supported by oath or affirmation, and particularly describing the places to be searched, and the persons or things be seized." The cause of seizure is not to be supported by a probable oath, or an oath that was probably taken, but by oath absolutely taken. This oath must be a legal oath; and if it must be a legal oath, it must legally appear to the court to be so. This provision is not made for a final trial; it is made for the very case now under consideration. In the cool and temperate moments of reflection, undisturbed by that whirlwind of passion with which in those party conflicts which most generally produce acts or accusations of treason the human judgment is sometimes overthrown, the people of America have believed the power even of commitment to be capable of too much oppression in its execution, to be placed, without restriction, even in the hands of the national legislature. Shall a judge disregard those barriers which the nation has deemed it proper to erect?

The interest which the people have in this prosecution, has been stated; but it is firmly believed, that the best and true interest of the people is to be found in a rigid adherence to those rules, which preserve the fairness of criminal prosecutions in every stage.

If this was a case to be decided by principle alone, the court would certainly not receive this paper; but if the point is settled by decision, it must be conformed to.

It has been said to be settled in the Supreme Court of the United States by admitting the affidavit of Wilkinson, to which an exception was taken, because it did not appear that the magistrate had taken the oaths prescribed by law. It was said, that as by law he could not act, until he had taken the oaths, and he was found acting, it must be presumed that this prerequisite was complied with; that is, that his acting as a magistrate under his commission was evidence that he was authorised so to act. It will not be denied that there is much strength in the argument; but the cases do not appear to be precisely parallel.

The certificate that he is a magistrate, and that full faith is due to his acts, implies, that he has qualified, if his qualification is necessary to his being a complete magistrate, whose acts are entitled to full faith and credit.

It is not usual for a particular certificate, that a magistrate has qualified, to accompany his official acts.

There is no record of his qualification, and no particular testimonial of it could be obtained.

These observations do not apply to the objections which exist. But it is said that the certificate is the same with that in Wilkinson's affidavit.

If this objection had been taken and overruled, it would have ended the question; but it was not taken, so far as is now recollected, and does not appear to have been noticed by the court. It is not recollected by the judge who sat on that occasion to have been noticed. A defect, if it be one, which was not observed, cannot be cured by being passed over in silence.

The case in Washington was a civil case, and turned upon the point, that no form of the commission was prescribed, and consequently, that it was not necessary to appear on the face of it that it was directed to magistrates.

That it was the duty of the clerk to direct it to magistrates, and he should not be presumed to have neglected his duty, in a case in which his performance of it need not appear on the face of the instrument.

That the person, intending to take this exception, ought to have taken it sooner, and not surprise the opposite party when it was too late to correct it.

But the great difference is, that the privy examination was a mere ministerial act: the administering an oath is a judicial act. The court is of opinion that the paper, purporting to be an affidavit made by Dunbaugh, cannot be read, because it does not appear to be an oath.

Mr. Hay observed, that as the examination of Colonel Burr for treason had already taken up much time without any progress in the business, and, from the disposition manifested by his counsel, it might last not only ten days, but even ten years longer, he considered it his duty, from information which he had received that morning, to suggest to the court the propriety of binding Colonel Burr in a further recognisance from day to day, till the examination could be ended. He stated, on the authority of a letter just come to hand from the secretary at war, that General Wilkinson, with several other witnesses, might be expected here between the 28th and 30th of this month. This circumstance, said he, renders it essential that he should be considered in custody, until he gives security that his person shall be forthcoming to answer the charge of treason against the United States. The gentlemen, who appear as counsel for Colonel Burr, may be, and no doubt are, sincere in the opinion they have expressed, that he will not shrink from the charges exhibited against him, and will not, in any conjuncture of circumstances which may occur, fly from a trial; but those gentlemen must pardon me for saying, that I entertain a very different opinion. I must believe, that his regard for the safety of his own life, would, if he perceived it in danger, prevail over his regard for the interest of his securities. I give notice therefore, that I consider him as being already in custody to answer the motion I have made for his commitment, and that he cannot be permitted to go at large without giving security for his appearance from day to day. His situation now is the same as that when he was first apprehended and brought before a single judge for the purpose of examination. Your honour at that time considered him as in custody, and bound him over from day to day; and I only contend, that the same course should be pursued at this time.

MR. WICKHAM.—The gentleman thinks he has obtained the effect of his motion, merely by having made it. I cannot perceive the propriety of a motion to compel Colonel Burr to give bail in any sum, before the probable cause to believe him guilty of treason has been shown. When he was brought before your honour for examination, you conceived the sum of 5000 dollars sufficient security for his daily appearance. But a recognisance has already been given in double that sum, binding him not to depart without the leave of this court. Yet now, although no probable proof of treason has been exhibited, Mr. Hay requires the court to demand of Colonel Burr additional security! I trust that such a motion will not prevail.

MR. MARTIN.—It has been already decided, by the supreme court of the United States, that not a single expression of Wilkinson's affidavit amounts to any proof of the charge of treason. The motion of the gentleman amounts to this: "We have no evidence of treason, and are not ready to go to trial for the purpose of proving it; we therefore move the court to increase the bail."

MR. RANDOLPH.—The first motion of the counsel for the United States was to commit Colonel Burr on the ground of probable cause only. This goes a step farther, and wishes the same thing to be done on the ground of a probable cause of a probable cause; but we trust that we shall not be deprived of our liberty, or held to bail on a mere uncertain expectation of evidence.

MR. MAC RAE.—The gentlemen seem to consider the recognisance already taken as sufficient for all circumstances, and that Colonel Burr will comply with it at any rate; but we have not the same expectation that he will appear, in case he discovers that sufficient evidence for his conviction has been obtained. When they speak of the sum in which he was bound on a former occasion, they do not recollect the circumstances which induced the judge to take bail in so small a sum; it was expressly mentioned by your honour, that his having been brought to a place at a distance from the circle of his friends, and the nature of the offence, (a misdemeanor only) induced you to hold him to bail in that sum; and the charge of treason was altogether excluded from view in taking the recognisance.

MR. WIRT.—Mr. Wickham, in saying that my friend Mr. Hay thought he had obtained the object of his motion merely by having made it, clearly misconceived the object of the motion now before the court. The motion we made yesterday was to commit Colonel Burr on a charge of treason: our motion today is to hold him in custody to abide the opinion which the court may pronounce upon the question of commitment. The gentlemen say, that we have secured the object we have in view by the recognisance already taken. The court expressly excluded the charge of treason from that recognisance, which applies only to the misdemeanor. Let us suppose that the motion to commit Colonel Burr was made out of court before a single magistrate: if the examination of witnesses in support of the motion occupied more than one day, would the magistrate let him go at large, while it was depending? Would he not rather, either have him retained in custody, or take security for his appearance, and renew it every evening until the motion should be determined? This is all that we ask of the court to do. The recognisance which has been given applies to the misdemeanor only. If therefore it should be forfeited by his going away, we should have had no security for his answering the charge of treason; a much more enormous offence, and attended with a very different punishment. We contend therefore that additional security ought to be taken.

MR. BOTTS.—I shall endeavour to place this subject in some measure in a new light. It has been said, that the former examination of Colonel Burr did not preclude this motion; if so, every new edition of the volume of evidence would justify a renewal of the motion to demand additional bail. Thus motions might be heaped upon motions, and bail upon bail, until the perpetual imprisonment of the accused might be the consequence.

It was a practice, in former times, to drown a person accused of being a witch, in order to try her. I think that practice is renewed on the present occasion, in another shape; a motion is made to commit Colonel Burr for treason, before the evidence can be gone through by which alone it can be ascertained that he ought to be committed. The court are requested to predetermine the effect of the evidence, and commit, before they have decided whether they ought to commit: besides, no warrant has been issued against Colonel Burr on the present occasion; he has not been arrested for treason, and therefore cannot be considered as in custody for that offence.

Mr. Hay then made some farther observations on the importance of the charge of treason (which is of the highest nature, involving the reputation and life of the prisoner,) and the great necessity therefore of the most ample security to compel his appearance to answer it. He stated that this examination might last many days; that after the court had made up an opinion that Colonel Burr ought to be committed, he might march off and leave the court to pronounce it; so that an order to commit might be made by the court, and no person found on whom it could be executed. Such an event, he said, would excite the laughter and scorn of all the people of the United States. He mentioned that an immense expense had been incurred by the government in collecting witnesses, and preparing for this trial;

that therefore he did not wish the whole of that expense to be thrown away.

General Wilkinson is expected to arrive between the 28th and 30th of this month: if he arrives, both the bills of indictment will be immediately sent to the grand jury. This is the first instance in which the ministers of the law have been requested to say to the accused, "You may do as you please, and go at large until we pronounce sentence." The gentlemen contend for new principles in favour of Colonel Burr; but, I trust that greater privileges will not be granted to him than to the humblest deluded victim of his ambition. The circumstance that he has already entered into a recognisance to answer for a misdemeanor, is no argument to exempt him from entering into another on a charge of treason. Shall the accused clear himself of a responsibility for one crime by his having committed or being charged with another? This would indeed be to violate that maxim of law, that no man shall be benefited by his own wrong.

Mr. Botts has contended that there is a difference between the case on the examination and that now before the court; that in the first instance a warrant had been issued, but none in the present; but a warrant is certainly unnecessary, now that the prisoner is before the court. The object of a warrant is to bring him before you. When this has been done, it is *functus officio*; here is Colonel Burr, before the court. It is therefore immaterial how he came before it; but he ought to be considered in custody, until discharged by the due course of law.

The Chief Justice delivered the opinion of the court, the substance of which was as follows: It is certainly necessary that a person accused should be retained in custody, or required to give security for his appearance while his examination is depending. The amount of the security to be required, must depend, however, upon the weight of the testimony against him. On a former occasion, Colonel Burr was held to bail for his daily appearance in the sum of five thousand dollars only, because there was no evidence before the judge to prove the probability of his having been guilty of treason. When the examination was completed, the sum of ten thousand dollars was considered sufficient to bind him to answer the charge of a misdemeanor only, because the constitution requires that excessive bail should not be taken; but that recognisance had no application to the charge of treason. Yet, whether additional security ought to be required in the present stage of this business, before any evidence has appeared to make the charge of treason probable, is a question of some difficulty.

It would seem, that evidence sufficient to furnish probable cause must first be examined, before the accused can be deprived of his liberty, or any security can be required of him. Yet, before this could be done, he might escape and defeat the very end of the examination. In common cases, where a person charged with a crime is arrested and brought before a magistrate, the arrest itself is preceded by an affidavit, which furnishes grounds of probable cause. The prisoner therefore is continued in custody, or bailed until the examination is finished: but here there has been no arrest for treason, and Colonel Burr is not in custody for that offence. The evidence then must be heard to determine whether he ought to be taken into custody; but as the present public and solemn examination is very different from that before a single magistrate; as very improper effects on the public mind may be produced by it; I wish, that the court could be relieved from the embarrassing situation in which it is placed, and exempted from the necessity of giving any opinion upon the case, previously to its being acted upon by the grand jury. It is the wish of the court, that the personal appearance of Colonel Burr could be secured without the necessity of proceeding in this inquiry.

Colonel Burr rose, and observed, that he denied the right of the court to hold him to bail in this stage of the proceedings; that the constitution of the United States was against it; declaring that no person shall be arrested without probable cause made out by oath or affirmation. But if the court were embarrassed, he would relieve them by consenting to give bail; provided it should be understood, that no opinion on the question even of probable cause was pronounced by the court, by the circumstance of his giving bail.

The Chief Justice said, that such was the meaning of the court.

Mr. Martin said, for his part, he should prefer that all the evidence should be fully gone into. Instead of fearing that public prejudice would thereby be excited against Colonel Burr, he believed it would remove all the prejudices of that sort which now prevailed.

THE CHIEF JUSTICE.—As a bill will probably be sent up to the grand jury, the court wishes to declare no opinion either way.

Some conversation then occurred relative to the quantum of bail; and Colonel Burr mentioned, that he would propose that the sum should be ten thousand dollars, if he should be able to find security to that amount, of which he expressed himself to be doubtful. Mr. Hay contended, that fifty thousand dollars would not be too much. But the court finally accepted of the offer made by Colonel Burr; who after a short interval, entered into a recognisance with four securities, to wit, Messrs. Wm. Langburn, Thomas Taylor, John G. Gamble, and Luther Martin; himself in the sum of ten thousand dollars, and each security in the sum of two thousand five hundred dollars, conditioned, that he would not depart without leave of the court.

Mr. Martin, when offered as security for Colonel Burr, said, that he had lands in the district of Virginia, the value of which was more than double the sum; and that he was happy to have this opportunity to give a public proof of his confidence in the honour of Colonel Burr, and of his conviction that he was innocent.

All further proceedings in the case were thereupon postponed, until the next day.

FRIDAY, MAY 29TH, 1807

The court met, but as the witnesses had not arrived, it was adjourned until Monday next, at 10 o'clock.

MONDAY, JUNE 1ST, 1807

The court met according to adjournment. Present, the Chief Justice and Judge Griffin.

The grand jury having been called over, Mr. Hay observed, that he felt great embarrassment and difficulty as to the course which ought to be pursued; he had confidently expected the arrival of General Wilkinson, and was disappointed. He was, therefore, unwilling to subject the grand jury to the inconvenience of further attendance: but he thought it proper to inform the court, that he had this morning received a number of affidavits of witnesses, residing in the neighbourhood of Chillicothe, and of Blennerhassett's island, which bore directly upon the charge of treason against Colonel Burr.

Those affidavits, however, had been taken in such a manner, that, according to the opinion lately given by the court, concerning the affidavit of Jacob Dunbaugh, they were not admissible as evidence, and would not be permitted to be read. He expected to hear from General Wilkinson, (if he should not appear in person) by the Lynchburg mail, which he understood would arrive on Wednesday morning. He, therefore, hoped, that the grand jury would not be unwilling to make a further sacrifice of a portion of their time for the public good, and would consent to wait with patience.

The grand jury were adjourned until Tuesday, ten o'clock.

TUESDAY, JUNE 2D, 1807

General Wilkinson not having arrived, no business was done today, but the court adjourned till tomorrow morning, ten o'clock.

WEDNESDAY, JUNE 3D, 1807

The court met according to adjournment.
The same judges present as yesterday.
The names of the grand jury being called over, they retired to their chamber. A few minutes after, the attorney for the United States entered, and observed, that he had a proposition to submit to the court, which he wished the grand jury to hear. He requested, therefore, that they might be called in.

COUNSEL FOR MR. BURR.—We have no objection.
The chief justice directed the marshal to call the jury into court.
Some minutes intervened before they appeared. In the mean time, Mr. Hay informed the court, that he only wished to know from the grand jury, at what time it would be most convenient for them to attend the court, if they were adjourned to some distant day, should such an adjournment equally suit the arrangements of the opposite counsel; that he had just made a calculation with his friend the marshal, which satisfied him that General Wilkinson had not, perhaps, sufficient time to reach this city. The distance from New-Orleans, on the map, was about 1370 miles; if he came by land, he must travel on horseback; but judging him by himself, he could not probably ride more than thirty miles per day: by these data he would require about forty-five days (besides a fragment of a few miles) to travel from New-Orleans to this city. This calculation would bring him to the 14th or 15th of this month. He was, therefore, willing, if it suited the wishes of the opposite counsel, to have the grand jury adjourned for about ten days; that General Wilkinson's situation called upon the court to make this arrangement; he need not expatiate upon the importance of his official duties, nor the perilous condition of that part of the country, where the head of the army ought always to be present; that General Wilkinson should be detained here as short a time as possible; and, that it would be particularly inconvenient for him to stay here until the meeting of an intermediate court for the present trial; that it was, therefore, the interest of the United States to have the trial concluded during the present term; and, that he had no doubt the very same considerations would lead every member of the grand jury, cheerfully to submit to any private inconvenience which they might sustain, but punctually to return at the time appointed by the court.
The Chief Justice observed, that there could be no difficulty on the part of the court.
MR. HAY.—General Wilkinson's situation, as commander in chief of the forces of the United States, is a very delicate one. His official duties may require him to return immediately after his arrival at this place. Our affairs in that part of the

union are also in a very unsettled state. If he should be compelled to return after the adjournment of the court, it may not be in his power to be here either at a special court, or at the next term. He hoped that the proposition to adjourn the grand jury to a distant day would meet with the approbation of Colonel Burr and his counsel.

Mr. Wickham owned, that this communication somewhat surprised him, as Mr. Hay had, but a few days before, announced to the court, from a letter of the secretary of war, that General Wilkinson would be here between the 28th or 30th of May.

Mr. Hay observed, that the letter from General Dearborn admitted of an easy explanation: that according to Mr. Minnikin's affidavit, the express could not have reached New-Orleans before the 3d or 4th of May, and that this exceeded the time which General Dearborn had allowed. His opinion was founded on the circumstance of the messenger leaving Washington on a certain day, and of course his reaching New-Orleans on a certain day. That Mr. Minnikin's affidavit had shown the calculations to be not altogether correct; that Mr. Minnikin had, therefore, given him some information, which General Dearborn could not have possessed. Mr. Hay was sorry he could not inform the court how General Wilkinson travelled, and of course how to make any calculation about the time of his arrival.

The Chief Justice said, that before the grand jury came in, he could not but express his regret at the great inconvenience which they were likely to sustain; but he believed, that less of it would arise from the course pointed out by the United States' attorney than from any other. The court would continue to sit as usual; its ordinary business would go on; and no further steps would be taken in the prosecution, until the return of the grand jury. The court would observe, that it seemed desirable, in every point of view, that this business should be closed during the present term; that a number of witnesses were not present, all of whom would not probably attend at any other term, and that it would be more convenient for the court itself to wait a fortnight longer after its usual period of adjournment, than to hold an intermediate court for this purpose.

Mr. Wickham had no doubt himself, that if General Wilkinson had intended to have come at all, he would have been here before this time; certainly the government had not failed in its duty in taking every necessary measure to have him here. If the grand jury was adjourned to some distant day, the great difficulty would be to collect them all again at the end of the time appointed; and that if General Wilkinson was to come at all, he may be expected here every day; and that of course, it was better to adjourn the grand jury only from day to day.

Mr. Hay stated, that a large allowance ought to be made for the distance and uncertainty of the journey; and that he should remind the court of a corresponding fact. Mr. Perkins, who escorted Colonel Burr, left Fort Stoddert about the 23d or 24th of March; but he himself did not reach this city before the thirty-third or thirty-sixth day. Now, Mr. Perkins certainly travelled with greater advantages than General Wilkinson would; as he pressed or purchased horses to expedite his journey. Admit, then, Mr. Perkins used due diligence, (and he has been even charged with too much) how can General Wilkinson be certainly expected? Gentlemen ought not to be so confident in their hopes. General Wilkinson will be here, as sure as he is a living man. Nothing but death will prevent him.

The Chief Justice observed, that a large calculation ought certainly to be made; as the distance was very considerable, and it was very uncertain when General Wilkinson set out, or how he travelled.

At this moment, the grand jury returned into court.

Mr. Hay addressed them in the following terms:

Gentlemen of the Grand Jury,—I have already stated to the court and the opposite counsel, that this business should be concluded, if possible, during your present session. I have moved the court, that you be called again at the end of ten days, or a fortnight. My calculation is, that General Wilkinson cannot be here before the 14th or 15th of this month. I am sorry to detain you here a single moment; but I flatter myself, that you will still continue to display the same praise-worthy patience which has hitherto marked your conduct. I am, therefore, anxious to consult your own convenience as much as possible; and I wish to know at what time it will be most convenient for you to return to this place, if you are adjourned to a distant day.

CHIEF JUSTICE.—Gentlemen of the grand jury, you will attend here on Tuesday, June 9th, at two o'clock.

TUESDAY, JUNE 9, 1807

The court met pursuant to adjournment, and all the grand jurors appeared. General Wilkinson not having yet arrived, after some conversation between the court and bar as to the probable time of his arrival, the grand jury were further adjourned to Thursday following.

Mr. Burr then addressed the court. There was a proposition which he wished to submit to them. In the President's communication to Congress, he speaks of a letter and other papers which he had received from Mr. Wilkinson, under date of 21st of October. Circumstances had now rendered it material that the whole of this letter should be produced in court; and further, it has already appeared to the court, in the course of different examinations, that the Government has attempted to infer certain intentions on my part from certain transactions. It becomes necessary, therefore, that these transactions should be accurately stated. It was, therefore, material to show in what circumstances I was placed in the Mississippi Territory; and of course, to obtain certain orders of the army and the navy which were issued respecting me. I have seen the order of the navy in print; and one of the officers of the navy had assured me that this transcript was correct. The instructions in this order were, to destroy my person and my property in descending the Mississippi.

Now I wish, if possible, to authenticate this statement; and it was for this purpose, when I passed through Washington lately, that I addressed myself to Mr. Robert Smith. That gentleman seemed to admit the propriety of my application, but objected to my course. He informed me that if I would apply to him through one of my counsel, there could be no difficulty in granting the object of my application. I have since applied in this manner to Mr. Smith, but without success. Hence I feel it necessary to resort to the authority of this court to call upon them to issue a subpoena to the President of the United States, with a clause, requiring him to produce certain papers; or, in other words, to issue the subpoena *duces tecum.* The attorney for the United States will, however, save the time of this court, if he will consent to produce the letter of the 21st October, with the accompanying papers, and also authentic orders of the Navy and War Departments.

Mr. Hay declared that he knew not for what this information could be wanted; to what purpose such evidence could relate; and whether it was to be used on the motion for commitment or on the trial in chief.

Mr. Burr, Mr. Wickham, and Mr. Martin observed that perhaps it would be used on both, according as circumstances might require.

Mr. Hay declared that all delay was unnecessary; but he pledged himself, if possible, to obtain the papers which were wanted; and not only those, but every paper which might be necessary to the elucidation of the case.

After some further conversation which did not result in any arrangement satisfactory to Mr. Burr's counsel—

The Chief Justice said: If the attorney for the United States is satisfied that the court has a right to issue the subpoena *duces tecum,* I will grant the motion.

MR. HAY.—I am not, sir.

CHIEF JUSTICE.—I am not prepared to give an opinion on this point, and therefore I must call for argument.

WEDNESDAY, JUNE 10, 1807

The subject of the subpoena *duces tecum* was resumed.

The following affidavit, drawn up and sworn to by Mr. Burr, was read in support of the motion for the subpoena:

"Aaron Burr maketh oath, that he hath great reason to believe that a letter from General Wilkinson to the President of the United States, dated 21st October, 1806, as mentioned in the President's message of the 22d January, 1807, to both Houses of Congress, to gether with the documents accompanying the said letter, and copy of the answer of said Thomas Jefferson, or of any one by his authority, to the said letter, *may* be material in his defence, in the prosecution against him. And further, that he hath reason to believe the military and naval orders given by the President of the United States, through the departments of war and of the navy, to the officers of the army and navy, at or near the New Orleans stations, touching or concerning the said Burr, or his property, will also be material in his defence.

AARON BURR.

"Sworn to in open court, 10th June, 1807."

Upon this motion a protracted debate arose, occupying two entire days, and extending into the third, in which the motion was supported by Messrs. Wickham, Botts, Randolph, Martin, and Burr, and opposed by Messrs. Hay, MacRae, and Wirt.

On the part of the prosecution it was insisted that the subpoena was unnecessary, because certified copies of any documents in the Executive Departments could be obtained by a proper application. It was said to be improper to call upon the President to produce the letter of General Wilkinson, because it was a private letter, and probably contained confidential communications, which the President ought not and could not be compelled to disclose. It might contain State secrets, which could not be divulged without endangering the national safety. It was argued that the documents demanded could not be material to the defence, and objected that the affidavit did not even state, in positive terms, that they would be material.

SATURDAY, JUNE 13, 1807

The Chief Justice delivered the following opinion on the motion for a subpoena *duces tecum*, directed to the President of the United States:

The object of the motion now to be decided is to obtain copies of certain orders, understood to have been issued to the land and naval officers of the United States for the apprehension of the accused, and an original letter from General Wilkinson to the President in relation to the accused, with the answer of the President to that letter, which papers are supposed to be material to the defence. As the legal mode of effecting this object, a motion is made for a subpoena *duces tecum,* to be directed to the President of the United States.

In opposition to this motion, a preliminary point has been made by the counsel for the prosecution. It has been insisted by them that, until the grand jury shall have found a true bill, the party accused is not entitled to subpoenas nor to the aid of the court to obtain his testimony.

It will not be said that this opinion is now, for the first time, advanced in the United States; but certainly it is now, for the first time, advanced in Virginia. So far back as any knowledge of our jurisprudence is possessed, the uniform practice of this country has been, to permit any individual, who was charged with any crime, to prepare for his defence, and to obtain the process of the court, for the purpose of enabling him so to do. This practice is as convenient and as consonant to justice as it is to humanity. It prevents, in a great measure, those delays which are never desirable, which frequently occasion the loss of testimony, and which are often oppressive. *That* would be the inevitable consequence of withholding from a prisoner the process of the court, until the indictment against him was found by the grand jury. The right of an accused person to the process of the court to compel the attendance of witnesses seems to follow, necessarily, from the right to examine those witnesses; and, wherever the right exists, it would be reasonable that it should be accompanied with the means of rendering it effectual. It is not doubted that a person who appears before a court under a recognizance, must expect that a bill will be preferred against him, or that a question concerning the continuance of the recognizance will be brought before the court. In the first event, he has the right, and it is perhaps his duty, to prepare for his defence at the trial. In the second event, it will not be denied that he possesses the right to examine witnesses on the question of continuing his recognizance. In either case it would seem reasonable that he should be entitled to the process of the court to procure the attendance of his witnesses. The genius and character of our laws and usages are friendly, not to condemnation at all events, but to a fair and impartial trial; and they consequently allow to the accused the right of preparing the means to secure such a trial.

The objection that the attorney may refuse to proceed at this time, and that no day is fixed for the trial, if he should proceed, presents no real difficulty. It would be a very insufficient excuse to a prisoner, who had failed to prepare for his trial, to say that he was not certain the attorney would proceed against him. Had the indictment been found at the first term, it would have been in some measure uncertain whether there would have been a trial at this, and still more uncertain on what day that trial would take place; yet subpoenas would have issued returnable to the first day of the term; and if after its commencement other subpoenas had been required, they would have issued, returnable as the court might direct. In fact, all process to which the law has affixed no certain return day is made returnable at the discretion of the court.

General principles, then, and general practice are in favor of the right of every accused person, so soon as his case is in court, to prepare for his defence, and to receive the aid of the process of the court to compel the attendance of his witnesses.

The Constitution and laws of the United States will now be considered for the purpose of ascertaining how they bear upon the question. The eighth amendment to the Constitution gives to the accused, "in all criminal prosecutions, a right to a speedy and public trial, and to compulsory process for obtaining witnesses in his favor." The right given by this article must be deemed sacred by the courts, and the articles should be so construed as to be something more than a dead letter. What can more effectually elude the right to a speedy trial than the declaration that the accused shall be disabled from preparing for it until an indictment shall be found against him? It is certainly much more in the true spirit of the provision which secures to the accused a speedy trial, that he should have the benefit of the provision which entitles him to compulsory process as soon as he is brought into court.

This observation derives additional force from a consideration of the manner in which this subject has been contemplated by Congress. It is obviously the intention of the national legislature, that in all capital cases the accused shall be entitled to process before indictment found. The words of the law are, "and every such person or persons accused or indicted of the crimes aforesaid, (that is, of treason or any other capital offence), shall be allowed and admitted in his said defence to make any proof that he or they can produce by lawful witness or witnesses, and shall have the like process of the court where he or they shall be tried, to compel his or their witnesses to appear at his or their trial as is usually granted to compel witnesses to appear on the prosecution against them."

This provision is made for persons accused or indicted. From the imperfection of human language, it frequently happens that sentences which ought to be the most explicit are of doubtful construction; and in this case the words "accused or indicted" may be construed to be synonymous, to describe a person in the same situation, or to apply to different stages of the prosecution. The word *or* may be taken in a conjunctive or a disjunctive sense. A reason for understanding them in the latter sense is furnished by the section itself. It commences with declaring that any person who shall be accused and indicted of treason shall have a copy of the indictment, and at least three days before his trial. This right is obviously to be enjoyed after an indictment, and therefore the words are, "accused *and* indicted." So with respect to the subsequent clause, which authorizes a party to make his defence, and directs the court, on his application, to assign him counsel. The words relate to any person accused and indicted. But, when the section proceeds to authorize the compulsory process for witnesses, the phraseology is changed. The words are, "and every such person or persons accused or indicted," &c., thereby adapting the expression to the situation of an accused person both before and after indictment. It is to be remarked, too, that the person so accused or indicted is to have "the like process to compel his or their witnesses to appear at his or their trial, as is usually granted to compel witnesses to appear on the prosecution against him." The fair construction of this clause would seem to be, that with respect to the means of compelling the attendance of witnesses to be furnished by the court, the prosecution and defence are placed by the law on equal ground. The right of the prosecutor to take out subpoenas, or to avail himself of the aid of the court, in any stage of the proceedings previous to the indictment, is not controverted. This act of Congress, it is true, applies only to capital cases; but persons charged with offences not capital have a constitutional and a legal right to examine their testimony; and this act ought to be considered as declaratory of the common law in cases where this constitutional right exists.

Upon immemorial usage, then, and upon what is deemed a sound construction of the Constitution and law of the land, the court is of opinion that any person charged with a crime in the courts of the United States has a right, before as well as after indictment, to the process of the court to compel the attendance of his witnesses. Much delay and much inconvenience may be avoided by this construction; no mischief, which is perceived, can be produced by it. The process would only issue when, according to the ordinary course of proceeding, the indictment would be tried at the term to which the subpoena is made returnable; so that it becomes incumbent on the accused to be ready for his trial at that term.

This point being disposed of, it remains to inquire whether a subpoena *duces tecum* can be directed to the President of the United States, and whether it ought to be directed in this case?

This question originally consisted of two parts. It was at first doubted whether a subpoena could issue, in any case, to the Chief Magistrate of the nation; and if it could, whether that subpoena could do more than direct his personal attendance; whether it could direct him to bring with him a paper which was to constitute the gist of his testimony. While the argument was opening, the attorney for the United States avowed his opinion that a general subpoena might issue to the president; but not a subpoena *duces tecum*. This terminated the argument on that part of the question. The court, however, has thought it necessary to state briefly the foundation of its opinion, that such a subpoena may issue.

In the provisions of the constitution, and of the statute, which give to the accused a right to the compulsory process of the court, there is no exception whatever. The obligation, therefore, of those provisions is general; and it would seem that no person could claim an exemption from them, but one who would not be a witness. At any rate, if an exception to the general principle exist, it must be looked for in the law of evidence. The exceptions furnished by the law of evidence, (with one only reservation) so far as they are personal, are of those only whose testimony could not be received. The single reservation alluded to is the case of the king. Although he may, perhaps, give testimony, it is said to be incompatible with his dignity to appear under the process of the court. Of the many points of difference which exist between the first magistrate in England and the first magistrate of the United States, in respect to the personal dignity conferred on them by the constitutions of their respective nations, the court will only select and mention two. It is a principle of the English constitution that the king can do no wrong, that no blame can be imputed to him, that he cannot be named in debate.

By the Constitution of the United States, the President, as well as any other officer of the Government, may be impeached, and may be removed from office on high crimes and misdemeanors.

By the Constitution of Great Britain, the crown is hereditary, and the monarch can never be a subject.

By that of the United States, the President is elected from the mass of the people, and, on the expiration of the time for which he is elected, returns to the mass of the people again.

How essentially this difference of circumstances must vary the policy of the laws of the two countries, in reference to the personal dignity of the executive chief, will be perceived by every person. In this respect the first magistrate of the Union may more properly be likened to the first magistrate of a State; at any rate, under the former confederation; and it is not known ever to have been doubted, but that the chief magistrate of a State might be served with a subpoena *ad testificandum*.

If, in any court of the United States, it has ever been decided that a subpoena cannot issue to the President, that decision is unknown to this court.

If, upon any principle, the President could be construed to stand exempt from the general provisions of the Constitution, it would be because his duties as Chief Magistrate demand his whole time for national objects. But it is apparent that this demand is not unremitting; and, if it should exist at the time when his attendance on a court is required, it would be sworn on the return of the subpoena, and would rather constitute a reason for not obeying the process of the court than a reason against its being issued. In point of fact it cannot be doubted that the people of England have the same interest in the service of the executive government, that is, of the cabinet counsel, that the American people have in the service of the Executive of the United States, and that their duties are as arduous and as unremitting. Yet it has never been alleged, that a subpoena might not be directed to them. It cannot be denied that to issue a subpoena to a person filling the exalted position of the Chief Magistrate, is a duty which would be dispensed with more cheerfully than it would be performed; but, if it be a duty, the court can have no choice in the case.

If, then, as is admitted by the counsel for the United States, a subpoena may issue to the President, the accused is entitled to it, of course; and whatever difference may exist with respect to the power to compel the same obedience to the process, as if it had been directed to a private citizen, there exists no difference with respect to the right to obtain it. The guard, furnished to this high officer, to protect him from being harassed by vexatious and unnecessary subpoenas, is to be looked for in the conduct of a court after those subpoenas have issued; not in any circumstance which is to precede their being issued. If, in being summoned to give his personal attendance to testify, the law does not discriminate between the President and a private citizen, what foundation is there for the opinion that this difference is created by the circumstance that his testimony depends on a paper in his possession, not on facts which have come to his knowledge otherwise than by writing? The court can perceive no foundation for such an opinion. The propriety of introducing any paper into a case, as testimony, must depend on the character of the paper, not on the character of the person who holds it. A subpoena *duces tecum*, then, may issue, directing him to bring any paper of which the party praying it has a right to avail himself as testimony; if, indeed, that be the necessary process for obtaining the view of such a paper.

When this subject was suddenly introduced, the court felt some doubt concerning the propriety of directing a subpoena to the Chief Magistrate, and some doubt also concerning the propriety of directing any paper in his possession, not public in its nature, to be exhibited in court. The impression that the questions which might arise in consequence of such process, were more proper for discussion on the return of the process than on its issuing, was then strong on the mind of the judges; but the circumspection with which they would take any step which would in any manner relate to that high personage, prevented their yielding readily to those impressions, and induced the request that those points, if not admitted, might be argued. The result of that argument is a confirmation of the impression originally entertained. The court can perceive no legal objection to issuing a subpoena *duces tecum* to any person whatever, provided the case be such as to justify the process.

This is said to be a motion to the *discretion* of the court. This is true. But a motion to its *discretion* is a motion, not to its *inclination*, but to its *judgment;* and its judgment is to be guided by sound legal principles. A subpoena *duces tecum* varies from an ordinary subpoena only in this; that a witness is summoned for the purpose of bringing with him a paper in his custody. In some of our sister States whose system of jurisprudence is erected on the same foundation with their own, this process, we learn, issues of course. In this State it issues, not absolutely of course, but with leave of the court. No case, however, exists as is believed, in which the motion has been founded on an affidavit, in which it has been denied, or in which it has been opposed. It has been truly observed that the opposite party can, regularly, take more interest in the awarding a subpoena *duces tecum* than in the awarding an ordinary subpoena. In either case he may object to any delay, the grant of which may be implied in granting the subpoena; but he can no more object regularly to the legal means of obtaining testimony, which exists in the papers, than in the mind of the person who may be summoned. If no inconvenience can be sustained by the opposite party, he can only oppose the motion in the character of an *amicus curiae,* to prevent the court from making an improper order, or from burthening some officer by compelling an unnecessary attendance. This court would certainly be very unwilling to say that upon fair construction the constitutional and legal right to obtain its process, to compel the attendance of witnesses, does not extend to their bringing with them such papers as may be material in the defence. The literal distinction which exists between the cases is too much attenuated to be countenanced in the tribunals of a just and humane nation.

If, then, the subpoena be issued without inquiry into the manner of its application, it would seem to trench on the privileges which the constitution extends to the accused; it would seem to reduce his means of defence within narrower limits than is designed by the fundamental law of our country, if an overstrained rigor should be used with respect to his right to apply for papers deemed by himself to be material. In the one case the accused is made the absolute judge of the testimony to be summoned; if, in the other, he is not a judge, absolutely for himself, his judgment ought to be controlled only so far as it is apparent that he means to exercise his privileges not really in his own defence, but for purposes which the court ought to discountenance. The court would not lend its aid to motions obviously designed to manifest disrespect to the Government; but the court has no right to refuse its aid to motions for papers to which the accused may be entitled, and which may be material in his defence.

These observations are made to show the nature of the discretion which may be exercised. If it be apparent that the papers are irrelative to the case, or that for state reasons they cannot be introduced into the defence, the subpoena *duces tecum* would be useless. But if this be not apparent, if they may be important in the defence, if they may be safely read at the trial, would it not be a blot in the page which records the judicial proceedings of this country, if, in a case of such serious import as this, the accused should be denied the use of them?

The counsel for the United States take a very different view of the subject, and insist that a motion for process to obtain testimony should be supported by the same full and explicit proof of the nature and application of that testimony, which would be required on a motion, which would delay public justice, which would arrest the ordinary course of proceeding, or would in any other manner affect the rights of the opposite party. In favor of this position has been urged the opinion of one, whose loss as a friend and as a judge I sincerely deplore; whose worth I feel, and whose authority I shall at all times greatly respect. If his opinions were really opposed to mine, I should certainly revise, deliberately revise, the judgment I had formed; but I perceive no such opposition.

In the trials of Smith and Ogden, the court in which Judge Patterson presided, required a special affidavit in support of a motion made by the counsel for the accused for a continuance and for an attachment against witnesses who had been subpoenaed and who had failed to attend.

Had this requisition of a special affidavit been made as well a foundation for an attachment as for a continuance, the cases would not have been parallel, because the attachment was considered by the counsel for the prosecution merely as a means of punishing the contempt, and a court might certainly require stronger testimony to induce them to punish a contempt, than would be required to lend its aid to a party in order to procure evidence in a cause. But the proof furnished by the case is most conclusive that the special statements of the affidavit were required solely on account of the continuance.

Although the counsel for the United States considered the motion for an attachment merely as a mode of punishing for contempt, the counsel for Smith and Ogden considered it as compulsory process to bring in a witness, and moved a continuance until they could have the benefit of this process. The continuance was to arrest the ordinary course of justice; and, therefore, the court required a special affidavit, showing the materiality of the testimony before this continuance could be granted. *Prima facie* the evidence could not apply to the case; and there was an additional reason for a special affidavit. The object of this special statement was expressly said to be for a continuance. Colden proceeded: "The present application is to put off the cause on account of the absence of witnesses, whose testimony the defendant alleges is material for his defence, and who have disobeyed the ordinary process of the court. In compliance with the intimation from the bench yesterday, the defendant has disclosed by the affidavit which I have just read, the points to which he expects the witnesses who have been summoned will testify.

"If the court cannot or will not issue compulsory process to bring in the witnesses who are the objects of this application, then the cause will not be postponed.

"Or, if it appears to the court, that the matter disclosed by the affidavit might not be given in evidence, if the witness were now here, then we cannot expect that our motion will be successful. For it would be absurd to suppose that the court will postpone the trial on account of the absence of witnesses whom they cannot compel to appear, and of whose voluntary attendance there is too much reason to despair; or, on account of the absence of witnesses who, if they were before the court, could not be heard on the trial." (See page 12 of the Trials of Smith and Ogden.)

This argument states, unequivocally, the purpose for which a special affidavit was required.

The counsel for the United States considered the subject in the same light. After exhibiting an affidavit for the purpose of showing that the witnesses could not probably possess any material information, Mr. Standford said: "It was decided by the court yesterday that it was incumbent on the defendant, in order to entitle himself to a postponement of the trial on account of the absence of these witnesses, to show in what respect they are material for his defence. It was the opinion of the court that the general affidavit, in common form, would not be sufficient for this purpose, but that the particular facts expected from the witnesses must be disclosed in order that the court might, upon those facts, judge of the propriety of granting the postponement." (P. 27.)

The court frequently treated the subject so as to show the opinion that the special affidavit was required only on account of the continuance; but what is conclusive on this point is, that after deciding the testimony of the witnesses to be such as could not be offered to the jury, Judge Patterson was of opinion that a rule, to show cause why an attachment should not issue, ought to be granted. He could not have required the materiality of the witness to be shown on a motion, the success of which did not, in his opinion, in any degree depend on that materiality; and which he granted after deciding the testimony to be such as the jury ought not to hear. It is, then, most apparent that the opinion of Judge Patterson has been misunderstood, and that no inference can possibly be drawn from it, opposed to the principle which has been laid down by the court. That principle will therefore be applied to the present motion.

The first paper required is the letter of General Wilkinson, which was referred to in the message of the President to Congress. The application of that letter to the case is shown by the terms in which the communication was made. It is a statement of the conduct of the accused, made by the person who is declared to be the essential witness against him. The order for producing this letter is opposed:

First, because it is not material to the defence. It is a principle, universally acknowledged, that a party has a right to oppose to the testimony of any witness against him, the declarations which that witness has made at other times on the same subject. If he possesses this right, he must bring forward proof of those declarations. This proof must be obtained before he knows positively what the witness will say; for if he waits until the witness has been heard at the trial, it is too late to meet him with his former declarations. Those former declarations, therefore, constitute a mass of testimony, which a party has a right to obtain by way of precaution, and the positive necessity of which can only be decided at the trial.

It is with some surprise an argument was heard from the bar, insinuating that the award of a subpoena on this ground gave the countenance of the court to suspicions affecting the veracity of a witness who is to appear on the part of the United States. This observation could not have been considered. In contests of this description, the court takes no part; the court has no right to take a part. Every person may give in evidence, testimony such as is stated in this case. What would be the feelings of the prosecutor if, in this case, the accused should produce a witness completely exculpating himself, and the attorney for the United States should be arrested in his attempt to prove what the same witness had said upon a former occasion, by a declaration from the bench that such an attempt could not be permitted, because it would imply a suspicion in the court that the witness had not spoken the truth? Respecting so unjustifiable an interposition but one opinion would be formed.

The second objection is, that the letter contains matter which ought not to be disclosed. That there may be matter, the production of which the court would not require, is certain; but, in a capital case, that the accused ought, in some form, to have the benefit of it, if it were really essential to his defence, is a position which the court would very reluctantly deny. It ought not to be believed that the department which superintends prosecutions in criminal cases, would be inclined to withhold it. What ought to be done under such circumstances presents a delicate question, the discussion of which, it is hoped, will never be rendered necessary in this country. At present it need only be said that the question does not occur at this time. There is certainly nothing before the court which shows that the letter in question contains any matter the disclosure of which would endanger the public safety. If it does contain such matter, the fact may appear before the disclosure is made. If it does contain any matter which it would be imprudent to disclose, which it is not the wish of the Executive to disclose, such matter, if it be not immediately and essentially applicable to the point, will, of course, be suppressed. It is not easy to conceive that so much of the letter as relates to the conduct of the accused can be a subject of delicacy with the President. Everything of this kind, however, will have its due consideration on the return of the subpoena.

Thirdly, It has been alleged that a copy may be received instead of the original, and the act of Congress has been cited in support of this proposition.

This argument presupposes that the letter required is a document filed in the Department of State, the reverse of which may be and most favorably is the fact. Letters addressed to the President are most usually retained by himself. They do not belong to any of the departments. But, were the facts otherwise, a copy might not answer the purpose. The copy would not be superior to the original, and the original itself would not be admitted, if denied, without proof that it was in the handwriting of the witness. Suppose the case put at the bar of an indictment on this letter for a libel, and on its production it should appear not to be in the handwriting of the person indicted. Would its being deposited in the Department of State make it his writing, or subject him to the consequence of having written it? Certainly not. For the purpose, then, of showing the letter to have been written by a particular person, the original must be produced, and a copy could not be admitted. On the confidential nature of this letter much has been said at the bar, and authorities have been produced which appear to be conclusive. Had its contents been orally communicated, the person to whom the communications were made could not have excused himself from detailing them, so far as they might be deemed essential in the defence. Their being in writing gives no additional sanctity; the only difference produced by the circumstance is, that the contents of the paper must be proved by the paper itself, not by the recollection of the witness.

Much has been said about the disrespect to the Chief Magistrate, which is implied by this motion, and by such a decision of it as the law is believed to require.

These observations will be very truly answered by the declaration that this court feels many, perhaps, peculiar motives for manifesting as guarded a respect for the Chief Magistrate of the Union as is compatible with its official duties. To go beyond these would exhibit a conduct which would deserve some other appellation than the term respect.

It is not for the court to anticipate the event of the present prosecution. Should it terminate as is expected on the part of the United States all those who are concerned in it should certainly regret that a paper which the accused believed to be essential to his defence, which may, for aught that now appears, be essential, had been withheld from him. I will not say, that this circumstance would, in any degree, tarnish the reputation of the Government; but I will say, that it would justly tarnish the reputation of the court which had given its sanction to its being withheld. Might I be permitted to utter one sentiment, with respect to myself, it would be to deplore, most earnestly, the occasion which should compel me to look back on any part of my official conduct with so much self-reproach as I should feel, could I declare, on the information now possessed, that the accused is not entitled to the letter in question, if it should be really important to him.

The propriety of requiring the answer to this letter is more questionable. It is alleged that it most probably communicates orders showing the situation of this country with Spain, which will be important on the misdemeanor. If it contains matter not essential to the defence, and the disclosure be unpleasant to the Executive, it certainly ought not to be disclosed. This is a point which will appear on the return. The demand of the orders which have been issued, and which have been, as is alleged, published in the Natchez Gazette, is by no means unusual. Such documents have often been produced in the courts of the United States and the courts of England. If they contain matter interesting to the nation, the concealment of which is required by the public safety, that matter will appear upon the return. If they do not, and are material, they may be exhibited.

It is said they cannot be material, because they cannot justify any unlawful resistance which may have been employed or meditated by the accused.

Were this admitted, and were it also admitted that such resistance would amount to treason, the orders might still be material; because they might tend to weaken the endeavor to connect such overt act with any overt act of which this court may take cognizance. The court, however, is rather inclined to the opinion that the subpoena in such case ought to be directed to the head of the department in whose custody the orders are. The court must suppose that the letter of the Secretary of the Navy, which has been stated by the attorney for the United States, to refer the counsel for the prisoner to his legal remedy for the copies he desired, alluded to such a motion as is not made.

The affidavit on which the motion is grounded has not been noticed. It is believed that such a subpoena, as is asked, ought to issue, if there exist any reasons for supposing that the testimony may be material, and ought to be admitted. It is only because the subpoena is to those who administer the Government of this country, that such an affidavit was required as would furnish probable cause to believe that the testimony was desired for the real purposes of defence, and not for such as this court will forever discountenance.

Mr. Burr called up the motion for a supplemental charge to the grand jury, in support of which he had, on yesterday, submitted a series of propositions, with citations of authorities.

The Chief Justice stated that he had drawn up a supplemental charge, which he had submitted to the attorney for the United States, with a request that it should also be put into the hands of Colonel Burr's counsel; that Mr. Hay had, however, informed him that he had been too much occupied to inspect the charge with attention, and deliver it to the opposite counsel; but another reason was, that there was one point in the charge which he did not fully approve. He should not, therefore, deliver his charge at present, but should reserve it until Monday. In the meantime, Colonel Burr's counsel could have an opportunity of inspecting it, and an argument might be held on the points which had produced an objection from the attorney to the United States.

(After some conversation between the court and bar, as to whether the arguments on the supplemental charge should be submitted in writing or orally, the subject was passed over, and it appears never to have been again called up.)

At the instance of the District Attorney, four witnesses, viz: Thomas Truxton, William Eaton, Benjamin Stoddert, and Stephen Decatur, were sworn to testify before the grand jury.

The clerk then proceeded to call four other witnesses to the book, but when Erich Bollman appeared, Mr. Hay addressed the court to the following effect:

Before Mr. Bollman is sworn I must inform the court of a particular, and not an immaterial circumstance. He, sir, has made a full communication to the Government of the plans, the designs and views of Aaron Burr. As these communications might criminate Dr. Bollman before the grand jury, the President of the United States has communicated to me this pardon (holding it in his hands) which I have already offered to Dr. Bollman. He received it in a very hesitating manner, and I think informed me that he knew not whether he should or should not accept it. He took it from me, however, as he informed me, to take the advice of counsel. He returned it in the same hesitating manner; he would neither positively accept nor refuse it. My own opinion is that Dr. Bollman, under these circumstances, cannot possibly criminate himself. This pardon will completely exonerate him from all the penalties of the law. I believe his evidence to be extremely material. In the presence of this court I offer this pardon to him, and if he refuses, I shall deposit it with the clerk for his use. Will you (addressing himself to Dr. Bollman) accept this pardon?

DR. BOLLMAN.—No, I will not, sir.

MR. HAY.—Then observe that Dr. Bollman must be carried up to the grand jury with an intimation that he had been pardoned.

MR. MARTIN.—It has always been Dr. Bollman's intention to refuse this pardon; but he has not positively refused it before, because he wished to have this opportunity of publicly rejecting it.

Several other witnesses were sworn.

Mr. Martin did not suppose that the pardon was real or effectual; if he made any confessions before the grand jury, they might find an indictment against him, which would be valid, notwithstanding the pardon; that the pardon could not be effectual before it was pleaded to an indictment in open court.

Mr. Hay inquired whether Dr. Bollman might not go to the grand jury?

The Chief Justice suggested that it would be better to settle the question about the validity of the pardon before he was sent to the grand jury.

MR. HAY.—I am anxious to introduce the evidence before the grand jury in a chronological order, and the suspension of Dr. Bollman's testimony will make a chasm in my arrangement. He ended that, however, it was not very important whether he was sent now or some time hence to the grand jury.

MR. MARTIN.—Dr. Bollman is not pardoned, and no man is bound to criminate himself.

The Chief Justice required his authorities.

MR. MARTIN.—I am prepared to show that a party even possessed of a pardon is still indictable by the grand jury, unless he has pleaded it in court.

The other witnesses were sent to the grand jury, and Dr. Bollman was suspended.

Four other witnesses were then sworn.

MR. HAY.—I again propose to send Dr. Bollman to the grand jury.

At this time the marshal entered, and Mr. Hay informed the court that the grand jury had sent for the article of the Constitution and the laws of Congress relating to treason, and the law relating to the misdemeanor.

Jacob Dunbaugh was sworn and sent to the grand jury.

Some desultory conversation here ensued between the bar and the court respecting Dr. Bollman, when Mr. Hay addressed the opposite counsel: Are you then willing to have Dr. Bollman indicted? Take care in what an awful condition you are placing this gentleman.

MR. MARTIN.—Doctor Bollman, sir, has lived too long to be alarmed by such menaces. He is a man of too much honor to trust his reputation to the course which you prescribed for him.

THE CHIEF JUSTICE.—There can be no question but Dr. Bollman can go up to the jury; but the question is, whether he is pardoned or not? If the Executive should refuse to pardon him, he is certainly not pardoned.

MR. MARTIN.—But there can be no doubt, if he chooses to decline his pardon, that he stands in the same situation with every other witness, who cannot be forced to criminate himself.

Some desultory conversation here ensued, when Mr. Hay observed that he should extremely regret the loss of Dr. Bollman's testimony. He believed it to be material. He trusted that he should obtain it, however reluctantly given. The court would perceive, that Dr. Bollman now possessed so much zeal as even to encounter the risk of an indictment for treason. Whether he should appear before the grand jury under the circumstances of a pardon being annexed to his name, might hereafter become the object of a distinct inquiry. In the meantime he might go up without any such notification.

The counsel of Mr. Burr acquiesced.

CHIEF JUSTICE.—Whether he be really pardoned or not I cannot at present declare. I must take time to deliberate.

MR. HAY.—Categorically then I ask you, Mr. Bollman, do you accept your pardon?

MR. BOLLMAN.—I have already answered that question several times. I say no. I repeat, that I would have refused it before, but that I wished this opportunity of publicly declaring it.

MR. HAY.—If the grand jury have any doubts about the questions that they put to Dr. Bollman, they can apply to the court for instructions. I assert, sir, that Mr. Bollman is a pardoned man. I wish the opposite counsel to prove that he is not. I therefore move, sir, that he be sent up to the grand jury, certified by you, that he is pardoned. I make this motion that gentlemen who wish to discuss the question may have an opportunity of adducing their arguments.

Mr. Williams appeared as counsel for Dr. Bollman, and addressed the court in his behalf, insisting that he was not bound to criminate or calumniate himself, although pardoned. He claimed, however, that the pardon having been refused, the court could take no notice of it. He also insisted that no pardon except by statute could protect a party against a criminal prosecution, as a pardon under the great seal was not effectual until it had been pleaded and allowed in court. He cited numerous authorities in support of his positions.

Mr. Martin supported the same positions. He said, another reason why Dr. Bollman had refused the pardon was that it would be considered an admission of guilt. He did not consider a pardon necessary for an innocent man. Dr. Bollman, sir, knows what he has to fear from the prosecution of an angry Government, but he will brave it all. The man who did so much to rescue the Marquis la Fayette from his imprisonment, and who had been known at so many courts, bears too great a regard for his reputation, to wish to have it sounded throughout Europe that he was compelled to abandon his honor through a fear of unjust prosecution.

After some remarks by Messrs. MacRae and Hay, Dr. Bollman was sent up to the grand jury without any particular notification; the questions as to the effect of the pardon tendered to him, and how far he could be compelled to testify, being reserved for future discussion and decision.

Mr. Hay requested leave to inform the grand jury that fatigue that day, but that he should appear before them on Monday.

The court then adjourned to Monday.

MONDAY, JUNE 15, 1807

The court met pursuant to adjournment.

Gen. Wilkinson was sworn and sent to the grand jury, with a notification that it would facilitate their inquiries if they would examine him immediately.

Mr. Wickham reminded the court that the attorney for the United States had pledged himself to send up no papers to the grand jury which had not previously passed the inspection of the court; but it had since occurred to Col. Burr's counsel that the witnesses themselves might carry up improper papers. He submitted to the court whether they ought not to instruct the grand jury to receive no papers, except through the medium of the court.

Upon this motion a running debate of considerable length ensued.

Finally, the Chief Justice remarked that he was not satisfied that a court ought to inspect the papers which form a part of a witness' testimony before he is sent to the grand jury. He had reduced to writing an opinion to be sent to the grand jury. It instructed them not to inspect any papers but such as formed a part of the narrative of the witness, and proved to be the papers of the person against whom an indictment was exhibited.

At the instance of Mr. Hay, the instruction was so amended as to admit such papers as tend to justify the witness, but not to bear upon the accused.

Mr. Hay informed the court that the grand jury had sent for Dr. Bollman; that they wanted him to decipher, if he could, a ciphered letter annexed to Mr. Willie's affidavit, and which he held in his hand; that Mr. Willie, the reputed secretary of Mr.

Burr, would prove the identity of the paper, and Dr. Bollman, it was expected, would interpret it.

At the suggestion of Mr. Martin, the affidavit was severed from the letter.

Mr. Willie appearing in court, Mr. Hay produced the ciphered letter annexed to his affidavit, and said: This is the letter which I wish to transmit to the grand jury. It is addressed, I understand, to Dr. Bollman, under a fictitious name, and is all in the handwriting of Mr. Willie.

Mr. Botts objected to its being sent up to the grand jury until both its materiality and its authenticity had been proved.

Mr. Hay said that a hard proposition, as it was written partly in ciphers and partly in German. He deemed it material, because he understood it was either dictated by the accused, or first written by him and afterwards written by his secretary, and at his request. It was addressed to Henry Wilbourn, alias Erick Bollman. He wished it to be sent up while Dr. Bollman was before the grand jury.

After considerable sparring between counsel, Mr. Willie was called to the stand.

Mr. Williams, his counsel, hoped that no question would be put the answer to which might tend to criminate himself.

MR. MACRAE.—Did you copy this paper?

MR. WILLIAMS, (after consulting with his client.)—He says that if any paper he has written have any effect on any other person, it will as much affect himself.

MR. WIRT.—He has sworn in his deposition that he did not understand the cipher of this letter. How, then, can his merely copying it implicate him in a crime when he does not know its contents?

MR. MACRAE.—We will change our question. Do you understand the contents of that paper?

MR. WILLIAMS.—He objects to answering. He says that though the question may be an innocent one, yet the counsel for the prosecution might go on gradually from one question to another, until he at last obtained matter enough to criminate him.

MR. MACRAE.—My question is not, "Do you understand this letter, and then what are it contents?" If I pursued this course, I might then propound a question to which he might object; but unless I take that course, how can he be criminated?

MR. BOTTS.—If a man know of treasonable matter, and do not disclose it, he is guilty of misprision of treason. Two circumstances, therefore, constitute this crime: knowledge of the treason, and concealment of it. The knowledge of the treason, again, comprehends two ideas: that he must have seen and understood the treasonable matter. To one of these points Mr. Willie is called upon to depose. If this be established, who knows but the other elements of the crime may be gradually unfolded so as to implicate him? The witness ought to judge for himself.

MR. MACRAE.—I did not first ask if he copied and then understood it? but first, if he understood it? Had he answered this question in the affirmative, I certainly should not have pressed the other question upon him, because that might have amounted to self-crimination; but, if he did not understand it, it could not criminate him.

MR. HAY.—I will simply ask him whether he knows this letter to be written by Aaron Burr, or by some one under his authority?

The Chief Justice said that that was a proper question.

MR. WILLIAMS.—He refuses to answer; it might tend to criminate him.

The court were of opinion that Mr. Willie should answer upon oath whether or not he thought that answering the proposed question might have a tendency to criminate himself.

Here a long desultory argument ensued.

CHIEF JUSTICE.—Has the witness a right to refuse to answer?

MR. WILLIAMS.—The knowledge of the treason and concealment of it, amount to a misprision of treason.

CHIEF JUSTICE.—The better question is, Do you understand it?

MR. WILLIAMS.—He ought not to have such a question put to him, because he might be obliged to answer "Yes." He ought not to be compelled to answer, if it might possibly criminate him. The witness is to judge him himself, though the question may not seem to affect him. He referred to the case of young Goosely, before referred to by Mr. Randolph.

MR. BOTTS.—I will give Mr. Hay the benefit of an authority, 1 MacNally, 257, 258, which shows that the possibility of crimination is sufficient to excuse the witness from answering.

MR. WILLIAMS.—What the witness says here tending to his own crimination, may be used as evidence against him on a prosecution. If he answer at all, he is deprived of the privilege given by the law, not to criminate one's self.

CHIEF JUSTICE.—If he be to decide upon this, it must be on oath. He asked Willie whether his answering the question, whether he understood that letter, would criminate himself? He answered, It may in a certain case.

CHIEF JUSTICE.—I wish to consider the question until to-morrow.

JUDGE GRIFFIN (to Mr. Williams).—The case of Goosely was not as you represented it. It was the court who knew that the witness was one of those who robbed the mail.

MR. HAY.—The doctrine is most pernicious and contrary to the public good.

MR. WILLIAMS.—The public good does not require the conviction of Colonel Burr so much as to dispense with the law.

It was then agreed that the point should be argued to-morrow, and Colonel Burr's counsel promised to produce their authorities to show that Willie could not be compelled to answer such questions as might, in his own opinion, tend to criminate himself.

The court then adjourned till to-morrow.

TUESDAY, JUNE 16, 1807

As soon as the court met, Mr. Hay produced and read the following letter from the President of the United States, in answer to his letter on the subject of the *subpoena duces tecum,* observing at the same time, that he read it to show the disposition of the Government not to withhold any necessary papers, and that if gentlemen would specify what orders they wanted, they would be furnished without the necessity of expresses.

Washington, June 12, 1807

SIR: Your letter of the 9th is this moment received. Reserving the necessary right of the President of the United States to decide, independently of all other authority, what papers coming to him as President the public interest permits to be communicated, and to whom, I assure you of my readiness under that restriction, voluntarily to furnish on all occasions whatever the purpose of justice may require. But the letter of General Wilkinson, of October 21st, requested for the defense of Colonel Burr, with every other paper relating to the charges against him, which were in my possession when the Attorney General went on to Richmond in March, I then delivered to him; and I have always taken for granted he left the whole with you. If he did, and the bundle retains the order in which I had arranged it, you will readily find the letter desired under the date of its receipt, which was November 25th; but lest the Attorney General should not have left those papers with you, I this day write to him to forward this one by post. An uncertainty whether he be at Philadelphia, Wilmington, or New Castle, may produce delay in his receiving my letter, of which it is proper you should be apprised. But as I do not recollect the whole contents of that letter, I must beg leave to devolve on you the exercise of that discretion which it would be my right and duty to exercise, by withholding the communication of any parts of the letter which are not directly material for the purposes of justice. With this application, which is specific, a prompt compliance is practicable; but when the request goes to copies of the orders issued in relation to Colonel Burr to the officers at Orleans and Natchez, and by the secretaries of the War and Navy Departments, it seems to cover a correspondence of many months, with such a variety of officers civil and military, all over the United States, as would amount to the laying open the whole executive books. I have desired the Secretary of War to examine his official communications, and on a view of these we may be able to judge what can and ought to be done towards a compliance with the request. If the defendant allege that there was any particular order which, as a cause, produced any particular act on his part, then he must know what this order was, can specify it, and a prompt answer can be given. If the object had been specified, we might then have had some guide for our conjectures, as to what part of the executive records might be useful to him. But with a perfect willingness to do what is right, we are without the indications which may enable us to do it. If the researches of the Secretary of War should produce anything proper for communication, and pertinent to any point we can conceive in the defence before the court, it shall be forwarded to you. I salute you with esteem and respect.

THOMAS JEFFERSON

GEORGE HAY, Esq.

Some conversation ensued about the specification of the papers wanted from the Executive.

Mr. Hay stated that in his communication to the President, to which this letter was a reply, he had mentioned these papers in the terms by which he thought the opposite counsel would probably have described them. The President, however, did not deem this description sufficient.

Colonel Burr's counsel then stated that they had sent an express to Washington for these papers, with a subpoena to the President, and that it would appear on the return whether they could obtain them or not.

Here a desultory conversation ensued, in which Mr. Hay insisted that Dr. Bollman was a pardoned man, and ought to communicate all he knew to the grand jury, which was denied by the other side; when Dr. Bollman, addressing himself to the court, said: I have answered every question that was put to me by the grand jury.

The Chief Justice inquired if there was any objection to asking Dr. Bollman if he could decipher the letter.

Mr. Martin said it would be time enough to discuss that question after the letter shall have been before the grand jury.

MR. MACRAE.—I wish the question now put. I asked Willie whether he undertook that part of the letter which is in cipher; he could not be criminal if he did not understand it. I wish the part which is written in German now to be explained, to show that there is nothing criminal in it. I wish Bollman to translate that part.

The Chief Justice said he would prefer to proceed with the other point; how far a witness may refuse to answer a question which he thinks would criminate himself.

Mr. Botts then addressed the court at some length on that point. In the course of his remarks he intimated that the letter in question had been obtained by the robbery of the post office, and referred to the mark "25" on its back, (which he said was the only post mark of many of the country post offices) as evidence that it had been taken from the post office.

Mr. Williams, counsel for Mr. Willie, followed Mr. Botts in support of the position that the witness was not bound to answer any question, the answer to which he believed would tend to criminate himself.

Messrs. MacRae and Hay replied at some length, after which the court adjourned.

WEDNESDAY, JUNE 17, 1807

At the meeting of the court Mr. Hay referred to the insinuations that had been thrown out yesterday, that the ciphered letter in question had been taken improperly if not feloniously from the post office; and said this was evidently done to affect the character of Gen. Wilkinson. He read a note which he had just received from Gen. Wilkinson, stating that the letter was delivered to him by Charles Patton, of the house of "Meeker, Williamson & Patton," New Orleans.

Mr. Martin then addressed the court on the question of the right of Mr. Willie to decline answering the questions propounded to him by the counsel for the prosecution. He contended that "a witness is not compelled to answer when it tends to criminate him, nor where it does not relate to the issue," and cited authorities in support of the proposition.

Mr. Wickham followed in an argument on the same side.

After some further desultory conversation, the Chief Justice asked whether there were any other questions before the court.

Mr. MacRae requested a decision on Dr. Bollman's case, as he wished to interrogate him about the ciphered letter.

Mr. Williams said he was ready to discuss the question.

MR. BURR.—There will arise some very important questions, affecting the very source of the jurisdiction of this country. I have several affidavits to produce to show that improper means have been used to procure witnesses, and thereby contaminate the public justice. When these proofs have been duly exhibited, it will be the province of the court to decide whether they will not arrest the progress of such improper conduct, and prevent the introduction of such evidence.

Mr. Botts rose to apprise the opposite counsel there were three or four questions of importance which the counsel for Mr. Burr should bring forward as soon as possible. Two or three days ago he had commented on the plunder of the post office, and he assured the counsel for the prosecution that he should probe the subject to the bottom, as no man could be more anxious than himself that the stigma which this transaction attached to the inferior or superior offices of the government should be wiped off.

CHIEF JUSTICE.—Unless these allegations affected some testimony that was about to be delivered, how can you introduce this subject?

MR. BURR.—The court has very properly demanded some proof of the relevancy of our proposition. Sir we are ready to prove the violation of the post office. We are ready to fasten it on individuals now here, and we are ready to name the post offices, if the court require it, which have been thus plundered. When it comes out that evidence has been thus improperly obtained, we shall say, sir, that it is contaminated by fraud. I will name three persons who have been guilty of improper conduct, in improperly obtaining letters from the post office to be evidence against me. These are Judge Toulmin, of the Mississippi Territory, John G. Jackson, a Member of Congress, and General Wilkinson. Two of these persons are within the reach of this court. As well as the improper manner in which they have procured affidavits and witnesses against me, I mention these circumstances for two reasons: first, that the facts may be proved to the satisfaction of the court; and second, that the court may lay their hands on testimony thus procured.

MR. BOTTS.—The circumstance of the post mark proves that the post office was robbed of that letter; therefore it is not evidence.

The Chief Justice said, let the consequences be as they may, this court cannot take cognizance of any act which has not been committed within this district. That mark is not necessarily a post mark. The court can only know the fact, in a case to which it applies, except to commit and send for trial.

MR. HAY.—Let some specific motion be made, and the evidence procured; and if there have been any crime committed, let the offenders be prosecuted according to law. These gentlemen know the course, and I most solemnly promise to discharge the duties of my office, whether they bear against General Wilkinson, or the man at the bar. If the crime have been committed, it is not the province of the court to notice it till after an indictment has been found.

MR. BOTTS.—We only wish to prove and prevent a repetition and continuance of this improper mode of proceeding. The proof will affect General Wilkinson.

CHIEF JUSTICE.—If it did affect General Wilkinson it could not prevent him from being a witness.

Some desultory conversation here ensued, when Mr. Burr observed that he was afraid he was not sufficiently understood, from mingling two distinct propositions together. As to the subject of the post offices, it might rest for the present; but as to the improper means employed in obtaining testimony, they were at this moment in actual operation. Some witnesses had been brought here by this practice, and it was one which ought immediately to be checked; he did not particularly level his observations against General Wilkinson. He did not say that the attorney for the United States ought to indict, or that such a crime, if committed out of this district, was cognizable by the court, unless it be going on while the court is in session, or the cause depending; in those cases improper practices relative to crimes committed out of the limits of this court may be examined, and the persons committing them attached. Such practices have been since I have been recognized here, and they ought to be punished by attachment.

MR. WIRT.—I do not yet understand the gentlemen. What is the object of their motion?

MR. BOTTS.—We shall hereafter make it; we have no other object by the present annunciation than to give gentlemen a timely notice of our intentions.

MR. BURR.—We have sufficient evidence on which to found our motion.

What motion? demanded Mr. Hay.

MR. BURR.—I thought, sir, I had sufficiently explained my intentions. I may either move for a rule to show cause why an attachment should not issue against Judge Toulmin, John G. Jackson, and General Wilkinson, or what is sometimes, though not so frequently practiced, I may directly move for an attachment itself.

MR. MACRAE.—At whose instance?

MR. BURR.—At the public's.

MR. MACRAE.—A pretty proceeding, indeed! that the public prosecution should thus be taken out of the hands of the public prosecutor, and that the accused should supersede the attorney for the United States!

MR. BURR.—A strange remark indeed! As if it were not the business of the injured person himself to institute the complaint.

MR. HAY.—I wish for further explanation. Let the specific charge on which their motion is founded be clearly pointed out and reduced to writing.

MR. BURR.—The motion will be for an attachment for the irregular examination of witnesses, practicing on their fears, forcing them to come to this place, and transporting them from New Orleans to Norfolk.

At this moment Mr. Randolph entered the court and observed that if he had been present he would have himself opened this motion, which was intended to operate immediately upon General Wilkinson, and ultimately upon some other persons. Mr. Randolph here read the motion which he would have submitted to the court.

Mr. Hay protested against this proceeding, which, he said, was calculated to interrupt the course of the prosecution, and was levelled at General Wilkinson alone.

After some further remarks from Mr. Hay and from Messrs. Randolph and Martin,

Mr. Hay said he should move to postpone the motion of the gentleman till the prosecution was over, because it would necessarily interrupt the business before the court, because it was intended to impeach the credit of a witness, and because this inquiry could as well be conducted after as before the prosecution.

Mr. Wickham replied to Mr. Hay. He said, among other things that General Wilkinson had brought witnesses with him from New Orleans by military force. He had taken their depositions entirely *ex parte* at the point of the bayonet, for the purpose of keeping their testimony straight. He would lay down the broad proposition that the man who goes about collecting affidavits upon affidavits in relation to a matter to be investigated in this court corrupts the fountains of justice. We have already seen a volume of such at this bar. He particularly referred to Mr. Jackson, who comes here with the depositions of witnesses who are thus bound hand and foot, thus tongue-tied, because their depositions had been taken. He had seen them in this very court examining witnesses with affidavits in their hands, and comparing the one with the other; depositions taken not by commission, but *ex parte*. When an interested agent thus goes about collecting depositions, and with ignorant men shaping them just as he pleases, he acts contrary to law and to the spirit and genius of our government; and such acts are a contempt of this court, if done during the prosecution, by interfering with the purpose of justice. Such men are liable to attachment from the very moment that the government took possession of Colonel Burr's person; not from the moment of first arrest, but from the time when they ordered Perkins to conduct his prisoner from Fredericksburg to Richmond. It was necessary to institute this proceeding now to prevent the repetition of such practices during the progress of the trial. At the conclusion of Mr. Wickham's remarks,

The Chief Justice said that the pendency of the prosecution was no objection to hearing the motion, but it was another question whether there were any grounds for it or not, and that the court would not say that a motion relating to the justice of the case ought not to be heard.

The court then adjourned.

THURSDAY, JUNE 18, 1807

As soon as the court met, the Chief Justice delivered the following opinion in the case of Willie:

In point of law, the question now before the court relates to the witness himself. The attorney for the United States offers a paper in cypher, which he supposes to have proceeded from a person against whom he has preferred an indictment for high treason and another for a misdemeanor, both of which are now before the grand jury, and produces a person said to be the secretary or clerk of the accused, who is supposed either to have copied this paper by his direction, or to be able to prove, in some other manner, that it has proceeded from his authority. To a question demanding whether he understands this paper the witness has declined giving an answer, saying that the answer might criminate himself; and it is referred to the court to decide whether the excuse he has offered be sufficient to prevent his answering the question which has been propounded to him.

It is a settled maxim of law that no man is bound to criminate himself. This maxim forms one exception to the general rule, which declares that every person is compellable to bear testimony in a court of justice. For the witness who considers himself as being within the exception it is alleged that he is, and from the nature of things must be, the sole judge of the effect of his answer; that he is consequently at liberty to refuse to answer any question if he will say upon his oath that his answer to that question might criminate himself.

When this opinion was first suggested, the court conceived the principle laid down at the bar to be too broad, and therefore required that authorities in support of it might be adduced. Authorities have been adduced, and have been considered. In all of them the court could perceive that an answer to the question propounded might criminate the witness, and he was informed that he was at liberty to refuse an answer. These cases do not appear to the court to support the principle laid down by the counsel for the witness in the full latitude in which they have stated it. There is no distinction which takes from the court the right to consider and decide whether any direct answer to the particular question propounded could be reasonably supposed to answer the witness. There may be questions no direct answer to which could, in any degree, affect him; and there is no case which goes so far as to say that he is not bound to answer such questions. The case of Goosely in this court is, perhaps, the strongest that has been adduced. But the general doctrine of the judge in that case must have referred to the circumstances, which showed that the answer might criminate him.

When two principles come in conflict with each other, the court must give them both a reasonable construction, so as to preserve them both to a reasonable extent. The principle which entitles the United States to the testimony of every citizen, and the principle by which every witness is privileged not to accuse himself, can neither of them be entirely disregarded. They are believed both to be preserved to a reasonable extent, and according to the true intention of the rule and of the exception to that rule, by observing that course which it is conceived courts have generally observed. It is this:

When a question is propounded, it belongs to the court to consider and to decide whether any direct answer to it can implicate the witness. If this be decided in the negative, then he may answer it without violating the privilege which is secured to him by law. If a direct answer to it may criminate himself, then he must be the sole judge what his answer would be. The court cannot participate with him in this judgement, because they cannot decide on the effect of his answer without knowing what it would be; and a disclosure of that fact to the judges would strip him of the privilege which the law allows, and which he claims. It follows necessarily then, from this statement of things, that if the question be of such a description that an answer to it may or may not criminate the witness, according to the purport of that answer, it must rest with himself, who alone can tell what it would be, to answer the question or not. If, in such a case, he says upon his oath that his answer would criminate himself, the court can demand no other testimony of the fact. If the declaration be untrue, it is in conscience and in law as much a perjury as if he had declared any other untruth upon his oath; as it is one of those cases in which the rule of law must be abandoned, or the oath of the witness be received.

The counsel for the United States have also laid down this rule according to their understanding of it; but they appear to the court to have made it as much too narrow as the counsel for the witness have made it too broad. According to their statement a witness can never refuse to answer any question unless that answer, unconnected with other testimony, would be sufficient to convict him of a crime. This would be rendering the rule almost perfectly worthless. Many links frequently compose the chain of testimony which is necessary to convict any individual of a crime. It appears to the court to be the true sense of the rule that no witness is compellable to furnish any one of them against himself. It is certainly not only a possible but a probable case that a witness by disclosing a single fact, may complete the testimony against himself, and to every effectual purpose accuse himself as entirely as he would by stating every circumstance which would be required for his conviction. That fact of itself might be unavailing, but all other facts without it would be insufficient. While that remains concealed within his own bosom he is safe; but draw it from thence, and he is exposed to a prosecution. The rule which declares that no man is compellable to accuse himself would most obviously be infringed by compelling a witness to disclose a fact of this description.

What testimony may be possessed, or is attainable, against any individual the court can never know. It would seem, then, that the court ought never to compel a witness to give an answer which discloses a fact that would form a necessary and essential part of a crime which is punishable by the laws.

To apply this reasoning to the particular case under consideration: To know and conceal the treason of another is misprision of treason, and is punishable by law. No witness, therefore, is compellable by law to disclose a fact which would form a necessary and essential part of this crime. If the letter in question contain evidence of treason, which is a fact not dependent on the testimony of the witness before the court, and therefore, may be proved without the aid of his testimony; and if the witness were acquainted with the treason when the letter was written, he may probably be guilty of misprision of treason, and, therefore, the court ought not to compel him to answer any question, the answer to which might disclose his former knowledge of the contents of that letter.

But if the letter should relate to misdemeanor and not to the treason, the court is not apprized that a knowledge and concealment of the misdemeanor would expose the witness to any prosecution whatever. On this account the court was, at first, disposed to inquire whether the letter could be deciphered, in order to determine from its contents how far the witness could be examined respecting it. The court was inclined to this course from considering the question as one which might require a disclosure of the knowledge which the witness might have had of the contents of this letter when it was put in cipher; or when it was copied by himself; if, indeed, such were the fact. But, on hearing the question more particularly and precisely stated, and finding that it refers only to the present knowledge of the cipher, it appears to the court that the question may be answered without implicating the witness, because his present knowledge would not, it is believed, in a criminal prosecution, justify the inference that his knowledge was acquired previous to this trial, or afford the means of proving that fact.

The court is, therefore, of opinion that the witness may answer the question now propounded.

The gentlemen of the bar will understand the rule laid down by the court to be this:

It is the province of the court to judge whether any direct answer to the question which may be proposed will furnish evidence against the witness.

If such answer may disclose a fact which forms a necessary and essential link in the chain of testimony, which would be sufficient to convict him of any crime, he is not bound to answer it so as to furnish matter for the conviction.

In such a case the witness must himself judge what his answer will be; and if he say on oath that he cannot answer without accusing himself, he cannot be compelled to answer.

Mr. Williams (counsel for Mr. Willie) stated that he had misunderstood him the other day in court, and in a subsequent conversation had obtained more accurate information. He does understand a part of that letter.

Mr. Hay requested that Mr. Willie should be called into court.

When he appeared Mr. Hay interrogated him. Do you understand the contents of that letter? Answer. No. Mr. Willie afterwards said that he understood the part of the letter which is written in Dutch.

MR. HAY.—Was this letter written by the hand or the direction of Aaron Burr?

Mr. Wickham objected to the question.

CHIEF JUSTICE.—The witness and his counsel will consult.

MR. HAY repeated the question. MR. WILLIE.—Yes. MR. HAY.—Which? by his hand or his direction? MR. WILLIE.— By his direction. It was copied from a paper written by himself.

MR. HAY.—I wish this paper to be carried to the grand jury, I presume there can be no objection.

MR. BOTTS.—No objection! We call upon you to show the materiality of that letter.

MR. HAY.—I deny the necessity of any such thing. Until this letter be deciphered it will be perfectly unintelligible to me and to the grand jury. It is no more than a blank piece of paper.

MR. WICKHAM.—I had always understood before that the testimony which is laid before a grand jury must not only be legal in itself, but proved to be material.

MR. WILLIAMS begged leave to interrupt the gentleman. Mr. Willie is anxious to be particularly understood. He says that this ciphered letter was first written by Colonel Burr, and afterwards copied. But it is the cipher only which has been copied from Colonel Burr's original.

MR. HAY.—It is quite sufficient sir. If Colonel Burr wrote the ciphered part, he will be considered the author of the whole.

MR. WICKHAM.—The gentleman has started a curious proposition indeed! I had always understood before that the whole included the part; but it seems now that the part is to comprehend the whole.

After some further discussion, in which several of the counsel participated,

The Chief Justice said he had in some measure anticipated this question, and had reflected upon it; his opinion was, that a paper to go before the grand or petit jury must be relevant to the case, even if its materiality were not proved. Why send this paper before the grand jury, if it cannot be deciphered? If it can be deciphered before the grand jury, why not before the court? Let it, then, be deciphered, and its relevancy may at once be established.

Mr. Hay then requested Dr. Bollman to be called, that he might be interrogated as to its contents; but before he appeared, Mr. John Randolph entered at the head of the grand jury, and addressed the court as follows:

May it please the court: One of the witnesses under examination before the grand jury has answered certain questions touching a letter in ciphers. The grand jury understand that this letter is in the possession of the court, or of the counsel for the prosecution. They have thought proper to appear before you, to know whether the letter referred to by the witness be in the possession of the court?

The Chief Justice then remarked that as the letter was wanted by the grand jury, a witness having referred to it, that was sufficient to establish its relevancy, and directed it to be delivered to them.

Mr. MacRae hoped that before the grand jury retired they would be informed that a witness had proved that this letter was originally written by Aaron Burr.

Mr. Wickham hoped that they would also be informed that the superscription on that letter has not been proved to have been written by Colonel Burr. The witness did not and would not say that he knew the superscription to have been written by him.

The grand jury retired and the court adjourned.

FRIDAY, JUNE 19, 1807

As soon as the court met, Mr. Burr addressed them. He stated that the express that he had sent on to Washington with the subpoena *duces tecum* had returned to this city on

Wednesday last, but had received no other than a verbal reply from the President of the United States that the papers wanted would not be sent by him, from which I have inferred, said Mr. Burr, that he intends to send them in some other way. I did not mention this circumstance yesterday to the court, under an expectation that the last night's mail might give us further intelligence on the subject. I now rise to give notice that unless I receive a satisfactory intimation on this subject before the meeting of the court, I shall to-morrow move the court to enforce its process.

Mr. Burr's counsel called James Knox and Chandler Lindsley, (two of the witnesses of the United States,) whose affidavits had been drawn and were intended as the ground on the motion for an attachment against General Wilkinson.

The Chief Justice asked if the papers could not be put into his hands, and the argument take place to-morrow; he wished to consider the question before it was discussed.

This led to a debate of considerable length, in which the counsel for the prosecution favored the course suggested by the Chief Justice, and the counsel for Colonel Burr opposed all delay.

At the close of the discussion, some conversation ensued relative to the form of the motion for an attachment against General Wilkinson. The counsel for the United States insisted upon a specification of the conduct for which it was to issue; that if generally expressed as a "contempt of the court" nothing but the spirit of divination could enable him to discover the specific offence charged against him, nor to prepare for his defence; that the precise circumstances which constituted the offence ought to be particularized.

Mr. Burr and his counsel said that the specification was to be found in the two affidavits, and that it was from delicacy to gentlemen, he had not attempted to make these affidavits matter of record, by introducing them on the face of the motion. The motion reduced to writing, stated the offence to be "for a contempt in obstructing the administration of the justice of this court."

The court then adjourned.

SATURDAY, JUNE 20, 1807

The court met according to adjournment. Present, the same judges as yesterday.

Mr. Randolph rose to proceed with his motion, when he was interrupted by Mr. Hay, who spoke to this effect:

I have a communication to make to the court, and to the counsel of the accused. The court will recollect the answer which I received from the President, to my letter respecting certain papers. He stated in that letter that General Wilkinson's letter of the 21st October had been delivered to Mr. Rodney, the Attorney General from whom he would endeavor to obtain it. By the last mail I have received this letter from the President on the same subject.

Washington, June 17, 1807

SIR: In answering your letter of the 9th, which desired a communication of one to me from General Wilkinson, specified by its date, I informed you in mine of the 12th that I had delivered it, with all other papers respecting the charges against Aaron Burr, to the Attorney General when he went to Richmond; that I had supposed he had left them in your possession, but would immediately write to him, if he had not, to forward that particular letter without delay. I wrote to him accordingly on the same day, but having no answer I know not whether he has forwarded the letter. I stated in the same letter that I had desired the Secretary of War to examine his office in order to comply with your further request to furnish copies of the orders which had been given respecting Aaron Burr and his property; and, in a subsequent letter of the same day, I forwarded you copies of two letters from the Secretary of War, which appeared to be within the description expressed in your letter. The order from the Secretary of the Navy you said you were in possession of. The receipt of these papers has, I presume, so far anticipated, and others this day forwarded, will have substantially fulfilled the object of a subpoena from the district court of Richmond, requiring that those officers and myself should attend the court in Richmond, with the letter of General Wilkinson, the answer to that letter, and the orders of the Department of War and the Navy therein generally described. No answer to General Wilkinson's letter, other than a mere acknowledgement of its receipt in a letter written for a different purpose, was ever written by myself or any other. To these communications of papers I will add, that if the defendant suppose there are any facts within the knowledge of the heads of departments or of myself, which can be useful for his defence, from a desire of doing anything our situation will permit in furtherance of justice, we shall be ready to give him the benefit of it, by way of deposition through any persons whom the court shall authorize to take our testimony at this place. I know indeed that this cannot be done but by consent of parties, and I therefore authorize you to give consent on the part of the United States. Mr. Burr's consent will be given of course, if he suppose the testimony useful.

As to our personal attendance at Richmond, I am persuaded the court is sensible that paramount duties to the nation at large control the obligation of compliance with its summons in this case, as it would should we receive a similar one to attend the trials of Blennerhassett and others in the Mississippi Territory those instituted at St. Louis and other places on the western waters, or at any place other than the seat of government. To comply with such calls would leave the nation without an executive branch, whose agency nevertheless is understood to be so constantly necessary that it is the sole branch which the constitution requires to be always in function. It could not, then, intend that it should be withdrawn from its station by any co-ordinate authority.

With respect to papers, there is certainly a public and private side to our offices. To the former belong grants of land, patents for inventions, certain commissions, proclamations, and other papers patent in their nature. To the other belong mere executive proceedings. All nations have found it necessary that, for the advantageous conduct of their affairs, some of these proceedings, at least, should remain known to their executive functionary only. He, of course, from the nature of the case, must be the sole judge of which of them the public interest will permit publication. Hence, under our constitution, in requests of papers from the legislative to the executive branch, an exception is carefully expressed, "as to those which he may deem the public welfare may require not to be disclosed," as you will see in the inclosed resolution of the House of Representatives, which produced the message of January 22d, respecting this case. The respect mutually due between the constituted authorities in their official intercourse, as well as sincere disposition to do for every one what is just, will always insure from the executive, in exercising the duty of discrimination confided to him, the same candor and integrity to which the nation has, in like manner, trusted in the disposal of its judiciary authorities. Considering you as the organ for communicating these sentiments to the court, I address them to you for that purpose, and salute you with esteem and respect.

TH. JEFFERSON

Accompanying this letter is a copy of the resolution of the House of Representatives containing the exception to which the President refers. I have also received a letter from Mr. Smith, the Secretary of the Navy, containing an authentic copy of the order which was wanted, precisely corresponding with the unauthenticated copy in my possession.

MR. WICKHAM.—I presume that these must be considered and noted as the return to the "*subpoena duces tecum.*"

MR. HAY.—So far as they go. When we receive General Wilkinson's letter, the return will be complete. I have also received a letter from the Secretary at War, which contains all the orders of his department relative to Aaron Burr. All which papers I shall deposit with the clerk of this court.

The following is the order of the Navy Department:

I certify that the annexed is a true copy from the records in the office of the Department of the Navy of the United States of the letter from the Secretary of the Navy to Captain John Shaw, dated 20th December, 1806.

In faith whereof, I Robert Smith, Secretary of the Navy of the United States of America, have signed these presents, and caused the seal of my office to be affixed hereto, at the city of Washington, this 17th day of June, anno Domini 1807, and in the 31st year of the independence of the said States.

(Registered,)   RT. SMITH
CH. W. GOLDSBOROUGH,   Secretary of the Navy.
Ch. Clk., N.D.

(Copy)

Navy Department, 20th December, 1806

SIR: A military expedition formed on the western waters by Colonel Burr will soon proceed down the Mississippi, and by the time you receive this letter will probably be near New Orleans. You will, by all the means in your power, aid the army and militia in suppressing this enterprise. You will, with your boats, take the best position to intercept and to take, and if necessary to destroy, the boats decending under the command of Colonel Burr, or of any person holding an appointment under him. There is great reliance on your vigilance and exertions.

I have the honor to be, sir, your most obedient.

(Signed) RT. SMITH.
Captain John Shaw,
Or the Commanding Naval Officer at New Orleans.

Mr. Randolph brought forward the motion, of which previous notice had been given, for a rule against Gen. Wilkinson, to show cause why an attachment should not issue against him for attempting to obstruct the free administration of justice. He said:

The ground on which we make the motion is this: that Gen. Wilkinson, who is now before the court, in a case depending between the United States and Mr. Burr, deliberately abused the process of the law relative to a witness who has been summoned in this case. He contrived, on his own affidavit, and by his own power, to obstruct the free course of legal testimony, and to intimidate and coercively bring to this court a witness by the abuse of military authority. For this illegal proceeding it is the duty of the court to take notice of Gen. Wilkinson. As the cases ought to be kept distinct, I speak of him only; but it may be necessary to carry the principle into immediate execution as to other persons. The grounds of this accusation are the depositions of James Knox and Chandler Lindsley, which will be read to the court.

Mr. Hay objected to the introduction of these affidavits, because he understood they had been written and dictated by the counsel of Colonel Burr. He did not pretend to say that they contained anything which they did not believe to be true, nor did he know their contents. He understood that those witnesses had voluntarily gone and given information to the counsel, upon which the counsel had written or dictated the terms of these affidavits. The legal authorities showed that a court would never issue an attachment founded on affidavits taken by the agent or attorney of the party applying for it. He cited the case of the King vs. Wallace, 3 Term Rep., 403, where the court had set aside an affidavit because it was sworn to before the attorney for the prosecution, and refused to grant an attachment.

Mr. Baker said: As to the affidavit of Knox, I know nothing; but as to the affidavit of Lindsley, it was written by himself. The facts are simply these: He called upon me with his affidavit already written, (I had never seen him before,) to know whether it was correctly written or not. I read it, corrected some inaccuracies in style, and wrote it over again. It was not sworn to when he brought it to me. After I had corrected those grammatical errors, and submitted it to Mr. Lindsley's inspection, he said that the statement was perfectly correct.

Mr. MacRae said, as the witnesses are now before the court, and can be examined *viva voce,* there is no inconvenience in the objection.

Mr. Wickham insisted that the regular and established practice is, that when in the course of a trial collateral points arise in which it is necessary that testimony should be heard, not to produce *viva voce* testimony, but affidavits in support of them.

Mr. Burr said that, if agreeable to the court, he would have no objection to the examination of the witnesses in court, although the practice is, on principles of convenience, otherwise. As to the origin of this business, it was not perfectly understood, and some unfounded insinuations had been made concerning it. James Knox had called on him, stated the usage which he had received, and asked whether any redress could be obtained. One of his counsel, who was present at the interview, had concurred with him in opinion that some notice should be taken of this proceeding. At first they thought of referring him to Mr. Hay, but on reconsideration they thought that perhaps Mr. Hay might think himself disqualified from acting. Mr. Knox's own idea was that he ought to come into court and complain himself of the treatment he had received.

Mr. Wirt spoke against receiving the affidavits, and urged that the witnesses ought to be examined before the court.

Mr. Botts observed that Mr. Burr had signified his acquiescence in that course.

James Knox was then called, when

Mr. MacRae said, that as the business was of importance to General Wilkinson, it was very desirable that he should be present at the examination of this and the other witnesses who might be introduced; that he was now before the grand jury, and he had applied to the gentlemen on the other side to postpone the motion until he could be present, but they objected to any delay. He therefore found it necessary to apply to the court to suspend the examination for a short time till the General could be present.

Mr. Martin said, the question was whether a rule should be granted to show cause, with which neither General Wilkinson nor his counsel had anything to do, and were not in fact, as much as supposed to be present.

This led to some further discussions, in which Messrs. MacRae, Wirt, and Martin participated, when

The Chief Justice observed, that if the motion were to be postponed until Monday, and the witnesses on both sides were then heard, it would answer every purpose; and it might be considered then as a motion for an attachment, not for a rule to show cause.

Mr. Randolph said, we shall move them immediately for an attachment.

The examination was then postponed till Monday, and the court adjourned to that day.

MONDAY, JUNE 22, 1807

The court met pursuant to adjournment.

Mr. Randolph directed that James Knox and Chandler Lindsley be called, and was proceeding to open the motion he had introduced on Saturday, when

Mr. MacRae objected to proceeding until General Wilkinson could be present, who was still under examination before the grand jury.

After some discussion as to the propriety of proceeding in the absence of General Wilkinson, the court adjourned.

TUESDAY, JUNE 23, 1807

The court met pursuant to adjournment.

General Wilkinson appeared in court, and took his seat among the counsel for the United States.

Mr. Burr observed to the court, that as General Wilkinson was then present, he would proceed with his inquiry. He would have it, however, distinctly understood, that if the charge could not be brought home to General Wilkinson himself, so as to support the motion against him, yet it must attach according to the testimony, to any of his subordinate officers, as Mr. Gains, or any other.

Mr. Hay objected to this extension of the motion, which he had undertook to be confined to General Wilkinson alone, particularly as they had not given any intimation of such an intention before, and as no other person had any notice.

Mr. Randolph insisted that the evidence to be introduced must attach to General Wilkinson or any of his subordinate officers, or other persons, according to what the witnesses should prove. He read the charge against General Wilkinson: then he, in conjunction with others, did wilfully and unlawfully cause compulsory process to be served on James Knox and Chandler Lindsley, whilst in the city of New Orleans, whence they were transported by water to the city of Richmond, to give testimony for the United States in the case of Aaron Burr: the effect of which unlawful measures was directly and essentially tending to obstruct the free course of testimony, and of the administration of justice in this court, and to invade the privileges of witnesses.

The witnesses were then introduced. James Knox was first sworn, and testified as follows:

He says that he went to New Orleans some time in March. Soon after his arrival he received a note from General Wilkinson, making some inquiry concerning Sergeant Dunbaugh. He waited on the General, who received and treated him handsomely, took him by the hand, and asked him if he were not afraid, after what had happened, and what had been said about him? He told him that he was not afraid. He asked him whether he were at liberty to reveal what has occurred in coming down the river? The witness said he was at liberty to reveal what he knew, but did not wish to do so. He inquired whether the witness were a freemason? He then began to take notes. The witness stopped him from taking down, and told him it was not his wish to have what he said taken down. He complained of distress; expected to be ruined. Said that there was a great force coming down the river. He asked the witness his circumstances; what money was due to him for his services in coming down? He answered, one hundred and fifty dollars. Asked him if he were in want of money, and offered to supply him, which the witness refused. He said he was very unhappy; had lost his wife; but all that was nothing to his trouble on account of the state of the country. The witness said that a subpoena had been served on him about the 12th of May, by Mr. Gaines, to attend this court; that he told him he was not prepared to come round then, but he expected to get money in ten or twelve days, and would then be ready. He went to Gaines's office about four days afterwards; was taken by a sheriff on Sunday morning, who took him to Judge Hall's. The judge was from home. He went again, and was told by the judge that he must give his deposition or go round to Richmond. He answered that he had no objection to going to Richmond, but, having no counsel, would not give his deposition, lest he should commit himself. No person but the sheriff was present. The Governor desired the sheriff to take his word if the judge could not be found; saw the judge, and was bailed until eleven o'clock; gave two securities, bond in five hundred dollars each, to avoid being put in gaol. When he appeared, the judge had before him a number of printed interrogatories. The witness asked the liberty of reading them. He permitted him to do so. The judge asked him if he would answer. The witness refused until he had counsel, but offered to be placed in confinement until he could procure counsel. He afterwards saw, as his counsel, Mr. Carr, who informed him that the judge had no right to demand such answers. The judge still persisted to interrogate him, to some of which interrogatories he answered in order to save trouble. The witness then related everything that passed from Meadville until his arrival in New Orleans. Mr. Fort was then sent for and interrogated. He made some observations, and refused to answer, (being, he said, about Tom, Dick, and Harry). After which the judge gave the deputy marshal a note, who put Fort and the witness into gaol, among forty or fifty negroes and criminals. Fort was bailed by his friends; but they required bail of the witness in five or six thousand dollars, and he remained in gaol until the vessel was ready in which he embarked. He requested leave to get his clothes. Dunbaugh then came with some men with belts and side arms. The witness asked if they were a guard? He was answered no, but that they were some acquaintances. That he has since been told by Dunbaugh they were a guard. They went with Dunbaugh and himself to the water edge. The witness asked whether Lieutenant Gaines were on board? They said no, but soon would be. When Dunbaugh came to the gaol he had an order, which was handed to the gaoler. While in gaol the witness wrote to Lindsley and Doctor Mulhollen to come and see him, and told them if they came to New Orleans what they might expect. He was informed by the gaoler that they would be confined. He did not send the note. He did not see Gaines until the next day. When Lieutenant Gaines came on board the vessel, he said the witness was in a bad humor. The witness told him he was; and Gaines said that he had better be satisfied, and bear his situation with patience. He asked Gaines for leave to go on shore for his clothes; he did not care what guard was sent with him. Gaines said that it was not in his power to grant it, but the power was in General Wilkinson. The witness was not permitted to get his clothes, and came without any except what he had on at the time, and except that Lindsley brought him one of his shirts, which he had lent him. Gaines, after having told him that he might put him in irons, and bring him round in that manner, offered him forty dollars. The witness said that if he would let him go on shore he did not want it; otherwise must take it. It was paid and sent on shore; twenty dollars were paid to his landlord, and the other twenty dollars returned to him by Governor Claiborne, who came on board and went with them six or eight miles on the passage. And also, when they came to anchor in Hampton Roads,

Gaines asked him if he had any objection to coming to Richmond? He answered that he never had any objection. Gaines said that he was sent by the authority of Judge Hall. General Wilkinson spoke to him next day and asked him if he had any objection to come to Richmond. He answered he had not, if properly treated; but he had been brought off without clothes or money. General Wilkinson had not heard of his not being permitted to bring his clothes until that morning. General Wilkinson agreed he was ill treated. Told him that he (witness) must understand that he was brought round by the direction of Judge Hall. General Wilkinson proposed to let the witness go to Richmond upon his parole of honor, which was refused. Wilkinson said, if the witness wanted twenty dollars he should have it. Afterwards he talked to Mr. Lindsley, and returned to the witness, and said if he wanted fifty dollars he might have it. Witness wanting money to purchase clothes, took it. He observed, in the first conversation, that he had twice asked favors of him and Gaines, and would never ask a third favor of any person. He came to Richmond with Moxley in a pilot boat. Moxley told him that he had orders from General Wilkinson to take charge of the passengers on board the Revenge, and bring them to Richmond, and there wait his (Wilkinson's) orders.

Cross-examination by the counsel for the United States.

Have you any military commission? *Answer.* None. Where were you born? *Answer.* In Maryland; left it very young; resided in Pennsylvania and left it some time in November last. Left Pennsylvania (Meadville) for New Orleans on the 24th or 25th of November; went down the Alleghany and Ohio to Beaver; went from thence, with about twenty or thirty to Blennerhassett's island, where he did not recollect to have staid but two days, or a day and a half; left that place some time in December, Blennerhassett and another with them, who were the only persons who joined them there. Stopped at Shawnee Town; went with about double the number to Cumberland island, just opposite to the mouth of Cumberland river; staid a day and a half; met with Colonel Burr and a few others; the whole number about fifty or sixty, about seven or eight boats, five fire-arms; went thence to Fort Massac; Serjeant [sic] Dunbaugh met them there with a musket, and after meeting with Colonel Burr, he considered himself under his direction; went to Natchez; Colonel Burr did not accompany them; went from Natchez to New Orleans. Some of the boats were chartered and others sold. They arrived at New Orleans on the 13th or 16th of March. The first notice he had, after seeing General Wilkinson, of the proceedings against him, was when he was carried before Judge Hall. He was said to be carried under an affidavit of General Wilkinson before Judge Hall. Captain Gaines requested him to write to him on shore, and he would get what he wanted. He was not permitted to send the letter. Never mentioned this to General Wilkinson till they arrived in Hampton Roads. That he was treated as others while on his way; that is, as well as some, not so well as some, and better than others. Arrived at Richmond on Friday evening; put up at the Bell tavern. Three days elapsed before he saw Colonel Burr. He mentioned the treatment he had received to Colonel Burr, and intended mentioning it to the court on his first appearance, but was told it was unnecessary. That General Wilkinson used no terror against him, and offered to relieve him if he wanted money. Whilst at the mouth of Cumberland river, and when Colonel Burr made his escape, he was one that took Colonel Burr in a wherry and carried him some distance, and left him in the woods; did not hear him address any one. The note written him by General Wilkinson, and sent by Dunbaugh, was left at his house sealed; the object was to obtain some information about Dunbaugh. Not letters. Carried Colonel Burr's things to a Parson Bruin's as he was told. They had but few guns, which were traded for as they descended the river. The vessel sailed from New Orleans in half an hour after General Wilkinson came on board. The one hundred and fifty dollars offered him by General Wilkinson, he was induced to believe, was to bribe him to give evidence against Colonel Burr, or it might be considered as a bribe. Said he could obtain from Colonel Tyler a sufficiency to carry him home under his agreement with the gentleman. This conversation took place before the subpoena was served.

Lieutenant Gaines was then sworn. He stated that he received a letter from Attorney General of the United States, enclosing subpoenas for witnesses against Colonel Burr. That he went to New Orleans in consequence, and arrived there on the 7th of May. Called several times at the house where James

Knox stayed with Mr. Lindsley and Dr. Mulhollon, and could not find them. He was told by the landlord that those gentlemen walked out whenever he approached; they supposed he had something against them. He told his business, and at length saw them. They said that the reason why they endeavored to keep out of his way, was that they had belonged to Burr's party, and did not wish to appear against him. He told them that the commander-in-chief offered them a passage in the United States vessel with him. He desired Knox and Lindsley to say whether they would come or not? Knox said he could not come until he had made some money arrangements, (though Lindsley seemed disposed to come on). That he then applied to Judge Hall; the judge directed him to obtain an affidavit of the refusal, and that he would take the proper steps. He said that the subpoena might be served by the marshal or sheriff, and proposed that he (Lieutenant Gaines) should be appointed by the marshal, a deputy. He refused, unless he could afterwards be released from any further service in that capacity. Next day the judge told him that the marshal had left a deputation for him, and asked him if he would act; he answered that he would, on the foregoing condition, and that he should not attend to Knox, at New Orleans. Knox appeared always ill-natured, which induced him to ask him if he could do anything for him. He obtained from the United States agent at the place forty dollars, and offered it to Knox, which he, after some hesitation, accepted. In reply to his inquiries, whether Knox wanted assistance, he hesitated, and then said that he wished to go on shore himself, to get some necessaries out of his trunk. He told him that as the vessel was going to sail so soon, he could not, but offered him pen, ink, and paper, and requested him to write to some friend on shore to do what he wanted done, or he would act for him himself. He was then in a very ill humor, and was so when the witness returned on board. James Knox was under no restraint from the time the vessel sailed till they arrived at Hampton Roads. To a question put by Mr. Burr's counsel, by whose authority he acted, Lieutenant Gaines answered, that in every step relative to Knox he acted under the authority of the marshal at New Orleans, except that he was authorized by the commander-in-chief to offer him a passage in a public vessel. In serving the subpoena he acted under the authority of the Attorney General. When at Hampton Roads he inquired of Knox whether he had any disposition to go to Richmond? He said that he wished to come to Richmond, but wished also to leave that vessel. He told him he should leave it, but had not determined how he would be conveyed to Richmond. General Wilkinson told him all would come in a vessel, except those who would come in the stage. His getting off gave him no concern, because he supposed that Knox could be caught again in some part of the country, if he attempted to go away. Whilst the witness was on shore, General Wilkinson procured a vessel in which Knox and others were sent to Richmond. He considered Knox under his authority, not as a military officer, but as deputy marshal. That he was committed to his charge as such, in virtue of a warrant of commitment issued by Judge Hall. He did not know the reason why the judge made such an order. That General Wilkinson never attempted to exercise any authority over Knox on his passage. That the deputation was not of his own procuring. That he had received an order from the Department of War to leave the garrison at which he commanded under the direction of some other person, and to attend to the orders of the Attorney General.

Question by COLONEL BURR.—Did you have previous conversation with General Wilkinson about this deputation? *Answer.* I had none. I never heard nor had any conception of such a deputation till it was mentioned by Judge Hall. He gave to Sergeant Dunbaugh an order at New Orleans to receive from prison and deliver to the commanding officer on board the United States schooner Revenge, the body of James Knox, and he was accordingly conveyed on board.

Question by MR. BAKER.—Was not Dunbaugh a sergeant in the army, and did you not consider him acting as such under you? *Answer.* I should not have considered any citizen of New Orleans bound to obey my order; I did not consider Sergeant Dunbaugh farther bound than in compliance with his promise. He was called Sergeant Dunbaugh, but I did not consider him under my authority, as a military officer. I took no oath of office; I gave no bond to perform the duties of a deputy marshal; I do not know that I shall get any pay; I have no promise of any. General Wilkinson made his affidavit at his own quarters, before Mr. Cenas. I do not recollect whom General Wilkinson consulted; an attorney had been with him. I delivered to General Wilkinson the subpoenas received from the Attorney General of the United States, and among them one for myself, another for Mr. Graham. I always consider myself bound to obey the orders of General Wilkinson. I was bound before the deputation to obey him, and I continued so. I considered General Wilkinson as having the power of controlling myself, and every person belonging to the army and navy of the United States, on board the Revenge, if he chose to exercise that control; but I do not consider that he did exercise such control.

The subpoenas which I delivered to General Wilkinson came into my hands afterwards, but nothing passed between the general and myself on the subject, except that I stated to him the orders I had received, and the power I possessed. My impression was that General Wilkinson must have been privy to the whole, and perhaps recommend that I should transact this business. I communicated to him what Judge Hall had said; that an affidavit must be made of the materiality of Knox as a witness before he could take any steps to compel his attendance. General Wilkinson knew that Knox was put on board the Revenge unwillingly.

On our way to Virginia we stopped at the Havana for fresh supplies of water and other necessaries. Some on board were sick; they prevailed on the officers to call. While preparing to go on shore, a shot was fired from the Moro castle, and orders given to come on shore. They went on shore at the request of the sick persons on board made to General Wilkinson and Captain Read. They did not land until after four o'clock in the afternoon, and a little after dark they set sail again. Had good provisions, &c., on board. Heard Captain Read direct the cook to let those people have their provisions regularly. To a question put by Mr. Burr's council, he answered that General Wilkinson pointed out the witness on whom the subpoenas must be served. He, on several occasions, received advice and instructions from the counsel whom he consulted how to act in executing the business in which he was engaged.

MR. RANDOLPH.—Upon what authority were the forty dollars received from the military agent? *Answer.* The money received from the military agent was applied for after several applications from Knox and General Wilkinson advised me to consult Judge Hall as to whether it were legal to demand money for him, and was told by the judge that it was regular to advance a reasonable sum; and was also told by the military agent that General Wilkinson had advised him to advance that sum. The General advised me to consult the Attorney General there, or Mr. Duncan, and the General's own idea corresponded on the subject.

Mr. Graham being sworn, gave the following testimony: A short time after the arrival of Captain Gaines at New Orleans, I was told that he had subpoenas for witnesses, and one for myself; that there was a public vessel that would carry us to Richmond. I then waited on General Wilkinson to know whether I could be accommodated in that vessel? My health was bad at that time; General Wilkinson agreed that I should, and then said that he understood that there were several witnesses in town, some of whom were unwilling, others unable to come round, and asked me whether I knew any legal means or process by which those who were unwilling could be compelled to come? I told him I did not know, but I supposed the federal judge could inform him. As there was a misunderstanding between the General and the judge, I offered to ask the judge myself whether there were such process, and I did so. At this, or some subsequent time, General Wilkinson told me to ask the judge whether there were any impropriety in advancing money to the witnesses, and in what amount? The judge said, that so far from being improper, the witnesses had a right to demand it. The judge said, in answer to the other question, that if the witness refused to enter into recognizance, or to answer such questions as would satisfy him of the materiality or relevancy of his evidence, from the law, (which he showed me,) he would be authorized to send such witness round under the care of the district marshal. He saw, a few days after, in an outer room at the judge's, Mr. Knox talking with Mr. Keene, a lawyer. Some short time after, when those gentlemen came into the room, the judge asked Knox if he were then willing to answer questions or enter into recognizance? He declined doing either. The judge had that clause of the law before him. He pointed it out to Mr. Keene, and a Mr. Fort, who was in the same situation with Knox, and advised them to do one of the two, or he should be obligated to act rigidly towards them; that he was very unwilling to act against them, but it was his duty, and he must do it. The same gentleman had a curiosity to know what questions they intended to put to him, and then the printed interrogatories were shown to him. The judge asked Mr. Fort to answer these interrogatories, which he refused to do. The judge then sent for the marshal, and committed both of them. In the afternoon Captain Fort gave security in five hundred dollars for his appearance at Richmond, and was released. He understood Captain Fort was going in the ship Amity to New York, in order to come to Richmond; but as Fort told the witness he could not leave New Orleans without injury to his business, it was his own opinion that he would not leave that place. Mr. Keene intimated to the judge that he did not appear as an attorney; but expressed some doubt of the correctness of the proceedings, and of the power of the judge to send Knox round. The ship's stores were good, and the persons treated civilly and not restrained. They slept where he did. They called in at the Havana on account of bad winds, and being chased close in by a British cruiser, Captain Read, who commands the vessel, Mr. Gaines, Mr. Smith, and himself, went on shore to procure fruit, &c. Remained there about three hours. His impression was, that if the gun had not been fired from the fort, they should not have gone in. That part of the navy of the United States which is at New Orleans, and was formerly under the control of the government, and the officers about New Orleans, when the country was considered to be in a state of danger, was put under the command of General Wilkinson. He saw no guard on his way to New Orleans. I went, said Mr. Graham, partly by land, and partly by water. I went down the river with Captain Fort, who said that he was one of a party whose object was to go against Mexico, of which declaration he made no secret. I do not know by what authority Fort was brought before the judge, but Judge Hall said he felt himself bound to act under the law. I advised Fort not to oppose the judge, who was a very determined man. Fort replied, that Mr. Alexander said that the judge had no right to send him. The judge and Mr.

Keene both requested him to request Mr. Gaines to remove Knox out of the prison to the vessel.

Lieutenant Gaines, upon being called up again, said he is an officer of the United States army; never consulted General Wilkinson about accepting the appointment of deputy marshal. He understood Fort was included in the same affidavit with Knox. He sailed from New Orleans in the Revenge; saw General Wilkinson exercise no kind of authority on the voyage.

Mr. Graham said, that General Wilkinson opposed their stopping at the Havana for two reasons; first, that it would occasion delay; and secondly, that his enemies might charge it against him as an improper act. The gun was fired from the Moro castle.

I understood that the judge had requested Mr. Gaines to accept the deputation. Gaines did not wish to act. He was urged by myself and others to accept it, and he did accept it, I believe, from motives of patriotism. General Wilkinson exercised no control over the persons on board, and no restraint was used, except what has been mentioned with respect to the witness, Mr. Knox.

After the testimony was closed, a dispute arose between the counsel which side should begin the argument, both parties claiming the right. After some observations by gentlemen on both sides, it was determined that the correct distinction was, that he who obtained a rule to show cause should close, and, of course, begin the argument.

The court then adjourned till to-morrow, eleven o'clock.

WEDNESDAY, JUNE 24, 1807

The court met according to adjournment.

Mr. Graham was called by Mr. MacRae, and questioned relative to the state of the public mind at New Orleans, and whether great alarms were not excited by the conspiracy. He answered, that he had not arrived at that place till the month of March, and at that time the public mind was much agitated.

To a question put by Colonel Burr, whether General Wilkinson himself had not contributed to excite those alarms by his violent measures, Mr. Hay objected as improper. Colonel Burr insisted on the propriety of his question.

The court was of opinion, that the witness was only bound to answer such questions as directly applied to the subject before them.

Mr. Graham said, that there was a considerable portion of the people at New Orleans who believed that there was another portion unfriendly to the government. He did not know the measures pursued by the executive at New Orleans. He was then interrogated as to the post offices being robbed of letters. He did not recollect that General Wilkinson particularly informed him how letters of information were received by him; only he observed, concerning a letter partly in cipher, that he had received it from a house at New Orleans; (which Mr. Graham named, but it is not inserted, as he was not distinctly heard;) that the practice of opening letters, if it existed at all, had ceased when he arrived at New Orleans; that General Wilkinson showed him three or four letters, He did not know how those letters were taken from the post office, but it was generally said at New Orleans that the postmaster there had given him those letters.

Colonel Burr asked him whether a considerable number of letters directed to himself, or to others, had not been taken from the post office? He answered that he knew not; but there was an impression on his mind that letters were improperly taken from the post office; whether by General Wilkinson or not, he knew not. He rather thought not.

MR. MARTIN.—Did you not understand that General Wilkinson had placed guards on the river, and on the roads, to stop travellers and passengers from passing?

MR. GRAHAM.—I did understand that he had placed guards at two points, near New Orleans, for the purpose of arresting suspected characters. I had understood, also, that certain persons had been seized.

MR. MARTIN.—Did General Wilkinson never tell you how he got those letters?

MR. GRAHAM.—He did not.

Captain Murray was then called and sworn.

Being interrogated by Colonel Burr, he stated that he was stationed by Ville Grove, two miles above New Orleans. His orders from Governor Claiborne were to stop boats coming down the river and examine them; to examine papers, but break no seal; but that from his orders he would have deemed it his duty to have transmitted letters addressed to suspicious persons to the executive at New Orleans.

COLONEL BURR.—Would you have obeyed the Governor, since, as an officer, you are strictly bound to obey General Wilkinson?

CAPTAIN MURRAY.—Yes, I should. The orders from Governor Claiborne originated with and always came through General Wilkinson.

The testimony being here closed, a protracted debate ensued, occupying two days, with the exception of some intervening business, which will hereafter be noticed. Mr. Randolph opened in support of the motion, and was replied to by Mr. MacRae. Mr. Botts then addressed the court in support of the motion, and was followed by Mr. Hay on the other side. Messrs. Wickham and Martin rejoined, the latter making the closing argument.

Mr. Randolph, in opening the argument, stated that this was a motion for an attachment against General Wilkinson, to bring him before the court to answer such interrogatories as might be put to him, for a contempt. It was customary, he believed, whenever strong suspicions were excited, that an attachment should go; because it was always within the power of the party charged to purge himself upon his own oath.

He commented upon the testimony at length. Great ingenuity was displayed by Mr. R. and the counsel who followed on the same side, in giving the facts testified to by the witnesses a coloring unfavorable to General Wilkinson. The acts of that aristocratic and imperious officer in inviting poor Knox to his house, offering him money, and treating him with so much apparent respect and kindness, were represented as mere acts to draw from him an *ex parte* deposition which might be held *in terrorum* over him, when he should come to testify before this court. Failing to get from him such a deposition as he desired, it was alleged that General Wilkinson had then caused him to be arbitrarily and illegally imprisoned with felons and negroes; not to secure his attendance upon this court, but because he had refused to give his deposition. Judge Hall, it was said, must be presumed to have acted under the influence of General Wilkinson, who was exercising a military dictatorship in New Orleans. Knox was taken from the jail to the "prison ship," it was contended, by mere military force. Captain Gaines was never clothed with any civil authority, under his pretended appointment as deputy marshal. The act of Congress required that a deputy marshal should qualify in the same way as his principal, by giving bond and taking an oath of office. Captain Gaines had done neither, and hence had no authority to act in the capacity of a deputy marshal. He was in reality acting in his military capacity, under the command of General Wilkinson. His order to Sergeant Dunbaugh, to take the witness from the jail and put him on board the vessel, was "in true military style," and was executed by Dunbaugh as a military command from his superior officer, which he was obliged to obey. The "rifling of private papers by unreasonable and illegal search," by General Wilkinson, was also made the subject of some very severe strictures, by Mr. Botts.

Messrs. Hay and MacRae defended General Wilkinson against all these charges with zeal and ability. They contended that he had acted with great moderation and caution, considering his situation; "threatened in New Orleans by traitors without and enemies within." That so far from exercising the military power reposed in him in an arbitrary manner, to compel the attendance of witnesses before this court, he had turned the whole matter over to the civil authorities. Even admitting that Judge Hall had acted arbitrarily and illegally, (which was denied), General Wilkinson could not be held responsible for his acts, as there was no evidence that he had exercised any influence over him. The contrary was presumable, from the fact that Judge Hall and General Wilkinson were not then on good terms, owing to a former difficulty between them. It was conceded that an attachment would lie for preventing or obstructing the attendance of a witness before the court, but denied that there could be any contempt in compelling a witness to come, in obedience to his summons, however illegal the means employed. If General Wilkinson had resorted to illegal means to compel the attendance of the witness, he might have his action against him; but it could not constitute a ground of contempt. It was also contended that the acts complained of were committed, if at all, without the jurisdiction of the court, and therefore could not be inquired into in this proceeding.

On Saturday, the 27th of June, Chief Justice Marshall, delivered the following opinion upon the motion for an attachment against General Wilkinson, which is here inserted out of its chronological order, to preserve the continuity of the subject:

The motion now under consideration was heard at this time, because it was alleged to be founded on a fact which might affect the justice of the case in which the court is about to be engaged, and because, while the bills were depending before the grand jury, the court might, without impending the progress of the business, examine into the complaint which has been made.

The motion is to attach General Wilkinson for a contempt of this court, by obstructing the fair course of justice, with regard to a prosecution depending before it. In support of this charge had been offered the testimony of Mr. Knox, who states a conversation between General Wilkinson and himself, obvious to his being served with a subpoena, the object of which was to extract from him whatever information he might possess, respecting the expedition which was the subject of inquiry in this court; and who states also, that he was afterwards summoned before Judge Hall, who examined him upon interrogatories, and committed him to gaol, whence he was taken by order of the deputy marshal, who was a military as well as civil officer, and put on board the Revenge, in which General Wilkinson sailed, for the purpose of being brought from New Orleans to Richmond.

That unfair practices towards a witness who was to give testimony in this court, or oppression under color of its process, although those practices and that oppression were acted in another district, would be punishable in the mode now suggested, provided the person who had acted therein came within the jurisdiction of the court, is a position which the court is not disposed to controvert; but it is also believed that this mode of punishment ought not to be adopted, unless the deviation from law could be clearly attached to the person against whom the motion was made, and unless the deviation were intentional, or unless the course of judicial proceeding were or might be so affected by it as to make a punishment in this mode obviously conducive to a fair and correct administration of justice.

The conversation which took place between General Wilkinson and the witness, on the arrival of the latter in New Orleans, was manifestly held with the intention of drawing from him any information which he might possess relative to the expedition which was then the subject of inquiry. In this intention there was nothing unlawful. Government, and those who represent it, may justifiably and laudably use means to obtain voluntary communications, provided those means be not such as might tempt the person making them to give an improper coloring to his representations, which might afterwards adhere to them when repeated in court. The address stated to have been employed, the condescension and regard with which the witness was treated, are not said by himself to have been accompanied with any indications of a desire to draw from him more than the truth. The offer of money, if with a view to corrupt, could not be too severely reprehended. It is certainly a dangerous species of communication between those who are searching for testimony, and the person from whom it is expected. But in this case the court cannot contemplate the offer as being made with immoral views. The witness had a right to demand from those he was expected to serve a small sum of money, sufficient to subsist him on his return to his home. He was asked whether, on receiving this sum, his objections to giving testimony would be removed. This was certainly a delicate question, but it might be asked without improper motives, and it was pressed no further. This is not shown to be an attempt to contaminate the source of justice, and a consequent contempt of the court in which it is administered.

The imprisonment of Mr. Knox, and the order for conveying him from New Orleans to Richmond, were the acts of Judge Hall. Whether his proceedings were legal or illegal, they are not shown to have been influenced by General Wilkinson, and this court cannot presume such to have been the fact; General Wilkinson, therefore, is not responsible for them. They were founded, it is true, on an affidavit made by him; but there was no impropriety in making this affidavit, and it remained with the judge to decide what the law would authorize in the case.

All the subsequent proceedings were directed by the civil authority. The agents who executed the orders of the judge were indeed military men, who most probably would not have disobeyed the commander-in-chief; but that officer is not responsible, in this way, for having failed to interpose his authority, in order to prevent the execution of the orders of the judge, even if those orders ought not to have been given.

Upon a full view of the subject, the case appears to have been this: General Wilkinson was desirous that the testimony of the witness should be obtained; and aware of the accusations which had before been brought against him for the use he had made of the military power, he was desirous of obtaining the testimony by lawful means, and therefore referred the subject to a judge of the territory, under whose orders all subsequent proceedings were taken. Whether the judge did or did not transcend the limits prescribed by law, those ministerial officers who obeyed his orders cannot be supposed to have acted with a knowledge that he had mistaken his power. Should it be admitted that this would be no defence for them in an action to obtain compensation for the injury, yet it furnishes sufficient evidence that no contempt was intended to this court by General Wilkinson, that he has not been guilty of any intentional abuse of its process, or of any oppression in the manner of executing it.

It is said that Captain Gaines, the gentleman who the marshal appointed as his deputy for this particular purpose, had not taken the oath of office, and was therefore not legally qualified to act in that character. However correct this observation may be in itself, it does not appear to the court to justify an attachment against General Wilkinson. The person who sees in the possession of another a commission as deputy marshal, and sees that others are acting under that commission, ought not to be subjected to a process of contempt for having made no inquiries respecting the oath which the law requires to be taken.

The attachment will not be awarded, because General Wilkinson cannot be considered as having controlled or influenced the conduct of the civil magistrate, and because in this transaction his intention appears to have been not to violate the laws. In such a case, where an attachment does not seem to be absolutely required by the justice due to the particular individual against whom the prosecution is depending, the court is more inclined to leave the parties to the ordinary course of law, than to employ the extraordinary powers which are given for the purpose of preserving the administration of justice in that purity which ought to be so universally desired.

On Wednesday, the 24th of June, while Mr. Botts was speaking on the motion for an attachment, the grand jury entered, when Mr. John Randolph, their foreman, addressed the court, and stated that they had agreed upon several indictments, which he handed in at the clerk's table. The clerk then read the endorsements upon them as follows:

"An indictment against Aaron Burr for treason. A true bill."

"An indictment against Aaron Burr for a misdemeanor. A true bill."

"An indictment against Herman Blannerhasset* for treason. A true bill."

"An indictment against Herman Blannerhasset* for a misdemeanor. A true bill."

The foreman then stated that the grand jury had still other subjects for their consideration, and had adjourned themselves to meet to-morrow at ten o'clock.

After Mr. Botts had concluded his argument,

Mr. Burr addressed the court, and observed that as bills had been found against him, it was probable the public prosecutors would move his commitment. He would, however, suggest two ideas for the consideration of the court: the one was, that it was within their discretion to bail in certain cases, even when the punishment was death; and the other was, that it was expedient for the court to exercise their discretion in this instance, as he should prove that the indictment against him had been obtained by perjury.

*So in the indictment. The correct spelling is "Harman Blennerhassett."

Mr. Hay moved for the commitment of Aaron Burr. He stated that if the court had power to bail by the 33rd section of the judicial act, it was only to be exercised according to their sound discretion, and that the prisoner was not to demand bail as a matter of right.

Mr. Martin said the counsel for the prosecution had admitted the right of the court to give bail according to its discretion.

Mr. MacRae did not understand from the judicial act that the discretion was to be exercised at this stage of the business, but only at the time of making the arrest.

After some further remarks by Messrs, Martin, Wirt, and Wickham,

The Chief Justice said: Mr. Martin, have you any precedents where a court has bailed for treason, after the finding of a grand jury, on either of these grounds; that the testimony laid before the grand jury had been impeached for perjury, or that other testimony had been laid before the court, which had not been in possession of the grand jury?

Mr. Martin said that he had not anticipated this case, and had not, therefore, prepared his authorities; but he had no doubt that such existed.

Mr. Burr said, if the court have no discretion, it is unnecessary to produce evidence. That question ought, therefore, to be previously settled.

Some further discussion ensued, as to the question whether the court had any discretion, when

Mr. Burr said, that if the court thought it had the power to bail in any case after bill found, it would then be necessary to show that it ought to exercise its discretion in this instance. That the finding of the jury was founded on the testimony of a perjured witness. That General Tupper would prove that there had been no such resistance of his authority as had been stated by that witness.

After some further conversation between counsel,

Mr. Burr wished to know whether the court would go into testimony extrinsic to the indictment.

The Chief Justice said he had never known a case similar to the present when such an examination had taken place.*

Mr. Martin would produce authorities if he had time allowed him.

The Chief Justice insisted upon the necessity of producing adjudged cases to prove that the court could bail a party against whom an indictment had been found.

Mr. Burr did not wish to protract the session of the court to suit his own personal convenience. There was no time at present to look for authorities.

The Chief Justice observed that he was then under the necessity of committing Colonel Burr.

Mr. Burr stated that he was willing to be committed, but hoped that the court had not forestalled its opinion.

CHIEF JUSTICE.—I have only stated my present impression. This subject is open for argument hereafter. Mr. Burr stands committed to the custody of the marshal.

He was accordingly committed to the gaol, and the court adjourned.

On Thursday, the 25th of June, while Mr. Hay was addressing the court on the motion for an attachment against General Wilkinson, the grand jury entered, and their foreman, Mr. John Randolph, addressed the court as follows:

May it please the court:

The grand jury have been informed that there is in the possession of Aaron Burr a certain letter, with the post mark of May 13th from James Wilkinson, in ciphers, which they deem to be material to certain inquiries now pending before them. The grand jury are perfectly aware that they have no right to demand any evidence from the prisoner under prosecution which may tend to criminate himself. But the grand jury have thought proper to appear in court to ask its assistance, if it think proper to grant it, to obtain the letter with his consent.

Mr. Burr rose and asked whether the court were about to give an opinion?

The Chief Justice stated that the court was about to say

---

*The court will in no instance inquire into the character of the testimony which has influenced the grand jury in finding an indictment. The State vs. Boyd, 2 Hill's S.C. Rep.

that the grand jury were perfectly right in the opinion, that no man can be forced to furnish evidence against himself; he presumed that the grand jury wished also to know whether the person under prosecution could be examined on other questions not criminating himself?

Mr. Burr declared that it would be impossible for him, under certain circumstances, to expose any letter which had been communicated to him confidentially; how far the extremity of circumstances might compel him to such a conduct, he was not prepared to decide; but it was impossible for him even to deliberate on the proposition to deliver up anything which had been confided to his honor, unless it was extorted from him by law.

MR. RANDOLPH.—We will withdraw to our chamber, and when the court had decided upon the question it will announce it to the grand jury.

The Chief Justice knew not that there was any objection to the grand jury calling before them and examining any man as a witness who laid under an indictment.

Mr. Martin said there could be no objection.

Mr. Randolph said he was afraid that the object of the grand jury had been misunderstood by the court. The grand jury had not appeared before the court to apply for the person of Aaron Burr, to obtain evidence from him, but for a certain paper which might or might not be in his possession; and upon that paper being or not being in his possession, and upon its being possible or not possible to identify that paper, it might depend whether Aaron Burr himself were or were not a material evidence before them; and then the grand jury withdrew.

When Mr. Hay had concluded his argument, Mr. MacRae addressed the court. He was solicitous he said, to lay a communication before it, or a circumstance which had lately transpired. The grand jury had asked for a certain letter in ciphers, which was supposed to have been addressed by General Wilkinson to the accused. The court had understood the ground on which the accused had refused to put it in their possession, to be an apprehension lest his honor should be wounded by his thus betraying matters of confidence. I have seen General Wilkinson, sir, since this declaration was made. I have informed him of the communication which has thus been made, and the General has expressed his wishes to me, and requested me to express those wishes, that the whole of the correspondence between Aaron Burr and himself may be exhibited before the court. The accused has now, therefore, a fair, opportunity of producing this letter; he is absolved from all possible imputation; his honor is perfectly safe.

MR. BURR.—The court will probably expect from me some reply. The communication which I made to the court, has led, it seems, to the present invitation. I have only to say, sir, that this letter will not be produced. The letter is not at this time in my possession, and General Wilkinson knows it.

Mr. MacRae hoped that notice of his communication would be sent to the grand jury.

Mr. Martin hoped that Colonel Burr's communication also would go along with it.

The Chief Justice was unwilling to make the court the medium of such communications.

Mr. MacRae hoped the Court would notify his communication to the grand jury, and for an obvious reason. When the grand jury came into court to ask for the paper, what did the accused say? Did he declare that it was not in his possession? No: he merely said that honor forbade him to disclose it. The inference undoubtedly was, that he had the paper, but could not persuade himself to disclose it. And what then must have been the impression of the grand jury? A cloud of suspicion must have fastened itself upon their minds; suspicion unjustly injurious to the character of General Wilkinson and which the present communication may at once disperse. It is but justice, therefore, to General Wilkinson, to whom the injuries of the grand jury may at present relate, to give them the benefit of this information.

MR. BURR.—General Wilkinson, sir, is extremely welcome to all the *eclat* which he may expect to derive from this challenge; but as it is a challenge from him, it is a sufficient reason why I should not accept it. But as the remarks of the last gentleman seem to convey some reproach against me, (which no man who knows me can believe me to deserve) it may be proper to say, that I did voluntarily, and in the presence of a witness, put the letter out of my hands, with the express view that it should not be used improperly against any one. I wished, sir, to disable any person, even myself, from laying it before the grand jury. General Wilkinson knows this fact.

The Chief Justice then reduced these communications to writing, and transmitted them to the grand jury.

MR. BURR.—Let it be understood, that I did not put this letter out of my possession because I expected the grand jury would take up this subject but from a supposition that they might do so.

Mr. Wickham, about to speak, was interrupted by the entrance of the grand jury when Mr. Randolph, their foreman, informed the court that they had agreed upon some presentments, which he then delivered into the hands of the clerk. The clerk read as follows:

The grand inquest of the United States, for the district of Virginia upon their oaths, present, that Jonathan Dayton late a Senator in the Congress of the United States, from the State of New Jersey; John Smith, a Senator in the Congress of the United States, from the State of Ohio; Comfort Tyler, late of the State of New York; Israel Smith, late of the State of New York; and Davis Floyd, late of the Territory of Indiana, are guilty of treason against the United States, in levying war against the same, to wit: at Blennerhassett's island, in the county of Wood, and State of Virginia, on the 13th day of December, 1806.

FRIDAY, JUNE 26, 1807

The court met about nine o'clock, and about ten o'clock, the grand jury entered, and Mr. Randolph, their foreman, presented ten indictments, found true bills; that is one indictment for treason, and another for a misdemeanor, against each of the following, individuals, viz: Jonathan Dayton, John Smith, Comfort Tyler, Israel Smith, and Davis Floyd.

The Chief Justice then made a short address to the grand jury, in which he complimented them upon the great patience and cheerful attention which they had performed the arduous and laborious duties in which they had been so long engaged, and concluded, by discharging them from all further attendance.

The court then adjourned till twelve o'clock. As soon as it met again,

Mr. Botts requested the court to remove Mr. Burr from the public gaol, to some comfortable and convenient place of confinement. He depicted, in very strong terms, the miserable state of the prison where he was then confined. The grounds of this motion are to be found in the following affidavit made by some of Mr. Burr's councel [sic], and laid before the court:

> We, who are counsel in the defence of Colonel Burr, at the suit of the United States, beg leave to represent to the court, that in pursuance of our duty to him, we have visited him in his confinement in the city gaol: that we could not avoid remarking the danger, which will most probably result to his health, from the situation, inconveniences and circumstances attending the place of his confinement; but we cannot forbear to declare our conviction, that we ourselves cannot freely and fully perform what we have undertaken for his defence, if he remain in the gaol aforesaid, deprived, as he is of a room to himself, in being scarcely possible for us to consult with him upon the various necessary occasions which must occur, from all which we believe that he will be deprived of that assistance from councel, which is given to him by the Constitution of the United States unless he be removed.
>
> EDMUND RANDOLPH,
JOHN WICKHAM,
BENJAMIN BOTTS.
>
> Sworn to in open court, by Edmund Randolph, John Wickham, and Benjamin Botts, Esquires. June 25th, 1807
>
> William Marshall, Clerk.

The counsel for the prosecution were perfectly silent on the motion.

After a long and desultory argument by Mr. Burr's counsel, the court determined that the prisoner should be removed to his former lodgings near the capitol, provided they could be made sufficiently strong for his safe keeping, being of opinion that the act of Congress authorized it, on the foregoing affidavit, to make the order of removal.

Mr. Latrobe, surveyor of the public buildings of the United States, was requested to inspect them; and upon his report the court passed the following order:

Whereupon, it is ordered, that the marshal of this district do cause the front room of the house now occupied by Luther Martin, Esq., which room has been and is used as a dining room, to be prepared for the reception and safe keeping of Colonel Aaron Burr, by securing the shutters to the windows of the said room by bars, and the door by a strong bar or padlock. And that he employ a guard of seven men to be placed on the floor of the adjoining unfinished house, and on the same story with the before described front room, and also at the door opening into the said front room; and upon the marshal's reporting to the court that the said room had been so fitted up and the guard employed, that then the said marshal be directed, and he is hereby directed, to remove to the said room, the body of the said Aaron Burr from the public gaol, there to be by him safely kept.

MR. HAY.—My only wish is, that this prosecution should be regularly conducted. Is it not the usual practice to read the indictment first and then move for the venire?

MR. BURR.—I have been furnished with a copy of the indictment; I have perused it and I am ready to plead not guilty to it.

MR. WIRT.—The usual form requires the actual arraignment of the prisoner; however, the court may dispense with it, if it think proper.

Mr. Hay was indifferent about the form, if the law could be substantially executed. He supposed that a simple acknowledgment of the prisoner was sufficient, without the customary form of holding up his hand.

CHIEF JUSTICE.—It is enough, if he appear to the indictment, and plead not guilty.

The clerk then read the indictment against Aaron Burr, for treason against the United States; which specifies the place of the overt act to be at Blennerhasset's island; and the time, the 10th day of December, 1806.

When he had concluded, Mr. Burr addressed the court: "I

acknowledge myself to be the person named in the indictment: I plead not guilty; and put myself upon my country for trial."

Mr. Hay then addressed the court on the venire that was to try the issue between the prisoner and the United States. He expressed some doubt whether the 29th section of the act of Congress called the judicial act, was still in force, which required twelve jurors, at least, to be summoned from the county where the offence was committed. If this law was still in force, it would be necessary to summon twelve petit jurors from the county of Wood, which would render it impossible to have the trial at an early day.

The Chief Justice said he had no doubt the law was still in force.

Mr. Burr said as this law was most probably intended for the benefit of the accused, he consented to waive the right.

Mr. Wirt suggested a doubt whether consent in such a case could take away error.

The Chief Justice believed that the provision was not absolutely obligatory, if both parties would waive the right.

Mr. Hay said he felt no disposition to delay the trial; but he could not think of pledging himself to such a measure without due deliberation. He would consult the gentlemen associated with him, and inform the court of the result.

The counsel for the prosecution then retired to consult. On their return, Mr. Hay informed the court that they could not assume the responsibility of consenting to such a proposition, as the law seemed imperative. He must therefore request the court to direct a venire of twelve men, at least, to be summoned from Wood county.

A long conversation ensued as to the time that would be necessary to summon the venire from Wood county, as it would be necessary to postpone the trial accordingly; opinions varying from twenty to thirty-five days.

The court made an order for a venire of forty-eight jurors, twelve of whom, at least, were to be summoned from Wood county.

Without fixing the time for the trial, the court adjourned.

On Saturday, the 27th of June, an order was made postponing the trial to the third day of August, and for the return of the venire on that day.

MONDAY, JUNE 29, 1807

Mr. Hay laid the following order of the executive council before the court:

In Council, JUNE 29, 1807

The board being informed that an affidavit has been filed in the circuit court of the United States, for the Virginia district, which states that the gaol for the county of Henrico and city of Richmond is inconvenient and unhealthy, and so crowded with state offenders and debtors that there are no private apartments therein for the reception of persons charged with offences against the laws of the United States, it is therefore advised that the Governor be requested to tender the said court, (through the Federal attorney of the district of Virginia,) apartments in the third story of the public gaol and penitentiary house for the reception of such persons as shall be directed under the authority of the United States to be confined therein.

Extract from the minutes:

DANIEL L. HYLTON,
Clerk of the Council.

The following was the order of the court on this subject:

"Which tender the court doth accept for the purpose above mentioned."

The final decision of the motion to commit Aaron Burr to the penitentiary was postponed until to-morrow.

TUESDAY, JUNE 30, 1807

After the court met the motion to commit Aaron Burr to the penitentiary was renewed.

It was objected to by his counsel, on the ground (and an affidavit was made by them to the same effect) that in so important a case it was essentially necessary for the most uninterrupted intercourse to subsist between the prisoner and his counsel; but that the distance of the pentitentiary, combined with their own professional avocations, would necessarily narrow and interrupt this intercourse. It was also said that, by particular regulations of the penitentiary, the custody of the prisoner would be transferred from the marshal to the superintendent, and that the communications of the prisoner with his counsel would be limited to the very same short period which was allowed to the other visitants: that is, from eleven to one o'clock.

The attorney for the United States replied to the objections.

The Chief Justice said when there was a public gaol not unreasonably distant or unfit for the reception of the prisoner, and when the court was called upon on the part of the United States to commit a prisoner to its keeping; that he conceived himself bound to comply with the requisition; that when he had given the order for his removal from the gaol to his own lodgings, it was under an expectation that the trial would be prosecuted immediately, and that the intercourse between the prisoner and his counsel would be necessarily incessant; but as a postponement had taken place, such an intercourse would not be absolutely necessary; under such circumstances, therefore, he should direct the removal of the prisoner to the penitentiary, if he were still to continue in the possession of the marshal, and if his counsel were to have free and uninterrupted access to him.

Some difficulty having thus occurred on these points, the executive council was immediately convened. In a short time the following letter was submitted to the court:

Council Chamber, June 30, 1807

SIR: In pursuance of an advice of the council of State. I beg leave, through you, to inform the circuit court of the United States, now sitting, that any persons who may be confined in the gaol and penitentiary house, on the part of the United States, will be considered as in the custody, and under the sole control of the marshal of the district; that he will have authority to admit any person or persons to visit the confined that he may think proper, and that he will be authorized to select for the purpose aforesaid, any apartment in the penitentiary now unoccupied, that he may deem most conducive to safety, health, and convenience.

I am, with great respect, sir, your obedient servant,

WM. H. CABELL.

George Hay, Esq.

The court then made the following order:

In consequence of the offer made by the executive of apartments in the third story of the penitentiary and state prison, for persons who may be confined therein, under the authority of the United States, and of the foregoing letter from the Governor of this commonwealth, it is ordered, on the motion of the attorney for the United States, that so soon as the apartments in the third story of the public gaol and penitentiary shall be fit for the reception and safe keeping of Aaron Burr, that he be removed thereto, and safely kept therein by the marshal, until the second day of August next, when he shall be brought back to the prison where he is now placed, there to be guarded in like manner as at present, until the further order of the court.

MONDAY, AUGUST 3, 1807

On this day the circuit court of the United States for the fifth circuit and district of Virginia, was held according to adjournment.

Present, the Chief Justice of the United States:

George Hay, William Wirt, and Alexander MacRae, Esquires, counsel for the prosecution.

The prisoner was brought into court from his apartment, near the Swan tavern, to which he had been removed on Saturday.

Edmund Randolph, John Wickham, Benjamin Botts, John Baker, and Luther Martin, Esquires, appeared as his counsel.

The court assembled at twelve o'clock. An immense concourse of citizens attended to witness the proceedings of this important trial.

Mr. Hay observed that he could take no steps in this business until he had ascertained whether the witnesses summoned on the part of the United States were present; he therefore requested that their names might be called over; they were more than one hundred in number. Their names were accordingly called.

Mr. Hay begged leave to mention that he had nothing more to submit to the court this day. There were many of the witnesses of whose place of residence he was ignorant; several had not appeared; many had been merely pointed out to him by the Attorney General of the United States. He observed that, therefore, he had not yet been able to furnish Colonel Burr with a list of the witnesses, and a statement of the places of their residence, as the law requires; that, as many of those who had been summoned and recognized had failed to appear, he was not ready to proceed with the trial immediately. He also informed the court that a list of the venire had been delivered on Saturday to Colonel Burr, but had since been discovered to be inaccurate. It became, therefore, necessary (an act of Congress having directed this to be done at least three days before the trial) to deliver a correct list on this day; and, of course, the trial would be postponed until the requisite time should have elapsed.

The Chief Justice inquired, then, to what day it would be proper to adjourn the court.

Mr. Hay could not possibly state by what day he should be able to prepare his lists.

Mr. Burr observed that it was not probable that he should avail himself of any privileges to which he might be entitled from any delay in furnishing him with the list of jurors, or of any incorrectness in the list: and therefore the court might adjourn to any day which was convenient to the attorney for the United States. If the day of adjournment depended on his own consent, he should not object to any adjournment, provided it did not extend further than Wednesday.

Mr. Hay had no objection to that day.

At the instance of Mr. Hay the names of the jurors were called, when forty-six answered to their names, two only being absent.

Mr. Burr reminded the court of the motion which he had made, on a former occasion, for a subpoena *duces tecum,* addressed to the President of the United States. That motion had been partly complied with. He wished to know of the court whether it were not a matter of right for him to obtain a subpoena *duces tecum.* If it were not, he should then lay a specific motion before the court.

The Chief Justice did not believe it to be the practice in Virginia to obtain such a subpoena upon a mere application to the clerk. The motion must be brought before the court itself.

Mr. Hay said that he would say nothing on this subject until he understood the object of the application; that if it were to obtain the letter which was not formerly furnished, he would inform the opposite counsel that he had it now among his papers, and was ready to produce it.

MR. BURR.—That is one object of the application. Another is, to obtain a certain communication from General Eaton to the President of the United States, which is mentioned in his deposition.

Mr. Hay said that he was not certain whether he had that communication, but believed that it was among his papers. If it were there, he would certainly produce it.

MR. BURR.—But if, after a search, the gentleman finds that he had not that paper, will he consent, out of court, to issue a subpoena to the President of the United States, under the qualification I have mentioned? I wish not, at the present exigency, to derange the affairs of the Government, or to demand the presence of the executive officers at this place. All that I want are certain papers.

Mr. Hay said that he could not consent to it; he would rather that a regular application should be made for it to the court.

MR. BURR.—Then, sir, I shall move for a subpoena *duces tecum,* to the President of the United States, directing him to attend with certain papers. This subpoena will issue as in the former instance. I shall furnish the clerk with the necessary specifications of the paper which I require.

The court was then adjourned till Wednesday, twelve o'clock.

WEDNESDAY, AUGUST 5, 1807

The court met, according to adjournment. Present, John Marshall, Chief Justice of the United States.

The names of the witnesses being called over, and many being still absent, Mr. Hay was not ready to proceed. He presumed all of the witnesses would be present in a few days.

After some conversation as to the time to which the court should adjourn,

Mr. Hay proposed an arrangement as to the mode of conducting the trial, in respect to the order in which counsel should speak.

The Chief Justice said the best mode appeared to him to be this: that the case should be opened fully by one of the gentlemen on the part of the United States; then opened fully by one of the counsel on the other side; that the evidence should be next gone through, and the whole commented upon by another of the gentlemen employed by the United States, who should be answered by the rest of the counsel for Colonel Burr; and only one of the counsel for the United States should conclude the argument.

Without coming to any arrangement, the court adjourned till Friday, twelve o'clock.

FRIDAY, AUGUST 7, 1807

The court met according to adjournment.

Present, John Marshall, Chief Justice of the United States, and Cyrus Griffin, Judge of the District of Virginia.

The witnesses were again called over, and several who had not been present before, appeared, and were recognized to attend until discharged by the court.

The counsel for the United States, however, not being as well prepared to go into the trial as they expected to be, (many of their witnesses being still absent,) the trial was farther postponed, and the court adjourned until Monday next, at twelve o'clock.

In the course of this day, a difficulty was suggested by Major

Scott, the Marshal of the Virginia District, as arising out of the order of the court, by virtue of which Colonel Burr had been removed from the penitentiary house to his present lodgings. He stated that he had been informed from good authority, that the Secretary of the Treasury had declared that he would not allow his charge of seven dollars per day, for the guards employed for the safe-keeping of the prisoner; and, therefore, he might lose that sum, which he had hitherto been advancing out of his own pocket.

The Chief Justice declared the firm conviction of the court, that the order, heretofore made, was legal and proper: that the payments made in pursuance thereof would be sanctioned by the court, and ought to be allowed by the Secretary of the Treasury. He could not believe that the Secretary would finally disallow those items in the marshal's account. But, as the officer of the court ought not to be subjected to any risk in obeying its directions, and if the Secretary should refuse to allow him a credit for the money paid, the court had no power to compel him to do so, and the situation of the marshal was such that he dared not enter into a controversy with the Secretary; the court was disposed to rescind the order, unless some arrangement could be made by Colonel Burr and his counsel, for the indemnification of the marshal.

Colonel Burr declared that an offer had already been made on his part to indemnify the marshal, and that he was still ready and willing to give him satisfactory security that the money should be paid him, in case the Secretary of the Treasury should refuse to allow the credit.

Some desultory conversation ensued, but nothing positive was agreed upon; but it appeared to be understood that security was to be given to Major Scott, and that Colonel Burr was to remain in his apartment near the Swan Tavern.

MONDAY, AUGUST 10, 1807

The court met pursuant to adjournment.

Harman Blennerhassett was brought into court, and Mr. Hay moved that he be arraigned for treason. Mr. Botts objected, on the ground that he had not been furnished with a copy of the indictment three days previously; and he was reconducted to his prison.

Four of the venire were excused on account of indisposition. The clerk informed Mr. Burr that he was at liberty to challenge such of the venire as he might object to.

Mr. Burr begged leave to inform the jurors, who were within hearing, that a great number of them may have formed and expressed opinions about him which might disqualify them from serving on this occasion. He expected that, as they came up, they would discharge the duties of conscientious men, and candidly answer the questions put to them, and state all their objections against him.

The deputy marshal then summoned first, Hezekiah Bucky.

MR. BOTTS.—We challenge you for cause. Have you ever formed and expressed an opinion about the guilt of Colonel Burr?

MR. BUCKY.—I have not sir, since I have been subpoened.

Question. Had you before?

Answer. I had formed one before in my own mind.

Mr. Hay wished that the question of the opposite counsel could assume a more precise and definite form. If this question were proposed to this man, and to every other man of the panel, he would venture to predict that there could not be a jury selected in the State of Virginia, because he did not believe that there was a single man in the State, qualified to become a juryman, who had not, in some form or other, made up, and declared an opinion on the conduct of the prisoner. The transaction in the West had excited universal curiosity; and there was no man who had not seen and decided on the documents relative to them. Do gentlemen contend that in a case so peculiarly interesting to all, the mere declaration of an opinion is sufficient to disqualify a juryman? A doctrine of this sort would at once acquit the prisoner; for where is the jury that could try him? Such a doctrine amounts to this: that a man need only to do enough to draw down the public attention upon him, and he would immediately effect his discharge. Mr. Hay concluded with a hope that the question would assume a more definitive form; he should not pretend to decide the form in which it should be proposed, for that was the province of the court; it was a privilege to which every court is entitled, and one which the court had exercised in the case of James T. Callender.

Mr. Botts considered it as a misfortune ever to be deplored, that in this country, and in this case, there had been too general an expression of the public sentiment, and that this generality of opinion would disqualify many, but he had never entertained a doubt, until the gentleman for the prosecution had avowed it, that twelve men might be found in Virginia, capable of deciding this question with the strictest impartiality. He still trusted that the attorney for the United States was mistaken, that the catastrophe was not completely fixed, and that every man in the State had not pledged himself to convict Colonel Burr whether right or wrong. He was not present at the trial of James T. Callender; but all America had heard the question which was then propounded to the juryman, and that was, whether he had made up and expressed an opinion respecting the guilt of the prisoner.

Mr. Hay said that he would put Mr. Botts right as to matter of fact. The court would recollect that on the trial of Callender, the question was, not whether the jurymen had formed and expressed an opinion on that case generally, but on the subject matter that was to be tried, and contained in the indictment. The question then in the present case should be, have you formed and expressed an opinion on the point at issue; that is, whether Aaron Burr be guilty of treason? On the trial of Callender, the court would particularly recollect that Mr. John Bassett having objected to himself, because he had read the libellous publication, was actually overruled, because it was not on the book itself, but on the subject-matter of the indictment, that he was called upon to say whether he had ever expressed an opinion?

Mr. Burr declared that there was a material distinction between that and the present case. Mr. Bassett's acknowledging that he had seen the book did not disqualify him from serving on the jury; in the same manner the person who had seen a murder committed would not be an incompetent juror in the prosecution for that crime. But if a man pretended to decide upon the guilt of a prisoner, upon mere rumor, he would manifest such a levity and bias of mind as would effectually disqualify him. Mr. Bucky, however, had not yet come out completely with his declarations. Let him be further interrogated.

Mr. Hay observed that the question would still be too general and vague, if it were even to be "Have you expressed any opinion on the treason of Aaron Burr?" for the case stated in the indictment was infinitely more specific. It was treason in levying war against the United States at Blennerhassett's island. Unless this particular allegation be proved, it defeats all the other parts of the accusation; and it was probably on this point that the juror had never made up any opinion.

Mr. Martin contended that it was the duty of every juryman to come to the trial of any case with the most perfect impartiality, and more particularly one where life and reputation were at stake; that it was a libel upon Virginia a blot upon the whole State, to assert, that twelve men could not be found to decide such a case, with no other knowledge than what they had picked up from newspapers; that there was a material distinction between this and Callender's case; the libel was a book in every man's hand, but does any juryman in the present case pretend to know the testimony on which this charge depends? The gentleman proposes to ask the juryman whether he has made up an opinion on Colonel Burr's treason? But it is extremely probable that most of them know not what treason is; and though they may decide upon the guilt of Colonel Burr, they may be ignorant whether it come under the name and description of treason.

The Chief Justice observed that it might save some altercation if the court were to deliver its opinion at the present time; that it was certainly one of the clearest principles of natural justice, that a juryman should come to a trial of a man for life with a perfect freedom from previous impressions, that it was clearly the duty of the court to obtain, if possible, men free from such bias; but that if it were not possible from the very circumstances of the case—if rumors had reached and prepossessed their judgments, still the court was bound to obtain as large a portion of impartiality as possible, that this was not more a principle of natural justice, than a maxim of the common law, which we have inherited from our forefathers, that the same right was secured by the Constitution of the United States, which entitles every man under a criminal prosecution, to a fair trial by "an impartial jury?" Can it be said, however, that any man is an impartial juryman who has declared the prisoner to be guilty and to have deserved punishment? If it be said that he has made up this opinion, but has not heard the testimony, such an excuse only makes the case worse; for if the man has decided upon insufficient testimony, it manifests a bias that completely disqualifies himself from the functions of a juryman. It is too general a question to ask, whether he has any impression about Colonel Burr. The impressions may be so light that they do not amount to an opinion of guilt, nor do they go to the extent of believing that the prisoner deserves capital punishment. With respect to Mr. Bassett's opinion, it was true he had read "The Prospect before Us"; and he had declared that it was a libel, but Mr. Bassett had formed no opinion about James T. Callender's being the author. It was the same principle in the present case. If a juryman were to declare that the attempt to achieve the dismemberment of the Union, was treason, it would not be a complete objection or disqualification; but it would be the application of that crime to a particular individual; it would be the fixing it on Aaron Burr that would disable him from serving in this case. Let the counsel then proceed with the inquiry.

MR. BOTTS.—Have you said that Colonel Burr was guilty of treason?

MR. BUCKY.—No. I only declared that the man who acted as Colonel Burr was said to have done, deserved to be hung.

Question. Did you believe that Colonel Burr was that man?

Answer. I did, from what I had heard.

MR. HAY.—I understand then, that the question proposed in Callender's case is to be overruled?

CHIEF JUSTICE.—My brother, Judge Griffin, does not recollect whether it particularly went to the indictment or not.

JUDGE GRIFFIN.—I think the question was, "relative to the matter in issue."

MR. HAY.—The very position that I have laid down.

CHIEF JUSTICE.—The simple question is, whether the

having formed an opinion, not upon the evidence in court, but upon common rumor, renders a man incompetent to decide upon the real testimony of the case?

MR. WIRT (addressing Mr. Bucky).—Did I understand you to say that you concluded upon certain rumors you had heard, that Colonel Burr deserved to be hung?

MR. BUCKY.—I did.

Question. Did you believe these rumors? *Answer.* I did.

Question. Would you, if you were a juryman, form your opinion upon such rumors? *Answer.* Certainly not.

MR. MACRAE.—Did you form and express your opinion upon the question whether an overt act of treason had been committed at Blennerhassett's island?

Answer. It was upon other rumors, and not upon that, that I had formed an opinion.

MR. MARTIN submitted it to the court, whether he could be considered an impartial juryman.

The court decided that he ought not to be so considered, and he was accordingly rejected.

James G. Laidly stated that he had formed and expressed some opinion unfavorable to Colonel Burr; that he could not pretend to decide upon the charges in the indictment, which he had not heard; that he had principally taken his opinions from newspaper statements; and that he had not, as far as he recollected, expressed an opinion that Colonel Burr deserved hanging; but that his impression was, that he was guilty. He was therefore set aside.

James Compton being challenged for cause and sworn, stated that he had formed and expressed an opinion from hearsay that Colonel Burr was guilty of treason, and of that particular treason of which he stood charged, as far as he understood. He was rejected.

Mr. Burr observed, that as gentlemen on the part of the prosecution had expressed a willingness to have an impartial jury, they could not refuse that any juryman should state all his objections to himself; and that he had no doubt, in spite of the contrary assertions which had been made, that they could get a jury from this panel.

Hamilton Morrison, upon being called, said that he had frequently thought and declared that Colonel Burr was guilty, if the statements which he had heard were true; that he did not know whether they were so, but only thought, from the great clamor which had been made, that it might be possible that they were true; that he had not passed any positive opinion, nor was he certain that he had always qualified it by saying, "if these things were true"; that he does not recollect to have said that Colonel Burr ought to be punished, without stating at the same time, "if he were guilty." Mr. Morrison was suspended for further examination.

Yates S. Conwell had formed and expressed an opinion, from the reports he had heard, that Colonel Burr must be guilty of high treason. He was accordingly set aside.

Jacob Beeson declared that he had for some time past formed an opinion as well from newspaper publications as from the boats which had been built on the Ohio that Colonel Burr was guilty; and that he himself had borne arms to suppress this insurrection. He was therefore set aside as incompetent.

William Prince declared he had merely the same impression as Mr. Beeson; that he too had borne arms, as well on Blennerhassett's island as on descending the river in search of Blennerhassett. He was set aside in like manner.

Nimrod Saunders declared that he had expressed an opinion previously to his being summoned on the jury, that the prisoner had been guilty of treason. He was therefore set aside as incompetent.

Thomas Creel had no declaration to make, and he was challenged for cause. Upon being interrogated, he stated that he had never asserted that the prisoner ought to be punished; that he had said that he was a sensible man, and if there were any hole left he would creep out of it; that he had conceived that Colonel Burr had seduced Blennerhassett into some acts that were not right; that he had never positively said the Colonel Burr was guilty; that he had said that Blennerhassett was the most blamable, because he was in good circumstances and well off in life, whereas Colonel Burr's situation was desperate, and that he had little to lose; that he had not said that Colonel Burr had directly misled Mr. Blennerhassett, but through the medium of Mrs. Blennerhassett; in short, that there was no determinate impression on his mind respecting the guilt of the prisoner.

The Chief Justice did not think that this was sufficient to set him aside, and suspended his case for further examination.

Anthony Buckner had frequently said that the prisoner deserved to be hung. He was therefore set aside.

David Creel had formed an opinion from the statements in the newspapers and if these were true the prisoner was certainly guilty. He had expressed a belief that he was guilty of the charges now brought against him, and that he ought to be hanged. He was therefore rejected.

The above named jurors were all from Wood County.

JURORS FROM THE BODY OF THE DISTRICT

John Horace Upshaw declared that he conceived himself to stand there as an unprejudiced juryman, for he was ready to attend to the evidence; but that as he had formed opinions hostile to the prisoner, (if opinions they can be called which are formed from newspaper testimony,) and had, he believed, frequently expressed them, that he was unwilling to subject himself to the imputation of having prejudged the cause.

MR. BURR.—We challenge Mr. Upshaw for cause.

MR. HAY.—Then sir, I most seriously apprehend that we shall have no jury at all. I solemnly believe Mr. Upshaw is an intelligent and upright man, and can give a correct verdict on the evidence; and I will venture to assert, (whatever credit my friends on the other side will allow to my assertion,) that I myself could do justice to the accused; I believe that any man can who is blessed with a sound judgement and integrity. We might as well enter at once a *nolle prosequi*, if he is to be rejected.

MR. WICKHAM.—Then according to the gentleman's doctrine, any honest man, no matter what his impression may be, is a competent juryman. Is this agreeable to the principles of law? Does the gentleman mean to insinuate that when we object to a juryman it is for his want of honesty? No, sir, every man is subject to partialities and aversions, which may unconsciously sway his judgment. Mr. Upshaw does no doubt deem himself an impartial juryman; but Mr. Upshaw may be deceived.

After some desultory argument between Messrs. Hay and Wickham, Mr. Wirt proceeded to ask Mr. Upshaw whether he had understood him to say that notwithstanding the hostile impressions he had taken up from newspaper reports, these impressions had not received that determinate character which might entitle them to the name of opinions?

Answer: I have received impressions hostile to Colonel Burr, and have expressed them with some warmth, but my impressions have not been induced by anything like evidence. They were predicated on the deposition of General Eaton and the Communications of General Wilkinson, to the President of the United States. I have conceived that the prisoner had been guilty of some criminal act against the public, and ought to be punished; and I believe, also, that I went on further to vindicate the conduct of those gentlemen who would appear as the principal witnesses against him, and also of the government in the measures which it had taken to suppress his plans. After some further and animated discussion on this point, Mr. Upshaw's case was suspended for subsequent examination.

William Pope declared that his impressions were nearly the same with those of the gentleman who had preceded him; that he had thought at first, from newspaper representations, that it was Colonel Burr's intention to make his fortune in the west by the settlement of lands; that when he had afterwards understood that he had formed a union with Wilkinson to proceed to Mexico, he had regarded the prisoner's conduct in such a light that, if he had proceeded to Mexico, he would have considered it as an excusable offence; but when he had afterwards understood that there was treason mixed with his projects, it was impossible for him to view his conduct without the deepest indignation. If these impressions could be called prejudices, he trusted that he should always retain them. What other sentiments could he feel against such a crime, perpetrated against the very best government on the surface of the earth? But Mr. Pope declared that from his heart he believed that he could divest himself of these unfavorable impressions, and give Colonel Burr a fair and honorable trial. He would add that, in pursuance of the spirit manifested by the constitution which required two witnesses to an overt act of treason, he should think it necessary that the evidence for the United States should be so strong as to make the scale preponderate.

MR. WICKHAM.—You will not misunderstand me, Mr. Pope, when I ask you whether you have not been a candidate for your county, and whether you be not now a delegate?

Answer. Yes.

Question. In canvassing among the people, have you not declared that the government had acted properly in commencing this prosecution?

Answer. Yes: I believe I have said generally that I thought Colonel Burr was guilty of high treason. Mr. Pope was therefore set aside.

Peyton Randolph declared that it has never been his wish or intention to shrink from the discharge of a public duty, but that he had peculiar objections to serve on this occasion, one of which only he should state. He had been enrolled and was qualified as a lawyer in this court; and he would submit it to the court whether this did not exempt, if not disqualify him, from serving.

Chief Justice admitted Mr. Randolph's privilege, unless there were an express interposition on the part of the prisoner to retain him and others of the venire who had privileges; for this would call a conflicting privilege into operation.

Mr. Burr said that he should be passive.

John Bowe did not recollect to have said that the prisoner was guilty of treason, but of something hostile to the peace and happiness of the United States. Upon being interrogated, he observed that he was a delegate from the county of Hanover, that there had been a competition at the last election, that he had had occasion to speak at that time of the views of the prisoner, but had always done it cautiously; had never asserted that he ought to be hung, but that he was guilty of something unfriendly to the peace of the United States.

MR. WICKHAM.—You have said that the prisoner was guilty?

Answer. Yes.

CHIEF JUSTICE.—Did you ever make up an opinion about his levying troops and making war against the United States?

Answer. Yes; but I have never expressed it.

MR. BURR.—Take the whole together, and it amounts to an opinion of treason. Mr. Bowe had said that Colonel Burr was guilty; and of what? Of that which in Mr. Bowe's mind amounts to the definition of treason. He was therefore set aside.

John Roberts had thought and declared, from the reports in the public newspapers, that the prisoner was guilty of treason, though he had no doubt that his opinion might be changed by the production of other testimony. He was set aside as incompetent.

Joshua Chaffin excused from indisposition.

Jervis Storrs observed that the state of his mind was like that of the gentleman who had gone before him, (Mr. Bowe); he was in the habit of reading newspapers, and could not but examine their statements relative to those transactions. If he could believe General Eaton's assertion, that the prisoner had threatened to turn Congress out of doors, and assassinate the President, he had said, and would still say, that Colonel Burr was guilty of treason. If General Wilkinson's letter were true, he had surely been guilty of something in the West that was hostile to the interest of the United States. He did not know whether in the multifarious conversations he had had on this subject he had always expressed this opinion of his guilt with that reservation. He had very often communicated his impressions, that he was plotting some hostile designs against the United States. Mr. Storrs confessed that he might be prejudiced against the prisoner, and that he might be judging too highly of his own mind to entertain the belief that he could divest himself of all his impressions; and upon the whole, he expressed a wish not to serve. he was then rejected.

Miles Selden declared that it was impossible not to have entered into the frequent conversations which had occurred on this topic and to have declared some opinion; that he had always said that Colonel Burr was guilty of something, and that if he was guilty of treason against such a government as that of the United States, he would deserve to be hung; that he could not assert that he had always accompanied his opinions with this reservation, but that he was not afraid to trust himself in the rendering of a verdict.

Upon being interrogated, he said that he had frequently jested on the subject, and particularly recollected to have said in a sportive conversation with Colonel Mayo, that this was a Federal plot, and that Burr had been set on by the Federalists. Colonel Selden was therefore suspended for further consideration.

Lewis Truehart had said that if the reports were correct, Colonel Burr had been guilty of something inimical to the country, and that he always qualified his opinions in that manner.

Colonel Tinsley was then called in as a witness, who stated that from a conversation with Mr. Truehart, he thought that he had discovered that he had a general prepossession against Colonel Burr. He did not expect to be called on, and had no very distinct recollection of the particulars; that this was before any of the proceedings of the trial; and when he heard that he was summoned as one of the venire, he then recollected their conversation and happened casually to mention it. Mr. Truehart was suspended.

William Yancey had expressed an opinion on newspaper testimony that Colonel Burr was guilty; that he had frequently said that he would believe the statements of newspapers till the contrary was proved, but that he had no doubt he should entertain a different sentiment, if other testimony were produced. He was set aside.

Thomas Prosser was next called. He said that he had made numberless declarations about Colonel Burr; that he had believed him to be guilty of a treasonable intention, but not of the overt act; on this point he had suspended his opinion, but he was rather inclined to believe that he had not committed it.

MR. MARTIN.—Can this gentleman be considered as an impartial juryman, when he thus comes with his mind made up on one half of the guilt? He was suspended for further consideration.

John Staples had been under the same impressions which had been described by others; that he dared to say that he had said Colonel Burr was guilty of levying troops and making war upon the United States. He was set aside.

Edward C. Stanard acknowledged that his prejudices against

Colonel Burr had been deep-rooted; that he had no doubt of the criminality of his motives, but that he had doubts of the commission of an overt act; he regretted that a man of his talents and energetic mind should be lost to his country. Upon being interrogated, he observed that he had doubts as to the overt act, because he believed him to be a man of such deep intrigue as never to jeopardize his own life till thousands fell before him. He was rejected.

Richard B. Goode was then called.

I have never seen, neither do I believe that I have heard correctly, the evidence in this prosecution. From common report and newspaper information I have formed an opinion unfavorable to Colonel Burr; that opinion has been strengthened by what I have heard from the lips of Colonel Burr in this court; but without arrogating myself more virtue than belongs to other men, if I know myself, I have formed no opinion which cannot be altered by the evidence.

MR. BAKER.—Did you not endeavor to displace Mr. Heth as Captain of the Manchester Cavalry, for becoming the bail of Colonel Burr?

Answer. I never did. (Here sundry witnesses were directed to be called.)

MR. GOODE.—I will state the circumstance to which you allude, unless you prefer to prove it.

THE COURT.—Do so, if you please.

MR. GOODE.—On the 4th of July 1806, I was a member of a committee with Captain Heth, appointed to prepare toasts to be drunk on that day by the Manchester cavalry. I profess to be attached to the present Administration of the General Government, and wished to express such a sentiment. Captain Heth declared that he had no confidence in the executive, and rather than expressed such a sentiment he would resign his commission. At that time, I thought Captain Heth and myself differed only as to measures, and not as to principles; and that it was an honest opinion. But in a few months after, when I understood that Captain Heth had become bail for Colonel Burr, and was his zealous friend, with whom he was neither connected nor acquainted, but a stranger who, three years ago, would have been consigned to the grave by Captain Heth, and those thinking with him upon political subjects, and when I recollected the charge preferred against Colonel Burr, I confess that the declaration and conduct of Captain Heth made such impressions upon my mind, that I refused to trust my person with him as a military commander, and I would do it again.

COLONEL BURR.—Pray, sir, did you not write a letter to Captain Heth?

Answer. I did; and I have reasons to believe that that letter is in your possession, or in the possession of your counsel. You are at liberty to show it to the court, or I will repeat that part of it which relates to Captain Heth and yourself.

THE COURT.—Do sir.

MR. GOODE.—A few weeks past, I received a letter from Captain Heth, commanding me to appear at a certain time and place, in order to take my proper command in the troop. I wrote him, in answer, that my post as a soldier would never be abandoned, and that my duty as a citizen forbade that I should silently approve of the conduct of those who have extended a favor to a traitor, which the justice of my country denied to an unfortunate debtor, or words to that effect.

Mr. Goode was then rejected.

Nathaniel Selden stated he had formed an opinion, particularly from General Eaton's deposition, that the intentions of the prisoner were hostile to the United States, but that he had also said he had seen no evidence to satisfy him that he had been guilty of an overt act. He was suspended for further consideration.

Esme Smock declared that he had formed and expressed an opinion that Colonel Burr had treasonable designs.

CHIEF JUSTICE.—To what time did your opinion relate?

MR. SMOCK.—I have formed my opinion from newspaper publications and common report; but I have constantly conceived that Colonel Burr's intentions were treasonable throughout.

MR. WICKHAM.—Have you ever formed an opinion that Colonel Burr was guilty of treason?

Answer. I have in my own mind. He was set aside.

Richard E. Parker said that he had, like every other person formed an opinion on the case, on newspaper statements, but he had heard very little of the evidence that may be adduced on this occasion. He had declared that if these newspaper statements were true, Colonel Burr had been guilty of some design contrary to the interest and laws of the United States. As to the doctrine of treason, he had not formed a conclusive opinion.

MR. BURR.—I have no objection to Mr. Parker. He is therefore elected.

A desultory argument here ensued about the propriety of swearing one juryman at a time. The counsel for the prosecution opposed, the counsel for the prisoner advocated, the doctrine. The court decided that it would adhere to the practice of Virginia, and swear four jurymen at a time.

John W. Ellis said that he had no doubt that the prisoner had been guilty of having treasonable designs. Whether he had proceeded to acts, he had doubts. He was suspended.

Thomas Starke, without any expectations of being summoned as a juryman, had stated his opinion to his neighbors, who had asked him questions on the subject, that Colonel Burr had been guilty of high treason. He was set aside.

William White stated that he had been in the western country in May last, and from Colonel Burr's character, and from the representations he had received of his conduct, he had been induced to say that he was guilty of treason, and that he ought to be hanged, or that hanging was too good for him. He was set aside.

William B. Chamberlaine stated that he stood in a very peculiar situation, if, as Mr. Wickham declared, any man were unfit to be a juryman who had asserted Colonel Burr to have been worthy of death. He was ready to confess that he himself came under this restriction. He had said uniformly that he had treasonable designs; but he did not now believe that Colonel Burr had committed an overt act of treason, though he believed him to be guilty of the intention. He, however, believed that he could do him justice, and that he could conscientiously pass between him and his country. He was rejected.

David Lambert wished to be excused on account of his indisposition, but the court rejected his plea. On being interrogated, he declared that he did not recollect to have formed an opinion for or against Colonel Burr. He was elected.

William Hoomes had no hesitation in saying that he had often declared his opinion that Colonel Burr was guilty of treasonable intentions, and, perhaps he might say, of treason itself. He had imbibed his impressions from everything he had seen, heard, or read. He had understood that Colonel Burr's counsel had made preparations to prove that he had disqualified himself by his own declarations. He should thank them to develop their objections.

MR. BURR.—I assure you, sir, no such preparation has been made. He was set aside.

Overton Anderson said that he had often expressed an opinion that Colonel Burr's views were inimical to the United States. These opinions he had principally formed upon newspaper statements. He did not recollect that he had ever asserted him to be guilty of treason; but he had sometimes given credit to the representations which he had heard, without particularly defining the degree of guilt in which they might involve the prisoner, and thought him guilty of the charge against him though he would not say it was treason. He was rejected.

Hugh Mercer, upon being called, said that it was his duty to state that an opinion which he had for some time past entertained of the character of Colonel Burr was unfriendly to a strictly impartial inquiry into his case; that he was entirely uninformed as to the testimony which would be introduced, and that he did not recollect to have even expressed a positive opinion either as to his guilt or innocence. He was elected.

Jerman Baker had entertained opinions unfavorable to Aaron Burr, which he had repeatedly expressed. He had spoken them with warmth, for it was his nature to be warm. He had no doubt that the prisoner had formed very unfriendly designs against the United States but, from his ignorance of the evidence, he could not venture to say that they had ripened into an overt act.

MR. BURR.—What opinion have you formed of me?

Answer. A very bad one, which I have expressed often when called upon, and often when not. He was set aside.

Edward Carrington, next called, said that he had formed an unfavorable opinion of the views of Colonel Burr, but these opinions were not definitive. Some had said that Colonel Burr's object was to invade the Spanish territories; others, that it was to dismember the Union. His own opinion had not been definitely fixed. There was another subject connected with this trial on which he had also expressed his opinions, and that related to the measures taken at New Orleans. His own opinion had been that it was impossible for any one at this remote scene to determine upon the state of affairs in that city; but if General Wilkinson did seriously believe what he said had been represented to him as the views of Colonel Burr, that he ought to consider it as an extreme case, and take extreme measures, and act somewhat in the manner that General Wilkinson had done. This has been the state of his mind for twelve months.

MR. BURR.—Have you, Colonel, any prejudice of a more settled kind and ancient date against me?

COLONEL CARRINGTON.—None at all.

MR. BURR.—He is elected.

Mr. Parker said that perhaps he had been misunderstood by the court and Colonel Burr. Perhaps he was disqualified, and he wished to be distinctly understood. He said that he had expressed no deliberate opinion on the subject, yet he had believed that Colonel Burr had some designs contrary to the interests of the United States; that he had formed no opinion of the truth of those depositions, but if they were true his designs were treasonable. Mr. Parker was retained as a juror.

The four jurymen that had been elected were then called to the book and sworn, viz; Messrs. Parker, Lambert, Mercer, and Carrington.

Robert Haskins had expressed an opinion that Colonel Burr was guilty, but does not recollect to what extent he went. He went so far as to say he was guilty of an intention of treason, but not of an overt act. He might have said that he deserved to be hung. He was set aside.

William R. Fleming had formed and frequently expressed an opinion that Colonel Burr was guilty of treasonable intentions, and might have made a general declaration, not only as to intentions but to acts. He was set aside.

George W. Smith suggested a right to the same exemption which had been granted to Mr. P. Randolph. The court said that this privilege would be incontestible unless the prisoner should urge his conflicting privilege. Mr. Burr then requested Mr. Smith to attend to-morrow. Mr. Smith wished to be excused, as he had some important business in another court to attend to. He should, however, attend on the trial to-morrow; but it might now be proper to state the general impressions which he had received from these transactions. He had generally been solicitous to avoid an expression of his opinions; and as in such cases, where the government commences a prosecution against an individual, there is always a preponderance of prejudice against him, he himself had not only been solicitous not to declare, but even not to form an opinion. No one can, however, avoid reading representations of these things in the public papers, and he had formed and declared his impressions that Colonel Burr had entertained designs offensive to the peace and laws of the United States. What was the species of guilt he had not pretended to define, but he had concluded from the newspaper reports and the testimony which he had heard in the other end of the capitol that his designs were of a military nature, and that they might amount at least to a misdemeanor. He was suspended for further consideration.

Armistead T. Mason had formed no deliberate opinion in regard to the actual commission of treason. But it was his deliberate opinion that Colonel Burr had designed, if not to subvert the government, at least to divide the country. He was suspended for further consideration.

Dabney Minor had often said that Colonel Burr's intentions were unfriendly to the United States; he had said that if he were guilty of what was charged against him he ought to be hanged, but had heard no positive testimony.

Some conversation here ensued between Mr. Minor and Mr. Botts, when Mr. Minor was suspended until to-morrow.

Thus, then, of the whole venire that appeared, four only were elected and sworn, and nine were suspended till arguments should be heard on the subject, in order to aid the court to form an opinion whether they were competent jurymen or not.

Here a discussion of considerable length took place on the propriety of confining or not confining, in the custody of the marshal, the jurors already sworn, till the other eight should be sworn.

The court then decided that there was no necessity for delivering the jurymen who had been or should be sworn, into the custody of the marshal, until the whole number had been impaneled and sworn.

Opinion of the Court

Delivered by the Chief Justice Marshall
AUGUST 31, 1807

The question now to be decided has been argued in a manner worthy of its importance, and with an earnestness evincing the strong conviction felt by the counsel on each side that the law is with them.

A degree of eloquence seldom displayed on any occasion has embellished a solidity of argument and a depth of research by which the court has been greatly aided in forming the opinion it is about to deliver.

The testimony adduced on the part of the United States to prove the overt act laid in the indictment having shown, and the attorney for the United States having admitted, that the prisoner was not present when the act, whatever may be its character, was committed, and there being no reason to doubt but that he was at a great distance, and in a different State, it is objected to the testimony offered on the part of the United States to connect him with those who committed the overt act, that such testimony is totally irrelevant, and must, therefore, be rejected.

The arguments in support of this motion respect in part the merits of the case as it may be supposed to stand independent of the pleadings, and in part as exhibited by the pleadings.

On the first division of the subject two points are made:

1st. That, conformably to the Constitution of the United States no man can be convicted of treason who was not present when the war was levied.

2nd. That if this construction be erroneous, no testimony

can be received to charge one man with the overt acts of others until those overt acts as laid in the indictment be proved to the satisfaction of the court.

The question which arises on the construction of the Constitution, in every point of view in which it can be contemplated, is of infinite moment to the people of this country and to their Government, and requires the most temperate and the most deliberate consideration.

"Treason against the United States shall consist only in levying war against them."

What is the natural import of the words "levying war?" and who may be said to levy it? Had their first application to treason been made by our Constitution they would certainly have admitted of some latitude of construction. Taken most literally, they are, perhaps of the same import with the words raising or creating war; but as those who join after the commencement are equally the objects of punishment, there would probably be a general admission that the term also comprehended making war or carrying on war. In the construction which courts would be required to give these words, it is not improbable that those who should raise, create, make, or carry on war, might be comprehended. The various acts which would be considered as coming within the term would be settled by a course of decision; and it would be affirming boldly to say that those only who actually constitute a portion of the military force appearing in arms could be considered as levying war. There is no difficulty in affirming that there must be a war or the crime of levying it cannot exist; but there would often be considerable difficulty in affirming that a particular act did or did not involve the person committing it in the guilt and in the fact of levying war. If, for example, an army should be actually raised for the avowed purpose of carrying an open war against the United States and subverting their government, the point must be weighed very deliberately, before a judge would venture to decide that an overt act of levying war had not been committed by a commissary of purchases, who never saw the army, but who, knowing its object, and leaguing himself with the rebels, supplied the army with provisions, or, by a recruiting officer holding a commission in the rebel service, who, though never in camp, executed the particular duty assigned to him.

But the term is not for the first time applied to treason by the Constitution of the United States. It is a technical term. It is used in a very old statute of that country whose language is our language, and whose laws form the substratum of our laws. It is scarcely conceivable that the term was not employed by the framers of our Constitution in the sense which had been affixed to it by those from whom we borrowed it. So far as the meaning of any terms, particularly terms of art, is completely ascertained, those by whom they are employed must be considered as employing them in that ascertained meaning, unless the country be proved by the contex. It is, therefore, reasonable to suppose, unless it be incompatible with other expressions of the Constitution, that the term "levying war" is used in that instrument in the same sense in which it was understood in England, and in this country, to have been used in the statute of the 25th of Edward III, from which it was borrowed.

1st. That this indictment, having charged the prisoner with levying war on Blennerhassett's island, and containing no other overt act, cannot be supported by proof that was levied at that place by other persons in the absence of the prisoner, even admitting those persons to be connected with him in one common treasonable conspiracy.

2dly. That admitting such an indictment could be supported by such evidence, the previous conviction of some person, who committed the act which is said to amount to levying war, is indispensable to the conviction of a person who advised or procured that act.

As to the first point, the indictment contains two counts, one of which charges that the prisoner, with a number of persons unknown, levied war on Blennerhassett's island, in the county of Wood, in the district of Virginia; and the other adds the circumstance of their proceeding from the island down the river for the purpose of seizing New Orleans by force.

In point of fact, the prisoner was not on Blennerhassett's island, nor in the county of Wood, nor in the district of Virginia.

In considering this point, the court is led first to inquire whether an indictment for levying war must specify an overt act, or would be sufficient if it merely charged the prisoner in general terms with having levied war, omitting the expression of place or circumstance.

The place in which a crime was committed is essential to an indictment, were it only to show the jurisdiction of the court. It is also, essential for the purpose of enabling the prisoner to make his defence. That at common law an indictment would have been defective which did not mention the place in which the crime was committed can scarcely be doubted. For this, it is sufficient to refer to Hawkins, b. 2, ch. 25 sec. 84, and ch. 23, sec. 91. This necessity is rendered the stronger by the constitutional provision that the offender "shall be tried in the State and district wherein the crime shall have been committed" and by the act of Congress which requires that twelve petit jurors at least shall be summoned from the county where the offence was committed.

A description of the particular manner in which the war was levied seems, also, essential to enable the accused to make his defence. The law does not expect a man to be prepared to defend every act of his life which may be suddenly and without notice alleged against him. In common justice, the particular fact with which he is charged ought to be stated, and stated in such a manner as to afford a reasonable certainty of the nature of the accusation and the circumstances which will be adduced against him. The general doctrine on the subject of indictments is full to this point. Foster, p. 149, speaking of the treason of compassing the king's death, says: "From what has been said, it followeth that in every indictment for this species of treason, and, indeed for levying war and adhering to the king's enemies, an overt act must be alleged and proved. For the overt act is the charge to which the prisoner must apply his defence."

On page 220, Foster repeats this declaration. It is, also, laid down in Hawk., b. 8 ch. 17, sec. 29; 1st Hale, 121; 1st East, 116, and by the other authorities cited, especially Vaughn's case. In corroboration of this opinion, it may be observed that treason can only be established by the proof of overt acts, and that by the common law as well as by the statute of 7th of William III, those overt acts only which are charged in the indictment can be given in evidence, unless, perhaps, as corroborative testimony after the overt acts are proved. That clause in the Constitution, too, which says that in all criminal prosecutions the accused shall enjoy the right "to be informed of the nature and cause of the accusation," is considered as having a direct bearing on this point. It secures to him such information as will enable him to prepare for his defence.

It seems, then, to be perfectly clear that it would not be sufficient for an indictment to allege generally that the accused had levied war against the United States. The charge must be more particularly specified by laying what is termed an overt act of levying war. The law relative to an appeal as cited from Stamford, is strongly corroborative of this opinion.

If it be necessary to specify the charge in the indictment, it would seem to follow, irresistibly, that the charge must be proved as laid.

All the authorities which require an overt act, require also that this overt act should be proved. The decision in Vaughn's case is particularly in point. Might it be otherwise, the charge of an overt act would be a mischief instead of an advantage to the accused. It would lead him from the true cause and nature of the accusation, instead of informing him respecting it.

But it is contended on the part of the prosecution that, although the accused had never been with the party which assembled at Blennerhassett's island, and was, at that time, at a great distance, and in a different State, he was yet legally present, and, therefore, may properly be charged in the indictment as being present in fact.

It is, therefore, necessary to inquire whether in this case the doctrine of constructive presence can apply.

It is conceived by the court to be possible that a person may be concerned in a treasonable conspiracy, and yet be legally as well as actually absent while some one act of the treason is perpetrated. If a rebellion should be so extensive as to spread through every State in the Union, it will scarcely be contended that every individual concerned in it is legally present at every overt act committed in the course, of that rebellion. It would be a very violent presumption indeed, too violent to be made with out clear authority, to presume that even the chief of the rebel army was legally present at every such overt act. If the main rebel army, with the chief at its head, should be prosecuting war at one extremity of our territory, say in New Hampshire; if this chief should be there captured and sent to the other extremity for the purpose of trial; if his indictment, instead of alleging an overt act which was true in point of fact, should allege that he had assembled some small party which in truth he had not seen, and had levied war by engaging in a skirmish in Georgia at a time when, in reality, he was fighting a battle in New Hampshire; if such evidence would support such an indictment by the fiction that he was legally present, though really absent, all would ask to what purpose are those provisions in the Constitution, which direct the place of trial and ordain that the accused shall be informed of the nature and cause of the accusation?

But that a man may be legally absent who has counselled or procured a treasonable act is proved by all those books which treat upon the subject, and which concur in declaring that such a person is a principal traitor, not because he was legally present but because in treason all are principals. Yet the indictment, speaking upon general principles, would charge him according to the truth of the case. Lord Coke says: "If many conspire to levy war, and some of them do levy the same according to the conspiracy, this is high treason in all." Why? because all were legally present when the war was levied? No. "For in treason," continues Lord Coke, "all be principals, and war is levied." In this case the indictment, reasoning from analogy, would not charge that the absent conspirators were present, but would state the truth of the case. If the conspirator had done nothing which amounted to levying of war, and if by our Constitution the doctrine that an accessory becomes a principal be not adopted, in consequence of which the conspirator could not be condemned under an indictment stating the truth of the case, it would be going very far to say that this defect, if it be termed one, may be cured by an indictment stating the case untruly.

This doctrine of Lord Coke has been adopted by all subsequent writers, and it is generally laid down in the English books that whatever will make a man an accessory in felony, will make him a principal in treason; but it is nowhere suggested that he is by construction to be considered as present when in point of fact he was absent.

Foster has been particularly quoted, and certainly he is precisely in point. "It is well known," says Foster, "that in the language of the law there are no accessories in high treason; all are principals. Every instance of incitement, aid, or protection, which in the case of felony will render a man an accessory before or after the fact, in the case of high treason, whether it be treason at common law or by statute, will make him a principal in treason." The cases of incitement and aid are cases put as examples of a man's becoming a principal in treason, not because he was legally present, but by force of that maxim in the common law, that whatever will render a man an accessory at common law will render him a principal in treason. In other passages the words "command" or "procure" are used to indicate the same state of things; that is, a treasonable assemblage produced by a man who is not himself in that assemblage.

In point of law, then, the man who incites, aids, or procures a treasonable act, is not, merely in consequence of that indictment, aid, or procurement, legally present when the act is committed.

If it does not result, from the nature of the crime, that all who are concerned in it are legally present at every overt act, then each case depends upon its own circumstances; and to judge how for the circumstances of any case can make him legally present, who is in fact absent, the doctrine of constructive presence must be examined.

Hale in his 1 vol., p. 615, says: "Regularly no man can be a principal in felony unless he be present." In the same page he says: "An accessory before is he that, being absent at the time of the felony committed, doth yet procure, counsel, or command another to commit a felony." The books are full of passages which state this to be the law. Foster, in showing what acts of concurrence will make a man a principal, says: "He must be present at the perpetration, otherwise he can be no more than an accessory before the fact."

These strong distinctions would be idle, at any rate they would be inapplicable to treason, if they were to be entirely lost in the doctrine of constructive presence.

Foster adds, (p. 349), "When the law requireth the presence of the accomplice at the perpetration of the fact in order to render him a principal, it doth not require a strict actual immediate presence, such a presence as would make him an eye or ear witness of what passeth." The terms used by Foster are such as would be employed by a man intending to show the necessity that the absent person should be near at hand, although from the nature of the thing no precise distance could be marked out. An inspection of the cases from which Foster drew this general principle will serve to illustrate it. Hale, 439. In all these cases, put by Hale, the whole party set out together to commit the very fact charged in the indictment; or to commit some other unlawful act, in which they are all to be personally concerned at the same time and place, and are, at the very time when the criminal fact is committed, near enough to give actual personal aid and assistance to the man who perpetrated it. Hale, on p. 449, giving the reason for the decision in the case of the Lord Dacre, says: "They all come with an intent to steal the deer: and consequently the law supposes that they came all with the intent to oppose all that should hinder them in that design." The original case says this was their resolution. This opposition would be a personal opposition. This case, even as stated by Hale, would clearly not comprehend any man who entered into the combination, but who, instead of going to the park where the murder was committed should not set out with the others, should go to a different park, or should even lose his way.

In both these cases stated in Hale, p. 534, the persons actually set out together, and were near enough to assist in the commission of the fact. That in the case of Pudsey the felony was, as stated by Hale, a different felony from that originally intended, is unimportant in regard to the particular principle now under consideration; so far as respected distance, as respected capacity to assist in case of resistance, it is the same as if the robbery had been that which was originally designed. The case in the original report shows that the felony committed was in fact in pursuance of that originally designed. Foster, p. 350, plainly supposed the same particular design, not a general design composed of many particular distinct facts. He supposes them to be co-operating with respect to that particular design. This may be illustrated by a case which is, perhaps, common. Suppose a band of robbers confederated for the general purpose of robbing. They set out together, or in parties, to rob a particular individual; and each performs the part assigned to him. Some ride up to the individual, and demand his purse. Others watch out of sight to intercept those who might be coming to assist the man on whom the robbery is to be committed. If murder or robbery actually takes place, all are principals: and all in construction of law are present. But suppose they set out at the same time or at different times, by different roads, to attack and rob different individuals or different companies; to commit distinct acts of robbery. It has never been contended that those who committed one act of robbery, or who failed altogether, were constructively present at the act of those who were associated with them in the common object of robbery, who were to share the plunder, but who did not assist at the particular fact. They do, indeed, belong to the general party; but they are not of the particular party which committed this fact. Foster concludes this subject by observing that " in order to render a person an accomplice and a principal in felony, he must be aiding and abetting at the fact, or ready to afford assistance if necessary"; that is, at the particular fact which is charged. He must be ready to render assistance to those who are committing the fact. He must, as is stated by Hawkins, be ready to give immediate and direct assistance.

All the cases to be found in the books go to the same point. Let them be applied to that under consideration.

The whole treason laid in this indictment is the levying of war in Blennerhassett's island; and the whole question to which the inquiry of the court is now directed is whether the prisoner was legally present at the fact.

I say this is the whole question; because the prisoner can only be convicted on the overt act laid in the indictment. With respect to this prosecution, it is as if no other overt act existed. If other overt acts can be inquired into, it is for the sole purpose of proving the particular fact charged. It is an evidence of the crime consisting of this particular fact, not as establishing the general crime by a distinct fact.

The counsel for the prosecution have charged those engaged in the defence with considering the overt act as treason, whereas it ought to be considered solely as the evidence of the treason; but the counsel for the prosecution seem themselves not to have sufficiently adverted to this clear principle; that though the overt act may not be itself the treason, it is the sole act of that treason which can produce conviction. It is the sole point in issue between the parties. And the only division of that point, if the expression be allowed, which the court is now examining, is the constructive presence of the prisoner at the fact charged.

To return, then, to the application of the cases.

Had the prisoner set out with the party from Beaver for Blennerhassett's island, or perhaps had he set out for that place, though not from Beaver, and had arrived in the island, he would have been present at the fact. Had he not arrived in the island, but had taken a position near enough to co-operate with those on the island, to assist them in any act of hostility, or to aid them if attacked, the question whether he was constructively present would be a question compounded of law and fact, which would be decided by the jury, with the aid of the court, so far as respected the law. In this case the accused would have been of the particular party assembled on the island, and would have been associated with them in the particular act of levying war said to have been committed on the island.

But if he was not with the party at any time before they reached the island; if he did not join them there, or intend to join them there; if his personal co-operation in the general plan was to be afforded elsewhere, at a great distance, in a different State; if the overt acts of treason to be performed by him were to be distinct overt acts—then he was not of the particular party assembled at Blennerhassett's island, and was not constructively present, aiding and assisting in the particular act which was there committed.

The testimony on this point, so far as it has been delivered, is not equivocal. There is not only no evidence that the accused was of the particular party which assembled on Blennerhassett's island, but the whole evidence shows he was not of that party.

In felony, then admitting the crime to have been completed on the island, and to have been advised, procured, or commanded by the accused, he would have been incontestably an accessory and not a principal.

But in treason, it is said, the law is otherwise, because the theatre of action is more extensive.

The reasoning applies in England as strongly as in the United States. While in '15 and '45 the family of Stuart sought to regain the crown they had forfeited, the struggle was for the whole kingdom, yet no man was ever considered as legally present at one place, when actually at another; or as aiding in one transaction, while actually employed in another.

With the perfect knowledge that the whole nation may be the theatre of action, the English books unite in declaring that he who counsels, procures, or aids treason, is guilty accessorially, and solely in virtue of the common law principle that what will make a man an accessory of felony makes him a principal in treason. So far from considering a man as constructively present at every overt act of the general treason in which he may have been concerned, the whole doctrine of the books limits the proof against him to those particular overt acts of levying war with which he is charged.

What would be the effect of a different doctrine? Clearly that which has been stated. If a person levying war in Kentucky may be said to be constructively present and assembled with a party carrying on war in Virginia at a great distance from him, then he is present at every overt act performed anywhere. He may be tried in any State on the continent, where any overt act has been committed. He may be proved to be guilty of an overt act laid in the indictment in which he has no personal participation, by proving that he advised it, or that he committed other acts.

This is, perhaps, too extravagant to be in terms maintained. Certainly it cannot be supported by the doctrines of the English law.

The opinion of Judge Patterson in Mitchell's case has been cited on this point, 2 Dall., 348.

The indictment is not specially stated, but from the case as reported, it must have been either general for levying war in the county of Allegany, and the overt act must have been the assemblage of men and levying of war in that county, or it must have given a particular detail of the treasonable transactions in that county. The first supposition is the most probable, but let the indictment be in the one form or the other, and the result is the same. The facts of the case are that a large body of men, of whom Mitchell was one, assembled at Braddock's field, in the county of Allegany, for the purpose of committing acts of violence at Pittsburgh; that there was also an assemblage at a different time at Couch's fort, at which the prisoner also attended. The general and avowed object of that meeting was to concert measures for resisting the execution of a public law. At Couch's Fort the resolution was taken to attack the house of the inspector and the body there assembled marched to that house and attacked it. It was proved by the competent number of witnesses that he was at Couch's fort armed; that he offered to reconnoitre the house to be attacked; that he marched with the insurgents towards the house; that he was with them after the action attending the body of one of his comrades who was killed in it. One witness swore positively that he was present at the burning of the house; and a second witness said that "it run in his head that he had seen him there." That a doubt should exist in such a case as this, is strong evidence of the necessity that the overt act should be unequivocally proved by two witnesses.

But what was the opinion of the judge in this case? Couch's fort and Neville's house being in the same county, the assemblage having been at Couch's fort, and the resolution to attack the house having been there taken, the body having for the avowed purpose moved in execution of that resolution towards the house to be attacked, he inclined to think that the act of marching was in itself levying war. If it was, then the overt act laid in the indictment was consummated by the assemblage at Couch's and the marching from thence; and Mitchell was proved to be guilty by more than two positive witnesses. But without deciding this to be the law, he proceeded to consider the meeting at Couch's the immediate marching to Neville's house, and the attack and burning of the house, as one transaction. Mitchell was proved by more than two positive witnesses to have been in that transaction, to have taken an active part in it; and the judge declared it to be unnecessary that all should have seen him at the same time and place.

But suppose not a single witness had proved Mitchéll to have been at Couch's, or on the march, or at Neville's. Suppose he had been at the time notoriously absent in a different State. Can it be believed by any person who observes the caution with which Judge Patterson required the constitutional proof of two witnesses to the same overt act, that he would have said Mitchell was constructively present, and might, on the straining of a legal fiction, be found guilty of treason? Had he delivered such an opinion, what would have been the language of this country respecting it? Had he given this opinion, it would have required all the correctness of his life to strike his name from that bloody list in which the name of Jeffries is enrolled.

But to estimate the opinion in Mitchell's case, let its circumstances be transferred to Burr's case. Suppose the body of men assembled in Blennerhassett's Island had previously met at some other place in the same county; that Burr had been proved to be with them by four witnesses; that the resolution to march to Blennerhassett's island for a treasonable purpose had been there taken; that he had been seen on the march with them; that one witness had seen him on the island; that another thought he had seen him there; that he had been seen with the party directly after leaving the island; that this indictment had charged the levying of war in Wood county generally—the case would, then have been precisely parallel; and the decision would have been the same.

In conformity with principle and with authority, then, the prisoner at the bar was neither legally nor actually present at Blennerhassett's island; and the court is strongly inclined to the opinion that without proving an actual or legal presence by two witnesses, the overt act laid in this indictment cannot be proved.

But this opinion is controverted on two grounds:

The first is, that the indictment does not charge the prisoner to have been present.

The second, that although he was absent, yet if he caused the assemblage, he may be indicted as being present, and convicted on evidence that he caused the treasonable act.

The first position is to be decided by the indictment itself. The court understands the allegation differently from the attorney for the United States. The court understands it to be directly charged that the prisoner did assemble with the multitude, and did march with them. Nothing will more clearly test this construction than putting the case into a shape which it may possibly take. Suppose the law be that the indictment would be defective unless it alleged the presence of the person indicted at the act of treason. If, upon a special verdict, facts should be found which amounted to a levying of war by the accused, and his counsel should insist that he could not be condemned because the indictment was defective in not charging that he was himself one of the assemblage which constituted the treason, or because it alleged the procurement defectively, would the attorney admit this construction of his indictment to be correct? I am persuaded he would not, and that he ought not to make such a concession. If, after a verdict, the indictment ought to be construed to allege that the prisoner was one of the assemblage at Blennerhassett's island, it ought to be construed now. But this is unimportant; for if the indictment alleges that the prisoner procured the assemblage, the procurement becomes part of the overt act, and must be proved, as will be shown hereafter.

The second position is founded on 1 Hale, 214, 228, and 1 East, 127.

While I declare that this doctrine contradicts every idea I had ever entertained on the subject of indictments, (since it admits that one case may be stated, and a very different case may be proved,) I will acknowledge that it is countenanced by the authorities adduced in its support. To counsel or advise a treasonable assemblage, and to be one of that assemblage, are certainly distinct acts, and, therefore ought not to be charged as the same act. The great objection to this mode of proceeding is, that the proof essentially varies from the charge in the character and essence of the offence, and in the testimony by which the accused is to defend himself. These dicta of Lord Hale, therefore, taken in the extent in which they are understood by the counsel for the United States, seem to be repugnant to the declarations we find everywhere that an overt act must be laid, and must be proved. No case is cited by Hale in support of them, and I am strongly inclined to the opinion that had the public received his corrected instead of his original manuscript, they would, if not expunged, have been restrained in their application to cases of a particular description. Laid down generally, and applied universally to all cases of treason, they are repugnant to the principles for which Hale contends, for which all the elementary writers contend, and from which courts have in no case, either directly reported or referred to in the books, ever departed. These principles are, that the indictment must give notice of the offence; that the accused is only bound to answer the particular charge which the indictment contains, and that the overt act laid is that particular charge. Under such circumstances, it is only doing justice to Hale to examine his dicta, and if they admit of being understood in a limited sense, not repugnant to his own doctrines nor to the general principles of law, to understand them in that sense.

"If many conspire to counterfeit, or counsel or abet it, and one of them doth the fact upon that counselling or conspiracy, it is treason in all, and they may be all indicted for counterfeiting generally within this statute, for in such case in treason all are principals."

This is laid down as applicable singly to the treason of counterfeiting the coin, and is not applied to Hale to other treasons. Had he designed to apply the principle universally he would have stated it as a general proposition; he would have laid it down in treating our other branches of the statute as well as in the chapter respecting the coin; he would have laid it down when treating on indictments generally. But he has done neither. Every sentiment bearing in any manner on this point, which is to be found in Lord Hale while on the doctrine of levying war or on the general doctrine of indictments, militates against the opinion that he considered the proposition as more extensive than he has declared it to be. No court could be justified in extending the dictum of a judge beyond its terms to cases which he had expressly treated, in which he has not himself applied it, and on which he, as well as others, has delivered opinions which that dictum would overrule. This would be the less justifiable if there should be a clear legal distinction indicated by the very terms in which the judge has expressed himself between the particular case to which alone he has applied the dictum and other cases to which the court is required to extend it.

There is this clear legal distinction: "They may," says Judge Hale, "be indicted for counterfeiting generally." But if many conspire to levy war, and some actually levy it, they may not be indicted for levying war generally. The books concur in declaring that they cannot be so indicted. A special overt act of levying war must be laid. This distinction between counterfeiting the coins and that class of treasons among which levying war is placed is taken in the statute of Edward III. That statute requires an overt act of levying war to be laid in the indictment, and does not require an overt act of counterfeiting the coin to be laid. If in a particular case, in which a general indictment is sufficient, it be stated that the crime may be charged generally according to the legal effect of the act, it does not follow that in other cases, where a general indictment would not be sufficient, where an overt act must be laid, that this overt act need not be laid according to the real fact. Hale, then, is to be reconciled to himself and with the general principles of the law only by permitting the limits which he has himself given to his own dictum to remain where he has placed them.

On page 238, Hale is speaking generally to the receiver of a traitor, and is stating in what such a receiver partakes of an accessory: 1st. "His indictment must be special of the receipt, and not generally that he did the thing, which may be otherwise in case of one that is procurer, counsellor, or consenter."

The words "may be otherwise" do not clearly convey the idea that it is universally otherwise. In all cases of a receiver, the indictment must be special on the receipt, and not general. The words "may be otherwise in case of a procurer," &c., signify that it may be otherwise in all treasons, or that it may be otherwise in some treasons. If it may be otherwise in some treasons without contradicting the doctrine of Hale himself as well as of other writers, but cannot be otherwise in all treasons without such contradiction, the fair construction is, that Hale used these words in their restricted sense; that he used them in reference to treasons in which a general indictment would lie, not to treasons where a general indictment would not lie, but an overt act of the treason must be charged. The two passages of Hale thus construed may, perhaps, be law, and may leave him consistent with himself. It appears to the court to be the fair way of construing them.

These observations relative to the passages quoted from Hale apply to that quoted from East, who obviously copies from Hale and relies upon his authority.

Upon this point Kelyng, p. 26, and 1st Hale, p. 626, have also been relied upon. It is stated in both that if a man be indicted as a principal and acquitted, he cannot afterwards be indicted as an accessory before the fact—whence it is inferred, not without reason, that evidence of accessorial guilt may be received on such an indictment. Yet no case is found in which the question has been made and decided. The objection has never been taken at a trial and overruled, nor do the books say it would be overruled. Were such a case produced its application would be questionable. Kelyng says an accessory before the fact is *quodam modo* in some manner guilty of the fact. The law may not require that the manner should be stated, for in felony it does not require that an overt act should be laid. The indictment, therefore, may be general; but an overt act of levying war must be laid. These cases, then, prove in their utmost extent no more than the cases previously cited from Hale and East. This distinction between indictments which may state the fact generally, and those which must lay it specially, bear some analogy to a general and a special action on the case. In a general action the declaration may lay the assumpsit according to the legal effect of the transaction, but in a special action on the case the declaration must state the material circumstances truly, and they must be proved as stated. This distinction also derives some aid from a passage in Hale, p. 625, immediately preceding that which has been cited at the bar. He says: "If A be indicted as principal and B as accessory before or after, and both be acquitted, yet B may be indicted as principal, and the former acquittal as accessory is no bar."

The crimes, then are not the same, and may not indifferently be tried under the same indictment. But why is it that an acquittal as principal may be pleaded in bar to an indictment as accessory, while an acquittal as accessory may not be pleaded in bar to an indictment as principal? If it be answered that the accessorial crime may be given in evidence on an indictment as principal, but that the principal crime may not be given in evidence on an indictment as accessory, the question recurs, on what legal ground does this distinction stand? I can imagine only this: an accessory being *quodam modo* a principal in indictments where the law does not require the manner to be stated, which need not be special, evidence of accessorial guilt, if the punishment be the same, may possibly be received; but every indictment as accessory must be special. The very allegation that he is an accessory must be a special allegation, and must show how he become an accessory. The charges of this special indictment, therefore, must be proved as laid, and no evidence which proves the crime in any form substantially different can be received. If this be the legal reason for the distinction, it supports the exposition of these dicta which has been given. If it be not the legal reason, I can conceive no other.

But suppose the law to be as is contended by the counsel for the United States. Suppose an indictment charging an individual with personally assembling among others, and thus levying war, may be satisfied with the proof that he caused the assemblage. What effect will this law have upon this case?

The guilt of the accused, if there be any guilt, does not consist in the assemblage, for he was not a member of it. The simple fact of assemblage no more affects one absent man than another. His guilt, then, consists in procuring the assemblage, and upon this fact depends his criminality. The proof relative to the character of an assemblage must be the same whether a man be present or absent. In the general, to charge an individual with the guilt of an assemblage, the fact of his presence must be proved; it constitutes an essential part of the overt act. If, then, the procurement be substituted in the place of presence, does it not also constitute an essential part of the overt act? Must it not also be proved? Must it not be proved in the same manner that presence must be proved? If in one case the presence of the individual make the guilt of the assemblage his guilt, and in the other case the procurement by the individual make the guilt of the assemblage his guilt, then presence and procurement are equally component parts of the overt act, and equally require two witnesses.

Collateral points may, say the books, be proved according to the course of the common law; but is this a collateral point? Is the fact, without which the accused does not participate in the guilt of the assemblage if it was guilty, a collateral point? This cannot be. The presence of the party, where presence is necessary, being a part of the overt act, must be positively proved by two witnesses. No presumptive evidence, no facts from which presence may be conjectured or inferred, will satisfy the Constitution and the law. If procurement take the place of presence and becomes part of the overt act, then no presumptive evidence, no facts from which the procurement may be conjectured or inferred can satisfy the Constitution and the law. The mind is not to be led to the conclusion that the individual was present by a train of conjectures, or inferences, or of reasoning; the fact must be proved by two witnesses. Neither, where procurement supplies the want of presence, is the mind to be conducted to the conclusion that the accused procured the assembly by a train of conjectures or inferences, or of reasoning; the fact itself must be proved by two witnesses, and must have been committed within the district.

If it be said that the advising or procurement of treason is a secret transaction, which can scarcely ever be proved in the manner required by this opinion, the answer which will readily suggest itself is, that the difficulty of proving a fact will not justify conviction without proof. Certainly it will not justify conviction without a direct and positive witness in a case where the Constitution requires two. The more correct inference from this circumstance would seem to be, that the advising of the fact is not within the constitutional definition of the crime. To advise or procure a treason is in the nature of conspiring or plotting treason, which is not treason in itself.

If, then, the doctrines of Kelyng, Hale, and East, be understood in the sense in which they are pressed by the counsel for the prosecution, and are applicable in the United States, the fact that the accused procured the assemblage on Blennerhassett's island must be proved, not circumstantially, but positively, by two witnesses, to charge him with the assemblage. But there are still other most important considerations which must be well weighed before this doctrine can be applied to the United States.

The 8th amendment to the Constitution has been pressed with great force, and it is impossible not to feel its application to this point. The accused cannot be said to be "informed of the nature and cause of the accusation" unless the indictment give him that notice which may reasonably suggest to him the point on which the accusation turns, so that he may know the course to be pursued in his defence.

It is also well worthy of consideration, that this doctrine, so far as it respects treason, is entirely supported by the operation of the common law, which is said to convert the accessory before the fact into the principal, and to make the act of the principal his act. The accessory before the fact is not said to have levied war. He is not said to be guilty under the statute, but the common law attaches to him the guilt of that fact which he has advised or procured; and as contended, makes it his act. This is the operation of the common law, not the operation of the statute. It is an operation then, which can only be performed where the common law exists to perform it. It is the creature of the common law and the creature presupposes its creator. To decide, then, that this doctrine is applicable to the United States would seem to imply the decision that the United States, as a nation, have a common law which creates and defines the punishment of crimes accessorial in their nature. It would imply the further decision that the accessorial crimes are not, in the case of treason excluded by the definition of treason given in the Constitution. I will not pretend that I have not individually an opinion on these points; but it is one which I should give only in a case which absolutely required it, unless I could confer respecting it with the judges of the Supreme Court.

I have said that this doctrine cannot apply to the United States without implying those decisions respecting the common law which I have stated; because, should it be true, as is contended, that the constitutional definition of treason comprehends him who advises or procures an assemblage that levies war, it would not follow that such adviser or procurer might be charged as having been present at the assemblage. If the adviser or procurer be within the definition of levying war, and, independent of the agency of the common law, do actually levy war, then the advisement or procurement is an overt act of levying war. If it be the overt act on which he is to be convicted, then it must be charged in the indictment; for he can only be convicted on proof of the overt acts which are charged.

To render this distinction more intelligible, let it be recollected that, although it should be conceded that since the statute of William and Mary he who advises or procures a treason may, in England, be charged as having committed that treason, by virtue of the common law operation, which is said, so far as respected the indictment, to unite the accessorial to the principal offence and permit them to be charged as one, yet it can never be conceded that he who commits one overt act under the statute of Edward can be charged and convicted on proof of another overt act. If, then procurement be an overt act of treason under the Constitution no man can be convicted for the procurement under an indictment charging him with actually assembling, whatever may be the doctrine of the common law in the case of an accessorial offender.

It may not be improper in this place again to advert to the opinion of the Supreme Court, and to show that it contains nothing contrary to the doctrine now laid down. That opinion is, that an individual may be guilty of treason "who has not appeared in arms against his country; that if war be actually levied that is, if a body of men be actually assembled for the purpose of effecting by force a treasonable object, all those who perform any, part, however minute, or however remote from the scene of action, and who are actually leagued in the general conspiracy, are to be considered as traitors."

This opinion does not touch the case of a person who advises or procures an assemblage, and does nothing further. The advising, certainly, and perhaps the procuring, is more in the nature of a conspiracy to levy war than of the actual levying of war. According to the opinion, it is not enough to be leagued in the conspiracy, and that war be levied, but it is also necessary to perform a part: that part is the act of levying war. That part, it is true, may be minute, it may not be the actual appearance in arms, and it may be remote from the scene of action, that is, from the place where the army is assembled; but it must be a part, and that part must be performed by a person who is leagued in the conspiracy. This part, however minute or remote, constitutes the overt act of which alone the person who performs it can be convicted.

The opinion does not declare that the person who has performed this remote and minute part may be indicted for a part which was, in truth, performed by others and convicted on their overt acts. It amounts to this and nothing more, that when war is actually levied, not only those who bear arms, but those also who are leagued in the conspiracy, and who perform the various distinct parts which are necessary for the prosecution of war, do in the sense of the Constitution, levy war. It may possibly be the opinion of the Supreme Court that those who procure a treason and do nothing further are guilty under the Constitution. I only say that opinion has not yet been given, still less has it been indicated that he who advises shall be indicted as having performed the fact.

It is, then, the opinion of the court that this indictment can be supported only by testimony which proves the accused to have been actually or constructively present when the assemblage took place on Blennerhassett's island; or by the admission of the doctrine that he who procures an act may be indicted as having performed that act.

It is further the opinion of the court that there is no testimony whether which tends to prove that the accused was actually or constructively present when that assemblage did take place; indeed, the contrary is most apparent. With respect to admitting proof of procurement to establish a charge of actual presence, the court is of opinion that if this be admissible in England on an indictment for levying war, which is far from being conceded, it is admissible only by virtue of the operation of the common law upon the statute, and therefore is not admissible in this country unless by virtue of a similar operation—a point far from being established, but on which, for the present, no opinion is given. If, however, this point be established, still the procurement must be proved in the same manner and by the same kind of testimony which would be required to prove actual presence.

The second point in this division of the subject is the necessity of adducing the record of the previous conviction of some one person who committed the fact alleged to be treasonable.

This point presupposes the treason of the accused, if any have been committed, to be accessorial in its nature. Its being of this description, according to the British authorities, depends on the presence or absence of the accused at the time the fact was committed. The doctrine on this subject is well understood, has been most copiously explained, and need not be repeated. That there is no evidence of his actual or legal presence is a point already discussed and decided. It is, then, apparent that but for the exception to the general principle which is made in cases of treason, those who assembled at Blennerhassett's island, if that assemblage was such as to constitute the crime, would be principals, and those who might really have caused that assemblage, although in truth the chief traitors, would in law be accessories. It is a settled principle in the law that the accessory cannot be guilty of a greater offence than his principal. The maxim is accessorious *sequitur naturam sui principalis*—the accessory follows the nature of his principal. Hence results the necessity of establishing the guilt of the principal before the accessory can be tried; for the degree of guilt which is incurred by counselling or commanding the commission of a crime depends upon the actual commission of that crime. No man is an accessory to murder unless the fact has been committed.

The fact can only be established in a prosecution against the person by whom a crime has been perpetrated. The law supposes a man more capable of defending his own conduct than any other person, and will not tolerate that the guilt of A shall be established in a prosecution against B. Consequently, if the guilt of B depends on the guilt of A, A must be convicted before B can be tried. It would exhibit a monstrous deformity indeed in our system, if B might be executed for being accessory to a murder committed by A, and A should afterwards, upon a full trial, be acquitted of the fact. For this obvious reason, although the punishment of a principal and accessory was originally the same, and although in many instances it is still the same, the accessory could in no case be tried before the conviction of his principal, nor can he yet be tried previous to such conviction, unless he require it, or unless a special provision to that effect be made by statute.

If, then, this were a felony, the prisoner at the bar could not be tried until the crime were established by the conviction of the person by whom it was actually perpetrated.

Is the law otherwise in this case, because in treason all are principals?

Let this question be answered by reason and by authority.

Why is it that in felonies, however atrocious, the trial of the accessory can never precede the conviction of the principal? Not because the one is denominated the principal and the other the accessory; for that would be ground on which a great law principle could never stand. Not because there was, in fact, a difference in the degree of moral guilt; for in the case of murder committed by a hardy villain for a bribe, the person plotting the murder and giving the bribe is, perhaps, of the two, the blacker criminal; and were it otherwise, this would furnish no argument for precedence in trial.

What, then, is the reason?

It has been already given. The legal guilt of the accessory depends on the guilt of the principal; and the guilt of the principal can only be established in a prosecution against himself.

Does not this reason apply in full force to a case of treason?

The legal guilt of the person who planned the assemblage on Blennerhassett's island depends not simply on the criminality of the previous conspiracy, but on the criminality of that assemblage. If those who perpetrated the fact be not traitors, he who advised the fact cannot be a traitor. His guilt, then, in contemplation of law, depends on theirs; and their guilt can only be established in a prosecution against themselves. Whether the adviser of this assemblage be punishable with death as a principal or as an accessory, his liability to punishment depends on the degree of guilt attached to an act which has been perpetrated by others; and which, if it be a criminal act, renders them guilty also. His guilt, therefore, depends on theirs; and their guilt cannot be legally established in a prosecution against him.

The whole reason of the law, then, relative to the principal and accessory, so far as respects the order of trial, seems to apply in full force to a case of treason committed by one body of men in conspiracy with others who are absent.

If from reason we pass to authority, we find it laid down by Hale, Foster, and East, in the most explicit terms, that the conviction of some one who has committed the treason must precede the trial of him who has advised or procured it. This position is also maintained by Leach in his notes on Hawkins, and is not, so far as the court has discovered anywhere contradicted.

These authorities have been read and commented on at such length that it cannot be necessary for the court to bring them again into view. It is the less necessary because it is not understood that the law is controverted by the counsel for the United States.

It is, however, contended that the prisoner has waived his right to demand the conviction of some one person who was presented at the fact, by pleading to his indictment.

Had this indictment ever charged the prisoner according to the truth of the case, the court would feel some difficulty in deciding that he had, by implication, waived his right to demand a species of testimony essential to his conviction. The court is not prepared to say that the act which is to operate against his rights did not require that it should be performed with a full knowledge of its operation. It would seem consonant to the usual course of proceeding in other respects in criminal cases, that the prisoner should be informed that he had a right to refuse to be tried until some person who committed the act should be convicted; and that he ought not to be considered as waiving the right to demand the record of conviction, unless with the full knowledge of that right he consented to be tried. The court, however, does not decide what the law would be in such a case. It is unnecessary to decide it; because pleading to an indictment, in which a man is charged as having committed an act, cannot be construed to waive a right which he would have possessed had he been charged with having advised the act. No person indicted as a principal can be expected to say I am not a principal. I am an accessory. I did not commit, I only advised the act.

The authority of the English cases on this subject depends, in a great measure, on the adoption of the common law doctrine of accessorial treasons. If that doctrine be excluded, this branch of it may not be directly applicable to treasons committed within the United States. If the crime of advising or procuring a levying of war be within the constitutional definition of treason, then he who advises or procures it must be indicted on the very fact; and the question whether the treasonableness of the act may be decided in the first instance in the trial of him who procured it, or must be decided in the trial of one who committed it, will depend upon the reason, as it respects the law of evidence, which produced the British decisions with regard to the trial of principal and accessory, rather than on the positive authority of those decisions.

This question is not essential in the present case; because if the crime be within the constitutional definition, it is an overt act of levying war, and, to produce a conviction, ought to have been charged in the indictment.

The law of the case being thus far settled, what ought to be the decision of the court on the present motion? Ought the court to sit and hear testimony which cannot affect the prisoner, or ought the court to arrest that testimony? On this question much has been said—much that may perhaps be ascribed to a misconception of the point really under consideration. The motion has been treated as a motion confessedly made to stop relevant testimony; and, in the course of the argument, it has been repeatedly stated, by those who oppose the motion, that irrelevant testimony may and ought to be stopped. That this statement is perfectly correct is one of those fundamental principles in judicial proceedings which is acknowledged by all, and is founded in the absolute necessity of the thing. No person will contend that, in a civil or criminal case, either party is at liberty to introduce what testimony he pleases, legal or illegal, and to consume the whole term in details of facts unconnected with the particular case. Some tribunal, then, must decide on the admissibility of testimony. The parties cannot constitute this tribunal; for they do not agree. The jury cannot constitute it; for the question is whether they shall hear the testimony or not. Who, then, but the court can constitute it? It is of necessity the peculiar province of the court to judge of the admissibility of testimony. If the court admit improper or reject proper testimony, it is an error of judgment; but it is an error committed in the direct exercise of their judicial functions.

The present indictment charges the prisoner with levying war against the United States, and alleges an overt act of levying war. That overt act must be proved, according to the mandates of the Constitution and of the act of Congress, by two witnesses. It is not proved by a single witness. The presence of the accused has been stated to be an essential component part of the overt act in this indictment, unless the common law principle respecting accessories should render it unnecessary; and there is not only no witness who has proved his actual or legal presence, but the fact of his absence is not controverted. The counsel for the prosecution offer to give in evidence subsequent transactions at a different place and in a different State, in order to prove—what? The overt act laid in the indictment? That the prisoner was one of those who assembled at Blennerhassett's island? No: that is not alleged. It is well known that such testimony is not competent to establish such a fact. The Constitution and law require that the fact should be established by two witnesses; not by the establishment of other facts from which the jury might reason to this fact. The testimony, then, is not relevant. If it can be introduced, it is only in the character of corroborative or confirmatory testimony, after the overt act has been proved by two witnesses in such manner that the question of fact ought to be left with the jury. The conclusion that in this state of things no testimony can be admissible is so inevitable that the counsel for the United States could not resist it. I do not understand them to deny that, if the overt act be not proved by two witnesses so as to be submitted to the jury, all other testimony must be irrelevant; because no other testimony can prove the act. Now, an assemblage on Blennerhassett's island is proved by the requisite number of witnesses; and the court might submit it to the jury whether that assemblage amounted to a levying of war; but the presence of the accused at that assemblage being nowhere alleged except in the indictment, the overt act is not proved by a single witness; and, of consequence, all other testimony must be irrelevant.

The only difference between this motion as made, and the motion in the form which the counsel for the United States would admit to be regular, is this; It is now general for the rejection of all testimony. It might be particular with respect to each witness as adduced. But can this be wished, or can it be deemed necessary? If enough be proved to show that the indictment cannot be supported, and that no testimony, unless it be of that description which the attorney for the United States, declares himself not to possess, can be relevant, why should a question be taken on each witness?

The opinion of this court on the order of testimony has frequently been adverted to as deciding this question against the motion.

If a contradiction between the two opinions exist, the court cannot perceive it. It was said that levying war is an act compounded of law and fact, of which the jury, aided by the court, must judge. To that declaration the court still adheres.

It was said that if the overt act were not proved by two witnesses, no testimony in its nature corroborative or confirmatory was admissible, or could be relevant.

From that declaration there is certainly no departure. It has been asked, in allusion to the present case, if a general commanding an army should detach troops for a distant service, would the men composing that detachment be traitors, and would the commander-in-chief escape punishment?

Let the opinion which has been given answer this question. Appearing at the head of an army would, according to this opinion, be an overt act of levying war. Detaching a military corps from it for military purposes might, also, be an overt act of levying war. It is not pretended that he would not be punishable for these acts. It is only said that he may be tried and convicted on his own acts in the State, where those acts were committed, not on the acts of others in the State where those others acted. Much has been said in the course of the argument on points on which the court feels no inclination to comment particularly; but which may, perhaps not improperly, receive some notice.

That this court dares not usurp power is most true.

That this court dares not shrink from its duty is not less true.

No man is desirous of placing himself in a disagreeable situation. No man is desirous of becoming the peculiar subject of calumny. No man might he let the bitter cup pass from him without self-reproach, would drain it to the bottom. But if he had no choice in the case, if there be no alternative presented to him but a dereliction of duty or the opprobrium of those who are denominating the world, he merits the contempt as well as the indignation of his country who can hesitate which to embrace.

That gentlemen, in a case the most interesting, in the zeal with which they advocate particular opinions, and under the conviction in some measure produced by that zeal, should, on each side, press their arguments too far, should be impatient at any deliberation in the court, and should suspect or fear the operation of motives to which alone they can ascribe that deliberation, is, perhaps, a frailty incident to human nature; but if any conduct on the part of the court could warrant a sentiment that it would deviate to the one side or the other from the lien prescribed by duty and by law, that conduct would be viewed by the judges themselves with an eye of extreme severity, and would long be recollected with deep and serious regret.

The arguments on both sides have been intently and deliberately considered. Those which could not be noticed, since to notice every argument and authority would swell this opinion to a volume, have not been disregarded. The result of the whole is a conviction, as complete as the mind of the court is capable of receiving on a complex subject, that the motion must prevail.

No testimony relative to the conduct or declarations of the prisoner elsewhere, and subsequent to the transaction on Blennerhassett's island, can be admitted; because such testimony, being in its nature merely corroborative and incompetent to prove the overt act in itself, is irrelevant until there be proof of the overt act by two witnesses.

This opinion does not comprehend the proof by two witnesses that the meeting on Blennerhassett's island was procured by the prisoner. On that point the court for the present withholds its opinion for reasons which have been already assigned; and as it is understood from the statements made on the part of the prosecution that no such testimony exists, if there be such let it be offered, and the court will decide upon it.

The jury have now heard the opinion of the court on the law of the case. They will apply that law to the facts, and will find a verdict of guilty or not guilty as their own consciences may direct.

As soon as the Chief Justice had concluded, Mr. Hay observed that the opinion just delivered by the court furnished matter for the serious consideration of the counsel for the prosecution; and he hoped the court would grant them time to consider it. After some desultory conversation, the Chief Justice, at Mr. Hay's request, delivered him the opinion, that he might read and consider it.

The court adjourned till six o'clock in the afternoon.

At six o'clock the court met, and adjourned till Tuesday.

TUESDAY, SEPTEMBER 1, 1807

The court met according to adjournment.

Mr. Hay informed the court that he had nothing to offer to the jury of evidence or argument; that he had examined the opinion of the court, and must levy the case with the jury.

The jury accordingly retired, and in a short time returned with the following verdict, which was read by Colonel Carrington, their foreman: "We of the jury say that Aaron Burr is not proved to be guilty under this indictment by any evidence submitted to us. We therefore find him not guilty."

This verdict was objected to by Colonel Burr and his counsel as unusual, informal, and irregular. Colonel Burr observed that whenever a verdict is informal the court will either send back the jury to alter it, or correct it itself; that they had no right to depart from the usual form; that the rule universally is to ask them on their return, "How say you? is he guilty or not guilty?" to which they give a direct answer of "guilty," or "not guilty." That this is correct and responsive to the charge always read to them by the clerk, "If you find him guilty, you are to say so, &c., if you find him not guilty, you are to say so and no more."

Mr. Hay thought the verdict ought to be recorded as found by the jury, which was substantially a verdict of acquittal; and that no principle of humanity, policy, or law, forbade its being received in the very terms used by the jury; that they were not bound to find a verdict in the shortest possible way; that the form did not affect the substance.

Mr. Martin said that it was like the whole play, "Much Ado about Nothing"; that this was a verdict of acquittal; that there was nothing to do but to answer the question of guilty or not guilty; that it was the case with every jury in every instance; they had or had not evidence before them. Did they wish to have the verdict entered in this form on the record, as a censure of the court for suppressing irrelevant testimony? That he was conscious they had no such meaning; and as they had not, the jury ought to answer the question judicially addressed to them simply by a verdict of not guilty, as that was their intention.

Colonel Carrington, one of the jury, observed that it was said among themselves that if the verdict was informal they would alter it; that it was, in fact, a verdict of acquittal.

The Chief Justice said that the verdict was, in effect, the same as a verdict of acquittal; that it might stand on the bill as it was if the jury wished it; and an entry should be made on the record of "not guilty."

Mr. Parker, another of the jury, said that if he were to be sent back he would find the same verdict; that they all knew that it was not in the usual form, but it was more satisfactory to the jury as they had found it; and that he would not agree to alter it.

After some further desultory remarks by several of the counsel, Mr. Hay, in answer to the observation that the only correct form was guilty or not guilty, reminded the court of the case of the *King* vs *Woodfall,* for a libel, where the jury departed from the usual form, added other words, and found a verdict in these words: "We find the defendant guilty of publishing only." This form, though preferred by the jury, was probably disapproved of by the counsel; but it was taken by the court as they presented it; and, in the case of *King* vs *Williams,* cited in Woodfall's case by the court, the jury added other words to the usual form of finding the defendant guilty; and as it did not affect the substance, it was entered up by the clerk "guilty"; and no objection was ever made.

The court then decided that the verdict should remain as found by the jury; and that an entry should be made on the record of "not guilty."

The Chief Justice politely thanked the jury for their patient attention during the whole course of this long trial, and then discharged them.

* * *

I think it was the long hours that we spent at the trial each day that bothered me most of all. The arguing of the lawyers, the rustling sound of a spectator moving in his chair, endless questioning of witnesses, an occasional rap of the gavel—these were the sounds that I could not escape. My nerves grew frayed, and the ache in my heart deepened each time that someone mentioned our island.

Was I already thinking of Neil that afternoon, before they called his name? I do not know. My mind had sought release from the strain of the crowded courtroom. For the moment, I was back on the island, seeing it again in all its beauty. As one in a daze, I heard a voice say, "The prosecution wishes to call Mr. Neil Colton to the stand."

The thoughts that flooded my mind as I watched Neil walk up that aisle were more than I can tell. Most of all did I feel the stabbing pangs of regret—regret that I had refused to heed Neil's admonitions, in the days before tragedy had destroyed us all.

At that time, I had thought only of loyalty to the Blennerhassett's. I was beginning to wonder if, through my loyalty, I had failed them. Had I been strong enough to oppose them and follow Neil's advice, might not my opposition have been the very means by which they could have been saved?

Perhaps, if I had tried to persuade them to listen to Neil,

their ruin could have been averted. At last I knew how right Neil had been in his distrust of such a venture. Such were the thoughts that tortured me as, through my tears, I watched him take his place in the witness chair. Such joy and such sorrow filled my heart at that moment as to make it almost unbearable.

Neil was here! He had come to help us! Of that I had no doubt as he answered the questions asked him by the lawyer. And once he had looked directly at me as he faced the crowded courtroom. For the first time since my father's arrest, I felt a little hopeful, a little encouraged. It was good to know that he had at least one friend who had remained loyal.

Neil's appearance was such a brief interlude in all that long trial, what he said was so limited as to be almost lost in the lengthy testimony of others, but to me it was the one bright spot in the entire trial.

Almost unbelievably, the long days of the trial had dragged themselves to an end. The jury had returned with their verdict, so unsatisfactory to Colonel Burr—"We of the jury say that Aaron Burr is not proved to be guilty under this indictment by any evidence submitted to us. We therefore find him not guilty."

At once, Colonel Burr and his counsel were on their feet, vigorously protesting the irregularity of such a verdict. How little we others cared how the verdict read. We were too tired to be even interested. We knew only that we wanted to escape from the hot courtroom, to get outside, to breathe the fresh, pure, outdoor air.

As Colonel Burr continued to protest against the jury's decision, I noticed that Neil, who had been sitting on the other side of the courtroom, had moved into a seat by the aisle. Until today, I had not seen Neil since that day when he had appeared on the witness stand so unexpectedly. At that time, we had not been permitted to talk together. Now I was certain that he was moving to a spot from where he could see me more clearly. I had been watching him for most of the afternoon. Suddenly I realized that he must also have been keeping an eye on me.

As people began moving out of the courtroom, I ignored what they might think and hurriedly crossed the aisle to be with Neil. I was headed for the vacant chair beside him but, instead, I found myself in his arms. He said nothing, but I felt his arms tighten about me in an embrace strong and warm as any I had known in those happier days back on the island.

As the crowd continued to thin, we were joined by my mother. She was tired and thoughtful but she looked as though a weight had been lifted from her mind. Her warm and friendly greeting for Neil surprised me. Until then I had never been sure that she had forgiven him.

"I am glad to see you, Neil," she said, extending her hand.

"Thank you, Madam," Neil answered. "I have come to offer my services if there is anything that I can do to help."

I wondered if my mother's worn and weary appearance had touched his heart. Was he perhaps remembering her as the beautiful lady she had once been?

"You are very kind," she answered him, "but for the moment I can think of nothing.

"Now that Colonel Burr has been cleared, they tell me that all charges against Harman will be dropped. Right now that is all I care about—just that Harman may be free.

"Melissa, dear," she turned to me, "we should be going now. Your father will join us later. He has asked that we not wait for him. I hope you will come with us, Neil."

The long days of waiting were over. At last we were free to go when, or where, we chose—at any time and at our own convenience.

We were approaching the stairs that led to the outside, when Mother paused by a door that led from the hall into the jury room. For some unknown reason the door stood slightly ajar. It may have been the open door that gave Mother her idea, or maybe it was the apparent emptiness of the darkened room. On a moment's impulse, and without a word, she turned and motioned us inside.

The door creaked in protest as she closed it behind her then turned to face Neil and me. A strange look in her eyes told me that I should try to stop her, but I was powerless to interfere.

"It is in this room," Mrs. Blennerhassett said with suppressed emotion, "that I want to talk to you both.

"No, Melissa, do not attempt to stop me. What I am about to say, I must say, and I ask you both to listen."

She looked around the room slowly, searchingly, as though she wished to impress its image on her mind forever. This horrible room, she was thinking. It has held so much of hope and fear, of life and death for all of us. Can we ever forget it?

"It is fitting," she said, turning back to Neil and Melissa. "It is cruelly fitting that this room should be the place I would find where I can talk with you. Perhaps in no other place would I be able to speak as freely."

She drew a sharp breath then continued, "Many months ago I made a decision, a decision that has brought you, me, all of us straight and surely to this very spot where we now stand."

"Mother, don't!" Melissa protested. "You were not to blame."

"I was to blame," Mrs. Blennerhassett said in a tone that forbade contradiction. "I, more than any other, am to blame. It was I who believed without question the fairy-tale stories of fabulous estates. It was I who insisted on sacrificing all of reality for a dream. All of you, including Harman, had doubts. I never did. I just believed.

"If just one time I had been willing to question what we were doing, we should not stand here today. Our lives and fortunes would not be in ruin."

"Mrs. Blennerhassett," Neil tried to stop her, "there is no point in your tormenting yourself now. It is all over. You will need to forget it as much as you can."

"I can never forget any part of it, Neil. Least of all, can I ever forget that I have caused you and Melissa so much unhappiness. I can only say that I am sorry.

"In my own defense, let me say that I never believed that Colonel Burr intended treason. Even today, I do not know!

"But we do know," she continued angrily, "that he tried to place all of the blame on Harman. I can never trust him again."

Mrs. Blennerhassett realized that she was making Melissa and Neil both very uncomfortable and she regretted it. However, she knew that she must finish what she had started. She must undo, in so far as she was able, the wrong she had done them.

"It is hard for me to tell you this, Neil," she said. "I must conquer my pride to do so, but I do want you to know that for many unhappy months I have known that you were right. I have wished many times that I had listened to your advice back on the island. This episode in Richmond has been agony for all of us. Except for me, it need never have happened to us."

"Mother," Melissa interrupted in a firm voice, "stop it. We will not listen to another word." Fondly she put her arms around her mother's shoulders.

"We love you; it is all over; we have already forgotten it. Neil and I are already thinking of happier things. We are going to be married. This must never be allowed to come between us again."

"We are going to be looking ahead now," Neil said, "and we want you to share our happiness."

Neil and I were married in Richmond. Two days after the wedding, we began the long journey back to our new home. Neil, in his optimism that everything would work out right, had built the new house just for me. We were sad that the Blennerhassetts were not returning with us, but we could not persuade them to come. That they would never return, was hidden in the future. Had I known that I should never see them again, it would have broken my heart.

The days of the journey seemed very long, so anxious was I to get home. I knew that the house Neil had built was below Parkersburg, on a bluff overlooking the island—Blennerhassett Island. How I longed to be there, to see the well-loved scenes once more.

More than three weeks went by before we had put the miles behind us and were home, at last. I was not prepared for the warm welcome we received from our neighbors. There they were to greet us—many of them the same dear friends who had come frequently to the island. More than one who now greeted us with a smile, I had last seen weeping on the shore as our flatboat left the island.

I could not feel that I was really home until I was finally able to steal away from the neighbors and stand at the edge of the bluff, looking down on our island. I saw our mansion home, more cold and stark than I had expected. Yet it was strangely the same, almost as we had left it. Neil came out and stood beside me, saying nothing.

In the days that followed, Neil and I found the happiness we had long been seeking. The friendships we made were many and warm, with people who, like ourselves, were ever ready to help a neighbor. Help was often needed here in this pioneer land.

I think I must always have known what the last episode would be, but I was not prepared for the strange feeling that swept over me when they told me that the mansion was burning. It was as though a fitting ending were at last being written to a tragic story. Once more the quiet and peace of nature were being allowed to return to the island that had known so much of sorrow and strife.

We stood there together, Neil and I, on the bluff above the river, and watched the flames so far below—flames that were to erase from that spot of beauty, tragic scars that had saddened us who knew the story.

The sorrow in my heart that night as we watched the mansion burn, came not from the scene of destruction below us. Instead, my mind went back in sadness to another night when not flames, but moonlight, relieved the darkness.

I saw once more a boat moving out from the shore of the island—a boat carrying a family into exile. Again, I beheld the desolation of the house that they had left behind—a house standing gaunt and alone in the moonlight. For me, the mansion had died that night, when the heart went out of it. And now, at last, nature would reign once again over a scene of peace and tranquility.

Interior of old hall of House of Delegates located in
Virginia State Capitol Building, scene of trial.

Chair occupied by Chief Justice John Marshall during trial.